POLITICAL
MARKETING

POLITICAL MARKETING

THEORETICAL AND STRATEGIC FOUNDATIONS

WOJCIECH CWALINA

ANDRZEJ FALKOWSKI

BRUCE I. NEWMAN

M.E.Sharpe
Armonk, New York
London, England

This book is dedicated to our families:

Wojciech Cwalina: Justyna Cwalina, Hanna Cwalina

Andrzej Falkowski: Ewa Falkowska, Justyna Falkowska, Zuzanna Falkowska

Bruce I. Newman: Judith Ann Newman, Todd Paul Newman, Erica Lynn Newman

The EuroSlavic and Transroman fonts used to create this work are © 1986–2011
Payne Loving Trust. EuroSlavic and Transroman are available
from Linguist's Software, Inc., www.linguistsoftware.
com, P.O. Box 580, Edmonds, WA 98020-0580 USA, tel (425) 775-1130.

Library of Congress Cataloging-in-Publication Data

Cwalina, Wojciech.
  Political marketing : theoretical and strategic foundations / by Wojciech Cwalina, Andrzej
Falkowski, and Bruce I. Newman.
    p. cm.
  Includes bibliographical references and index.
  ISBN 978-0-7656-2291-4 (hardcover : alk. paper)—ISBN 978-0-7656-2916-6 (pbk. : alk. paper)
  1. Campaign management. 2. Political campaigns. 3. Marketing—Political aspects.
I. Falkowski, Andrzej. II. Newman, Bruce I. III. Title.

JF2112.C3C93 2011
324.7'3—dc22   2010040044

Printed in the United States of America

The paper used in this publication meets the minimum requirements of
American National Standard for Information Sciences
Permanence of Paper for Printed Library Materials,
ANSI Z 39.48-1984.

∞

| IBT (c) | 10 | 9 | 8 | 7 | 6 | 5 | 4 | 3 | 2 | 1 |
| IBT (p) | 10 | 9 | 8 | 7 | 6 | 5 | 4 | 3 | 2 | 1 |

Contents

Introduction

Democracy is full of paradoxes. One of its premises is the freedom of citizens, which creates favorable conditions to create more and more sophisticated marketing strategies whose goal is to make the voter vote for a certain political option. We face then a paradoxical situation because a side product of these strategies is the limitation of the voters' choices in their voting decisions; in other words, the developing democracy creates mechanisms that limit democracy.

One may wonder how it might be possible to handle such a situation. First of all, one should discover how social and psychological mechanisms controlling citizens' behavior operate. These mechanisms are the basis of the applied marketing strategies. Thus the main concern of this book is the demonstration that political marketing analysis is virtually impossible without substantial knowledge of psychology. The theoretical and practical knowledge of political marketing is analyzed with particular emphasis on psychological mechanisms of voter behavior. It is obvious that the psychological research in the domain of cognitive and emotional processes is commonly used to create politicians' or parties' images as well as to construct persuasion messages for political campaigns. Such efforts lead to stronger and stronger control of people's attitudes and preferences on the automatic level—that is, beyond their conscious control. Thus, voters do not realize that their behavior is often shaped by those who deliberately use sophisticated marketing techniques.

The present book provides a complete and profound view of political marketing. Apart from instructing readers how to use the research tools of political marketing, it teaches them to understand social and political reality and encourages them to participate in shaping this reality. This is especially important for well-established as well as emerging democracies, in which the dynamic development of information technology, resulting in the development of the Internet and new technologies used for wireless multimedia transmission and increasingly available to ordinary people, is creating a new information society. The rapid development of the media and the possibility of reaching each person with information encourage individuals to construct in their minds a certain way of perceiving the surrounding reality.

One might wonder then who may be interested in such constructing. In the first place, it is managers responsible for marketing strategies in business and also political marketing consultants. The first group uses the achievements of modern social science for influencing customer behavior, whereas the other group uses them for influencing voter behavior. The increasingly sophisticated promotional campaigns used by both groups influence the cognitive and emotional spheres of the voters, creating a certain image of reality in their minds. In this way voters become puppets in the hands of the manager who, by controlling their behavior, is limiting their freedom.

The content of the book is put within the theoretical framework of social psychology with particular emphasis on cognitive-emotional processes. Such an approach is especially important in creating the flexibility of the political campaign consultant not only in using the market research tools discussed in detail in this book, but also in creating and controlling the surrounding social reality.

The first chapter presents political marketing as a separate discipline and analyzes current definitions of the field, which leads to proposing our own, original definition of this domain of research in theory and practice. The second chapter introduces an advanced theory of political marketing in the context of existing models. The third chapter is devoted to the marketing tools of segmentation of the voting market and positioning of parties and politicians. Special attention is paid to three positioning methods, the first one based on triangulation, the second on the associative affinity index, and the third on contrast theory of similarity. The following four chapters discuss in detail particular problems related to candidate image, direct campaigns, debates, permanent campaigns, and maintaining relationship with voters. The final, eighth, chapter is a special one. It undertakes the problem of democracy and freedom of citizens which, in a sense, is limited as a result of advanced marketing strategies used to convince voters to vote for a particular political option. It seems that the only way to eliminate such paradoxes is through social education. The increase of political awareness and the popularization of the knowledge of economy and law should ensure that an increasing number of those entitled to vote will start making rational political choices. Popularization of political marketing will, on the one hand, equalize the election chances of all political subjects on the scene and, on the other hand, lead to citizens' becoming less enslaved and manipulated.

The book is aimed not only at students and researchers working in marketing, business, and political sciences. It is also aimed at psychologists, sociologists, and those who are professional in the humanities. It can certainly be helpful to consultants working on political campaigns as well as politicians who would better understand their chances of success or failure.

The completion of this book would not have been possible without the support and constructive editing of several people. We first want to thank Harry Briggs, executive editor at M.E. Sharpe. Harry served as a guiding light throughout the process, providing necessary feedback and excellent leadership. It should be noted that Harry served as the editor on two previous books on political marketing, dating back to 1994, a clear indication of his foresight in the promise of the field. We also want to thank Andrzej Antoszek from Catholic University of Lublin for his careful reading of the manuscript that proved to be invaluable. Furthermore, we want to thank several colleagues for their contribution to the field of political marketing. They organized conferences and wrote important articles and books, all of which had an influence on the subjects and problems we addressed in our book: they include Costa Gouliamos from European University, Cyprus; Phil Harris from University of Chester, England; Stephan Hennebergu from University of Manchester, Manchester Business School, England; Nicholas O'Shaughnessy from Queen Mary University of London; Paul Baines from Cranfield University, England; Dominic Wring from Loughborough University, England; Dennis Johnson from George Washington University, United States; and Wayne Steger from DePaul University, United States. We want to thank Yuanyun Peng (Ella) from DePaul University for her help with the proofreading of each draft of the manuscript. We want to also thank the administrative and editorial staff at M.E. Sharpe for their support of this project. Finally, we thank our families for their continued love and their support of our professional lives.

POLITICAL MARKETING

1

Metatheory in Social Science
and Political Marketing

Theory development in political marketing has borrowed from several different social science disciplines. At the very heart of this pursuit is the understanding of human behavior that encompasses the various activities involved in political marketing. The sum total of those activities is put forward in the following definition of political marketing: "the applications of marketing principles and procedures in political campaigns by various individuals and organizations. The procedures involved include the analysis, development, execution and management of strategic campaigns by candidates, political parties, governments, lobbyists and interest groups that seek to drive public opinion, advance their own ideologies, win elections and pass legislation and referenda in response to the needs and wants of selected people and groups in society" (Newman 1999a, xiii).

Metatheory in Social Science

The various activities that encompass the human behaviors related to political marketing will be analyzed in this book in an effort to understand how democracies around the world use these methods to accomplish the many political goals that allow a society to increase the quality of life for its citizens. The theorists from the different social science disciplines that we have borrowed from all approach theory development in a slightly different way, with each approach unique to the study of activities that pertain to the human behavior in question. However, it is possible to study the contribution of a theory in social science by outlining the various functions that theory serves into four different categories: integration, description, delimitation, and generation (see Howard and Sheth 1969; Rychlak 1968). Each of these functions will be described and used to evaluate how a theory in political marketing should be developed to better understand the technopolitical shift that has taken place in democracies around the world over the past twenty years.

The Integrative Function

One of the most important parts of theory development in the social sciences is the integration of constructs, propositions, and existing models that seek to explain the phenomenon in question. Perhaps the most important function to use to test a theory in political marketing is its ability to bring together the various constructs that define a discipline made up of two different worlds: politics and marketing. We find ourselves at a very exciting stage of theoretical development in the field of political marketing where scholars from around the world are contributing to the knowledge base of the field on a regular basis (see *Journal of Political Marketing*, published by Taylor & Francis, in its eighth year in 2009). It is not surprising that the research most widely referenced in the field is from two disciplines: political science and marketing. However, it is fair to say that scholars have borrowed from many other disciplines to explain the very wide range of human behaviors that make up the field of political marketing, including, but not limited to, cognitive and social psychology, sociology, advertising, cultural anthropology, economics, management, and political management. Each of these different disciplines seeks to explain and predict the behavior of the many actors involved in the functioning of democracies.

We believe the theoretical structure put forward in this book pulls together the relevant empirical and conceptual findings in several different disciplines that have been tapped to contribute to the current thinking in the field. This statement is made with an understanding that theoretical developments have come from disciplines in democracies around the world. Furthermore, it acknowledges the importance that must be placed on developing theory from empirical works that allow us to bridge the global network of democracies that rely on similar constructs to understand the thinking and actions of the voter in society (Cwalina, Falkowski, and Newman 2008).

The Descriptive Function

Like other theories in the social sciences, theory in political marketing should be explained by the integration of constructs and propositions that allow one to get an understanding of the human behavior in question. Key to describing the central constructs of the theory in this discipline is the ability to integrate the environmental forces that play a role in shaping the behaviors in question. Because the phenomenon in question can have global idiosyncratic characteristics, it is critically important in the description of theory in this field to account for the broad commonalities that do exist in all democracies around the world. This is perhaps the most compelling aspect of the work presented in this book, which to date has not been accomplished by any other scholar in the field.

We believe the theoretical contribution made in this book moves the field forward because human political behaviors around the world do have many features in common, but at the same time have some unique features. For example, some democracies are driven by governments as opposed to political parties. In other words, governments are so powerful that they are able to pick and choose the political party that is in charge of day-to-day operations of the society. At the same time, in some democracies individual politicians may be put in power without the consent of the government, or a political party may gain control through the sheer power of money and advertising that are used to drive the choice of candidates. Furthermore, it has been well established in the field that the set of activities and actors may vary or stay the same as a democracy moves from precampaign, to campaign, to postcampaign status. Finally, the actual use of marketing tools and strategies can also have a differential impact on the outcome of campaigns depending on the democracy being studied. It is therefore imperative that a theory be developed that describes and accounts for all the conditions that might impinge on the uniqueness of a democracy. We believe our theory can be used to fully describe the human behavior we are studying.

The Delimiting Function

In light of the fact that theory in the social sciences must be limited to a selection of constructs that describe the phenomenon from a specific vantage point, and the fact that we are attempting to provide a theory that has a global reach, the selection of constructs is very important (see Figure 2.6 in Chapter 2). Our goal in this book is not to attempt to explain the unique features of political marketing in each and every democracy around the world, but rather to present an array of constructs and propositions that can give meaning to the common human behaviors and activities that cut across the discipline. The question then arises how we went about selecting those constructs that could give meaning to anyone who might have an interest in this phenomenon around the world. The best answer to this question lies in the fact that we relied on both empirical and conceptual works in the development of our theoretical linkages.

By definition, the field of political marketing is an applied science that relies on the application of constructs that are measured in paper-and-pencil questionnaires. Yes, these measurements come from models and conceptual frameworks that fit into the phenomenon being studied. Therefore, it is quite possible that the selection of constructs (from empirical studies) in our theory may be limited to the execution of the research carried out and reported in the literature. We are naturally constrained by the relationships that show statistical significance in the reporting of results, and by the modeling that is developed from these research studies. It must also be recognized that there may be constructs that should be included in our theory, but because they cannot be measured, we are limited to their exclusion. This is the nature of an applied discipline and naturally delimits the choice of constructs that describe and explain the phenomenon in question. As the methodological sophistication of a discipline advances through multivariate statistical testing, it becomes possible for theorists to use more rigorous tests to validate the meaning of the constructs and their relationships. Ultimately, it is the ability to predict the human behaviors in question that allows us to extract meaningful explanations and ultimately a choice of constructs to use in our theory. We are of the opinion that we have successfully selected out those constructs that delimit the field.

The Generative Function

The ability to test a theory, and parts of it, is a measure of the generative function. In the social sciences, testing hypotheses that are generated from theory is one measure of the richness of the thinking. The development of our theory in this book is based on preexisting models, some of which have been tested across people, time, and places. However, we have gone a step beyond the traditional thinking in the field by expanding the phenomenon to be tested across global boundaries. For example, we have borrowed from models that have been conceptualized in one country, but never tested. We also have borrowed from some models that have been operationalized in selected democracies, but not in others. Finally, we have also borrowed from conceptual frameworks that have not been tested, but have been compared between countries.

It is our goal to generate much thinking and research from scholars around the world on the subject of political marketing. We expect that to happen because the theory provides for an unlimited number of relationships that could exist between constructs in the model (see Figure 2.6 in Chapter 2). For example, it will be very interesting to see how the strategic use of social networking moves from the United States (as witnessed in the Obama campaign of 2008) to other democracies around the world as the Internet becomes more popular and more economical to use compared with traditional communication tools, such as television advertising. We also expect to see some very interesting research carried out longitudinally within democracies from precampaign to campaign to postcampaign as constructs are more clearly delineated and able to be measured by researchers. This function should serve to advance the field of political marketing in a significant way, and we believe that the theoretical propositions put forward will serve to do that well.

Political Marketing as a Separate Discipline of Science and Practice

Politicians are in the business of selling hope to people. This hope is related to convincing people that it is this particular politician or political party that guarantees, as Jenny Lloyd (2005) puts it, successful management of national security, social stability, and economic growth on behalf of the electorate. From this perspective, the major challenge to political marketing is to connect a politician's words, actions, and vision into a realistic transformation of the electorate's dreams and aspirations (Newman 1994).

According to Stephen Dann, Phil Harris, and their collaborators (2007), political marketing faces four main challenges. First, we need to turn political marketing into political marketing science. Implementing this goal requires, above all, developing background research and core datasets to utilize for constructing advanced insights into the political marketing process. Second, political marketing needs to be modernized. The research agenda for marketers and academics is to test the applicability of the principles in the context of the local political system so as to identify independent and nation-dependent political marketing strategies and campaigns. This step is necessary to develop a general theory of political marketing. Third, we need to define the relations between political marketing, lobbying, and government. Fourth, any theory of political marketing should include changes taking place in modern democracies, especially the shift from citizenship to spectatorship, and assess and point new ways to increase citizen involvement.

Paraphrasing the words of Phil Harris and Patricia Rees (2000, 368), "political marketing needs to regenerate itself and not fear change or ambiguity in its quest to seek the truth. It needs to avoid shibboleths, false and unarmed prophets, learn from history and show passion and courage or be deemed beyond redemption."

Mainstream and Political Marketing

The first conceptualizing efforts related to political marketing referred to or represented the transferring of classical product marketing to the plane of politics (e.g., Farrell and Wortmann 1987; Kotler 1975; Niffenegger 1988;

Shama 1975), defined by Stephan C. Henneberg (2003) as "instrumental" or "managerial" interpretation of political marketing activities. The starting point for this approach was the assumption that it would be a gross mistake to think that election campaigns have taken on marketing character only in recent years. Campaigning for office has always had a marketing character, and what has only increased in the course of time is the sophistication and acceleration of the use of marketing methods in politics (Kotler 1975; Kotler and Kotler 1999). From this perspective, political marketing was defined as "the process by which political candidates and ideas are directed at the voters in order to satisfy their political needs and thus gain their support for the candidate and ideas in question" (Shama 1975, 793). Applying mainstream marketing to politics was justified by a number of similarities—similarities of concepts (e.g., consumers, market segmentation, marketing mix, image, brand loyalty, product concept and positioning) and similarities of tools (e.g., market research, communication, and advertising). On the other hand, attempts were made to prove that the differences between marketing and politics were only ostensible and that they disappeared under a more thorough analysis (see Egan 1999; Kotler 1975).

One of the consequences of identifying political marketing as product marketing was that candidates or political parties often were compared to particular consumer products, such as toothpaste or a bar of soap, and the media played an important part in popularizing that myth. As Philip Kotler and Sidney Levy (1969, 10) state, "political contests remind us that candidates are marketed as well as soap." However, as Alex Marland (2003) demonstrates, such comparisons are outdated and hardly appropriate in modern political marketing. The notion that parties and candidates can be promoted in the same manner as soap has become the mechanism for decrying the side effects of political marketing. This outdated axiom still continues to be used by political actors and observers alike. The "selling soap" analogy presumes that candidates are sold with a selling concept rather than promoted within a marketing concept. According to Marland (2003, 106), "only amateur, underfunded, and small-scale election campaign teams are still involved in a selling concept." Candidates are not "sold"; they are "marketed," as are realtors (i.e., real estate agents) and other service providers.

This idea is also strongly emphasized by Nicholas O'Shaughnessy (1987, 63): "politics deals with a person, not a product." Rather, politicians should be treated as vendors hired for a particular period of time—like doctors or lawyers. In other words, political marketing is mainly concerned with people and their relationships with each other, whereas mainstream marketing is often concerned with people's interaction with products. Therefore, attitude and impression formation in reference to political candidates also has a number of characteristics distinguishing it from consumer brands. The results of a series of psychological experiments conducted by Sarah Hampson, Oliver John, and Lewis Goldberg (1986) suggest that category membership is fuzzier with persons than in the domain of natural objects. It means, for instance, that the category "politician" is more blurred or less unequivocal than the category "soft drink." There are many more features politicians are characterized by and the associations with them are less predictable than those with the category of products. Furthermore, the results of neuropsychological research suggest that different brain regions are activated during forming impressions of people and inanimate objects (Mitchell, Macrae, and Banaji 2005). Also, Geeta Menon and Gita Johar (1997) demonstrate that judgments related to nonsocial product experiences trigger processes that are different from those established for social stimuli. Product experiences are inherently less ambiguous than personal experiences, thereby entailing more concrete and less self-referent processing. Judgments of social stimuli (e.g., person, party) are likely to depend on inferred, abstract information (e.g., traits); whereas judgments of nonsocial stimuli (e.g., products) are likely to depend on concrete attributes, which, in turn, leads to the manifestation of positivity effects (tendency to recall positive experiences from the past rather than negative ones) in personal but not product experiences. Menon and Johar (1997) suggest then that consumer researchers need to be cautious when applying knowledge of structure and processes dealing with person memory to the domain of products. Furthermore, the results of John Lastovicka and E.H. Bonfield's research (1982) suggest that although consumers are likely to hold attitudes about a politician's stands on familiar social and political issues, attitudes are less likely to be held about familiar branded products, since, in general, consumer products are less involving than social issues.

The above differences suggest that identifying political candidates with consumer brands may lead to errors if mainstream marketing knowledge is directly applied to politics. It does not mean, though, that there are no similarities between these two concepts, but that the differences stress the specificity of human reactions to political objects as opposed to consumer goods. According to Bruce Newman (1994), in reality the candidate is rather like a service provider, whereas parties can be compared with service-providing companies (see also Bauer, Huber, and Herrmann 1996). From this perspective, candidates offer a service to their voters, much in the same way that insurance agents offer a service to their consumers. In this case, the insurance policy becomes the product sold by the agent. Therefore, to convey the impression that the marketing of candidates is similar to traditional fast-moving consumer goods marketing is to oversimplify and minimize the uniqueness of the marketing application to politics.

First of all, as Newman (1994) proves, consumption of soap does not require nearly as much time and effort in a consumer's decision to buy one brand over another as a voter spends when deciding to cast a ballot for a candidate. As a result, a buyer of soap will be less involved in the acquisition of information than is a voter. Second, by taking note that a candidate really is a service provider, the distinction between campaigning and governing becomes clearer. The actual delivery of a service that candidates offer to the voter does not occur until they begin to govern. Finally, candidates operate in a dynamic environment—fast, changing, and full of obstacles—which present marketing challenges that require flexibility. Like corporations around the world that alter their services to respond to more demanding consumers in the commercial marketplace, candidates have to respond to the fast-paced changes that take place in the political marketplace (Newman 1994). From the perspective of service marketing, G. Lynn Shostack (1977, 79) presents a similar idea: "services are often inextricably entwined with their human representatives. In many fields, a person is perceived to *be* the service."

Service Marketing and Political Marketing

These clearly defined differences between political and product marketing suggest that political marketing may have much more in common with service and nonprofit organizations marketing than with product marketing (see Kotler and Andreasen 1991; Lloyd 2005; Scammell 1999). This approach is defined by Henneberg (2003) as "functional" marketing analysis of political management. Service marketing incorporates a whole host of strategic issues that are not applicable in the marketing of products because services have unique characteristics that products do not have. According to Stephen Vargo and Robert Lusch (2004, 2), services may be defined as "the application of specialized competences (knowledge and skills) through deeds, processes, and performances for the benefit of another entity or the entity itself." Services are intangible (no physical product is exchanged and repeat purchases may be based on reputation and recollection of previous services), heterogeneous (the provision of services is variable—depending on the service provider, the quality of the service can vary), perishable (they are instantaneous and cannot be stored for any length of time), and inseparable (service requires the presence of the producer, and its production often takes place at the same time as consumption—either partial or full), nonstandardized (there is difficulty in consistency of service delivery), and they have no owner (customers have access to but not ownership of service activity or facility) (see Berry 1980; Kearsey and Varey 1998). These characteristics can be referred, to a large extent, to the area of politics (Butler and Collins 1994; Lloyd 2005).

The service-centered view of marketing perceives marketing as a continuous learning process. From this perspective, according to Vargo and Lusch (2004), the application of specialized skills and knowledge is the fundamental unit of exchange. Thus, people exchange to acquire the benefits of specialized competences or services, and not for specific goods. The service-centered view of marketing is customer-centric and market-driven. This means collaborating with and learning from customers and adapting to their individual, dynamic needs. In consequence, "value" is defined by and co-created with the consumer rather than embedded in particular products. In other words, value is perceived and determined by consumers on the basis of "value in use"—the result of the transformation of "matter" into a state from which they could satisfy their desires. The enterprise can only offer a value proposition, and goods are simply a distribution mechanism from service provision (Vargo and Lusch 2004).

These unique service features result in specific marketing problems that need to be resolved by marketing strategists. According to Valerie Zeithaml, A. Parasuraman, and Leonard Berry (1985), these strategies involve, especially, using personal communication (word-of-mouth) tools more than nonpersonal and engaging in postpurchase communications. Furthermore, it is necessary to create a strong organizational or corporate image and not only a particular brand or brand family image. Due to inseparability of service production and consumption, it is necessary then to focus on selection and training of public contact personnel and use multisite locations of providers.

This approach is developed with the concept of perceived service quality (Boulding et al. 1993; Parasuraman, Zeithaml, and Berry 1985), relationship marketing (Grönroos 1994, 1998; Gummesson 2002), and customer relationship management (Boulding et al. 2005; Payne and Frow 2005). Christian Grönroos (1998) introduced the concept of "interactive marketing function" to cover the marketing impact on the customer during the consumption of usage process, where the consumer of a service typically interacts with systems, physical resources, and employees of the service provider. From this perspective, the goal of a company (and political party or candidate too) is to establish, maintain, and enhance relationships with customers and other partners (voters and other political power brokers), at a profit, so that the objectives of the parties involved are met. This goal is achieved by a mutual exchange. Thus, according to Grönroos (1996), three important strategic issues of the relationship marketing approach are (1) to redefine business as a service business; (2) to look at the organization from a process management perspective and not from a functionalistic perspective; and (3) to establish partnerships and a network in order to be able to handle the whole service process. Three tactical elements correspond to these three strategies: (1) seeking direct contacts with customers and other stakeholders; (2) building a database covering information about customers; and (3) developing a customer-oriented service system.

Grönroos (1997) believes that in every market situation latent relationships always exist and that either the firm or the customer, or both, may choose to activate that latent relationship, depending on their strategies, needs, wishes, and expectations, or choose not to do it. Individual and organizational customers can thus be seen as interested in either a relational (active or passive) or transactional contact with firms. Consumers in an active relational mode seek contact, whereas consumers in a passive mode are satisfied with understanding that the firm is available if needed. In addition, from the firm's perspective, the main thing is not whether a relational strategy is possible or not, but whether a firm finds it profitable and suitable to develop a relational strategy or a transactional strategy. These four modes of consumers (active and passive relational and transactional) and two types of firm marketing efforts (relational and transactional intent/strategy) can be combined into a relationship configuration matrix. Consumer transactional intent independent of the strategies adopted by a company leads to the exchange of product for money, because this creates the value the customers are looking for. In fact, anything else would be a waste of effort. Then, if the consumers are in relational mode (active or passive), they are looking for something in addition to the product to satisfy their value needs. This value goes beyond the product. But if a company adopts a relational strategy, the customer may engage in a long-term relationship.

From this perspective, an integral element of the relationship marketing (but also political marketing) approach is the "promise concept." The key functions related to it are giving promises, fulfilling promises, and enabling promises. A firm that is preoccupied with giving promises may attract new customers and initially build relationships. However, if promises are not kept, the evolving relationship cannot be maintained and enhanced. Therefore, an important element of building stable relations is trust, which is a willingness to rely on an exchange partner in whom one has confidence (Grönroos 1994). This belief in the partner's trustworthiness results from his or her expertise, reliability, and intentionality. In the commitment-trust theory of relationship marketing, Robert Morgan and Shelby Hunt (1994) claim that trust is central to all relational exchanges in relationship marketing with suppliers, internal partners, buyers, and lateral partners (competitors, government, and nonprofit organizations). It is also the foundation of developing relationship commitment, where an exchange partner believes "that an ongoing relationship with another is so important as to warrant maximum efforts at maintaining it"; that is, the "committed party believes the relationship is worth working on to ensure that it endures indefinitely" (23). This commitment has three basic aspects referring to behavior, affect, and time (San Martín, Gutiérrez, and Camarero 2004). The behavioral dimension of commitment refers to the repeat buying and loyalty of consumers and their investment in the relationship. The affective dimension indicates the extent to which each partner wishes to maintain relations with the other, and the temporal dimension refers to the desire for continuity in the relationship and stability through time.

In the political market, Bauer, Huber, and Herrmann (1996, 156) stress that "when referring to a political party as an association of citizens, it is important to remember that according to the parties' view of themselves, their services have no 'consumers.' Instead, the parties' efforts are aimed at inducing citizens to put their political ideologies into practice in every aspect of their daily lives." These authors emphasize that one of the major strategies used by political parties to win support should be reducing voters' risk and uncertainty by gaining their trust and developing one's reputation.

However, these clear similarities between service and political marketing do not mean that they are identical. As elements distinguishing political marketing, Lloyd (2005) suggests the following: (1) political outcomes are standardized at the point of "production," whereas variations arise from the way they are perceived, based upon electors' experiences and expectations; (2) political outcomes may refer to individuals or groups and they either function independently or sum up; and (3) voters are stakeholders in the resources that create political outcomes.

Besides, it seems that most contemporary voters demonstrate, to use Grönroos's terminology (1997), passive relational mode, and in most cases they are in transactional mode. It is represented by such phenomena as low election turnout, growing cynicism of citizens toward politics and politicians, and voters failing to identify with particular parties (see Cwalina, Falkowski, and Newman 2008). In this way, citizens no longer seek to develop long and stable relationships with parties. They are rather focused on a short-term perspective. The consequence is candidates' and parties' adopting of a transactional strategy: "Vote for us now; what is going to happen later is difficult to predict."

Political Marketing: A Definition

Despite many similarities between political marketing and mainstream (product, service, not-for-profit, and relationship) marketing, identifying them cannot be justified. In order to understand the specificity of marketing actions in politics, one should take a closer look at the differences between mainstream and political marketing. A detailed analysis was conducted by Andrew Lock and Phil Harris (1996), who point out seven major differences between the two spheres.

First, those eligible to vote always choose their candidate or political party on the same day that the voting takes place. Consumers, on the other hand, can purchase their products at different times, depending on their needs and purchasing power. Very seldom do the majority of consumers simultaneously want to purchase a certain product. Besides, although one can talk about similarities between opinion polls and tracking measures, the latter often refer to the purchasing decisions that have already been taken, unlike poll questions referring to the future and unknown reality. Besides, declaration of support for political parties is often accompanied by what Elisabeth Noelle-Neumann (1974, 1977) calls a "spiral of silence." It is related to the fact that some voters are ashamed to reveal their actual political views or preferences. They subject themselves to some form of self-censorship by trying to hide their actual views, although still following them. In this way, their responses included in a poll may be congruent with the responses of the majority (for instance, support for a particular political party), but their behaviors will be congruent with their beliefs (for instance, voting for a completely different political party). The phenomenon of the "spiral of silence" may be one of the explanations of "unexpected" election successes of particular political parties that are heavily criticized in the media. In such cases people seem to follow the rule that it is better to say nothing at all or not to tell the truth rather than get exposed to social isolation and scorn (see Price and Allen 1990).

Second, while the consumer purchasing a product always knows its price—the value expressed in financial terms—for voters there is no price attached to their ability to make a voting decision. Making a voting decision may be the result of analyzing and predicting the consequences of this decision, which can be considered as possible losses and gains in the long-term perspective between elections. In this respect, there is great similarity between postpurchase behavior and voting behavior. In both cases, one may regret taking a particular decision; the product one purchased or the candidate one chose might not meet the expectations of the customer or voter. Of course, one may also feel satisfaction after making a decision. However, it seems that such a state is much more often experienced by customers than voters. Besides, it would be odd if, before going to the polls, voters were informed how much they need to pay to be able to choose a party or a politician, while it is natural that such a price be attached to consumer products.

Third, voters realize that the choice is collective and that they must accept the final voting result even if it goes against their voting preference. Geoffrey Brennan and James Buchanan (1984) even claim that the relation between how an individual voter votes and the final result of the election is hardly relevant. What is really important is the distribution of support across the whole society. In other words, this is a social rather than an individual choice. This is very different from consumer choices, where the purchasing decision is independent of the attitude toward a given product that other consumers may have.

Fourth, winner takes all in political elections. This is the case in first-past-the-post elections. The closest equivalent to commercial marketing in this case would be gaining a monopoly on the market.

Fifth, the political party or candidate is a complex, intangible product that the voter cannot unpack to see what is inside. Although in commercial marketing there are also products and services that the consumer cannot unpack and check while buying them, the proportion of such packages that cannot be unpacked is much greater in the political market. Besides, consumers may change their minds and exchange products or services almost immediately for others, if they do not like the ones that they have purchased; such exchanges may be quite expensive, though. If voters decide to change their minds, they have to wait till the next election, at least a few years.

Sixth, introducing a new brand in the form of a political party is quite difficult and always remote in time. Furthermore, it always takes place only at the national level. There are many short-lived parties (in Poland, for instance: Center Agreement, Liberal-Democratic Congress, and Solidarity Election Action). Furthermore, in politics there are no supranational parties, although there are transnational groupings in the European Parliament, for instance. In commercial marketing, on the other hand, there are many brands that have acquired international status, including the supermarket chain Géant, for instance, which is present in many European countries, or the Coca-Cola company, which is represented all over the world.

Seventh, in mainstream marketing, brand leaders tend to stay in front. In political marketing, many political parties begin to lose support in public opinion polls after winning the election, because the new ruling party often makes decisions that are not well received by various social groups (e.g., unfavorable budget decisions or tax increases).

In addition, Newman (1994) points out further differences between mainstream and political marketing, stressing that in business the ultimate goal is financial success, whereas in politics it is strengthening democracy through voting processes. Using various marketing strategies in economic practice is the result of conducting market research that promises satisfactory financial profits. In politics, on the other hand, a candidate's own philosophy often influences the scope of marketing strategies. This means that although marketing research may suggest that a politician's chances will improve if she concentrates on particular political or economic issues, she does not have to follow these suggestions if her own conception of political reality is incongruent with these issues. The distinguishing feature of political marketing is continuous and increasing use of negative advertising, attacking directly rival political candidates (O'Shaughnessy 1987).

Then, Paul Baines, Ross Brennan, and John Egan (2003) emphasize that in the political market, the key form of transaction is the election, which occurs infrequently and does not constitute a legal contract between the "buyer" and the "seller." The most tangible product is the electoral manifesto, but voters have yet to sue their elected representatives for failing to deliver on manifesto promises. It is not clear what price the voters are paying, nor what product they are buying. Furthermore, oligopoly and monopolistic competition predict a high degree of sunk cost expenditure for corporate communications because prices are particularly rigid and firms prefer to compete by almost any other means (notably advertising and sales promotion). In the political market, the very notion of price competition is problematic, so that nonprice competition becomes particularly important.

The differences between mainstream and political marketing are big enough to make one think about developing an independent concept for studying voting behaviors. And despite the fact that, as Lock and Harris (1996) conclude, political marketing is at a "craft" stage, the assumption that there is direct transferability of mainstream marketing theory to political marketing is questionable. They claim that political marketing has to develop its own frameworks by adapting the core marketing literature and develop its own predictive and prescriptive models (see also Dann et al. 2007; Henneberg 2008).

Newman (1994) believes that the key concept for political marketing is the concept of "exchange." When applying marketing to politics, the exchange process centers on a candidate who offers political leadership in exchange for a vote from the citizen. In other words, when voters cast their votes, a transaction takes place. They are engaged in an exchange of time and support (their vote) for the services that the party or candidate offers after election through better government. Aron O'Cass (1996, 38) believes then that "marketing is applicable to political processes as a transaction occurs and is specifically concerned with how transactions are created, stimulated and valued." In this way, marketing offers political parties and candidates the ability to address diverse voter concerns and needs through marketing analyses, planning, implementation, and control of political and electoral campaigns. According to Dominic Wring (1997, 653), political marketing is "the party or candidate's use of opinion research and environmental analysis to produce and promote a competitive offering which will help realize organizational aims and satisfy groups of electors in exchange for their votes."

Baines, Brennan, and Egan (2003) propose a multipart definition of political marketing. It is the means by which the political organization (1) communicates its messages, targeted or untargeted, directly or indirectly, to its supporters and other electors; (2) develops credibility and trust with supporters, other electors, and other external sources to enable the organization to raise finances and to develop and maintain local and national management structures; (3) interacts with and responds to supporters, influencers, legislators, competitors, and the general public in the development and adaptation of policies and strategies; (4) delivers to all stakeholders, by means of diverse media, the level of information, advice, and leadership expected and/or required in a social-democratic state; (5) provides training, information resources, and campaign material for candidates, agents, marketers, and/or other local party activists; and (6) attempts to influence and encourage voters, the media, and other important influencers to support the organization's candidates and/or to refrain from supporting the competition.

The emphasis on the processes of election exchanges cannot obscure the fact that political marketing is not limited only to the period of the election campaign. In the era of the permanent campaign, in reality there is no clear difference between the period directly before the election and the rest of the political calendar (Harris 2001a; Newman 1999c). Governing between and in the period of election campaign secures politicians' legitimacy by stratagems that enhance their credibility (Nimmo 1999). Taking this into consideration, Lock and Harris (1996, 21) define political marketing as "a discipline, the study of the processes of exchanges between political entities and their environment and among themselves, with particular reference to the positioning of those entities and their communications. Government and the legislature exist both as exogenous regulators of these processes and as entities within them." Political marketing should thus have strong emphasis on long-term interactive relationships rather than simple exchange. It should also focus on party allegiance, electoral volatility, civic duty, government quality, responsible legislating, or new public management (Bauer, Huber, and Herrmann 1996; Butler and Collins 1999; Collins and Butler 2003; Lees-Marshment 2003).

Based on these differences and similarities between mainstream and political marketing and the concepts proposed so far, we propose our own definition of political marketing: "the processes of exchanges and establishing, maintaining, and enhancing relationships among objects in the political market (politicians, political parties, voters, interests groups, institutions), whose goal is to identify and satisfy their needs and develop political leadership" (Cwalina, Falkowski, and Newman 2009, 70).

Political Marketing Orientation

Together with the development of political marketing and the changes in the voter market, there also took place the evolution of the marketing approach to political campaigns. Newman (1994) discusses in four stages how American presidential campaigns have gone from organizations run by party bosses (the party concept) to organizations that have only one goal: to find the best possible candidate to represent the party (the product concept). Next, the organization shifts from an internally to an externally driven operation (i.e., focus on the voter's reaction to the candidate—the selling concept) to an organization run by marketing experts. This type of organization identifies voters' needs and then develops political platforms to meet those needs (the marketing concept). The evolution of the marketing concept is depicted in Figure 1.1.

In *the party concept* the organization has internal focus, which means that it is operated on information generated from the people within the organization and run by party bosses whose only allegiance is to the political party. Grassroots efforts to get the vote out are at the heart of the power of the political party. The candidates have no choice but to rely on the party bosses within the organization in order to become slated as a nominee. The party concept in political elections was the leading element of voting strategies in former communist countries of Eastern Europe. Any characteristics that were not congruent with the party's political profile destroyed the candidate's electoral chances. Any departures from the party's line were treated as manifestations of disloyalty and usually led to the immediate removal of the politician from office. However, one may have the impression that the majority of Polish voting campaigns are still based on the party way of management. In the United States, presidential elections up through the Eisenhower presidency featured campaign organizations that also followed the party concept.

In time, however, attention shifted from the party to the candidate representing it. The major effort during political campaigns no longer focuses on the party's ideology. Although candidates are usually put up by a particular party, it is their own characteristics that are important for wielding power, and these are emphasized in the electoral strategy. They include, for instance, competence or an ability to run the country's economic policy. This shift was caused by the decline in the number of people who considered themselves partisans and the increase in the number who considered themselves independents (see, e.g., Cwalina, Falkowski, and Newman 2008; Hayes and McAllister 1996; Holbrook 1996; Wattenberg 1991).

Marketing has developed the notion of *product concept* that stresses the importance of manufacturing a quality product. For example, Henry Ford went into manufacturing the Model T Ford with only one idea in mind: to build a quality automobile. Likewise, in politics, the product concept would apply to campaign organizations that have only one goal: to find the best possible candidate to represent the party. In contrast to the party concept in which allegiance is to the party, here it is directed to the candidate.

Figure 1.1   **The Evolution of the Marketing Concept**

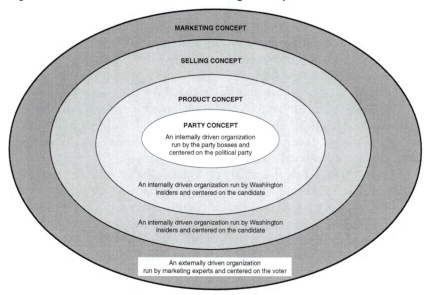

Source: Newman (1994, 32).
Note: The focus of the political campaign or organization has evolved. Once centered on the political party, the political campaign became candidate-centered and then voter-centered.

The next stage in the evolution of the marketing concept involves a *selling concept* in which the focus of the campaign organization shifts from an internally to an externally driven operation. Here the voter's reaction to the candidate's media appearances becomes critical. However, as with the product concept, the focus is still on the candidate. The best example of this concept comes from Joe McGinniss (1969) on the Nixon presidency. McGinnis describes how great efforts were made to sell Richard Nixon to the electorate by relying on media experts. Work went into making Nixon look as good as possible on television by using persuasive appeals in commercials to convince people to vote for him.

The *marketing concept* goes a step further by first identifying consumer needs and then developing products and services to meet those needs. The marketing concept is based on a very different philosophy than the party concept, the main difference being that the marketing concept centers on the voter as the primary focus of the campaign. The delivery of promises once the candidate begins to govern is also pivotal to the philosophy behind the marketing concept. In business, to avoid failure and ensure that consumers

get what they want, companies must address their needs. This same orientation can be found in the political marketplace as well and is used to help the
candidate avoid failure and win the election. The marketing concept begins
with the voter, not with the candidate. As in the business world, the marketing
concept dictates what candidates do, and, as in business, candidates want to
create and retain their customers. Several differences between party-driven and
voter-driven campaigns have been described in detail by Newman (1994).

A similar approach to the evolution of marketing in politics was proposed
by Jennifer Lees-Marshment (2001a, 2001b, 2003) for British political parties. She points out three stages, from product-oriented party, to sales-oriented
party, and to market-oriented party.

What is crucial for the specificity of political marketing is defining what
"political product" actually is. Patrick Butler and Neil Collins (1994, 1999)
believe that it can be described as a conglomerate consisting of three parts:
the multicomponent (person/party/ideology) nature of the offer; the significant degree of loyalty involved; and the fact that it is mutable—that is, it can
be changed or transformed in the postelection setting. According to Lees-
Marshment (2003, 14–15), a party's "product" is its behavior that "is ongoing
and offered at all times (not just elections), at all levels of party. The products
include the leadership, MP's (and candidates), membership, staff, symbols,
constitution, activities such as party conferences and policies."

According to Newman (1994), the real "political product" is the campaign
platform. It consists of a number of elements, including (1) the general election program of the candidate based on the political and economic guidelines
of the party he belongs to or the organization set up for the time of the elections; (2) his positions on the most important problems appearing during the
campaign; (3) the image of the candidate; (4) his reference to his political
background and the groups of voters supporting him (e.g., labor unions, associations, NGOs) or the authorities. Such a platform is flexible and evolves
together with the development of the voting campaign and changes in the
voting situation.

Marketing Versus Market Orientation

Kotler and Kotler (1999) state that to be successful, candidates have to
understand their markets—that is, the voters and their basic needs and
aspirations—and the constituencies that the candidates represent or seek to
represent. Marketing orientation means that candidates recognize the nature
of the exchange process when they strive for votes. If a candidate is able to
make promises that match the voters' needs and is able to fulfill these promises once in office, then the candidate will increase voter, as well as public,

satisfaction. It is obvious then that it is the voter who should be the center of attention during political campaigns.

Philip Kotler and Alan Andreasen (1991) maintain that the difficulty in transposing marketing into public and nonprofit organizations is a function of its placement on the continuum from organization-centered (internal) orientation to customer-centered (external) orientation. An organization-centered orientation counters the organization's ability to integrate marketing. From this perspective, marketing is viewed as a marketing mind-set of customer-centeredness and is seen in organizations that exhibit customer-centeredness and heavy reliance on research, are biased toward segmentation, define competition broadly, and have strategies using all elements of the marketing mix.

We want to stress that "marketing orientation" is not the same as "market orientation." "Market orientation" refers to acceptance of the importance of relationships with all stakeholders and aims at being responsive to internal and external markets in which an organization operates. The emphasis here is on building and maintaining stakeholder relationships by the entire organization. Ajay Kohli and Bernard Jaworski (1990, 6) define market orientation as "the organizationwide generation of market intelligence pertaining to current and future customer needs, dissemination of the intelligence across departments, and organizationwide responsiveness to it." Furthermore, the responsiveness component is composed of two sets of activities: response design (i.e., using market intelligence to develop plans) and response implementation (i.e., executing such plans) (Jaworski and Kohli 1993). While this definition of market orientation is concerned with a specific group of organizational behaviors (behavioral approach), John Narver and Stanley Slater (1990, 21; see also Slater and Narver 1994) define it as "the organizational culture that most effectively and efficiently creates the necessary behaviors for the creation of superior value for buyers and, thus, continuous superior performance for the business." It consists of three components: customer orientation (understanding one's target buyers in order to be able to create superior value for them continuously), competitor orientation (understanding the short-term strengths and weaknesses and long-term capabilities and strategies of both the key current and the key potential competitors), and interfunctional coordination (coordinated utilization of company resources in creating superior value for target customers). Furthermore, market orientation has primarily a long-term focus both on the relation to profits and on implementing each of the three components. For businesses, the overriding objective in market orientation is profitability. For nonprofit organizations, the analogous objective is survival, which means earning sufficient revenues to cover long-run expenses and satisfying all key constituencies in the long run.

With politics, according to Robert P. Ormrod (2006, 113; see also Ormrod

2005; Ormrod and Henneberg 2009), political market orientation refers to "all party members' responsibility for taking part in both development of policies and their implementation and communication." O'Cass (2001) additionally emphasizes that market orientation is the key mechanism for implementing the marketing concept, while marketing orientation is the underlying mind-set or culture of approaching the operations and processes of the organization through marketing eyes. As such, a marketing orientation is a necessary pre-requisite for both being market-oriented and adopting the marketing concept. The essence of marketing is a marketing mind-set of customer-centeredness, which is fundamentally a marketing orientation.

Market-Driven Versus Market-Driving Orientation

Another important distinction for marketing orientation in politics is juxtapos-ing market-driven versus market-driving business strategies (see Day 1998; Hills and Sarin 2003). The aim of a market-driven organization is to possess a culture that focuses outward on the customer in an attempt to build and sustain superior customer value. Then, market-driving organizations anticipate the changing nature of the market in the future and develop strategies to adapt the organization to ensure long-term success. Hence, a market-driven organiza-tion is one that aims to satisfy consumers by responding to their needs, which are derived through market research and market scanning. This suggests that as a longer-term strategic option, the focus on being market-driven leads to managerial complacency in that the focus remains on the existing customer base without being aware of the changing nature of the consumer base in the future. According to George Day (1994, 45), the objective of market-driven organization is "to demonstrate a pervasive commitment to a set of processes, beliefs, and values, reflecting the philosophy that all decisions start with the customer and are guided by a deep and shared understanding of the customer's need and behavior and competitors' capabilities and intentions, for the purpose of realizing superior performance by satisfying customers better than competitors." The market-driven development process combines an understanding of the market situation and technological possibilities with deep insights into customer problems and requirements; it then seeks new opportunities to deliver superior customer value. Market-driven firms are not oriented only to the external customer. They give equal emphasis to the employees who define and deliver the customer value, because employee satisfaction is closely correlated with customer satisfaction. According to Day (1998), market-driven firms achieve and sustain this orientation by making appropriate moves along four interwoven dimensions: (1) values, beliefs, and behaviors; (2) superior market sensing and customer-linking capabilities; (3)

strategic thinking processes that build a commitment to superior customer value proposition; and (4) organization structures, systems, and incentives that facilitate alignment of all aspects and activities with the market.

In the political marketplace, as Peter Reeves, Leslie de Chernatony and Marlyn Carrigan (2006) suggest, there is currently a move toward a market-driven standpoint in that the political parties attempt to design their brands on the basis of the needs of the electorate through market research and polling evidence. Political parties also need to be market-driving in predicting and taking action on longer-term programs that are not immediately important, but will have longer-term consequences. In other words, successful political marketing requires a balanced approach. Driving the market or being driven by it are antagonistic concepts on a continuum, but this is not the case of political marketing orientation. These two dimensions, as Stephan C. Henneberg (2006a, 2006b) demonstrates, constitute the specific strategic posture of a political party and its behavior in the political marketplace: the Relationship Builder (high in market-driving and high in market-driven), the Convinced Ideologist (high/low), the Tactical Populist (low/high), and the Political Light-weight (low/low; in fact it does not participate in the competition).

The Convinced Ideologist (CI) scores high on the leading-scale while its following capabilities are not fully developed. This posture is characterized by a clear focal point for policy-making—implementing ideological postulates. Preferences of voters or opinion shifts are secondary. The CI party concentrates on persuading and convincing voters to follow its proposals, without, however, paying too much attention to how they react to those proposals.

The Tactical Populist (TP) party is characterized by following more than leading. Recognizing the political pulse of the electorate is its most important strategic aim. Therefore, strategic marketing techniques (microsegmentation and concentration on marginal seats and swing voters) are applied to ensure that its political propositions are best fitted to voters' current needs and opinions. It requires employing many electoral professionals—consultants, pollsters, and advisers—and handing over control of the whole campaign to them (see Baines and Worcester 2000).

The Relationship Builder (RB) party scores relatively high on both dimensions of marketing: leading and following. The political offer is developed using political marketing concepts while a clear and trustworthy proposition is created through incorporating brand heritage, such as ideological roots or long-held overarching political beliefs. Furthermore, the RB party is focused on long-term relationships with voters and other players from the political scene.

According to Henneberg (2006a), before and during an election campaign, political parties modify their postures by increasing emphasis on the following-dimension. But during terms in government, they increase emphasis on the leading-dimension. However, depending on the situation, the ruling party may introduce corrective measures or even change its strategic postures, a shift that is confirmed by the analysis of perceptions of British prime minister Tony Blair, conducted by Henneberg (2006b). Then, being out of office (e.g., in opposition) for a long time increases the likelihood of the adoption of a TP (or RB) approach.

Candidate and Political Party as a Brand

A brand is a multidimensional construct involving the blending of functional and emotional values to match consumers' performance and psychosocial needs. A brand can be defined as "a name, term, sign, symbol, or design, or combination of them which is intended to identify the goods and services of one seller or group of sellers and to differentiate them from those of competitors" (Kotler and Keller 2006, 274). One of the goals of branding is to make a brand unique on dimensions that are both relevant and welcomed by consumers. Success in a market depends on effective brand differentiation, based on the identification, internalization, and communication of unique brand values that are both pertinent to and desired by consumers (de Chernatony 2001). Therefore, it is important to understand the content and structure of brand knowledge because they influence what comes to mind when a consumer thinks about a brand. Consumer brand knowledge relates to the cognitive representation of the brand. Consistent with an associative network memory model, brand knowledge is conceptualized as consisting of a brand node in memory to which a variety of associations are linked (Cwalina and Falkowski 2008b; Keller 1993, 2003).

In the political marketplace—as Leslie de Chernatony and Jon White (2002) stress—a political party can consider itself as a brand, to be developed to offer functional and emotional values to an electorate as part of its appeal (see also Smith 2001). Based on the analogy between a political party and brand, one may use the same marketing tools to develop their integrated images. The brand equity pyramid is a standard tool for understanding a brand's associations and customers' (voters') response. Kevin Lane Keller's brand pyramid (2001) establishes four steps in building a strong brand, with each step conditional on successfully achieving the previous step. The pyramid is presented by Figure 1.2.

The foundation step is establishing identity. It involves creating brand salience. Developing deep, broad brand awareness should ensure identification of the brand with customers and an association with a specific product class or customer need. Salience influences mainly the formation and strength of brand associations that make up the brand image and give the brand mean-

Figure 1.2   **Brand Equity Pyramid**

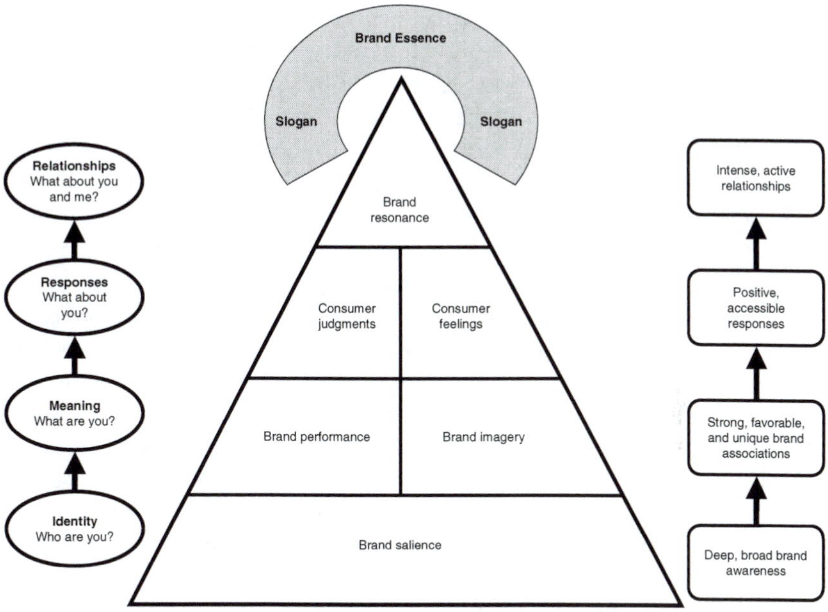

Source: Adapted and modified from Keller (2001).

ing. Brand awareness is related to the strength of the brand node or trace in memory, as reflected by consumers' ability to identify the brand under different conditions (Keller 1993). It plays an important role in consumer decision-making because it increases the likelihood that the brand will be a member of the consideration set for purchase. Furthermore, brand awareness also affects consumer choice by influencing the formation and strength of brand associations in the brand image. Therefore, a necessary condition for the creation of a brand image is that a brand node should be established in memory, and the nature of that brand node affects how easily different kinds of information can become attached to the brand in memory.

With political parties, establishing their identities is mainly about positioning a party as left- or right-wing (see Chapter 3). In other words, a party or its members must perform self-identification. This goal can be achieved in many, not mutually exclusive, ways. First, it can be achieved through the party manifesto and its detailed political program. When a party supports social and economic solutions increasing the role of the state over the individual initiative, it locates a party on the left side of the political stage. Stressing the importance of individual initiative, reducing taxes, or emphasizing some national values may indicate that a party is positioned on the right side of the poetical political stage. Another element connected with developing the identity of a party is choosing its name. In many cases, particularly in Europe, the names of political parties send clear messages to the voters about the beliefs a party represents. Examples include the Democratic Left Alliance, the Polish Peasants' Party, and the League of Polish Families in Poland, the Christian Democratic Union and the Social Democratic Party in Germany, and the Conservative Party and the Labour Party in the United Kingdom.

Another component of building the brand is establishing the meaning of the brand—creating a strong, favorable, and unique brand association. Another goal here is establishing a brand image—that is, what the brand is characterized by and should stand for in the minds of customers. Brand image means perceptions of the brand as reflected by the brand associations held in consumer memory. Brand associations are the other informational nodes linked to the brand node in memory; they contain the meaning of the brand for consumers (Keller 1993). These associations differ according to how favorably they are evaluated. The success of a marketing program is reflected in the creation of favorable brand associations. That is, consumers believe the brand has attributes and benefits that satisfy their needs and wants such that a positive overall brand attitude is formed.

According to Keller (2001), the third step should seek to develop positive, accessible responses to brand identity and meaning. Brand responses refer to how customers respond to the brand, its marketing activity, slogans, and other sources of information—in other words, what customers think (judgments) or feel (feelings) about the brand. The activities within that level of the pyramid are focused on developing positive attitudes toward the brand.

The pinnacle of the pyramid should build strong customer relationships to develop loyalty. The final step of Keller's model focuses on the ultimate relationship and level of identification that customer has with the brand. Brand resonance is characterized in terms of the intensity or depth of the psychological bond that customers have with the brand as well as the level of activity engendered by this loyalty—for example, repeat purchase rates or, during political elections, voting for the same party or candidate in subsequent elections. One of the consequences of building strong relations is also developing a sense of community among customers of a given brand or voters.

The strongest brands exhibit both "duality" (emotional and functional associations) and "richness" (a variety of brand associations or "equity" at every level, from salience to resonance). The more brand elements a brand has, generally the stronger the brand will be. Understanding a brand's equity elements and those of its competitors is the first step in developing effective brand-building.

The vision of the brand is completed by expressing all its components through a brief statement defining brand essence (Cwalina and Falkowski, in press; de Chernatony 2001). Most often it becomes the foundation of a slogan whose major goal is to help one particular brand stand out in the consumer's mind at the point of purchase.

Political Marketplace

The political arena is very diverse. It consists of groups with various interests, likings, preferences, and lifestyles. Efficient and successful political campaigns need to accommodate this diversity by creating strategies for various market segments. There are issue-oriented voters, but also there are voters influenced by the candidate's personal charm. The politicians often face a difficult task then; they have to build a voting coalition based on and reflecting a certain compromise among various social groups. This requires a lot of skills on the part of the candidate in creating a cognitive map of different opinions, emotions, or interests. Then the candidate has to assign them to particular groups and refer to such a map while constructing information messages in order to establish the foundations of the agreement between various voter groups and the candidate.

Andrew Lock and Phil Harris (1996) point out that political marketing is concerned with communicating with party members, media, and prospective sources of funding as well as the electorate. Similarly, Philip Kotler and Neil Kotler (1999) distinguish five voting market segments playing key roles in organizing political campaigns and establishing a political market:

1. active *voters* who are in the habit of casting ballots in elections;
2. *interest groups*, social activists, and organized voter groups who collect funds for election campaigns (e.g., labor unions, business organizations, human rights groups, civil rights groups, ecological movements);
3. *the media* that make candidates visible by "foregrounding" them during the campaign or keeping them in the shadows of the campaign;
4. *party organizations* that nominate candidates, express opinions about them, and provide the resource base for the campaign; and
5. *sponsors*, who are private persons making donations for the candidate and the campaign.

These factors are graphically presented in Figure 1.3.

Among these five elements, the media are the most important for the success of a political campaign. The media influence the ultimate image of

Figure 1.3   **Factors Influencing the Political Voting Market**

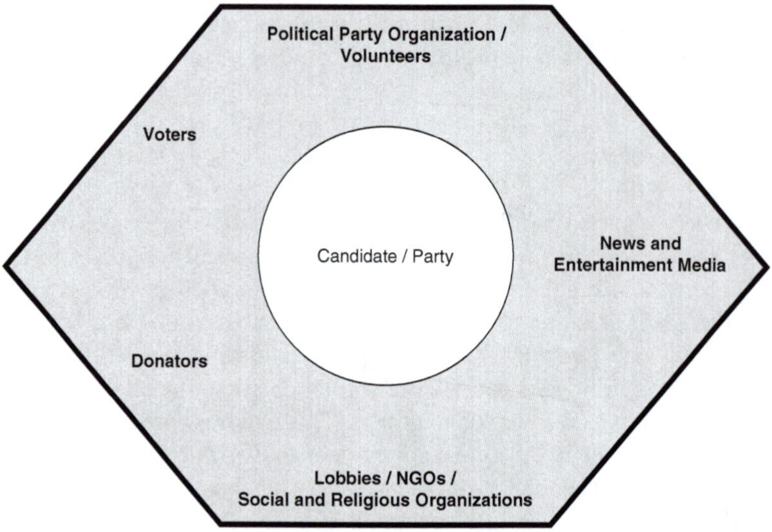

Source: Adapted from Kotler and Kotler (1999).

the candidate in the direct process of communication with the voters. The media's influence on voting preferences can be either open or hidden (e.g., Kaid and Holtz-Bacha 2006; Newman 1994). The media's open influence may be demonstrated by their supporting a given political option and sponsoring and publicizing various events connected with the political campaign. The media's hidden influence is represented by the extent to which a given candidate appears in the media. Becoming known to the voters is an important factor that has an influence on voting preferences. The media may also manipulate the message, exaggerating or marginalizing a candidate's position on various social and political issues. They may also shape the candidate's personality and emotional image, highlighting positive or negative features in information programs.

Political marketing campaigns are integrated into the environment and, therefore, related to the distribution of forces in a particular environment (Cwalina, Falkowski, and Newman 2008; Newman 1994; Scammell 1999). It can then be stated that the environment in which marketing and political campaigns take place consists of three fundamental component groups: (1) technological elements (direct mail, television, the Internet, and other means of voting communication, such as spots); (2) structural elements connected mainly with the election law, but also with the procedure of nominating candidates, financial regulations for the campaign, and conducting political debates; and (3) the forces influencing the development of the campaign (candidate, consultants, media, political parties, interest groups setting up political and election committees, polling specialists, and voters).

Each of these elements represents an area where dynamic changes have taken place in the past few decades. These changes facilitate the development of marketing research and are becoming more and more important for the election process. Technological changes, for instance, have revolutionized a candidate's contacts with voters (for example, through email, cable televisions, and cell phones). Structural changes in the development of political campaigns make candidates pay more attention to marketing strategies and rely more on the opinions of the experts developing them.

In order to understand political marketing, one should also understand specific political marketing concepts. Above all, marketing as a process involves creating exchange, where the two sides involved are the candidate or party and the voters or/and other market segments. The majority of political marketing strategies are analyzed with reference to the classic 4Ps (production, price, place, and promotion) marketing model (e.g., Harris 2001a; Kotler and Kotler 1999; Niffenegger 1988; Wring 1997). More extended approaches go beyond the marketing mix, trying to relate it to service and relationship marketing, nonprofit organization marketing, as well as knowledge of political science, communication analyses, and psychology (Baines, Harris, and Lewis 2002; Henneberg 2003; Lees-Marshment 2001a, 2001b, 2003; Newman 1994, 1999c; Wymer and Lees-Marshment 2005).

2

An Advanced Theory of Political Marketing

What Is Missing?

It is hardly possible to understand modern political marketing without following its evolution. Analyzing the concept of political marketing from different perspectives will furnish a uniform picture, which will be the basis of the new, advanced theory of political marketing proposed here.

A Model of Political Marketing

Earlier theories of political marketing originated, to a large degree, from theories of marketing developed for the consumer goods market (Kotler 1975; Reid 1988; Shama 1975; Wring 1997). However, in the course of time, important differences have emerged between the practice and efficiency of marketing theories used for political and economic purposes. Political marketing, to a larger and larger extent, drew from disciplines such as sociology, political science, and psychology (Cwalina, Falkowski, and Newman 2008; Lees-Marshment 2003; Scammell 1999). That led to defining political marketing as a separate branch of science, with its own subject matter and methodology of research (Lock and Harris 1996; Newman 1994).

Process of Political Marketing According to Niffenegger

Phillip B. Niffenegger (1988) proposed a concept of political marketing showing the use of the classic marketing mix tools for political campaigns. He stresses that political marketing includes efforts aimed at integration within the *marketing mix*, known as the four *P*s—traditionally product, promotion, price, and place—to control the voters' behaviors efficiently. Advertising is not set apart here as an independent research discipline; rather it is closely connected to the process of marketing research, in which the segmentation of the voting market plays an important role. The framework integrating ele-

Figure 2.1   **The Political Marketing Process**

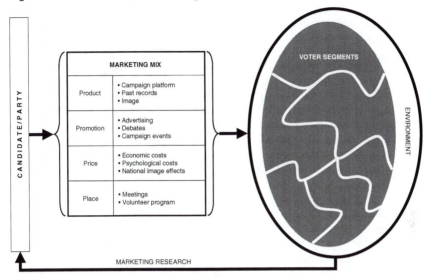

Source: Adapted from Niffenegger (1988).

ments of political marketing emphasizes the importance of market research, as shown in Figure 2.1.

It is evident that the political marketing concept is based on Kotler's approach to marketing research for nonprofit organizations. According to this approach, a political party participating in parliamentary elections or a candidate running for president must identify the needs, interests, and values of voters and present himself in such a way so as to best fit these requirements. Even if the candidate is able to identify the country's key social, economic, or political problems, without systematic research he is not able to determine how various voter groups perceive these problems. It can be assumed that the problems hold different weight for particular groups. Therefore, the candidate should try to fit his voting strategy to different voter segments—that is, to find the best position for himself in each of them.

Such a procedure requires marketing research, which is illustrated by the arrow in Figure 2.1, connecting the four *P*s marketing program with voter segments. This link is mediated by marketing research whose results, given to the candidate, show him what marketing mix he should use to be most successful. In political marketing, being successful mainly means expanding one's electorate.

Niffenegger described his concept using the example of the election committee in U.S. presidential campaigns. In 1952, Dwight Eisenhower's staff first conducted marketing research in the form of prevoting polls whose goal was to position the candidate. The purpose of the research was to define Eisenhower's position relative to the position of his main rival, Adlai Stevenson. The research procedure was quite simple. First, the voters were presented with thirty-second political spots. Then, an interview was conducted to determine which problem presentation made the greatest impression on the voters. The interviewers could then predict the voters' behavior by controlling the problems presented in the spot.

Prevoting marketing polls very quickly began to be commonly used to position candidates in various voter segments. Richard Nixon's consultants used them in the presidential campaign of 1968. They first tried to determine the voters' ideas of the ideal U.S. president, and then the next step was to position, in such a context, the images of Nixon and his main opponents, Hubert Humphrey and George Wallace. Defining the differences between the image of an ideal president and his own, Nixon was able to determine which characteristics should be improved and presented in TV spots in such a way as to approach as closely as possible the voters' expectations. Nixon's main goal was to reach undecided, floating (or swing) voters. The assumption was that those voters were most open to the persuasion message of the campaign; therefore, the whole effort was focused on convincing them, even at the expense of brand-loyal voters, to whom less attention was paid (see Chapter 3).

Ronald Reagan used a slightly different approach in poll marketing research in 1984. Using prevoting polls, his political consultants tried to define the characteristics of the image of an ideal candidate, major social and economic problems of the country, and ways presidential candidates might solve them. Entering the data into their Political Information System (PINS), which was set up for the purpose of the campaign, the consultants could track the dynamics of the changes of voters' attitudes toward particular candidates.

In his model, Niffenegger distinguishes four fundamental marketing stimuli by using the same names that the classical commercial marketing mix uses: product, promotion, price, and place. According to Niffenegger, the *product* offered by the candidate is a complex blend of the many benefits voters believe will result if the candidate is elected. The major voting promises are spelled out in the candidate's party platform. Then they are publicized through political advertising, press releases, and the candidate's public appearances. Whether the offer is recognized as reliable and acceptable to their expectations mainly depends on voters' knowledge about the candidate and his achievements, his personal profile formed by his staff, and the evaluation of the state's economic condition connected with the previous ruling team. For instance, in his presidential campaign in 1984, Ronald Reagan very cleverly used the arguments of his Democratic opponent, Walter Mondale, for increasing taxes. Reagan showed what the consequences of such a policy might be by referring to the economic crisis during Jimmy Carter's presidency. This tactic led to a decrease in the support for Mondale.

Whereas creating the product in political marketing is the purpose of the candidate and his staff, the "packaging" part is almost solely the task of political consultants. An example showing how various packaging is created for various situations is the changing of strategy by Reagan's consultants during his presidential campaign in 1980. They were quick to spot that in his speeches, the Republican candidate was perceived as a political warmonger and as dangerous and uncaring. Instead of using the phrase the "defensive position," the candidate began to talk about the "peace position." The "armaments race" was replaced by the phrase "a need to restore a margin of safety." After such changes, the image of Reagan came closer to the image of an ideal president. He was perceived as a politician who would strengthen peace.

The *price* of the product offered by the candidate refers to the total costs that voters would bear if the candidate were elected. It includes economic costs, such as tax increases or budget cuts. Other costs listed by Niffenegger include national image effects: whether the voters will perceive the new leader as a strong one, someone who will increase people's national pride, or someone who will be a disgrace to his compatriots on the international stage. There are also psychological costs: will voters feel comfortable with the candidate's religious and ethnic background? The general marketing strategy for the price consists in minimizing the candidate's own costs and maximizing the opposition's. In his presidential campaign, John F. Kennedy recognized a potential cost in being the first Catholic president, a prospect that made some non-Catholics feel uneasy. But he was able to successfully minimize this cost with TV spots in which he was shown meeting Protestant audiences. During the presidential campaign in Poland in 1995, Aleksander Kwaśniewski similarly stressed that he would be the president of all Poles—irrespective of their religion and views.

The concept of the candidate's price is thus similar to the price of a product in mainstream marketing. Selecting a candidate on the political market or buying a product or service on the economic market, one must incur some costs. The major difference is the fact that on the political market, these costs are to a large extent intangible or psychological, whereas in the economic market they are tangible and represented by the money or products for which the money is exchanged.

Place (distribution) is the marketing stimulus that refers to the candidate's ability to get his message across to voters in a personal way. The marketing strategy for the distribution of the campaign's message combines the personal appearance program with the work of volunteers who are used as a personalized extension of the candidate into local markets. This includes the work of activists ("door to door") who by canvassing, distributing the candidate's badges, registering voters, and soliciting funds familiarize the voters with the candidate's program and his image during direct contact with the electorate. The places and forms of a candidate's meeting with voters can vary—from rallies in city centers to club meetings and meetings at workplaces. Since the goal of the politician on the campaign trail is to meet as many voters as possible, he tries to be in as many places as possible in the shortest possible time. Gary Hart, a candidate for the Democratic presidential nomination in 1984, used a plane to move quickly from one town to another. His press conferences were staged in every airport he flew into, and listening to the evening news gave voters the feeling that Hart was in many towns at the same time. More recently, satellite technology makes it easy for candidates to stage interviews with journalists who are in a remote place.

Promotion consists, to a large extent, of advertising efforts and publicity, through free media coverage of the candidate, his program, and the campaign. Niffenegger distinguishes four fundamental promotion strategies:

1. *concentration strategy*—concentrating a disproportionate amount of money and promotion efforts on particular voter segments (for instance on regions or provinces);
2. *timing strategy*—spending the heaviest promotion money and the highest promotion activity where it does the candidate the most good, thus forcing the opposition to increase their activity and thus deplete their resources;
3. *strategy of misdirection*—avoiding a frontal assault against a stronger opponent and trying to catch the opponent off balance to make her commit a mistake (this may be a particularly successful strategy for underdogs); and
4. *strategy of negative campaign*—staging a direct or indirect comparative assault against the position of the opponent and/or her personal characteristics.

Recognizing the reasons for his poor showings in political debates in 1980, during the next election Ronald Reagan decided to change the strategy he had been using and focus in his political spots on evoking positive emotions in his voters. His spots featured sunrises, colorful parades, landscapes, and friendly faces. They contrasted with Walter Mondale's spots, which gave rise to negative emotions by presenting the visions of atomic holocaust, starvation, and poverty. A detailed analysis of advertising strategies used in political campaigns will be presented in Chapter 6.

Specific marketing programs based on the four Ps are prepared separately for different voting market segments. A particularly important role in this division is played by the segment of undecided voters, irrespective of the demographic and psychographic criteria of segmentation. It is these voters at whom the marketing mix should be directed. Richard Nixon's staff, for instance, used marketing research to look for ways of reaching undecided voters. This segment is considered most susceptible to marketing influence; hence it is this segment at which the greatest efforts of a political campaign should be directed. Less attention can be given to decided and loyal voters whose preferences are hard to change. Nixon's approach to the strategy of voting market segmentation was congruent with the position of Jay Blumler and Denis McQuail (1968), who stated that the image of political reality could be formed only among undecided voters, whereas voters with a clearly defined political stance are very resistant to marketing efforts.

In the presidential campaign in 1980, when Jimmy Carter and Ronald Reagan competed against each other, the segment of undecided voters (amounting to nearly 20 percent of the electorate) decided the results of the election. Maintaining a strong position among current supporters is also important. During the 1984 presidential campaign, the PINS showed that Reagan needed to improve his image among blue-collar workers, Catholics, and Latinos. The support of these groups for the current leaders was decreasing, which turned this segment into undecided voters. These undecided voters were an easy segment for the challenger to take over. A detailed marketing strategy in a voting campaign based on the segment of undecided voters will be presented in Chapter 3.

The implications of the political marketing model proposed by Niffenegger suggest that a candidate's staff should create and update advanced marketing information systems, including collecting and analyzing data from political market research, segmentation, and channels of distributing the promotion message to target groups. In addition, it is important to introduce regional variants to the general strategy of the campaign and use microsegmentation, as well as take into account the specificity of local voting markets. Candidates should also consider focusing the marketing effort on some "showroom" target areas. A spectacular success in a given area may have a positive influence on the campaign in other areas. Niffenegger suggests that negative advertising be used only as a last resort because it might produce a backlash. Political campaign workers should also use the specific qualities and limitations of television to gain competitive advantage (e.g., organize rallies or meetings that can make headlines).

Despite the fact that it attempts to show the efficiency of using marketing strategies for political campaigns, Niffenegger's concept of political marketing is in fact a copy of the concepts used in commercial marketing. It seems, then, that it does not distinguish to a sufficient extent between consumer and political choices.

Marketing the Political Product According to Reid

David Reid's concept (1988) is also an attempt to apply some concepts from mainstream marketing to political marketing. It focuses on this element of the voting process that refers to voting understood as a buying process. Reid stresses that by looking at the problem from a consumer perspective, a broader marketing approach could make a useful contribution toward a better theoretical knowledge of the "voting decision process." The core of the buying process involves the following stages:

1. *Problem recognition.* This stage refers to motivation, which triggers the recognition that there is a problem to be considered. In its essence, the process boils down to asking the voter the following question: "Whom will I vote for?" Recognition of the problem is determined by the voter's needs, which, to a different extent, refer to the candidate's voting problems. For instance, if the voter has problems finding employment, he will be sensitive to a program in which the politician stresses lower unemployment as one of her major goals.
2. *Search.* At this level, the voter seeks various sources of information (TV, radio, newspapers, magazines), which highlight the recognition of a problem. Naturally, each source may have a different influence on the voter's opinions.
3. *Alternative evaluation.* The voter must weigh the accumulated information against a set of evaluative criteria. These criteria are linked with the voter's motivation, which refers to the first stage of the decision-making process: problem recognition. If the voters' evaluative criteria match their motivation very well, then it is very difficult to cause any change in their voting behavior. For instance, a businessman will be interested in lower taxes because the current level inhibits the development of his company. The candidate will then be evaluated through the tax policy she is proposing.

    This stage of the decision-making process is also related to the segmentation of the voting market. Candidates and political parties have to identify various evaluative criteria among the voters and use marketing strategies that will reach segments of voters with similar

Figure 2.2   **Buyer Decision Processes**

Steps between evaluation of alternatives and a purchase decision

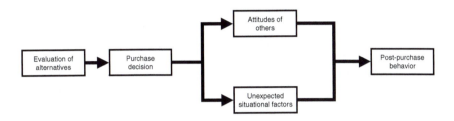

preferences. This stage is connected with the candidate's creating a political platform that will promote issues important for these voters and might attract voters from other politicians' electorates.

4. *Choice.* Choice is a particularly important element of the decision-making process. Seemingly, it should be logically connected to alternative evaluation. However, the voter may change it in the very last moment due to last-minute influences such as an article read, a news broadcast viewed, or a debate with a friend. Such unexpected situational factors are particularly related to last-minute voters, belonging to the segment of undecided, floating voters (see Chapter 3).

5. *Outcomes.* This element corresponds exactly to postpurchase behavior in consumer behavior. A politician needs to maximize the satisfaction of voters, including those who did not vote for her. Ongoing public relations activities and political patronage of influential groups can achieve this goal.

The multistage approach to the voter's decision-making process proposed by Reid is the direct transfer of the classical consumer decision-making process introduced by Kotler and Armstrong (1990). It is presented by Figure 2.2.

Reid's approach to political marketing corresponds very well to the marketing concept, which is the last stage of the evolution process in which presidential candidates have gone from campaign organizations run by party bosses to organizations run by marketing experts (see Figure 1.1. in Chapter 1). Its analysis is a pretty accurate reflection of the concepts developed in mainstream marketing and used for political behavior. However, this approach excludes a number of specific characteristics both of the political market and of different strategies of running political campaigns.

Kotler and Kotler's Model of a Candidate's Marketing Map

Philip Kotler and Neil Kotler (1999) present a six-stage process of marketing activities related to political campaigns. The analysis of these activities creates a *candidate marketing map*, presented in Figure 2.3. A professionally planned political campaign consists of (1) environmental research, (2) internal and external assessment, (3) strategic marketing, (4) setting the goals and strategy of the campaign, (5) planning communication, distribution, and organization, and (6) defining key markets for the campaign.

Environmental Research

Environmental research, the first step in preparing a candidate marketing map, consists of a thorough analysis of the social environment in which the political campaign is to be conducted. This research focuses on the opportunities the campaign may explore and threats it may encounter. The environment also includes the current economic condition of the candidate's constituency as well as the economic situation in the whole country, the electorate's feelings, and those social, economic, and political issues that provoke most emotions and disputes among the electorate. The environment also includes what political analysts and consultants call the electorate's *psychological profile*. It includes such elements as the voters' activity and involvement (what percentage of the voters participates in the elections), their ideological orientation (e.g., left, center, or right), and their attitude toward the incumbent and the challenger. This stage also includes checking the degree to which a particular party organization dominates in a particular voting district.

Social environment is also defined by such demographic variables of the electorate as age, income, and education, as well as psychographic variables including lifestyles, values, and attitudes toward many current issues that result from them. These variables become the basis of demographic and psychographic segmentation, which is one of many marketing strategies employed for the purpose of political campaigns. At this stage of developing a marketing map, the candidate should invest most resources in research.

Internal and External Assessment

In any marketing effort, including political marketing, the seller needs to assess her own strengths (internal assessment) as well as the strengths of her rival candidates (external assessment). Internal assessment is about assessing the candidate's strengths and weaknesses as well as the strengths and weak-

Figure 2.3   **Candidate Marketing Map**

Environmental Research

Internal and External Assessment Analysis

Strategic Marketing

Goal Setting and Campaign Strategy

Communication, Distribution, and Organization Plan

Key Markets and Outcomes

Source: Adapted from Kotler and Kotler (1999).

nesses of her campaign. Such an assessment is strictly related to the context in which the candidate functions in relation to her competition. She may be the *incumbent*, trying to get reelected, or may be the *challenger*, running for the first or another time. Like internal assessment, external assessment looks at the competition's strengths and weaknesses. Both internal and external assessment can help to position the candidate.

Strategic Marketing

The primary goal of marketing is to describe the society not as homogeneous but as consisting of a number of voter segments. At this stage of a candidate marketing map, the organizers of the campaign focus on analyzing the electorate in various districts. Some characteristics of the voters remain stable for a long time; however, other characteristics change from campaign to campaign. For instance, an attractive and active candidate planning new reforms may develop a new segment of voters and reconfigure the value they ascribe to the issues she aims to promote in her voting program.

Organizers of political campaigns first define all the segments of the voters in a particular district, highlighting those who are intending to vote and those who are not. Then the organizers try to divide the potential voters into particular segments for which they prepare a particular marketing strategy. For instance, the incumbent may seek to work with older, affluent, and conservative voters who supported her in the previous elections. A new candidate who is thinking about conducting fundamental reforms may develop a coalition with young and liberal voters who are open to changes, which requires strong identification with the issues included in his voting program as well as developing a new personality and identity on the political scene.

The third stage of developing a candidate marketing map is a segmentation of the voting market (see Chapter 3) and defining the candidate's strengths and weaknesses in each segment.

Goal Setting and Campaign Strategy

This stage of preparing a candidate marketing map is based on earlier research results influencing the way in which the candidate's image is going to be constructed and the way socioeconomic issues are going to be presented. This, in turn, influences the ways of transmitting voting information in order to efficiently promote the politician. At the same time, a monitoring program is prepared, allowing the introduction of any corrective measures if the campaign does not go according to plan and the candidate encounters some negative influences.

Communication, Distribution, and Organization Plan

At this stage particular marketing tools are developed. Kotler and Kotler suggest that the strategies of the standard *marketing mix* be followed here, which, in relation to competing in the political market, they define as the *campaign mix*. Here, the candidate's actions are quite similar to mainstream marketing. She defines her best *organizational resource mix*, including a detailed task division for members of her staff (collecting funds, contacts with interest groups, engaging volunteers) to create a so-called *retail campaign*.

A Candidate's Key Markets—Voters, Donors, and Media

The final stage of preparing a candidate marketing map is developing ways of reaching the fundamental market segments (see Figure 1.3.) and ways of building a media image. In the simplest form, the importance of the media in the voting campaign is defined by the amount of candidate coverage in mass media (including TV, newspapers, and magazines), the support the candidate gains, and the amount of money spent on advertising. At this level the candidate uses the results of earlier conducted market research and usually knows how a message should be constructed, where it should be placed, and how often it should be repeated to mobilize voters. She also knows what number of voters needs to be mobilized in different voting districts in order to be successful.

It should be stressed that the candidate marketing map proposed by Kotler and Kotler is compatible with the process of planning and organizing political campaigns described by Gary Mauser (1983). According to him, this process includes three stages: (1) the preparation process during which the candidate assesses his and his competition's strengths, (2) the process of developing a strategy of influencing voters, and (3) the process of implementing the strategy.

Lees-Marshment's Theory of Comprehensive Political Marketing

The comprehensive political marketing (CPM) described by Jennifer Lees-Marshment (2001a, 2001b, 2003; see also Wymer and Lees-Marshment 2005) is also consistent with the development of the concept of product in economic marketing. She believes that a candidate's or party's comprehensive political marketing should be based on five fundamental principles. First, CPM is more than political communication. It applies to whole political organizations' behaviors and activities—not only to political campaigns, but also to the way in which product is designed. Second, CPM uses marketing concepts and not only techniques. Third, it also includes elements of political sciences to better utilize and adapt such knowledge for the purpose of marketing. Fourth, it adapts marketing theory to the nature of politics. Finally, it applies marketing to all political organizational behavior, including interest groups, politics, the public sector, media, parliament, and local governments, as well as parties and candidates.

According to Lees-Marshment, the product—following the marketing process discussed above—is the complex behavior of the party, represented all the time (not only during the elections) by all the levels of its actions. The product includes the leaders, members of parliament (and the candidates), representatives in the government, party members, party officers, symbols, statues, and such activities as party conferences and conducting a particular policy.

What is particularly valuable about Lees-Marshment's concept is her presentation of the integrated and comprehensive theoretical framework of how political parties behave when they use political marketing following the example of the behaviors of the British Labour Party. Her general concept boils down to analyzing the particular stages of marketing evolution, from a product-oriented party to a sales-oriented party to a market-oriented party. This evolution was analyzed by Lees-Marshment using the examples of the British Conservative Party (2004; Lees-Marshment and Quayle 2001) and, in more detail, the British Labour Party, which went through all three orientations from 1983 to 1997 (Lees-Marshment 2001b).

A product-oriented party tries to convince the society to support its political program. Such a party assumes that voters will embrace its idea and—in consequence—will support it during the elections. Such an attitude of the party toward elections precludes any possibility of changing the idea or product, even if no support is won during the elections or the number of the party's members decreases. Unfortunately, what seems right in the eyes of the party bosses is not necessarily what the voters consider right too. In 1983, for example, the Labour Party lost the election because the party was not concerned with designing its product to respond to voters. Such an attitude leads to false appreciation of political reality by party members, who believe that the reason for their failure is that their policies were presented inappropriately or that the voters have not understood the party. A quote from Oscar Wilde can very well paraphrase such a product orientation: "The play had been a great success; it was the audience which was at fault" (Lees-Marshment 2001b).

A sales-oriented party focuses on "selling" its arguments to the voters. It maintains its leading product design but is able to recognize that the desired supporters may not want it. It utilizes marketing intelligence to understand the reactions of the voters to the party's behavior and uses advertising and communication techniques to convince the voters. Such a party does not change its behavior to convince voters to accept its program but tries to make them accept what it offers. One example of such behavior was the Labour Party in 1987, which attempted to win the election utilizing the sales orientation. It focused its efforts on designing the most professional and effective communication and campaign. However, the party focused not on changing the design of the product to suit voters' demands but on achieving a more effective presentation. In this respect, the sales-oriented party does not differ from the product-oriented party. In both cases, the product remains unchanged. One should not be surprised then that the concept of sales did not meet the expectations of the Labour Party when it failed in the election again. The number of Labour seats in Parliament after the 1987 election even decreased compared to the previous election.

A marketing-oriented party designs its behaviors to meet the voters' needs and provides them with satisfaction. It uses marketing intelligence to identify the voters' needs and then designs a product that will satisfy them. Such activities are supported and implemented by an internal organization and distributed by governing. The major implication of such an orientation is that a party does not attempt to change what people think, but to deliver what they need and want.

Tony Blair completely followed the marketing concept while leading the Labour Party during the 1997 election. His party was highly successful, wining 419 seats in Parliament, where the majority is 179 seats. The number of party members increased from 280,000 to 400,000 from 1993 to 1997.

The concept of adapting party programs to the voters' needs rather than persuading the voters to follow an already developed program (following the concept of product and sales) as part of the marketing effort is at variance with the traditional concept of politics. However, the greater sensitivity of the parties to the expectations of the voters is very good for democracy. Politicians feel more responsible for providing the product—that is, meeting their election promises. The marketing concept also prevents parties from developing such internal qualities as arrogance, self-satisfaction, or dogmatism, which often come out in the cases of the parties following the concept of the product.

Focusing on the voter in political campaigns has led to an important shift of attention, from nominated candidates or party bosses to the media, consultants, marketing and poll specialists, and members of political and voting committees. Their importance for the campaign is still growing; therefore, a carefully planned set of activities combining such procedures in the marketing effort is becoming more and more important.

Harris's Modern Political Marketing

According to Phil Harris (2001a), the changes taking place in modern democracies, in the development of new technologies, and in citizens' political involvement significantly influence the theoretical and practical aspects of political marketing efforts. Above all, modernization causes changes from direct involvement in election campaigns to spectatorship. Campaigns are conducted primarily through mass media and citizens participating in them as a media audience. In this way, politicians more and more often become actors in a political spectacle rather than focus on solving real problems that their country faces. They compete for the voters' attention not only against their political opponents but also against talk shows or other media events. For instance, during the Polish presidential campaign in 2005, the debate between two major candidates—Lech Kaczyński and Donald Tusk—was rescheduled for another day because otherwise it would have competed for the viewer against the popular TV show *Dancing with the Stars*. And it is doubtful whether it would have attracted a large audience.

This modernization process leads to changes in voting strategies that candidates and political parties have been following. According to Harris (2001a), the key elements of modern political campaigning include the following:

1. *The personalization of politics*, where the voters' choice depends increasingly on their relationship with the individual candidate, which replaces ideological bonds with a political party.
2. *The politicians' image*, whose importance is still growing. According to Harris, even if the candidates present their position on the issues, they do so, to a large extent, to reinforce the existing image because the image rather than substance is central in political marketing.
3. *The role of public relations*, particularly in candidate image creation. Political public relations are the inevitable consequence of the process in which mass media have become the center of opinion formation and decision-making. On the one hand, the goal of these activities is not only to initiate changes in voters' opinions but also to influence the media. On the other hand, the goal of public relations is to react to events with potential negative consequences for the candidate, limiting the potential damage. Public relations may then be a vital component in the political marketing mix, concerned with image and persuasion.
4. *The scientificization of politics*, which makes politicians use technical and scientific expertise in conducting their campaign but also in taking political decisions.

Furthermore, modern political campaigns are more and more characterized by direct linkage between political marketing and interest lobbying (Harris and Lock 1996, 2002).

Harris's concept of political marketing (2001a) is thus consistent in its fundamental assumptions with Niffenegger, Kotler and Kotler, and Lees-Marshment's assumptions. In his model, he includes the function of placement strategy, which is based on such traditional activities as canvassing and leafleting and "getting the vote out" on the polling day. Besides, his model stresses that the key element of success is not the development of persuasion activities, but the possibility of identifying and contacting potential supporters. As for price, Harris believes that in the case of voters it is shifted to the psychological domain and not expressed through money (the so-called feel-good factor). Following Dominic Wring (1997) in his concept of product, he assumes that it consists of three fundamental elements: the party image, the image of the leader, and policy commitments (manifesto). As opposed to the previous models, he attaches much more importance to the area of political promotion activities, which play the crucial role in the political marketing mix.

According to Harris, political promotion consists of a number of components, the most important of which are advertising (particularly, negative advertising), direct mail, public relations, and news management, as well as debates and pseudo-events planned to gain publicity and attention. Harris stresses that debates, like other pseudo-events, are meant to look spontaneous but in fact are carefully staged in order to attract the attention of the media and gain publicity for the political players.

In summary, in his concept of modern political marketing, Harris stresses the need to adapt both marketing theory and practice to the changing requirements of the modern world and politics. He also points out that political marketing cannot only be a copy of the solutions developed within mainstream marketing because the area it applies to has different constraints and often requires more complex and advanced strategies. Harris and Rees (2000) believe that marketing must strike a balance between beautiful academic reasoning and the realpolitik of what the constituents of marketing need. Marketing should be wary of throwing out the marketing mix or marketing concept in favor of outright replacement by new shibboleths such as relationship marketing. In other words, "marketing needs to regenerate itself and not fear change or ambiguity in its quest to seek the truth" (Harris and Rees 2000, 368).

Newman's Model of Political Marketing

Bruce I. Newman's concept of political marketing (1994, 1999c) is the most thorough model of those discussed so far describing the marketing approach in political behavior. It provides procedures for a number of concepts related to marketing activities on the voting market. It has also been the source of inspiration for a number of empirical researches expanding the theory (Cwalina, Falkowski, and Newman 2008).

In his model, Newman (1994) introduces a clear distinction between the processes of a marketing campaign and those of a political campaign. The marketing campaign helps the candidate go through the four stages of the political campaign, including everything from the preprimary stage of a politician's finding his own place in politics to his already formed political image at the general election stage. It is natural then that both campaigns are closely connected. The process of a marketing campaign is the foundation of the model because it includes all the marketing tools needed to conduct the candidate through all the levels of the political campaign. Figure 2.4 presents a schematic representation of Newman's model.

Despite the fact that foundations such as market (voter) segmentation, candidate positioning, and strategy formulation and implementation are also the foundation of consumer market mainstream marketing, their definition and meaning are distinctly different and fitted to the specificity of the voting market.

At the heart of the political marketing campaign is the candidate's realization that he is not in a position to appeal to all voters of every persuasion. This means that he must break down the electorate into distinct voting segments and then create a campaign platform that appeals to the candidate's following. It is obvious that the unemployed or those who may lose their jobs will be more sensitive to messages in which the candidate stresses those elements of his program that refer to fighting against unemployment and to such economic changes that will create more jobs. Entrepreneurs with high income, on the other hand, will be more sensitive to the messages presenting the candidate's position on the taxation system. It is not only demographic characteristics, including the citizens' economic status, for instance, that are important for the division of the political market, but also their needs, attitudes, interests, and preferences, all of which are part of psychographic segmentation and play an important role in the division of the market into segments.

An important criterion of voter segmentation in political marketing is also the time voters take to make their decisions. Some voters know for a long time whom they are going to vote for, and any persuasion efforts will inevitably fail in their case. But there are also floating voters, who make up their minds during the campaign or just before the act of voting. Because their behavior is more impulsive then reasoned, it is relatively easy to convince them by particular arguments, but it is much more difficult to reach them because usually they are not interested in politics (see Chapter 3).

After identifying voting segments, the candidate needs to define his position with each of them in the multistage process of positioning. It consists of assessing the candidate's and his opponents' strengths and weaknesses. The key elements here are (1) creating an image of the candidate emphasizing his particular personality features and (2) developing and presenting a clear position on the country's economic and social issues. Such an image and program should follow the strategy of the election fight.

For instance, a candidate competing against the incumbent has an advantage because he can try to attract the voters' attention to a new, completely innovative approach to economic and social problems in his voting program. No

Figure 2.4   **Newman's Model of Political Marketing**

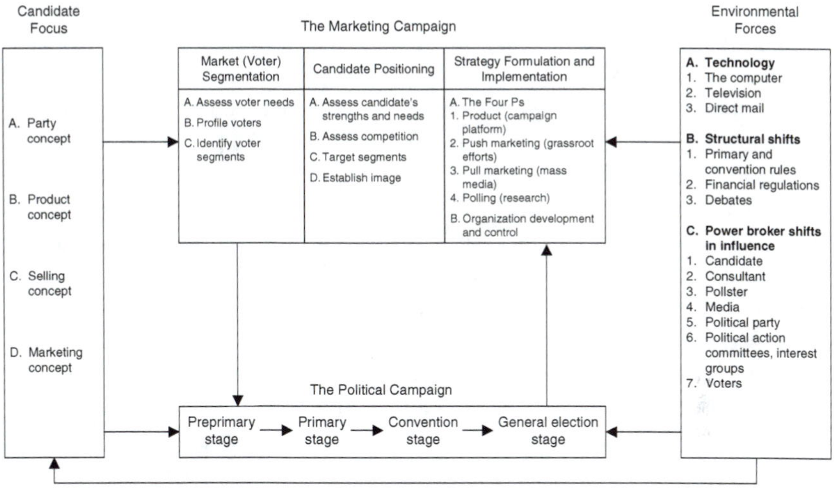

Candidate Focus	The Marketing Campaign			Environmental Forces
	Market (Voter) Segmentation	**Candidate Positioning**	**Strategy Formulation and Implementation**	**A. Technology** 1. The computer 2. Television 3. Direct mail
A. Party concept **B. Product concept** **C. Selling concept** **D. Marketing concept**	A. Assess voter needs B. Profile voters C. Identify voter segments	A. Assess candidate's strengths and needs B. Assess competition C. Target segments D. Establish image	A. The Four Ps 1. Product (campaign platform) 2. Push marketing (grassroot efforts) 3. Pull marketing (mass media) 4. Polling (research) B. Organization development and control	**B. Structural shifts** 1. Primary and convention rules 2. Financial regulations 3. Debates **C. Power broker shifts in influence** 1. Candidate 2. Consultant 3. Pollster 4. Media 5. Political party 6. Political action committees, interest groups 7. Voters
	The Political Campaign			
	Preprimary stage →	Primary stage →	Convention stage →	General election stage

Source: Newman (1994, 12).

matter whether the candidate will be able to implement those changes—voters are always sensitive to changes fitting their beliefs. Regarding this point, the candidate can highlight the weaknesses of the incumbent who does not fulfill her promises and attribute to her the failures in the area of the economy or social policy. The new approach to particular subjects should be accompanied by such characteristics of the candidate as being innovative, firm, conscientious, or open to experiences.

In order to position the candidate in voters' minds, the campaign should apply the political marketing mix used for the implementation of a marketing strategy. The typical strategic plan consists of the "four Ps," a strategy commonly followed in the commercial marketplace. For a company marketing a product, the four Ps include: product, promotion, price, and place. However, according to Newman, they need to be considerably modified if they are to be applied to the political market, both at the level of defining particular components and implementing them.

Product is defined in terms of candidate leadership and campaign platform, particularly issues and policies that the candidate advocates. Such factors as the people in his organization, the party, and the voters influence the product in addition to the candidate himself. When the campaign's platform is being formed, two key information flow channels are created through which a candidate can promote himself and his platform.

The first channel, called *push marketing*, is related to the concept of place or distribution channel. It refers to the grassroots effort necessary to build up a volunteer network to handle the day-to-day activities in running the campaign. Push marketing centers on communicating the candidate's message from his organization to the voter.

The second channel is *pull marketing*, which focuses on the use of the mass media to get the candidate's message out to the voters. Instead of the person-to-person channel used with a push marketing approach, this channel makes use of mass media outlets such as television, radio, newspapers, magazines, direct mail, computer, and any other forms of promotion that are available.

Polling, the last P, is conducted throughout the political process to provide the candidate with the information necessary to develop the marketing campaign. It represents the data analysis and research that are used to develop and test new ideas and determine how successful the ideas will be.

The marketing campaign is conducted simultaneously with the political campaign and serves to help the candidate get through each of the four stages—preprimary, primary, convention, and general election—successfully. Both the marketing and the political campaigns are influenced by the candidate's strategic orientation (see Chapter 1) and by forces in the environment. It is obvious then that both campaigns are tightly connected and interdependent, and one cannot analyze a political campaign without reference to particular elements of the marketing campaign. Those elements of political marketing are presented in Figure 2.4 at the right and left panels, accordingly.

Marketing and political campaigns are integrated into the environment and, therefore, they are related to the distribution of forces in a particular environment. The shift in power in politics—from dominance of party organization to dominance of political consultants—has resulted from two basic forces: technology and structural shifts in the political process. The three influential areas of innovation in technology include the computer, television, and direct mail. Each of these areas directly affects the way presidential candidates run their campaigns, forcing candidates to utilize the expertise of marketing specialists who guide them through the complex processes of marketing and political campaigning.

The structural shifts influence primary and convention rules, financial regulations, and debates. Complex primary and convention rules have altered the way candidates run for president. Limitations on individual contributions have forced candidates to rely not only on fund-raising experts but on direct-mail experts as well.

Advances in direct-mail technology have given candidates the ability to carefully target selected voter blocs with appropriate messages. The coffers of national party headquarters no longer solely finance their campaigns, as they are also dependent on individual contributors. These shifts have further pressured candidates to rely on the expertise of direct-mail wizards to navigate through each stage of the political campaign. The technological and structural changes have resulted in dramatic shifts in influence among the power brokers.

It can then be stated that the environment in which marketing and political campaigns take place consists of three fundamental component groups:

1. technological elements, including the mail, television, the Internet, and other means of voting communication (e.g., spots, direct mail);
2. structural elements involving election law, the procedure of nominating candidates, financial regulations for the campaign, and the conduct of political debates; and
3. the forces influencing the development of the campaign, including the candidate, consultants, media, political parties, interest groups, political and election committees, polling specialists, and voters.

Each of these elements represents an area where dynamic changes have taken place in the past few decades; these changes facilitate the development of marketing research and are becoming more and more important for the election process. Technological changes, for instance, have revolutionized a candidate's contacts with voters (for example, through email, cable televisions, and cell phones). Structural changes in the development of political campaigns make candidates pay more attention to marketing strategies and rely more on the opinions of the experts developing them. One should also note the growing importance of polling specialists. The results of their analyses given to the general electorate not only reflect the electorate's general mood, but also influence the forming of public opinion. It can thus be stated that polls are a controlled attempt to influence voter behavior.

The common element of the theories of political marketing presented here is their focus on the voter as a starting point for any actions undertaken by political consultants in the competitive voting market. An in-depth analysis of the similarities and differences between these theories may contribute to the development of a new and advanced theory of political marketing. This new concept will then be the foundation of the problems and research on modern political marketing presented here.

Challenges for Political Marketing

Political marketing campaigns are integrated into the environment and, therefore, related to the distribution of forces in a particular environment

(Cwalina, Falkowski, and Newman 2008; Newman 1994; Scammell 1999). In this way, changes in societies, legal regulations, or the development of new technologies force modifications of particular marketing strategies and make marketing needs regenerate as well (Harris and Rees 2000; Vargo and Lusch 2004). Each of these elements represents an area where dynamic changes have taken place in the past few decades. These changes facilitate the development of marketing research and are becoming more and more important for the election and governing processes. Therefore, as Stephen Dann, Phil Harris, and their collaborators (2007) and Stephen Henneberg (2008) postulate, political marketing needs to be modernized both as far as marketing practice and theoretical and empirical research are concerned. This modernization should include changes taking place in modern democracies, such as the shift from citizenship to spectatorship, and assess and show new ways of increasing citizen support. Besides, the relations between political marketing and such areas of knowledge as practice, public relations, and political lobbying also need to be clearly defined (Baines, Harris, and Lewis 2002; Harris 2001a).

The emphasis on the processes of election exchanges cannot obscure the fact that political marketing is not limited only to the period of the election campaign. In the era of the permanent campaign, in reality there is no clear difference between the period directly before the election and the rest of the political calendar (Harris 2001a). The emphasis on the processes of election exchanges cannot obscure the fact that political marketing is not limited only to the period of the election campaign. In the era of the permanent campaign there is no difference between the period of governing and election campaigning. David Dulio and Terri Towner (2009, 93) state that modern campaigning extends to governing: "each day is election day."

Permanent Campaign

Nicholas O'Shaughnessy (2001) argues that through the concept of the permanent campaign, political marketing has become the organizing principle around which parties and government policies are constructed. Political marketing is no longer a short-term tactical device used exclusively to win voters' support; it has become a long-term permanent process that aims to ensure continued governance (Smith and Hirst 2001). According to Dan Nimmo (1999), the permanent campaign is a process of continuing transformation. It never stops. From this perspective, the perpetual campaign remakes government into an instrument designed to sustain an elected official's public popularity.

Nimmo (1999) argues that the line between political campaigning and governance was crossed during Margaret Thatcher's and Ronald Reagan's 1980 political campaigns. It was exactly then that the era of total campaigning started. Political marketing began to occupy the total environment of politics, reaching and encircling the whole of every citizen and providing a complete system for explaining the world. The media, especially television and, more recently, the Internet, play a dominant role in political marketing.

Together with the political changes, a number of changes in the ways the media operate took place (see Kaid 1999a, 1999b). The legal regulations of the media market opened it up to commercial broadcasters; new technologies were introduced and the quality of the broadcast was improved (see Kaid and Holtz-Bacha 2006). According to Edwin Diamond and Stephen Bates (1992), the development of television production, marketing methods, and public opinion polls led to the establishment of today's high-tech political communication.

These developments led Jay Blumler and Dennis Kavanagh (1999) to announce the *third age of political communication*. According to them, modern and efficient political communication must follow and react to a number of changes taking place all the time in the media and social environment. The change is mainly about *modernization* and is connected with increased social differentiation and specialization, interests, and identities and proliferating diverse lifestyles and moral stances, which undermine traditional structures of social inclusion and aggregation (e.g., church, trade unions). According to Margaret Scammell (1999), the major consequences of modernization for political marketing are twofold: (1) the development of increasingly nonideological or populist "catch-all parties" (or the Tactical Populist; see Henneberg 2006a, 2006b), and (2) the transformation of media from essentially a channel of communication to an increasingly autonomous power center and a major actor in the campaigning process (see, e.g., Entman 2007; Gamson et al. 1992; Graber 2004). Thus candidates must look for media and communication channels (e.g., twenty-four-hour information channels, the Internet) in order to reach all segments of society with their message.

According to Blumler and Kavanagh (1999), modernization involves several challenges in political communication. The first is growing *individualization*. Citizens' personal views, beliefs, and aspirations are becoming increasingly important. Various traditional institutions (the family, for instance) and value systems are losing their importance. A second social trend that modern political communication takes into account is *secularization*. It contributes to the decreasing importance of ideological divisions and, as a consequence, to the marginalization of political parties. It also impairs the authority of political power. As a result of secularization the distance between the elites and the masses decreases and the masses become increasingly important. It fosters the development of political and media populism.

Third, the importance of the issues connected with the economy is also on the rise. The *economization* of life manifests itself by the growing importance of economic factors in political agendas' functioning and fulfilling their mission. The political sphere is constantly being made to conform to the institutions having financial capital.

Fourth, social life has been undergoing *aestheticization*. As a result of this, political communication has more and more to do with popular culture and the entertainment industry. This can be illustrated by the fact that television news stations are adopting tabloid news magazine production techniques for newscasts. They reflect sensational news practice, or "infotainment," where production style overpowers substantive information (see Grabe et al. 2000).

Fifth, more emphasis is put on *rationalization*, which forces politicians to adopt a marketing orientation based on facts and citizens' opinions and not on the politicians' own intuitions. The main focus here is on following public opinion and presenting the views of ordinary citizens rather than politicians. The last social change Blumler and Kavanagh point to is *mediatization*. The mass media have moved into the center of all social processes and begun to construct the public sphere and the world of politics (Gamson et al. 1992; Shapiro and Lang 1991). The processes of mediatization are presented metaphorically by William Gamson and his collaborators (1992, 374): "We walk around with media-generated images of the world, using them to construct meaning about political and social issues. The lens through which we receive these images is not neutral but evinces the power and point of view of the political and economic elites who operate and focus it. And the special genius of this system is to make the whole process seem so normal and natural that the very art of social construction is invisible."

Political marketing and political communication reacted to those changes gradually. Recognizing current trends, politicians tried to take advantage of them to win and then maintain power. According to Blumler and Kavanagh (1999), these efforts may be divided into three subsequent stages of the political communication era: the "golden age" of parties, the television age, and the third age of political communication. The "golden age" of political parties included the first two decades after World War II. Political communication was based on stable and permanent party identification. That is why it was focused on communicating positions on particular issues and opinions about them. The differences between a party's own views and the views of the opposition were presented and discussed. Political debate was substantial and based on ideological foundations.

An important shift in ways of conducting political communication took place in the 1960s, when television became the main medium. It was then that political parties lost control over the content that their supporters received.

Viewers had access to information about various political parties, with a lot of details about their strengths and weaknesses. That led to the development of a bigger and bigger segment of ideologically neutral citizens. The television age also led to the development of audiences whose support politicians were trying to win. This communication channel reached groups that before were not of much interest for those competing for power. Their growing importance made their votes more and more desirable.

The "third age" of political communication is related to the emergence of more and more mass media. The multiplicity of channels providing information led—according to Blumler and Kavanagh (1999)—to politicians' beginning to treat the new system of the media as a hydra with many heads always hungry for food. Such a situation leads politicians who want to gain support to hire professional assistants to maintain contacts with the media. Their main task is to provide the media with information about the politicians and their actions (or prevent such information from spreading) and to criticize political opponents. Such contacts with the media have consequences for the organization of government or party structures. The role of the party leader or premier grows and her task is to centralize and coordinate communication with citizens. This communication is no longer limited to television; other ways of presenting politicians are used more and more often: the Internet, billboards, press articles under a politician's name, or events that attract the attention of journalists and society. Intensive contacts with the society make politicians flatter citizens. Therefore, populist slogans become more and more widespread.

A similar view is also expressed by Philip Howard. In his opinion, information technologies have played a role in campaign organization since the 1970s, but it is only over the last decade that adopting new technologies also became an occasion for organizational restructuring within political parties and campaigns. As a result, a completely new and different way of planning and conducting the campaign emerged, which Howard (2006, 2) defines as the *hypermedia campaign,* "an agile political organization defined by its capacity for innovatively adopting digital technologies for express political purposes and its capacity for innovatively adapting its organizational structure to conform to new communicative practices." It is not simply that political campaigns employ digital information technologies in their communications strategies. Integrating such technologies becomes an occasion for organizational adaptation, effecting organizational goals and relationships among professional staff, political leadership, volunteers, financial contributors, citizens, and other political campaigns. According to Howard, this rising prominence of hypermedia campaigns is related to three factors. First, a service class of professional political technocrats with special expertise in information technology (IT) arose. Unlike other campaign managers, the consultants specializing in IT focus mainly on building new communication technologies for citizens and candidates. Second, the political consulting industry replaced mass-media tools with targeted media tools, ranging from fax and computer-generated direct mail to email and website content, which allowed the industry to tailor messages to specific audiences. Third, the engineers of political hypermedia made technical decisions about political hypermedia that constrained subsequent decisions about the production and consumption of political content. Howard argues that the hypermedia campaign has succeeded the mass media campaign, such that the 1988 campaign was the beginning of an important transition in the organization of political information in the United States.

There is a traditional view that the media constitute the "fourth estate," (the other three are legislative-parliament, judical, and executive-government) suggesting their importance as an element in the political fight and a way of influencing society. John B. Thompson (1994), trying to define the mutual relations between social development and mass communication, suggests that the media play an important role in the mechanisms of power. The close relation between the world of politics and the media is made even closer by the specific characteristics of mass communication. In this context, the power of the media using symbolic forms while transferring information in order to influence events becomes a temptation for those who want to use it to achieve particular ideological, economic, or political benefits (see Scammell 1999).

No matter how the mass media are organized, how they function, and what information they provide citizens with, they are a part of the political system. Therefore, all the strategies of political actors, both before and between the elections, include using the mass media for their own purposes, distributing particular messages and influencing the society. Finding mutual relations between the mass media and political institutions and society became a starting point for Ralph Negrine (1994) to propose his own model of political communication, presented in Figure 2.5.

According to Negrine, the key elements of the political communication process include media content, the influence of political institutions and other political and social actors on the context of the messages, the specific audience and interaction processes between sources of information, and the media diffusing information.

The content of media messages is the result of the work of media practitioners (owners of media corporations, editors, journalists, reporters, etc.) and political actors or events covered by the media. Despite clear quality standards of information distributed by mass media, the real quality of the media and thus their influence on society do not necessarily meet these standards. The

Figure 2.5   **Model of Political Communication**

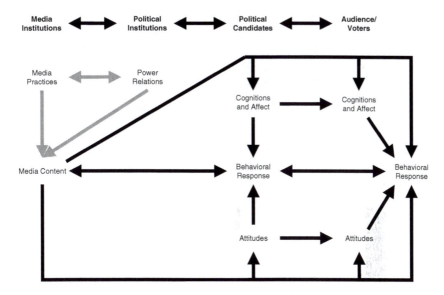

Source: Based on Negrine (1994, 13).

reasons for this discrepancy are connected with the uncertainty about what an appropriate or reliable information supply (offer) might be. That is, what information should be found in every news service and what information should not be distributed? Besides, there are still controversies about what constitutes "objectivity of information presentation" (McQuail 1994), and mass communication researchers often make distinctions between "real world" and "news world" (Wu 2000).

Negrine (1994) stresses that groups that influence the content of political communication have different levels of power in this area. In their interactions with the media, political actors, including parties, certain politicians, the government, and so on, try to achieve their own goals, and sometimes they manage to do so by dominating the content of the message. On the other hand, society at large does not have such influence. Society does not play an active role in creating messages, and the feedback from the messages is also very limited. In fact, the influence of the recipients of media messages can only be indirect. This happens when certain ideas of the audience are included by the specialists designing the message to make it fit the audience. The specialists often make use of various social studies on reading or viewing figures, dominant problems (e.g., pedophilia), or society's opinions about certain issues (e.g., the presence of Polish and American troops in Iraq). In this way, the creators of media messages are also indirectly the agents of citizens' influence on the content of political communication.

The third important component of the model proposed by Negrine is recognizing that there is no one uniform public political communication, but that it is rather a collection of different segments of viewers. Each of them has its own preferences related to newspapers or television channels from which it gains knowledge of the surrounding world.

The fourth characteristic of political communication is that the process of creating news requires some level of interaction or strategic negotiations between the sources of information and the media that diffuse it. For instance, such relations can be based on the promise that the informer will remain anonymous. On the other hand, media representatives may have the exclusive right to report some events. Such relations are then based on feedback. What finally reaches the audience is the result of such agreements or negotiations.

Media and Politics

Gamson and his collaborators (1992) state that a wide variety of media messages act as teachers of values, ideologies, and beliefs, providing images for interpreting the world whether or not the designers are conscious of this intent. It seems, however, that in relation to politics, developers of media messages are fully aware of what content and in what form they are trying to communicate to society.

Media Bias

Robert M. Entman (2007, 166) believes that content bias is "consistent patterns in the framing of mediated communication that promote the influence of one side in conflicts over the use of government power." These patterns of slant regularly prime audiences, consciously or unconsciously, to support the interests of particular holders or seekers of political power. Dave D'Alessio and Mike Allen (2000) distinguish three types of media bias: gatekeeping bias, coverage bias, and statement bias.

Gatekeeping bias. The *gatekeeping bias* means that editors select from a body of potential stories those that will be presented to the public and, by extension, also deselect those stories of which the mass audience will hear nothing. Thus, the gatekeeper is any person or formally organized group that is directly involved in relaying or transforming information from one individual to another through a mass medium (Bittner 1980; White 1950). The gatekeeper's activities consist in limiting information by selective editing, increasing the amount of information by expansive editing, or reorganizing the information through reinterpretation. Such activities should be implemented not only by the editor but also by the moderator—not only for television programs, but also for blog or chat on the Internet. Another modern form of gatekeeping is using Internet search engines as gatekeepers of public communication (Schulz, Held, and Laudien 2005). Despite the fact that the number of channels the citizen can get information from increases, this may lead to the collapse of media gatekeeping; its forms change, too (Williams and Delli Carpini 2000). Gatekeeping evolves and takes on more and more subtle forms. An example may be applying gatekeeping for online newspapers. Daniela Dimitrova and her collaborators (2003) conducted a study of the online coverage of American terrorist Timothy McVeigh's execution on the websites of the top fifteen American print newspapers. Using content analysis, the study compared the fifteen newspapers' websites by measuring the number, destination, and characteristics of hyperlinks that accompanied these stories. The results suggest that online newspapers use hyperlinks as a gatekeeping device because they are unlikely to offer external hyperlinks.

One of the consequences of gatekeeping is media bias toward supporting or not supporting particular political parties. For example, Tim Groseclose and Jeffrey Milyo (2005) found a systematic tendency for U.S. media outlets (press and TV) to slant the news to the left; the most liberal are *CBS Evening News* and the *New York Times*, and the most conservative are the *Washington Post* and *Fox News' Special Report*. However, the media outlets are fairly centrist relative to members of Congress, and according to Daniel Ho and Kevin Quinn (2008), about half the newspapers they analyzed take relatively moderate positions on issues coming before the American Supreme Court. From this perspective, an important supplement and extension of media bias analyses are the results of research conducted by James Druckman and Michael Parkin (2005). Combining comprehensive content analyses of two competing newspapers (*Star Tribune* and *St. Paul Pioneer Press*) with an Election Day exit poll, they found that editorial slant influenced voters' decisions in the 2000 Minnesota Senate campaign (see also Mondak 1995a).

Coverage and statement biases. According to D'Alessio and Allen (2000), the *coverage bias* refers mainly to physical features of media message. Ten media biases were codified by measuring the physical amount of coverage each side of some issue receives. This is typically measured in column inches for newspapers and magazines (with or without photographs and headlines), whereas analyses of television include the number of appearances and time devoted to each side of the issue. But the *statement bias* suggests that members of the media can interject their own opinions into the text of coverage of an issue. This type of bias can take many forms and is usually expressed

by whether media coverage is favorable or unfavorable to a particular politician or party.

Jeffrey Peake (2007) conducted a comparative study of coverage of the
George W. Bush presidency on the front pages of 100 American newspapers
during a five-month period in 2006. He found clear media slant. Newspapers
that endorsed Bush's reelection in 2004 tended to write more, and more favorably about the president, and newspapers in states where Democrats are
strong politically tended to write less, and less favorably (see also Groeling
and Kernell 1998).

The OSCE/ODIHR Election Assessment Mission Final Report (2008)
referring to preterm parliamentary elections in Poland in 2007 also showed
a lack of qualitative balance by the public television broadcaster during the
broadcasts monitored. While all three public TVP channels devoted the largest
news coverage to the Civic Platform party (30 percent on TVP1 and TVP2,
and 32 percent on TVP Info), the party's portrayal was characterized by mostly
neutral and negative information, especially on TVP1 and the informative TVP
Info. The Law and Justice party, by comparison, was presented on all public
channels in a qualitatively balanced way (with 24 percent on TVP1 and TVP2,
and 19 percent on TVP Info). Of the private broadcasters, Polsat, during the
timeframe monitored by the OSCE/ODIHR mission, overall showed a degree
of lack of balance in coverage of the main parties, with some 35 percent of
balanced (generally equally positive, neutral, and negative) political news
coverage for the CP, while it gave some 30 percent to L&J, with a neutral
and negative tone prevailing in party-related information.

The Instytut Monitorowania Mediów [Institute of Media Monitoring] monitored the Polish presidential campaign in 2000 (see Cwalina and Falkowski
2006). From August 1 to October 6, 2000, all the television programs of four
stations—two public (TVP1 and TVP2) and two private (Polsat and TVN)—
were analyzed. The researchers focused on the number of appearances of all
thirteen presidential candidates on television programs and on how long their
presentations were. The same analyses were performed for the presentations
of their aides and spokespersons. In addition, the number and duration of the
programs dedicated to the candidates and to the main subjects of the campaign
were registered too.

The unquestionable media leader given the frequency of his appearances
was the incumbent, President Aleksander Kwaśniewski. During the analyzed
period, he appeared on television more than 300 times. Marian Krzaklewski
was far behind him (about 160 appearances), as was Lech Wałęsa (over 120)
and—the second person in the voting struggle—Andrzej Olechowski (over
110). The duration time of the candidates' presentations was distributed slightly
differently. Although the leader here was still President Kwaśniewski, he owed

his position mainly to the public media. TVP1 and TVP2 gave almost as much time to Jarosław Kalinowski and Lech Wałęsa as they did to Kwaśniewski. This breakdown shows clearly that the presentations of the presidential candidates in the presidential campaign of 2000 were biased. Television stations—both private and public—had their favorites and sentenced the other politicians to "nonexistence." However, in the case of Kwaśniewski, one should remember that his presentations were the result of an overlap between his functions as the president in office and as presidential candidate. The proportions of appearing in one or the other role changed as the election campaign progressed. In August, 60 percent of his appearances were connected with his office, whereas in September and October, it was 51 percent. One of the issues he raised most often was . . . the Olympic Games in Sydney! Most of these statements were presented by public television channels that broadcast the games. So the viewers had a chance to watch and listen to Aleksander Kwaśniewski's statements on the Olympic Games and see him with Polish athletes—particularly those who were successful.

Media Effects

There are three main forms of media communication's influence on citizens: agenda-setting, priming, and framing.

Agenda-setting. The idea of *agenda-setting* influence by the mass media is a relational concept specifying a positive, causal relationship between the key themes of mass communication and what members of the audience come to regard as important. According to Maxwell McCombs (1981, 126; see also McCombs and Shaw 1972), "the salience of an issue or other topic in the mass media influences its salience among the audience." Newspaper and television stories often make explicit statements about the importance of an issue (e.g., global economic crisis, terrorist threat) in order to justify attention to it. However, as Joanne Miller and Jon Krosnick (2000) emphasize, even when such issue statements are not made, most readers and viewers recognize that devoting attention to an issue means that editors and reporters believe the issue is a significant one for the country. Consequently, people may infer from the media that an issue is nationally important.

The mechanism of agenda-setting resembles, to some extent, the process of fashion. Its natural consequence is that politicians and parties try to exert pressure on media to highlight those issues that present them in a good light and are positive for them. Manfred Holler and Peter Skott (2005) suggest that the incumbent or governing party can manage agenda-setting better since it holds power and has access to resources (e.g., confidential information, experts). The authors stress that decisions regarding this field have to be made before the start of the election campaign. The opposition also makes precampaign decisions, but, almost by definition, the incumbent dominates the political arena before the election campaign.

Keeping a particular issue on top of the agenda, or agenda control, requires further effort on behalf of the politicians. It also depends on political and policy context and previous media attention and public concern. Jeffrey Peake and Matthew Eshbaugh-Soha (2008) tried to answer the question: Are televised presidential speeches effective in increasing news coverage of presidential priorities? They analyzed television news stories shown on the nightly news programs of the three broadcast networks (ABC, CBS, and NBC) in the context of American presidents' speeches over four issue areas (economy, energy policy, drugs, and Central America) from 1969 to 2000. They found that 35 percent of the president's national addresses increased media attention in the short term, while only 10 percent of the speeches increased media attention beyond the month of the speech.

Politicians are not the only subjects trying to mark their presence in the media. Their competition includes all kinds of interest groups. The results of content analysis of American network television news from 1969 to 1982 suggest that although most attention is given to the president and his partisans and opponents in Congress (51.9 percent), other interest groups were also present in the news (14.4 percent). The most important ones were corporations and business groups (36.5 percent) and citizen action groups (32 percent), creating, as the authors of the research—Lucig Danielian and Benjamin Page (1994)—put it, "the heavenly chorus" on TV news.

Furthermore, as the results of a study conducted by Phil Harris, Ioannis Kolovos, and Andrew Lock (2001) confirm, during the campaign for the European Parliament in Greece in 1999, it was not enough if a party managed to initiate coverage of a specific issue and "made it" to their voters' minds. It was necessary to subsequently manage to adopt the overall media agenda to party-specific priorities or manifestos. The relationship between media and politicians is then a bilateral relationship; politicians try to include their message in the media, but in order to be successful they need to adapt to the content distributed by the media.

Public issues, however, are not the only objects of communication. The objects defining the media and public agendas also can be the political candidates competing in elections. When the mass media present an object, they also tell something about the attributes of the object. According to McCombs and his collaborators (1997), when the agendas of objects (issues, candidates) are the first level of agenda-setting (object salience), the agenda attributes are the second level (attribute salience). This distinction is supported by the results of their study conducted in Pamplona during Spain's general election in 1996. They found a high degree of correspondence between the attribute agenda of seven different mass media (newspapers and TV channels) and the voters' attribute agendas for each of the three candidates: Felipe Gonzalez (the incumbent prime minister at the time of the election and candidate of the Spanish Socialist Workers Party), Jose Maria Aznar (the candidate of the Popular Party, who won the election), and Julio Anguita (the candidate of the United Left). The median correlation between these two agendas was 0.72.

In this way, the media can not only "create fashion" for particular issues, but also set trends about what features of a candidate are most desirable for the position of the president—for instance, moral or competent, dominant or affiliative (see Chapter 4).

Media priming. The effect of agenda-setting is making particular issues, objects, or their attributes more salient for the audience. The consequence of it may be and often is the phenomenon called *priming*. Priming refers to changes in the standards people use to make political evaluations. According to Shanto Iyengar and Donald D. Kinder (1987, 63), "by calling attention to some matters while ignoring others, television news influences the standards by which governments, presidents, policies, and candidates for public office are judged." Priming presumes that when evaluating complex political phenomena, people do not take into account all that they know. Instead, they consider what comes to mind, those bits and pieces of political memory that are accessible. The media messages might help to set the terms by which political judgments are reached and political choices are made.

For example, Iyengar and Kinder (1987) found that the news media's sudden preoccupation with the Iranian hostage issue in the closing days of the 1980 presidential campaign caused voters to think about the candidates' ability to control terrorism when choosing between Jimmy Carter and Ronald Reagan. This phenomenon proved disadvantageous to President Carter.

Political parties also "specialize" in offering "the best solutions" to particular social and economic problems. This means that, according to voters, a certain political group is more efficient in solving certain issues than other groups. Such a phenomenon was described by John R. Petrocik (1996) with reference to American parties in his theory of issue ownership. According to this theory, a party's "owning" of a certain problem is connected with a relatively stable social background and is also connected with political conflicts. The results of Petrocik's analysis suggest that American voters consider issues connected with general social welfare, including the homeless, public schools, the elderly, national minorities, unemployment, health care, and the environment, as owned by the Democratic Party. The Republican Party is associated with better achievements in the areas of crime, defense of moral values, running foreign policy, defense, inflation, taxes, and government spending. The theory of issue ownership has certain consequences for running a successful campaign. According to Petrocik, the campaign will bring the desired result if the candidate or political party manages to limit voting decisions to those issues that the country faces (decisions' criteria) that the candidate is better able to solve than his opponent. In other words, to the degree that candidates or parties enjoy a favorable reputation on some issue, their support is likely to be boosted by news coverage on this issue. In an experimental study, Stephen Ansolabehere and Shanto Iyengar (1994) found that news coverage of crime was an asset to the Republicans. In addition, Republican advertising on crime was more effective in shaping viewers' perceptions of the sponsor as tough on crime, while Democratic advertising on unemployment was more effective in influencing perceptions of the sponsor as a supporter of jobs programs and in influencing voting preference.

Priming, like agenda-setting, may concern both particular issues and attributes of candidates' image. Important data concerning the problem was provided by the research conducted by James Druckman (2004) during the 2000 campaign for the U.S. Senate in Minnesota. The content analysis of local newspapers allowed him to define the major subjects of this campaign. It was focused on social security and health-care issues and the integrity of candidates. Druckman also used data from the Election Day exit poll for his analysis. The results of these analyses show that the noncampaign voters did not rely on social security and integrity; rather they based their votes on taxes and leadership effectiveness—an issue and an image that were not particularly emphasized in the campaign. In contrast, campaign voters focused mainly on the central issue and image in the campaign. Thus, campaign priming effects manifested themselves only among voters who attended to and discussed the campaign. Miller and Krosnick (2000) also reached similar conclusions. In two experiments they found that for priming to occur, citizens must have the requisite knowledge to interpret, store, and later retrieve and make inferences from news stories they see, hear, or read. In addition, knowledge facilitates priming only among people who trust the media. In this context, sole accessibility information in memory (e.g., as a result of agenda-setting) did not determine the weight people placed on an issue when evaluating a particular object (e.g., the president).

Media framing. According to Entman (2007, 164), *framing* is the "process of culling a few elements of perceived reality and assembling a narrative that highlights connections among them to promote a particular interpretation." However, media framing, as defined by William Gamson and Andre Modigliani (1996, 143), is "a central organizing idea or story line that provides meaning to an unfolding strip of events, weaving a connection among them. The frame suggests what the controversy is about and the essence of the issue." James Druckman and Kjersten Nelson (2003) state specifically that framing effects occur when in the course of describing an issue or event, a media emphasis on a subset of potentially relevant considerations causes individuals to focus on these considerations when constructing their opinions. Therefore, at a general level, the concept of framing refers to subtle alterations in the statement or presentation of judgments or choice problems, and, as Iyengar (1991) emphasizes, framing effects refer to changes in decision outcomes resulting from these alterations.

This phenomenon was first researched and described by the cognitive psychologists Daniel Kahneman and Amos Tversky. They demonstrated in a series of experiments that choices between risky prospects could be powerfully altered merely by changing the terms in which equivalent choices are described. In one experiment, subjects were asked to define their preferences for various solutions of the problem presented in two ways (Kahneman and Tversky 1984, 343):

> Imagine that the U.S. is preparing for the outbreak of an unusual Asian disease, which is expected to kill 600 people. Two alternative programs to combat the disease have been proposed. Assume that the exact scientific estimates of the consequences of the programs are as follows:
> If Program A is adopted, 200 people will be saved.
> If Program B is adopted, there is a one-third probability that 600 people will be saved and a two-thirds probability that no people will be saved.
> Which of the two programs would you favor?

The formulation of the problem implicitly adopts as a reference point a state of affairs in which the disease is allowed to take its toll of 600 lives. The outcomes of the programs include the reference state and two possible gains, measured by the number of lives saved. A clear majority of respondents (72 percent) prefer saving 200 lives for sure over a gamble that offers a one-third chance of saving 600 lives (28 percent).

An alternative presentation of the same two options looked as follows:

> If Program C is adopted, 400 people will die.
> If Program D is adopted, there is a one-third probability that nobody will die and a two-thirds probability that 600 people will die.

Options C and D are undistinguishable in real terms from options A and B. The second version, however, assumes a reference state in which no one dies of the disease. The best outcome is the maintenance of this state, and the alternatives are losses measured by the number of people that will die of the disease. People who evaluated the options in these terms preferred a risky choice (option D; 78 percent) over the sure loss of 400 lives (option C; 22 percent).

Frames are never neutral. They may provide different ways of presenting situations, attributes, choices, actions, issues, responsibility, and news (Hallahan 1999). According to Iyengar (1991), all television news stories can be classified as either episodic or thematic. The episodic news frame takes the form of a case study or event-oriented report. It presents a particular issue by concrete cases. The thematic frame places public issues in some more general or abstract context. It refers to more analytical, contextual, or historical coverage. In a series of experiments, researchers found that, for example, episodic media framing of poverty increased attributions of individualistic responsibility, while thematic framing increased attributions of societal responsibility. Attributions of responsibility for unemployment, however, were unaffected by the type of frame. Citizens understood unemployment primarily in economic terms under conditions of both episodic and thematic framing.

Holli Semetko and Patti Valkenburg (2000) distinguish five media frames that occur most often in media reports about politics:

- *conflict frame*—emphasizes conflict among individuals, groups, or institutions;
- *human interest frame*—brings a human face or an emotional angle to the presentation of an event, issue, or problem;
- *economic consequences frame*—reports an event or issue in terms of the consequences it will have economically on an individual, a group, an institution, a country, or a region;
- *morality frame*—puts an event or issue in the context of religious tenets or moral prescriptions;
- *responsibility frame*—presents an issue in such a way to attribute responsibility for its cause or solution either to the government or to an individual, a group, or to uncontrolled external conditions or powers.

Semetko and Valkenburg used these five frames in their content analysis of the Dutch national media news (newspapers and TV news programs) from May 1 to June 20, 1997, the period leading up to the meeting of the heads of government of the European Union countries, held in Amsterdam during June 16–17, 1997. The European leaders met to finalize agreement on monetary union. Semetko and Valkenburg found that television news coverage in Holland was predominantly episodic, focusing on specific events in the past twenty-four hours. Only 8 percent of the news coverage was thematic, taking information from different points in time and providing a context or interpretation for an event. Most often the media used a responsibility frame and then the following frames: conflict frame, economic consequences frame, human interest frame, and morality frame. The subjects attributed responsibility for most of the discussed problems to the government. Also the relations concerning the monetary union were most often presented through this perspective and were supplemented only to a small extent by references to conflict or economic consequences.

Despite some similarities, Miller and Krosnick (2000) state that framing and priming are substantively different effects—the former deals with how changes in the *content* of stories on a single issue affect attitudes toward relevant public policy, the latter with how changes in the *number* of stories about an issue affect the ingredients of presidential performance evaluations. However, both ways of influencing citizen beliefs by the media do influence considerably people's preferences toward particular ways of solving problems and attribution of responsibility for and, thus, support for particular political parties.

Political Public Relations and Lobbying

Philip Kotler and Kevin Lane Keller (2006) believe that public relations (PR) is one of six major modes of communication within the *marketing communications mix*. Public relations is company-sponsored activities and programs designed to create daily or special brand-related interactions. It involves a variety of programs designed to promote or protect a company's image or its individual products. Public relations includes communications directed internally to employees of the company and externally to consumers, other firms, the government, and the media. According to these authors, the appeal of public relations is based on three distinctive qualities: (1) high credibility (the news stories and features are more authentic and credible to readers than ads); (2) ability to catch buyers off guard (PR can reach prospects who prefer to avoid salespeople and advertisements); and (3) dramatization (PR has the potential for dramatizing a company or product). The major tools in marketing PR include, according to Kotler and Keller, publications (e.g., reports, press and web articles, company newsletters), events (e.g., news conferences, seminars, outings), sponsorships (sports and cultural events), news (media releases), speeches, public service activities (e.g., contributing money and time to good causes), and identity media (e.g., logos, stationery, business cards, buildings, uniforms).

Political Public Relations

In accordance with changes in modern societies, public relations has expanded into a communication strategy that is increasingly permeating all areas of society. According to Ulrich Saxer (1993), PR gradually separated itself from the business advertising system, becoming interinstitutional and reaching beyond the economic sector. In consequence, professional communicators come with expertise in a variety of fields (e.g., media, business, polling), including also politics. In this context they usually perform the function of political press officers but are commonly defined as "spin doctors." Their main task is to control the news agenda. Joy Johnson, a former director of the British Labour Party, and cited by Ivor Gaber in the April 1999 edition of *Red Pepper* magazine (274), defines spin as "characterized as either (a) malign and dealing in deceit or (b) benign by throwing morsels to the lobby. It was born with the end of ideas. Politicians hold belief that what happens in the political world does not matter—only perceptions matter."

John Brissenden and Kevin Moloney (2005) believe that political PR should be viewed as much as defensive activity by parties against critical journalism as an offensive of self-serving publicity. Parties are focused on preventing media and thus voters from getting particular information unfavorable to the parties while attracting voters with positive policy and image. The media respond to political PR by reporting not simply political strategy and issues but on the attempts by politicians to manage their presentation, although according to Brian McNair (2004) the techniques of PR are value-neutral. However, they may be and are used to manipulate public opinion, and in this case it is not the problem of techniques but intentions and goals for which they are employed. Besides, some PR techniques seem "neutral" whereas others are based on sheer communication strategies to exert social influence. Given those procedures, Gaber (1999, 264, 265) proposes to characterize spin as being "above the line" or "below the line." Above-the-line activities might be defined "as those more or less overt initiatives that in very simple terms would have caused an 'old-fashioned' press officer no great difficulty." Then, below-the-line activities are those "usually more covert and as much about strategy and tactics as about the imparting of information."

The first group of techniques includes, according to Gaber,

- government or party announcements—issue press releases, press conferences, making announcements via interviews or speeches;
- reacting to government or party announcements ("re" and "prebuttal")—usually assuming the same forms as the above category;
- publicizing speeches, interviews, and articles;
- reacting to interviews or speeches; and
- reacting to breaking news events (and "staying on message").

The below-the-line techniques include

- spinning—managing the way (e.g., the sequence), form, and content of disseminated messages;
- setting the news agenda—dissemination and control of information that appears in media;
- dividing the news agenda—sustaining the campaign of driving the news in a particular direction over a period of time; a string of related stories;
- firebreaking—deliberatively constructing diversions to take journalists off the scent of an embarrassing story;
- stoking the fire—finding and publicizing the material to keep an opponent's awkward story running;
- building up a personality—creating a politician's own positive image (see Chapter 4);
- undermining a personality—creating a negative image of the opponent;
- preempting—anticipating negative media reports about to appear (e.g., admitting in advance to some mistake);
- kite-flying—floating a proposal in order to test reaction;
- raising or lowering expectations—preparing for a worse (or better) course of action than was predicted (e.g., that the politician's year budget will be particularly problematic);
- milking a story—extracting as much positive media coverage out of a given situation as possible;
- throwing out the bodies—disseminating bad news without attracting too much attention (e.g., in the context of other events that are very interesting to the public);
- laundering—finding a piece of good news that can be released at the same time as bad news (see Chapter 6);
- creating the "white commonwealth"—a favored group of correspondents who receive special treatment and access, above and beyond that available to other correspondents;
- bullying and intimidation—accusing certain media of partiality in order to discredit them.

From another perspective, these techniques may also be described as focused on the following: creating media relations, framing favorite narratives, photo opportunities, event management, and sloganeering (Brissenden and Moloney 2005). Their main goal is, above all, to build a positive image of a party or politician or repair the image after some negative events (see Chapter 4).

It should also be emphasized that PR actions are not always an efficient tool for winning the support of voters. Their efficiency depends not only on the professionalism of spin doctors but also on particular situations in which they are undertaken, on the activities of political opponents, and also on the media, the key channel of message dissemination. An important element of success is the object on which PR focuses, something that former British prime minister John Major (Bale and Sanders 2001) learned, as did U.S. president George W. Bush, conducting a series of domestic travels to promote his reforms (Barrett and Peake 2007; Eshbaugh-Soha and Peake 2006) and the British government in its communication on the so-called BSE crisis (Harris and O'Shaughnessy 1997).[1]

Spin is the current dominant form of political presentation, but changes in journalism, particularly an alluring treatment of fact and opinion, were an incubatory environment for it (Moloney 2001). Although it is most often connected with manufacturing politicians' false images and cheating society, spin could also be said to have some benefits related to it. Kevin Moloney (2000) believes that the benefits created by PR in politics are those that come from information flowing between parties, government, and the public. PR and other political marketing techniques make politics more attractive to contemporary electorates.

PR, although considered one of the elements of the marketing communication mix (see Kotler and Keller 2006), is in fact something more than a pure promotion tool. It has become an important supplement to political marketing campaigns resulting from their permanent character. It also occupies a particularly important place in postelection communication strategies (see Chapter 6). Despite the threats related to using PR techniques to manipulate people, it may significantly support the communication of those in power with citizens by presenting clearly the goals, policy, and reforms realized by politicians. It may also contribute to higher transparency and accountability of those in power (see Gaber 2004). Moloney (2001, 125) believes that "spin style represents an opportunity for politicians to re-assess the relative importance they give to the substance of policy and to their private and public behavior" and to "and rebalance their time and energies in favor of policy substance."

Another dimension of PR in politics is, as Moloney (2000) puts it, "PR as lobbying." PR as lobbying is a technique with the potential to add strength to weak, outsider groups seeking policy advantage. It may equip these groups with a set of low-cost techniques, thanks to which they will be able to publicize their interests. But it also raises acute concerns about access by powerful interests to elected governments.

Political Lobbying

Conor McGrath (2007) believes that political lobbying can be considered a form of political communication and—as Phil Harris and Andrew Lock

(1996) add—a part of the broader field of public relations. It is related to the "stimulation and transmission of a communication, by someone other than a citizen acting on his/her own behalf, directed to a governmental decision-maker with the hope of influencing his/her decision" (McGrath 2007, 273). And the most powerful form of lobbying is the supply of information on your lobbyist case, and the issues surrounding it, on a regular basis to those within the decision process.

The results of interviews and research conducted by Harris and Lock (1996, 326) allowed them to formulate five main reasons for the growth and increased importance of commercial campaigning in the United Kingdom:

1. the increased internationalization and competition in business markets and the consequent pressure to have influence over the legislature and to maintain competitive positioning in the business environment;
2. the growing importation of a more structured corporate lobbying system from the United States and Washington, DC, designed in particular to influence legislation affecting business markets;
3. the increased activities of lobbyists on behalf of clients as a result of increased corporate acquisitions, mergers, and joint-venture activity;
4. the radical nature of British government in the 1980s and 1990s, which effectively broke down earlier consensus politics and required that those affected by proposals should seek to ensure that their views are communicated as competently as possible or lose influence; and
5. the growth of transnational government (e.g., the European Union), which has generated substantial legislation affecting businesses (e.g., environmental legislation).

According to Leighton Andrews (1996), lobbying means two things. First, lobbying is working the system—that is, representations based on careful research, usually followed by negotiation with several elements of central or local government. Second, it means pressure on government—that is, mobilization of public and media opinion around a particular problem.

Phil Harris (2001b) believes that there are two competing views on the legitimacy of lobbying. The first view is that lobbyists abuse the democratic system for their selfish interests and that their activity requires the imposition of greater controls over lobbying activities. It is often related to campaign contributions for candidates, who, in return for such donations, will support particular bills beneficial to the interests of either individual or corporate donors. The second perspective assumes that lobbying is an intrinsic part of the democratic process because it can create a counterbalance to potentially ill-informed, unthought-out policy decisions.

The first of these views is supported by the results of a meta-analysis of research and campaign contributions' impact on roll call voting conducted by Douglas Roscoe and Shannon Jenkins (2005). They found that it is not true that the apparent connection between money and roll call voting is just a reflection of friendly giving. Money had a statistically significant impact on how legislators voted: one in three roll call votes exhibited the impact of campaign contributions. The authors state that legislators are inundated with legislative proposals, many of which have little connection to their own policy interests or the interests of their constituency. Lawmakers themselves may have little information about these bills and they may rely on cues from their political and social environment. In these conditions, according to Roscoe and Jenkins, it is not surprising that they would be willing to trade their votes for a resource critical to their goal of reelection (see also Harris and Lock 2005; Wray 1999).

Political lobbying by companies and other pressure groups at the British parties' conferences may also evoke similar doubts. Summing up their research in this field, Harris and Lock (2002) state that there is only a limited portion of overt lobbing at party conferences and that much lobbying at these events is difficult to monitor. The one area of limited information is of private meetings between politicians and representatives of business organizations or pressure groups.

The other view on political lobbying is supported by widely described cases of efficient activities not directly related to supporting particular politicians financially. Examples are the Davenport Naval Dockyard campaign in the United Kingdom (Andrews 1996; Harris 2001b; Harris, McGrath, and Harris 2009), the campaign by the Shopping Hours Reform Council to change Sunday trading laws in the United Kingdom (Harris, Gardner, and Vetter 1999), and the Fawcett Society's "Listen to My Vote" campaign to discover and articulate women's political opinions across Britain and to use this information to influence the political process (Lindsay 1999).

The growth of corporate lobbying and campaigning is a response to the complexities of modern business society caused by more pervasive government and increased need for competitiveness in a global market (Harris 2001b). It seems then that the government's higher influence on the economy and passing new laws forces in a way the development of political lobbying. Phil Harris, Conor McGrath, and Irene Harris (2009) propose a taxonomy of situations in which government is involved and postulate the relative importance of lobbying in influencing outcomes. These situations are linked and conditioned by the roles that modern governments are supposed to perform: as a purchaser or allocator (e.g., purchasing procedures and infrastructure and offering large public work contracts); as legislator and framer of regulations;

as initiator of action; as partner and mediator with international organizations (e.g., the European Union or NAFTA); as decision-maker; and as employer.

Political Consultants

Today, politics has become a big, profitable business to consultants who help manufacture politicians' images. Shaun Bowler, Todd Donovan, and Ken Fernandez (1996) even talk about the emergence and dynamic development of the "political marketing industry." In California, the first permanent organization devoted to political campaigning, Whitaker and Baxter's Campaigns Inc., was founded in 1930. Sixty years later, the 1990 *California Green Book* listed 161 general campaign consultants, 14 polling firms, 3 petition management companies, 22 professional fundraising firms, and 15 legal firms offering legal and accounting device to campaigns (Bowler, Donovan, and Fernandez 1996). Nicholas O'Shaughnessy (1990, 7) describes political consultants as "the product managers of the political world."

Some say the by-product of these consultants is cynicism in the electorate and growing armies of people involved in opposition research (see Kavanagh 1996). The consultants have become important because they are in a position to help a politician craft a winning television image that resonates well with citizens. As we move from the television era to the Internet era, the expertise necessary to be a successful consultant will have to change. As Philip Howard (2006) states, while pollsters supply campaigns with important information about the electorate and fund-raising professionals generate revenue, information technology experts have also had significant influence on campaign organization. Information technology experts build their political values into the tools and technologies of modern campaigns, with direct implications for the organization and process of campaigning.

At the level of overall strategic thinking, the candidate is involved, but when it comes to creating a campaign platform, conducting polls, and setting up a promotional strategy, very few candidates get involved. The services offered by consultants include several different activities, such as direct mail, fund-raising, television and radio spots, issue analysis, and print advertising (see Plasser 2009). The ability to lead in the high-tech age we live in hinges on the careful selection of the right consultants to run the candidate's campaign, both before and after entering the political office.

Results from a nationwide survey of political consultants reveal the increasingly important role they are

1. 40 percent said candidates are neither very involved nor influential when it comes to setting issue priorities.

2. 60 percent said their candidates were neither very involved nor influential in the day-to-day tactical operation of the electoral campaign.
3. Consultants emphasize campaign activities such as fund-raising, advertising strategies, and analysis of voter preferences.
4. Consultants believe a winning campaign does not hinge on the competence of the candidate, political organization, or the recruitment and use of volunteer workers.
5. The majority of consultants do not provide services such as precinct walking, phone banking, or "get-out-the-vote" efforts (all of which are hallmarks of grassroots politicking).
6. Major services that consultants offer are direct mail, fund-raising, television and radio spots, issue analysis, and print advertising.
7. The "permanent campaign" means that consultants do not stop consulting after Election Day, but continue to provide advice on policy-making activities in anticipation of the next reelection campaign and follow their clients into office as formal advisers or political appointees.

This increasing power of consultants is a very serious issue concerning the general health of democracies around the world. In the past in the United States, when the political party bosses were the ones in control, there was a screening process that was put in place to choose these people. Local officials, who were voted into office themselves, were the ones who had positions of power in a campaign.

Today, consultants are hired and fired by campaigns in the same way that a corporation might hire a consultant, based on word-of-mouth recommendation and relative success in the past. The consultants have not been exposed to the public, nor have they been screened by voters in the same way that party officials have been. So as we become a more market-driven democracy, and the power shifts from public officials to hired guns, there is an inherent danger to society that the basis on which candidates are elected will be determined by the ability, both monetarily and otherwise, to hire the right consultant. This is a serious issue that will only be perpetuated by the rising costs of running for public office and the need to hire consultants to manufacture images for politicians.

An Advanced Theory of Political Marketing

The processes described above show clearly the shift in the focus and range of political marketing. It has expanded to become a permanent strategic element of governance. These changes facilitate the development of marketing research and are becoming more and more important for the election and governing processes. They also require the development of more appropriate models of political marketing that include these processes.

Phil Harris (Dann et al. 2007; Harris and Rees 2000; Lock and Harris 1996) calls for regenerating political marketing and turning political marketing into political marketing science. Many scholars point to multiple possibilities and paths through which this transition may occur (Baines, Brennan, and Egan 2003; Baines, Harris, and Lewis 2002; Cwalina, Falkowski, and Newman 2009; Davies and Newman 2006; Harris 2001a, 2001b; Harris and Rees 2000; Henneberg 2008; Henneberg and O'Shaughnessy 2007; Lock and Harris 1996; Newman 1994, 1999c; O'Shaughnessy and Henneberg 2009; Wring 1997, 1999). They are also the foundation for the advanced theory of political marketing formulated in this book, presented in Figure 2.6.

The starting point for developing the advanced model of political marketing is the model elaborated by Bruce Newman (1994). It includes the concepts introduced in Chapter 1 and related to service and relationship marketing, as well as a discussion of market and marketing orientation and market-driven versus market-driving marketing orientation.

The advanced model of political marketing presented in this book brings together into a single framework the two campaigns: the permanent marketing campaign and the political marketing process. These two components are realized within a particular country's political system, and the system depends, above all, on political tradition as well as the efficiency of the developed democratic procedures. In this way "democracy orientation" determines how the functions of the authorities are implemented and, also, who is the dominant object in the structure of government. On the other hand, democracy orientation also defines whom the voters focus on during elections. From this perspective, we distinguish four fundamental types of such orientation: candidate-oriented democracy, party leader–oriented democracy, party-oriented democracy, and government-oriented democracy.

A good example of a candidate-oriented democracy is the United States, where the choice in an election is very much a function of the sophisticated use of marketing tools to move a person into contention. It is characterized by the electorate's attention shifts from political parties to specific candidates running for various offices, particularly for president. The shift is accompanied by the growing importance of a candidate's individual characteristics, of which his image is made up. American parties have little direct control over either candidate selection or the running of campaigns. Key decisions about campaign strategy are made at the level of the individual candidate. Although the national party committees play a supportive role, candidate image, character,

Figure 2.6   **The Advanced Model of Political Marketing**

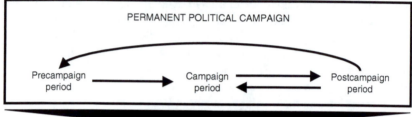

DEMOCRACY ORIENTATION			
Candidate	Party leader	Party	Government

PERMANENT POLITICAL CAMPAIGN		
Precampaign period	Campaign period	Postcampaign period

POLITICAL MARKETING PROCESS			
Message development		Message dissemination	Relationship building
Voter segments determination	Candidate/party positioning and targeting (branding)		
A. Primary segmentation B. Secondary segmentation (assess voter needs) C. Profile voters D. Voter segments identification E. Target segments identification	A. Assessing candidate/party image and issues strengths and weaknesses B. Assessing competition C. Candidate position in target segments D. Campaign platform establishing (image, issues, promises)	A. Personal (direct) campaign (grass-roots efforts, election events and meetings) B. Mediated (indirect) campaign (printed and electronic materials) C. Public Relations D. Campaign development and control (polling) E. Social networking	A. Platform delivery (policy implementation, public sector services) B. Mutual trust building C. Permanent communication D. Lobbying

and policy pledges are the prime "products" on offer in elections rather than party behaviors and platforms (see Wattenberg 1991).

Party leader–oriented democracy seems to be characteristic of the United Kingdom and Mexico, where although there is still a focus on the individual in the campaign, the choice in an election is more a function of the "approval" of a superbody of influentials who decide who will run for office. To a great degree, the political party is in a very powerful position, but there is still active use of marketing techniques once the party chooses who the nominee will be. British parties are ideologically cohesive and disciplined, with centralized and hierarchical national organizations, and their leaders are focused on directing the behavior of the whole party in the search for office (Ingram and Lees-Marshment 2002). While analyzing the data from parliamentary elections in Britain between 1979 and 1987 collected in the archives of the Economic and Social Research Council (ESRC) and from TV polls conducted by the BBC together with Gallup, Ron Johnston, Charles Pattie, and Graham Allsopp (1988) stated that, all other things being equal, the most popular leaders will be those with the most popular policies. However, some leaders are much more popular than the policies they stand for, whereas others are less popular. Thus, a voter may prefer the Labour Party's policies but, because of the quality of the party's leader, does not believe that the promises in those policies will be delivered; as a consequence, another party may get that person's vote, because it has a leader who is believed better equipped to fill the role of prime minister. To some voters, the leadership may be even more important than the direction in which it leads. For example, Johnston and his collaborators found that about three-quarters of those who thought Margaret Thatcher would make the best prime minister voted for her at each of the three analyzed elections. Another piece of evidence confirming these results is the data from the 1987 British Campaign Study (BCS) conducted by Marianne C. Stewart and Harold D. Clarke (1992). They found that favorable perceptions of Thatcher as competent and responsive enhanced, while similar perceptions of other leaders reduced, the likelihood of the Conservative voting. Similar interrelations were also found for leaders of the other parties. The dominant position of the leader in relation to her party is also confirmed by the results of the polls conducted by MORI in the context of the 1987–2001 British general elections analyzed by Robert M. Worcester and Roger Mortimore (2005). They showed that leader image was a greater determinant of voting behavior than party image: the respective figures were 35 percent and 21 percent in 1987; 33 percent and 20 percent in 1992; 34 percent and 23 percent in 1997; and 32 percent and 24 percent in 2001. In this context it seems justifiable to assume that a political party and voters' identification with it are an important factor influencing voting decisions. However, its image is to a large degree based on how its leader is perceived. It is the leader that voters focus on and it is the leader whose promotion is the main goal of the campaign.

Party-oriented democracy is characteristic of such countries as Poland, Finland, Czech Republic, and Romania, where the political party presents itself to the voters as the real choice being made. The Polish political system is based on a party system. Therefore, in the parliamentary, presidential, and local elections, candidates supported by significant political parties have a better chance of success. The politics of Poland takes place in the framework of a parliamentary representative democratic republic, whereby the prime minister is the head of government and of a multiparty system. The president, as the head of state, is chosen during elections based on the majority rule and has the power to veto legislation passed by parliament, but otherwise has a mostly representative role. During general parliamentary elections the citizens of Poland elect their representatives, who belong to various political parties. These parties then take seats in the Sejm and Senate (lower and higher chambers of parliament) depending on the number of votes they receive during an election. For a particular candidate to be elected, his party (or election committee) must get at least 5 percent of the votes across the whole country, and if he represents a coalition of various parties it has to be 8 percent of the votes cast in the whole country. So a situation may occur (and does occur) that a candidate who won most votes in his constituency will not become an MP because his party was below the 5 percent or 8 percent threshold in the whole country. Such legal regulations lead to campaigns being mainly concentrated on political parties. Obviously their leaders are an important element of winning such support; however, even their personal success does not guarantee the party's success. Besides, the person that the winning party designates as its candidate for prime minister does not have to be the party's leader but only a person nominated by the party.

Government-oriented democracy seems to be characteristic of countries like Russia and China, where governing is dominated by one party. Such a system is defined on the website of the China Internet Information Center (www.china.org.cn) as "democratic centralism." The Communist Party of China (CPC) has established formal organizations (through elections within the Party) and informal organizations within the Chinese government and various levels and walks of life in the country. According to the principle of democratic centralism, the individual CPC member is subordinate to a party organization, the minority is subordinate to the majority, the lower level organization is subordinate to the higher level, and each organization and all members of the entire CPC are subordinate to the Party's National Congress and the Central Committee. Furthermore, leading bodies at various levels of the party, except for their agencies and for leading party groups in nonparty organizations, are all elected, and the party prohibits personality cults in any form. Such elections are two-tier elections: direct and indirect. Direct elections are applicable to the election of deputies to the people's congresses of the counties, districts, townships, and towns. They adopt the competitive election method, which means that a candidate wins the election when she receives more than half of the votes cast. Indirect elections, then, are applicable to the election of deputies to people's congresses above the county level, deputies among the armed forces at the same level, and deputies to the National People's Congress (NPC) elected from special administrative regions. Candidates may be nominated by political parties or mass organizations jointly or independently or by more than ten deputies. Expenses for the election of the NPC and local people's congresses at various levels are to be provided from the national treasury. In the case of government-oriented democracy, the major tasks of the political campaign focus on the communication between the government and citizens rather than on the direct election struggle between candidates or political parties.

The permanent campaign is a process of continuing transformation that never stops. Therefore, distinguishing the particular stages of the campaign (precampaign period, campaign period, and postcampaign period) is in a sense artificial because those particular stages often merge into one another and there is no clear division line between them.

The permanent marketing campaign is the heart of the model because it may be successfully conducted only within the political marketing process. It contains three key elements: politician or party message development, message dissemination, and relationship building. Message development refers to distinguishing particular groups of voters for whom an individualized and appropriate campaign platform will be designed. Voter segments determination is a process in which all voters are broken down into segments, or groupings, that the candidate then targets with her message. Political marketing can distinguish two levels of voter segmentation: primary and secondary (Cwalina, Falkowski, and Newman 2009). *The primary segmentation* focuses on dividing voters based on the two main criteria: (1) voter party identification (particular party partisanship vs. independency), and (2) voter strength (from heavy partisans to weak partisans to floating voters). From the perspective of the whole marketing campaign, the goal of the campaign should be to reinforce the decisions of the supporters and win the support of those who are uncertain and whose preferences are not crystallized, as well as those who still hesitate or have poor identification for a candidate or party that is close ideologically. It is these groups of voters that require more study—*the secondary segmentation*.

These elements may be used jointly for positioning politicians or puts it: The goal of message development is elaboration and establishing the campaign platform. It evolves over the course of the permanent political campaign (the time of the election and during governing). The campaign platform is defined in terms of candidate leadership, image, and issues and policies she advocates. It is influenced by several factors, including the candidate herself, the people in her organization, the party, and, especially, the voters.

The established politician or party message is then distributed on the voter market. The personal (direct) campaign primarily refers to the grassroots effort necessary to build up a volunteer network to handle the day-to-day activities in running the campaign. The grassroots effort that is established becomes one information channel that transmits the candidate's message from her organization to the voter, and feedback from the voters to the candidate. The goal here is then not only the distribution of the candidate's message, but also an attempt to establish and/or enhance relationships with voters and other political power brokers. Direct marketing consists of the candidate's meetings with voters and power brokers, such as lobbyists and interest groups.

The mediated (indirect) campaign becomes a second information channel for the candidate. Instead of the person-to-person channel used with a direct marketing approach, this channel makes use of electronic and printed media outlets such as television, radio, newspapers, magazines, direct mail, the Internet (e.g., email, websites, blogs), campaign literature (e.g., flyers, brochures, fact sheets), billboards, and any other forms of promotion that are available. Political marketing also adopts new ways of communicating with the voter, mainly related to the development of new technologies such as social networking or mobile marketing. After the so-called digital revolution, which mainly involved the development and spread of the Internet, initiating convergence between traditionally separated technologies, we are currently experiencing some kind of "mobile revolution" in which all information and communication technologies (ICT) and media usage seem to be going mobile. Mobile marketing is the use of wireless media as an integrated content delivery and direct-response vehicle within a cross-media marketing communications program. The wave of mobile telephony is largely behind us, but has created an environment in which almost everybody suddenly owns a personal mobile device and is always "on" and reachable. In today's fragmented political market, it is evident that traditional mass market (and mass media) approaches need to make way for a more differentiated and personalized approach of (micro) segment targeting. In order to achieve this, and given the fact that almost everyone has a personal mobile device, the advertising and marketing sector is rigorously experimenting with a diversity of new mobile marketing paths (De Marez et al. 2007). The ubiquity of the mobile phone extends the traditional media model of time and space. Mobile advertisers can deliver timely short message service (SMS) ads to consumers based on their demographic characteristics and geographic information. Worldwide, wireless advertisers have already integrated SMS into the media mix. SMS has started its ascent toward reaching critical mass as a direct marketing medium (Scharl, Dickinger, and Murphy 2005). In political campaigning, through the use of SMS, politicians try to influence voters directly. They can inform citizens about campaign events, invite them to participate in the campaign, and ask for their vote. The results of research conducted by Ifigeneia Mylona (2008) between December 2004 and January 2005 among Greek MPs suggest that 40 percent of them use SMS for communicating with their voters. However, younger politicians use this communication tool more than older ones. Mobile technology seems a potent political tool because it appeals to voters' emotions, is individualized, and reaches voters immediately.

The use of social networking by the Barack Obama campaign as both a personal and mediated information outlet in 2008 was integral to his victory. A comparison of the websites of the two presidential candidates showed that Obama understood the power of this form of message dissemination. For example, Obama had links on his website to Facebook, Myspace, YouTube, Flickr, Digg, Twitter, Eventful, LinkedIn, BlackPlanet, Faithbase, Eons, and Glee. John McCain by contrast had none until the very late stages of his campaign when it was too late to leverage the impact of this technology.

Obama won in 2008 in part because he made better use of the Internet and other marketing-related technologies to support his marketing efforts. Through the use of Facebook, Flickr, Twitter, and other social networking sites, the Obama strategists successfully targeted young voters who wanted change in the U.S. political system. These technological outlets were first used by Howard Dean in 2004, even though he was unsuccessful in his bid to win the Democratic presidential nomination. The use of social networking by the Dean campaign organization was beneficial in getting volunteer support and some fund-raising, primarily as a personal, targeted approach to interested voters and citizens.

The Obama campaign's use of these same technologies was boosted to a level never before attained in a presidential campaign, with hundreds of millions of dollars raised over the Internet and thousands of hours of support received. The funds were raised through both personal requests to individual donors who had signed up at events during the course of the campaign and through Internet channels targeted at selected segments of voters who followed the campaign over the Internet. Millions of supporters gave less than $300 each, on average, enough to build a multimillion-dollar campaign that would support the advertising that eventually worked to defeat the McCain campaign. At the same time, messages sent through mediated Internet outlets were used to allow supporters to keep track of the campaign at all times. Any interested party could tap into a website like Flickr or Twitter and both follow and be alerted to the daily activities of the campaign. Social networking at both the personal and mediated levels will continue to play an integral role in campaigns in democracies around the world in the future.

These activities should be supported by public relations efforts that are coordinated with them. The main goal of public relations activities is to strengthen the image of the candidate and his message by creating positive media relations, framing favorite narratives, event management, and sloganeering.

The foundation of message dissemination is organizational tasks connected with assembling staff for the campaign team, defining their tasks, and monitoring their activities where soliciting funds for the campaign plays an important role. Then, polling represents the data analysis and research that are used to develop and test new ideas and determine how successful the ideas will be. Polls are conducted in various forms (benchmark polls, follow-up polls, tracking polls) throughout the whole voting campaign and implemented by various political entities among the campaigns. One should also note the growing importance of polling specialists. The results of their analyses given to the general electorate not only reflect the electorate's general mood, but also influence the forming of public opinion.

The third element of the political marketing process and the goal of the political party or candidate is to establish, maintain, and enhance relationships with voters and other political power brokers (media, party organizations, sponsors, lobbyists, interest groups, etc.), so that the objectives of the parties involved are met. And this is achieved by a mutual exchange—both during the election campaign and after it, when the candidate is either ruling or in opposition. The integral element of the relationship building is the "promise concept." The key functions related to it are to give promises, to fulfill promises, and to enable promises. Therefore, an important element of building stable relations is trust, which is a willingness to rely on an exchange partner in whom one has confidence (Grönroos 1994). Trust is also the foundation of developing relationship commitment, when an exchange partner believes that an ongoing relationship with another is so important as to warrant maximum efforts at maintaining it. That is, the committed party believes the relationship is worth working on to ensure that it endures indefinitely. In order to achieve that, one also needs to establish communications channels functioning on a constant basis.

The advanced model of political marketing presented here will be further developed in subsequent chapters of the book and supported by the results of empirical research related to its particular components. The model is an attempt to include the changes taking place in modern democracies and to turn political marketing into political marketing science.

Note

1. Bovine Spongiform Encephalopathy (BSE) was first reported being found in the UK beef herd in April 1985 in Ashford, Kent, and scientifically confirmed in September 1986. Its origins are uncertain, but it has been widely reported that it developed from the use of meat-and-bone meal (especially sheep scrapie-infected carcasses and offal) in animal feed. In March 1996, the potential link between BSE and Creutzfeldt-Jakob Disease (CJD), the human equivalent of BSE, was officially announced, and a worldwide export ban on British beef followed (Harris and O'Shaughnessy 1997, 30).

3

The Campaign Message Development

Segmentation and Positioning on the Voting Market

The major challenge for the marketing campaign is the candidates' realization that they are not in a position to appeal to all voters of every persuasion. This means that the candidate must break down the electorate into segments or groupings and then create a campaign platform that appeals to these targets. The process of dividing the whole electorate into many different groups is called voter segmentation (Baines 1999). The goal of segmentation is to recognize and assess voter needs or characteristics that become the foundation for defining the profile of the voters in order to plan efficient communication with them. In other words, marketing planning aims at identification and creation of competitive advantage; in politics, its goal is to determine how to generate and retain public support for the policies and programs of the party and its candidate (Baines, Harris, and Lewis 2002).

After identifying voting segments, the candidate's position needs to be defined in each stage of the multistage process of positioning. It consists of assessing the candidate's and his opponents' strengths and weaknesses. The key elements here are (1) creating an image of the candidate emphasizing his particular personality features and (2) developing and presenting a clear position on the country's economic and social issues. These elements may be used jointly for positioning politicians or, as Smith (2005) puts it, *positioning via policies on issues* or *image and emotional positioning* (see also Baines 1999; Johnson 1971) or based on the model of the "political triangle" proposed by Worcester (Worcester and Baines 2004; Worcester and Mortimore 2005).

Voting Market's Segmentation Strategy

Market segmentation is related to all the activities undertaken by the candidate's election staff in the competitive market. The goal of the marketing campaign is to develop the *campaign marketing mix* that will best fit the needs of particular age groups. The segmentation process is presented in Figure 3.1.

Figure 3.1   **The Essentials of Marketing Segmentation**

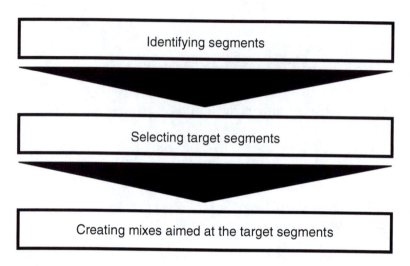

In mainstream marketing many segmentation methods have been advanced to identify viable market segments and select those that are likely to purchase and use the product. Once segments are identified, the next step is to prioritize them in terms of their marketing viability. According to Philip Kotler and colleagues (1998), common criteria used in prioritizing the segments are measurability, sustainability, accessibility, and actionability. Measurability is defined as the degree to which the size and purchasing power of all segments can be assessed. Sustainability is the degree to which the segments are large and profitable. Accessibility is the degree to which the segments can be effectively reached and served. Actionability is traditionally defined as the degree to which effective programs can be formulated for attracting and serving the segments.

The same rules lay the foundations of electoral market segmentation. The goal of a candidate is not only to identify voters, because she can win and develop a strategy to achieve that. She also has to determine whether the size of these segments is big enough to allow her to participate in the voting race. And although there are significant differences in the characteristics based on which the consumer and political markets are segmented, the concept of segmentation and most of the segmentation research approaches are to some extent applicable to both of them.

The basic division in the case of segmentation is between *a priori* and *post hoc* (or *clustering-based*) segmentation (Wind 1978). A priori segmentation involves the marketer choosing some cluster-defining descriptors (e.g., demographic or psychological characteristics) in advance of the research itself. In post hoc or *a posteriori* segmentation, there is no prejudgment by choosing the basis at the outset. Respondents are placed into groups by using statistical techniques (e.g., cluster analysis or multidimensional scaling), according to their similarity with those in the same group and their dissimilarity with those in other groups (Smith and Saunders 1990). Those who behave in a similar way—for instance, people who follow rationality in the decision-making process while buying something or voting for someone—constitute one segment of the market. They are different from other groups, such as impulse buyers who wait until the last day of a supermarket sale or voters who decide to support a particular party or candidate at the very last minute of a political election (they are called *last-minute deciders*).

What is crucial for those two approaches is to determine the characteristics that will become the basis for segmentation. Most often they include consumers' and voters' diverse characteristics that can, however, be grouped into two most general categories: demographic and psychographic. Therefore, both a priori segmentation and a posteriori segmentation are used together in the marketing practice or constitute related stages in the whole process of market segmentation.

With political marketing we can distinguish two levels of voter segmentation: primary and secondary (Cwalina, Falkowski, and Newman 2009).

Primary Segmentation

Primary segmentation divides voters according to two main criteria: (1) voter party identification (particular party partisanship vs. independency), and (2) voter strength (from heavy partisans to weak partisans to floating voters). Primary segmentation is a type of a priori segmentation that allows a candidate to initially select those voter groups with which communication may be successful, thus influencing the planning of marketing strategies and improving the allocation of resources for marketing campaigns.

Partisanship Schemata

The primary and natural segment of the voter market is a particular electorate. Voter partisanship is the criterion of dividing the market into electorates; the candidates develop a platform for their campaign that identifies problems that are relevant for their voters and that can attract voters from rival electorates, which are not very remote ideologically. Angus Campbell, Gerald Gurin, and Warren Miller (1954, 90) believe that political parties serve as standard-setting groups for a significant proportion of the people, who "associate themselves psychologically with one or the other of the parties, and this identification has predictable relationships with their perceptions, evaluations, and actions" (90). The concept of party identification explains how the average individual manages the complexities of democratic politics. Partisanship is then a heuristic for organizing political information, evaluations, and behaviors (Conover and Feldman 1981; Cwalina, Falkowski, and Newman 2008). It is a kind of "perceptual screen" through which individuals interpret and evaluate political experiences (Dalton 2007). Party identification includes also cues about the party background of issue options, ideological position (liberal, conservative, communist, socialist, nationalist or, more broadly, left and right), and so-called ideology by proxy, whereby an ideological vote may be multiplicated by personal admirers of a charismatic ideologue or party leader (Converse 2000). Another characteristic here is that voters' ideological self-identifications are highly accessible, and people with accessible points of partisan orientation are more likely to invoke it in formulating political judgments and resisting efforts at political persuasion (Huckfeldt et al. 1999).

Partisan information or cues also affect individual voting behavior in nonpartisan elections or referenda. Using data from a 1982 California Poll survey on state Supreme Court confirmation elections, Peverill Squire and Eric R.A.N. Smith (1988) demonstrated that nonpartisan elections are easily turned into partisan contests in the mind of voters. Partisan information increased the probability of an individual holding an opinion on the elections, resulting in votes based on the respondent's partisan identification and opinion of the governor who appointed the justice. Thus nonpartisan elections do not fulfill their promise if voters approach them with an activated heuristic (or frame) of partisan orientation.

Being a partisan of a particular party is also connected with sharing stereotypes about the party one supports as well as the other parties on the political market. Results of two experiments conducted by Lisa Farwell and Bernard Weiner (2000) demonstrate that American liberals are perceived as generous but not judicious, while conservatives are seen as as judicious but not generous, regardless of voters' own ideology. Both liberal and conservative study participants viewed conservatives as somewhat heartless, giving less than liberals whether the needy were responsible or nonresponsible for their plights (i.e., were less or more deserving). On the other hand, another commonly shared stereotype was the stereotype of a bleeding-heart liberal. Overall, subjects overestimated liberals' generosity toward the people responsible for their plight, but this effect was strongest among conservatives. Farwell and Weiner label this finding the "Limbaugh effect," after the conservative media personality who has acquired fame as a critic of liberal excess.

According to Wendy Rahn (1993), partisan stereotypes appear to be quite robust cognitive categories with considerable influence in many political information-processing tasks. In her experimental research she found that in the absence of the party label, individuals can and do respond to the implications of the candidates' messages. They use policy positions in making their evaluations of the candidates and in reaching inferences about their stands on issues. However, when voters have both particular policy information and a party label, they neglect the first and use the label in drawing inferences and evaluating candidates. Even when individuating policy information is made available in conjunction with party stereotypes, it is ignored and even distorted.

Strength of Partisanship

An important factor related to partisanship's influence on voting decisions is its formal aspect: the strength of the voter's attachment to her party or the level of her party involvement. In contrast to weak attitudes, the strong ones are persistent over time, are resistant to change, have a strong impact on information processing, and have a strong impact on behavior (Krosnick et al. 1993). If an individual is a strong partisan of a particular party, then her support for the party will be stable across subsequent elections. Information about the party's proposals and its candidates may be processed in a biased manner so that even random and inconsistent information or events can appear to lend support to an entrenched position and, as a result, lead to an increase of attitude polarization (Lord, Ross, and Lepper 1979). Besides, persuasion activities whose goal is to change those attitudes (for instance, a campaign of a candidate from another party) will most likely be inefficient. But the appeals supporting these attitudes sent by "our own" politicians will strengthen them. Therefore, it is very useful to distinguish a priori voters with strong and weak attitudes toward particular parties in order to figure out in which cases the promotional activities cannot be narrowed down only to those groups in which they can be efficient. It would, on the other hand, allow candidates to skip those segments that are most likely to be very resistant to persuasion activities. As a result, only the first group will be subject to further marketing focus. It is of this group that the following question will be asked: "Who are these voters and what are they characterized by?" The answer to this question is the goal of the secondary segmentation of the electoral market.

However, such narrowing and directing of the strategy of segmentation require using precise indicators of partisanship strength. Jon Krosnick and his collaborators (1993) believe that attitude strength is a metaphor to describe attitudes rather than a formal construct that is defined conceptually and readily operationalized. The strength of an attitude may be represented by such distinct features as extremity, intensity, certainty, importance, interest in relevant information, knowledge, accessibility, direct experience, latitudes of rejection and noncommitment, and affective-cognitive consistency. Joanne Miller and David Peterson (2004) supplement this list by attitude ambivalence.

From the perspective of segmentation of the electoral market, the key issue seems to be two dimensions of strong attitudes: accessibility and certainty. Accessibility is the strength of the object-evaluation link in memory, and certainty refers to the degree to which an individual is confident that his attitude (and/or behavior) toward an object is correct (Krosnick et al. 1993).

Attitude accessibility is measured by the length of time it takes people to report their attitudes toward an object as indexed by response latency. In a number of studies, Russell Fazio (2007) has demonstrated that attitudes that are expressed quickly are more predictive of subsequent behavior than attitudes that are expressed slowly. In measuring voter intentions, the methodology for measuring accurately the time it takes voters to answer questions in a computer-assisted telephone interview (CATI) was developed by John N. Bassili (1993; Bassili and Bors 1997; Bassili and Fletcher 1991). The methodology, which is completely invisible to respondents, comprises a computer clock capable of timing responses with millisecond accuracy and a voice-key that converts sounds emitted by respondents into signals capable of triggering the computer clock. The results of the analysis of survey data conducted in Canada by Bassili (1993) during the 1990 Ontario provincial election and by Bassili and Bors (1997) during the 1993 federal election show that response latency is a better predictor of discrepancies between individuals' voting intentions and voting behavior than their certainty measured by a "second choice" question or by self-reported intention. Voting intentions that were expressed slowly were less stable (more respondents switched their vote in the election) than voting intentions that were expressed quickly. However, the improvement in the accuracy of forecasting based on response latency did not extend beyond two months prior to the election. When the intentions of only those who were polled prior to the announcement of the 1993 federal election (four and three months before election day) were examined, there was a notable difference between the pattern of intentions and that of the actual vote. Besides, an important limitation of this research is the fact that the authors of the study excluded respondents who were undecided, who supported a minor party, who said that they would support none of the parties. Despite the fact that Bassili and Bors claim that in a multiparty system, knowledge of voters' second choice is unreliable and of little use in forecasting, relying on this aspect of attitude accessibility measurement has clear limitations. It seems that it is not very useful in segmentation research conducted at the beginning of the campaign but can be an efficient way of monitoring voters' preferences as the campaign develops.

Attitude certainty is usually gauged by individuals' self-reports of certainty or confidence (Krosnick et al. 1993). For voting preferences, this variable is also operationalized by a "second choice" question (i.e., showing a second choice candidate or party) (Bassili and Bors 1997; Cwalina and Falkowski 2005) and by differences in voters' attitudes toward candidates measured by a feeling thermometer (Falkowski and Cwalina 1999). In the latter case, if the voter's attitude toward two competing candidates varies considerably (one is liked and the other one is not), it points to certainty of the attitudes. If, on the other hand, the voter's attitude toward both politicians is similar, this suggests uncertainty. The aggregated way of calculating the uncertainty index as well as its analysis for groups supporting particular candidates is discussed by Wojciech Cwalina and Andrzej Falkowski (1999; Cwalina, Falkowski, and Kaid 2000; Falkowski and Cwalina 1999). The studies refer to the 1995 Polish and French presidential elections and the 1994 German national election.

Another indirect way of measuring attitude certainty which seems most useful for voter segmentation is determining the moment during the voting cycle when the voter makes the decision to support a particular candidate (see, e.g., Chaffee and Rimal 1996; Fournier et al. 2004). It is assumed that the sooner the decision is taken, the stronger the attitude certainty or strength will be. From this perspective, stronger and more persuasion-resistant attitudes are represented by precampaign deciders, weaker and less resistant attitudes are represented by campaign deciders, and the voters who are most uncertain about whom to support are last-minute or Election Day deciders.

In their pioneer research, Paul Lazarsfeld, Bernard Berelson, and Hazel Gandet (1944) divided their voters into "early" and "late" deciders. They also assumed that the time of taking the decision was a relatively stable quality of the voter depending on such factors as partisanship, interest in the election, and social class. The research conducted thirty years later by Garrett O'Keefe, Harold Mendelsohn, and Jenny Liu (1976) investigated "early" voters, who, before the U.S. presidential campaign in 1972, knew whom to vote for; two years later, during the Senate and Ohio governor elections, nearly half of these voters did not reach their final decision for either governor or senator until well after the nominations. On the other hand, 40 percent of those classified as late deciders in 1972 had their minds made up for a gubernatorial or senatorial candidate by the primary nominations in 1974. According to O'Keefe and his collaborators, the difficulty of voter decision-making appears primarily to be a function of the circumstances of a particular campaign (e.g., the aftermath of the Watergate scandal) rather than a characteristic of certain voters per se.

We should stress here, however, that the American presidential election is completely different from the U.S. Senate or House of Representatives elections. Besides, the fact that voters' change their decisions every following election does not mean that making the decision early in a particular election is changeable. The reported time of decision appears especially highly reliable within the context of a short election campaign (Fournier et al. 2004). Thirdly, the results are also consistent with attitudes perceived as constructions (e.g., Fazio 2007). Situational demands sometimes force individuals to make evaluative judgments and decisions regarding novel entities (e.g., voting for a newly emerging candidate) or some new information (e.g., reports about corruption or political scandals), and they may modify earlier beliefs. In such cases, attitudes need to be constructed. However, Fazio (2007) emphasizes that the outcomes of any such construction efforts are not forgotten. To the contrary, they facilitate automatic activation of object evaluation when it is encountered. Voter segmentation based on the time voters take to decide whom they are going to support seems a useful criterion then, particularly for analyzing a particular election rather than across elections. Of course, the accuracy and predictive power of this procedure might be stronger if indexes of partisanship strength (e.g., reaction time to answer questions in CATI) are used simultaneously (for other operationalizations of political attitude strength, see Miller and Peterson 2004).

A more detailed division of voters based on the time they take to make up their minds can be found in the section of the chapter dedicated to undecided or floating voters.

In sum, the primary segmentation assumes a priori division of voters based on the party they support (the content of the identification) and the power of this support or certainty in making decisions (identification potency). The strategy allows candidates to conduct an initial market division and to distinguish those segments of the market to focus on from those that are out of reach. In this way, primary segmentation refers to Kotler and his collaborators' (1998) criterion of actionability—that is, the degree to which effective programs can be formulated for attracting and serving the segments.

Secondary Segmentation

From the perspective of the whole marketing campaign, the goal of the campaign should be to reinforce the decisions of the supporters and win support of those who are uncertain and whose preferences are not crystallized, as well as of those who still hesitate or have poor identification for a candidate or party that is close ideologically (for more detailed discussion, see Newman and Sheth 1985). It is these groups of voters that require more study—*the secondary segmentation.* It can be both a priori and post hoc segmentation. Besides, it may only focus on analyzing the voters' individual characteristics or whole sets of them. In political marketing the segmentation methods that are most frequently used refer to four groups of variables (see Smith and Saunders 1990): geographic (e.g., Johnston, Pattie, and Allsopp 1988), demographic (e.g., Yorke and Meehan 1986), behavioral and psychographic (e.g., Cwalina and Falkowski 2005). Some approaches to political market segmentation go beyond these groups of variables, are based on more complex models (Cwalina, Falkowski, and Newman 2008; Cwalina, Falkowski, Newman, and Verčič 2004; Newman 1999b; Newman and Sheth 1985), and also refer to benefit segmentation applied in mainstream marketing (Baines, Worcester, Jarrett, and Mortimore 2003, 2005).

In theory, the number of combinations of different voter groups that can be distinguished based on various demographic and personal characteristics as well as needs and lifestyles is unlimited. However, from a practical point of view, not every such group would be useful for the purposes of a political campaign. A particular segment is useful in planning a promotional campaign mix only when two fundamental criteria are met:

1. Group identity—voters in the same segment are similar to each other and different from other voter groups.
2. Similarity of behavior—voters from the same segment react in a similar manner to the marketing strategies of particular staffs.

These criteria lay the foundation for segmenting voters according to two sets of related variables: demographic traits and psychographic traits.

Demographic Segmentation

Demographic segmentation is a way of grouping voters (and customers) based on features that are easy to define, including gender, age, education, profession, and income. Such a combination is often used to create a complex demographic classification, such as family life cycle or social class. The importance of such segmentation for marketing strategy seems obvious. William D. Wells (1975, 196) states that "marketing researchers collect demographics as a matter of routine, and marketers feel comfortable using them." Many products on the market are addressed to customers meeting particular demographic criteria. Many candidates or political parties appeal to citizens belonging to a particular social group (Forma 2000), gender (Kaufmann and Petrocik 1999; Newman and Sheth 1984; Randall 1987), or age group (Davidson 2005; Stephens and Merrill 1984) while constructing voting messages or developing their voters' support or even promoting themselves as representing the interests of such groups. Such representatives include the Polish Peasants' Party, Croatian Peasant Party, and Centre Party of Finland. The National Party of Retirees and Pensioners in Poland, Party of United Pensioners of Serbia, and Gil-Pensioners of Israel are set up to win the support of the elderly and retired.

However, segmentation based on a single criterion (e.g., social class or age) is hardly useful from a marketing perspective. For instance, in Great Britain, the division of social classes has begun to no longer matter in the segmentation of the voting market. When analyzing parliamentary elections, David Butler and Dennis Kavanagh (1984) discovered a shift of a few percentage points among working-class voters moving from supporting the Labour Party to the electorate of the Conservative Party. As a consequence, they developed a division of the voting market that would simultaneously include a number of sociodemographic characteristics. Such a promising division of the voting market was the concept of ACORN (A Classification of Residential Neighbourhoods), a relatively new segmentation tool available to management.

D.A. Yorke and Sean Meehan (1986) examined ACORN in detail as a suitable basis for segmenting the electoral marketplace. According to them, in the 1983 general election in the United Kingdom, it emerged that the link between political parties and social classes was rapidly eroding: nearly 40 percent of the electorate did not vote for the party related to their social class.

The ACORN market segmentation system classifies people according to the type of area in which they live. It separates voters according to combinations of such demographic characteristics as location of residence, age, household types, housing, and social and employment status. Yorke and Meehan distinguished eleven different neighborhood groups, three of which they tested for their voter behavior:

1. *Older housing of intermediate status.* This division consists of older voters who are less mobile and live in houses close to city centers. The absence of large gardens and modern amenities is compensated for shopping accessibility and local employment.
2. *The less well-off council estate.* This segment includes manual, semi-skilled, and unskilled workers. This group tends to consist of older couples and pensioners rather than younger couples, although average incomes are increased by multiple earners and by low housing costs.
3. *Affluent suburban housing.* This is an older, high-income group inhabiting interwar suburban private housing, detached, and developed in low densities. Disposable income is spent on luxury items and invested in home improvements. Attributes of the neighborhood that particularly attract residents are quietness, privacy, and exclusiveness.

The goal of Yorke's and Meehan's analysis was to answer the following question: Are voters from these segments different from one another because of their attitude toward political choices? Their results (referring to the elections to the European Parliament in 1984) showed some small, statistically significant differences between the voting intentions of the voters from the tested social groups. However, it should be stated that the tested individuals had a similar attitude to such questions and statements as "When are the next European Parliamentary elections?" "The outcome of the Euro Election does not affect me at all" and "I know little or nothing about the European Parliament, so I don't feel qualified to vote."

A different approach to segmenting the electoral marketplace is offered by Russell Dalton (2007). The primary segmentation assumes a priori division of the voters according to whether they support a political party at all and if so which party it is (identification content) and the strength of this support and decision certainty (identification potency). Dalton suggests that these two voter characteristics should be supplemented by such criteria as voters' political sophistication, which is closely related to the level of their education.

According to him, a better understanding of citizens' voting behavior and their consistency over time is only possible when such elements as the level of citizens' partisan mobilization and cognitive mobilization are included. Based on these two criteria, Dalton presents and empirically analyses a mobilization typology of voters based on the cross-classification of both variables. This typology yields four ideal groups, characterized by various patterns of political behavior. *Apoliticals* are neither attached to a political party nor cognitively involved in politics. They have a limited store of political knowledge and limited information about electoral campaigns. Apoliticals participate in elections less often than the other groups and display somewhat higher levels of vote switching and split-ticket voting between their presidential and congressional voting choices. *Apartisans* are political independents with cognitive skills and resources necessary to orient themselves to politics without depending on party labels. They are less supportive of party-based politics; thus their voting abstention or vote switching is more likely to evolve from a deliberative decision-making process. It is also characteristic of their voting behavior that they are more likely to divide their party support between presidential and congressional offices. *Ritual partisans* are guided by their political identity and party cues in the absence of cognitive sophistication. Their party support is almost habitual, but very stable across elections. *Cognitive partisans* have strong party attachments and rich cognitive resources. Since the partisan and cognitive dimensions overlap, both influence their perceptions and behaviors. They are focused on both party stereotypes and the analysis of party policy proposals. Their partisanship is reinforced by extensive political information.

These four types of citizens bring very different decision-making criteria into their electoral choices and that is why a priori segmentation may be an important factor allowing politicians to develop precise, efficient strategies for winning their voting support.

Despite that, demographic variables seem to have limited use for voting market segmentation. In every group distinguished by such characteristics as age, gender, education, social group, or place of living, there are people who also differ on their party or candidate preferences. Naturally, there may be more or less supporters of a particular political option in a given group, but these proportions do change even during a short period of the campaign. So despite the fact that demographic segmentation is an important element of marketing strategy, psychologists and marketing specialists had long known that the key to such a segmentation that allows for successful prediction of consumer preferences of different product brands and voter preferences of political parties or candidates is a personal profile of the consumer and the voter (Mowen and Minor 1998; Wells 1975; Wilkie 1994; Ziff 1971).

Personality has therefore become the foundation of the division of the market based on psychographic variables. It has inspired a number of research projects on consumer and voter behavior that resulted in various proposals of psychographic segmentation.

Psychographic Segmentation

A homogeneous segment, due to various demographic variables, may be very diverse as far as psychological features are concerned. Psychographic segmentation, unlike the study of measurable demographic features, consists of studying unobservable psychological traits. Voting preferences are analyzed as, for instance, conditioned by voters' personality traits (Caprara and Zimbardo 2004; Eysenck 1956), particular patterns of motivated social cognition (Jost et al. 2003), value systems (Braithwaite 1997; Rokeach 1973), or risk propensity (Morgenstern and Zechmeister 2001). Segmentation analyses include standardized personality inventories, methods of clinical psychology, or specially designed methods measuring lifestyle, values, attitudes, emotions, and motivations (Wells 1975).

A detailed proposal of psychographic segmentation of the voting market is offered by Bruce Newman (1999b). It stems from the model of voter behavior developed by Newman and Jagdish Sheth (1985). The authors distinguished seven cognitive domains that determine citizen's voting behavior: issues and policies, social imagery, emotional feelings, candidate image, current events, personal events, and epistemic issues. When segmenting the voting market, Newman used four cognitive domains of the behavior model referring to different values sought by the voters from a candidate. On this basis he separated voters into four groups:

1. *Rational voters*. This segment of the electorate corresponds to the social domain of Political Issues referring to the problems and directions of social and political actions. In the questionnaire developed by Newman, fields from this domain referred to the economy, foreign policy, and social issues and were measured on binary scales: "I agree—I disagree" (e.g., "I am convinced that the candidate I voted for will decrease inflation"). It was determined that social and economic concerns are the main issues that rational voters consider when making their voting decisions.

2. *Emotional voters*. Candidate Personality belongs to this group, which includes particular emotions that a candidate evokes among voters. Such emotions include happiness, appreciation, anxiety, pride, and disappointment. When making political choices, emotional voters follow their feelings.

3. *Social voters*. This segment refers to the domain of Social Imagery. The voters from this segment vote for a particular candidate associated with a particular social group, including, for instance, a national minority, a particular religion, the affluent, or the educated.

4. *Situational voters*. This segment, to which Situational Contingency corresponds, is particularly sensitive in its choices to anything that has or might have happened recently. Negative events include, among others, a higher rate of inflation or unemployment or increased corruption among civil servants. Positive events include citizens' increased access to education, lower costs of living, or fewer racial tensions. In the questionnaire, the domain of Situational Contingency is operationalized by statements pointing to voters' changing their voter decisions provided certain conditions take place (e.g., "I will vote for another candidate if he or she gives people more access to education").

These segments describe voters' psychological characteristics and belong to the psychographic segmentation of the voting market. Currently, however, they are still hypothetical constructs, and we do not in fact know whether such groups really exist in political campaigns. That is why Newman designed a survey that helped to determine whether the proposed voting segmentation concept is valid. In addition to using the questionnaire referring to cognitive domains, the author asked: "To what extent does each of the candidates make it easier or harder for you to achieve your dreams?"

This question related directly to the concept of creating the president's image that Newman presented to Clinton in 1995 in the White House. He proposed a certain vision of the president focused around the subject "The Restoration of the American Dream." This concept, supported by detailed research, was then presented by Newman to the president's spokesman George Stephanopoulos in 1996. It became the foundation for creating Clinton's new position in voters' minds. The new position defined the way in which the president was to restore dreams to his compatriots. Of course, "restoring dreams" is a certain metaphor operationalized by cognitive domains in the model of voter behavior.

The first stage of the research compared the importance of the four domains (Political Issues, Candidate Personality, Social Imagery, and Situational Contingency) in forming the voting intentions of three electorates: those of Bill Clinton and two politicians competing for the Republican Party nomination, Bob Dole and Colin Powell. Although the latter did not participate in the election campaign, he was included in the research because of the high popularity he enjoyed among the voters. The research was conducted when Powell was still considering running for the Republican presidential nomination in the 1996 election. The research demonstrated that the importance of these domains was similar among all the electorates. Each domain was almost equally important for Dole's, Clinton's, and Powell's supporters. At this stage of the research, Newman could not determine whether the proposed voter segmentation was valid.

The decisive step in determining the validity of the psychographic model of voting market segmentation was the use of discrimination analysis. The criterion variable was the respondent's opinion regarding whether or not a particular candidate would make it possible for Americans to achieve their dreams. Obviously, in each of the electorates, most voters set their hopes on "their" politicians, despite the fact that some respondents answered that the opponent could make these dreams come true as well.

At that point, the fundamental problem needing to be solved was to determine which domains were important in explaining the voter's opinion on the candidate's ability to make it possible for the voters to achieve their dreams. In order to use the language of discrimination analysis, the researcher should find out what questions differentiate from these questions significantly and what the indicator is that predicts these proportions. The results showed that a number of detailed domain items predicted the proportions of answers to the question about the dreams in each of the electorates quite well. However, they often belonged to different areas and, therefore, it was not possible to determine the types of voters in an empirical and unequivocal way by using Newman's model of psychographic segmentation.

In Clinton's electorate, three important items predicting why this candidate might help Americans achieve their dreams came from three domains: "Clinton makes me happy" (domain: Candidate Personality), "Clinton will help me have more time for myself" (domain: Political Issues), "Clinton will contribute to the development of social equality" (domain: Situational Contingency). The items predicting why the candidate could make it harder for people to achieve their dreams also belonged to different domains: "My candidate will not stop the spread of crime," "will not create conditions for general access to education" (both statements belong to the domain of Situational Contingency), and "will not contribute to my financial stability" (the domain of Political Issues). Expressing an opinion on these six issues allowed respondents to predict the candidate's ability to make it possible for voters to achieve their dreams in 76.8 percent of the cases.

The concept of psychographic segmentation proposed by Newman was developed in cross-cultural analyses by Cwalina, Falkowski, and Newman (2008). It is also consistent with the approach to segmentation presented in the well-known proposal of the consulting company SRI International on consumer behavior—*Values and Life Styles* (VALS) (Kahle, Beatty, and Homer 1986). Although the research on psychographic segmentation of the voting market described here does not achieve results that are as good as VALS on the consumer market, attempts continue to create voter groups based on psychological characteristics (Fiedler and Maxwell 2000).

These two variants of the secondary segmentation—demographic and psychographic—are closely related to each other in marketing practice. Therefore, we should rather talk here about a hybrid approach. The most important goal of segmentation is to get to know the potential voters as far as their personal and psychological characteristics in the context of a priori primary segmentation are concerned. From this perspective, the major focus of the campaign is to get to know and understand the broadly understood segment of floating or undecided voters.

Undecided Voters as a Strategic Segment

For many years voter behavior analyses assumed that a considerable majority of voters knew quite well before the election whom they were going to support and, therefore, they were not susceptible to any persuasion actions during the campaign. The group of undecided voters was thought to be so small that, although they were susceptible to candidates' and parties' information policy, their importance seemed to be quite small. This approach changed only with a considerable increase in the number of voters all over the world who did not identify with any party or candidate, who were undecided, or who changed their decision during the campaign (see Cwalina, Falkowski, and Newman

2008, Chapter 1; Dalton and Wattenberg 2000; Diamanti and Lello 2005; Hayes and McAllister 1996; Holbrook 1996; Wolfsfeld 1992).

Following stronger and stronger polarization in the voting market, including voters' certainty and uncertainty about their decisions, Steven Chaffee and Rajiv Rimal (1996) suggested a *dichotomous model*, which is a simple way of dividing voters into a relatively high segment of voters knowing whom they are going to vote for and a smaller but still growing segment of undecided voters. Voters from the first segment have already made up their minds whereas those from the second segment may decide at the very last moment. Voters from the first segment demonstrate strong party identification and/or agreement on its agenda. Therefore, they are more resistant to political marketing activities of the other party, despite the fact that they follow the campaign closely. Voters from the second segment have not made up their mind yet, which means that they are more susceptible to campaign communication. These assumptions were fully confirmed by Patrick Fournier and his collaborators (2004) during the 1997 Canadian parliamentary election. Their analyses were based on two sources of data: the 1997 Canadian Election Study and a content analysis of televised news broadcasts and party leaders' debates. They found that the link between time of decision and stability of vote choice held even if the influence of strength of partisan identification, political sophistication, and various sociodemographic characteristics was controlled. Furthermore, in terms of political attitudes and interests, precampaign and campaign deciders were surprisingly similar. Precampaign and campaign deciders were similarly interested in politics, similarly attentive to media coverage, similarly informed about general and campaign political facts. The only characteristic distinguishing these groups was strength of partisanship. Individuals who decided during the campaign were less attached to political parties. Besides, campaign deciders turned out susceptible to campaign persuasion. Over half of the Canadian citizens in the Canadian Election Study said they made their voting decisions over the course of the campaign, and they formed a relatively interested, attentive, informed, and less committed group that was more likely to be reached by, to be receptive to, and to be responsive to campaign stimuli. Their vote intentions were strongly affected by campaign events such as party leaders' debates and media coverage. This segment corresponds then to the characteristics of partisans distinguished by Dalton (2007).

Dalton's analyses suggest that at least among some undecided voters one may expect the pattern of behavior that is characteristic of apoliticals. In other words, some voters' indecision may result from their lack of interest in the political situation, which may lead to a situation that Chaffee and Sun Yuel Choe (1980) define as a paradoxical relationship between media use and the time at which voters make their final decision. It means that although undecided voters are less opinionated and more persuadable than the early deciders, they are also less interested and consequently pay little attention to political news. In this way they are a segment that is relatively difficult to reach with campaign messages. These are volatile voters who may change their decisions several times and whose final decision is often made when they are about to cast their ballot.

It is for these reasons that Chaffee and Rimal (1996) further characterized the segment of undecided voters, dividing it into two subgroups: (1) *campaign deciders* and (2) *last-minute deciders*. This division also has important consequences on voting segmentation. Since each of these groups has distinct characteristics, different campaign appeals and distribution channels need to be developed for each of them. Both groups are susceptible to voting persuasion, but for different reasons. The last-minute decisions, made by voters usually on Election Day, are to a large degree unpredictable. Quite often they are the result of accidentally watched spots on which the opponent is attacked. The analysis conducted by Lawrence Bowen (1994) confirms that only 18 percent of voters making up their mind a week before the election watch political advertisements, compared to 79 percent of voters making up their mind a day before the election. Campaign voters make up their minds before the final days of the campaign. They follow the voting competition, learning a lot about the candidates and their programs, so their decisions are the result of the information they have processed. Therefore, the decisional uncertainty that both subgroups of the segment are characterized by has a different character. On the one hand, it is caused by the excessive amount of information the campaign decider has to process. On the other hand, it is caused by the insufficient amount of information that gets to the last-minute decider.

Empirical data confirming this assumption were collected by Chaffee and Choe (1980). They developed a model analyzing voting decisions in which such variables as partisanship, television and newspaper campaign attention, education, income, and age as well as the image of the candidates and the issues they discussed allowed for predicting voters' behavior. Analyzing the image, the authors used scales allowing categorizing the candidates on such dimensions as honesty and integrity, strength and decisiveness, capacity for effective leadership of the government, and ability to inspire confidence by the way the candidate speaks. Issues taken up by the candidates included problems important at that time for the country, such as the reform of the tax system, government efforts to alleviate unemployment, and defense expenditures. The basic variable differentiating the voters was their decision time: precampaign, campaign, and last-minute deciders. The authors conducted their research immediately after the 1976 U.S. presidential election with Gerald Ford competing against Jimmy Carter.

Chaffee and Choe found that the important factors differentiating precampaign deciders from the combined two groups' undecided voters included education, partisanship, discussion about the campaign, and candidates' image discrimination. Precampaign deciders strongly identified themselves with a particular party, were better educated, more often talked about elections, and distinguished well between candidates relative to their images. The probability of the correct classification of voters into a particular group based on these variables was 78 percent.

The goal of another discriminate analysis was to capture the differences between campaign deciders and last-minute deciders. Two important variables turned out to be important here: attention to the campaign via TV and candidates' image discrimination. Based on them, a correct voter classification could be performed (with 69 percent probability). According to the voting media paradox, it turns out that campaign deciders follow campaign programs closely and can distinguish well between candidates. Last-minute deciders are not politically sophisticated and they are not particularly interested in the elections.

To complete these results, Chaffee and Rimal (1996) analyzed data from four waves of election panel surveys in four districts in southern and northern California in 1992, during the U.S. presidential election as well as two-year and six-year-term Senate elections. The voters were divided into three groups relative to the time they spent making up their minds: precampaign deciders, campaign deciders, and last-minute deciders. The goal of the study was to determine the extent to which uncertainty was a stable characteristic of an individual voter. If it was, then voters should behave in a similar way during various political elections. However, this did not happen. The results clearly showed that almost half of the voters who belonged to a particular group during the presidential election because of the time of their decision were in a different group during the Senate elections. For instance, 57 percent of last-minute voters during the presidential election were a "decided" group in the Senate election. A voter may thus be a "decided voter" in one election but susceptible to persuasion during another election. The results showed that in fact it is not possible to predict a voter's behavior in a particular election based on previous elections. Therefore, the time of making a decision should not be considered as a voter's individual feature, but ascribed to the situation in which such decisions occur. This was confirmed twenty years ago by O'Keefe, Mendelsohn, and Liu (1976).

Bernadette Hayes and Ian McAllister (1996) conducted an analysis of undecided voters for the 1992 British general election. As in other democracies, in Great Britain the number of voters loyal toward political parties is constantly decreasing (from 77 percent in 1964 to 60 percent in 1992). At the same time, the segment of floating voters is constantly growing: in 1992

Figure 3.2 **Age and Gender of Campaign Deciders in the British General Election, 1992**

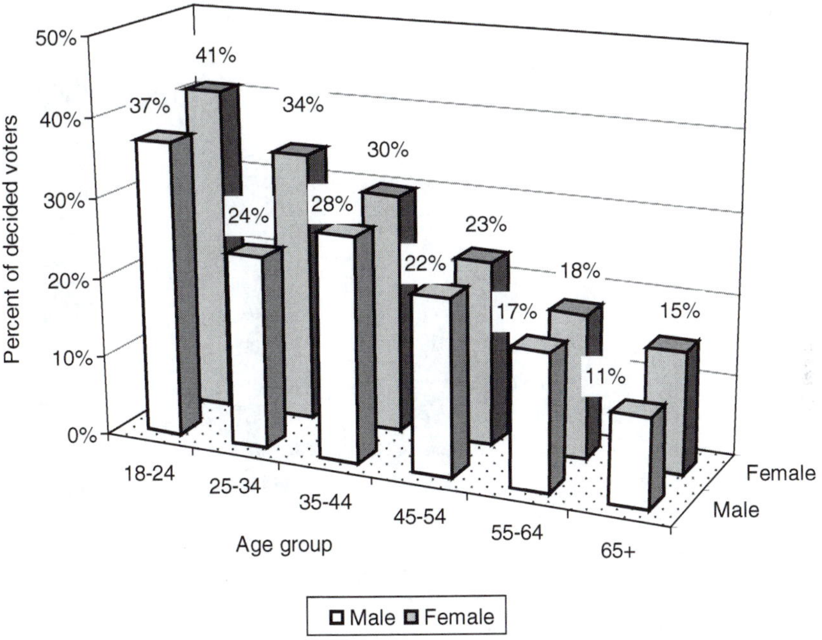

Source: Based on British Election Study 1992 supplied by the UK Data Archive.

it was already 24 percent of all the voters. This shift is accompanied by more and more resources spent on marketing action during political campaigns. Private advertising agencies are also involved in the process and their goal is to appeal to undecided voters. For example, the Conservative Party spent 9 million pounds on its campaign in 1987, and although it seemed that the record could hardly be broken, five years later it spent more than 10 million pounds. The spending of the Labour Party was increased considerably too; in 1987 it invested slightly more than 4 million pounds, or $6.4 million in the campaign whereas in 1992 it spent over 7 million pounds, or $11.2 million.

The analyses of voting behaviors conducted by Hayes and McAllister on the British political market and based on the British Election Surveys from 1974 to 1990 show that undecided voters not only have limited political knowledge but also are not involved in any ideology either. Besides, they are relatively young. The correlation between gender and age in British campaign deciders during the 1992 election is presented by Figure 3.2.

Figure 3.3   **The Strength of Partisanship Among Precampaign and
Campaign Deciders in the British General Election, 1992**

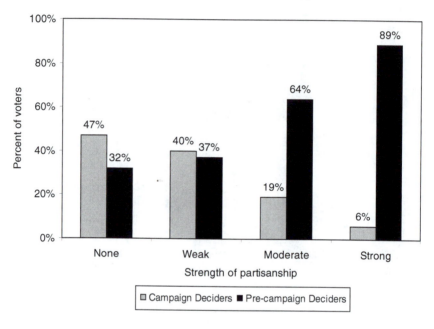

Source: Based on British Election Study 1992 supplied by the UK Data Archive.

The percentage of campaign deciders clearly falls together with age. Using the terminology of demographic segmentation of the voting market, we can conclude that undecided voters are rather young. Half of them are between 18 and 24 years, whereas in the age group of 55 to 64 years there are less than 20 percent of them. Women show a slight tendency to be more undecided than men.

Confirming the results of previous studies, Hayes and McAllister also observed very weak partisanship of voters making up their mind during the election campaign compared to those who made a decision a long time ago. This finding is presented in Figure 3.3.

Only 6 percent of very strong partisans made up their mind about whom to vote for in the last minute, which is contrasted with the 47 percent of undecided voters who do not identify with any party. A reverse result may be observed in undecided voters who do not identify with any party. Almost 90 percent of them are characterized by very strong partisanship, whereas slightly more than 30 percent of those who make up their minds long before the election have no such ties. One should also note that weak partisanship does not differentiate voters according to their decision time. The percentages of decided and undecided voters are almost identical (37 percent vs. 40 percent).

Hayes and McAllister (1996), like Chaffee and Choe (1980), claim that despite the fact that British undecided voters are less knowledgeable politically, lack political involvement, and are more susceptible to persuasion than voters decided before the campaign, they cannot be easily influenced during a political campaign. Less politically aware voters also pay less attention to political information and consequently are as difficult to convert as the most committed and knowledgeable voters.

We also note another aspect of the behavior of floating voters. Even if we assume that this particular segment is most susceptible to persuasion during a campaign, then we should also remember that it is susceptible to all the sides participating in the election contest. The fluctuation of voters' becoming members of the electorate of a particular party but also leaving it is quite high. The strategic persuasion of the competing parties during the campaign period, even if it is efficient, leads to offsetting the voter shift among competing electorates, so it does not influence the results of the election.

We may wonder, however, if someone may actually take advantage of such voter shifts among electorates. The shift of the electorate of a particular party to the electorate of another party at the other end of the political spectrum is not very likely. However small it is, the segment—defined by Gadi Wolfsfeld (1992) as "external floaters"—is so specific that it requires a separate promotion strategy. Such a shift happens either within different parts of a similar political spectrum (e.g., from one left-wing party to another) or toward the parties that are at its center. Such a party benefits the most from the process if it maximizes the number of its electorate and minimizes the number of voters fleeing to another party. Candidates could then consider using a marketing strategy in order to take over the supporters of another party by using the so-called triangulation model in positioning.

In sum, as Fournier and his collaborators (2004) note, we can speculate that if the decline in partisanship persists in the future, then the proportion of campaign and last-minute deciders and the frequency of campaign effects could also continue to increase. However, if this is also accompanied by an increase in cognitive mobilization of citizens, it may push the electoral process toward the ideal of democratic theory. Then, as Dalton (2007) suggests, it will emerge that voters make independent judgments on the candidates and issues of the day, rather than vote on the basis of habitual party loyalties inherited from their parents.

Figure 3.4   **Electoral Segmentation Logic**

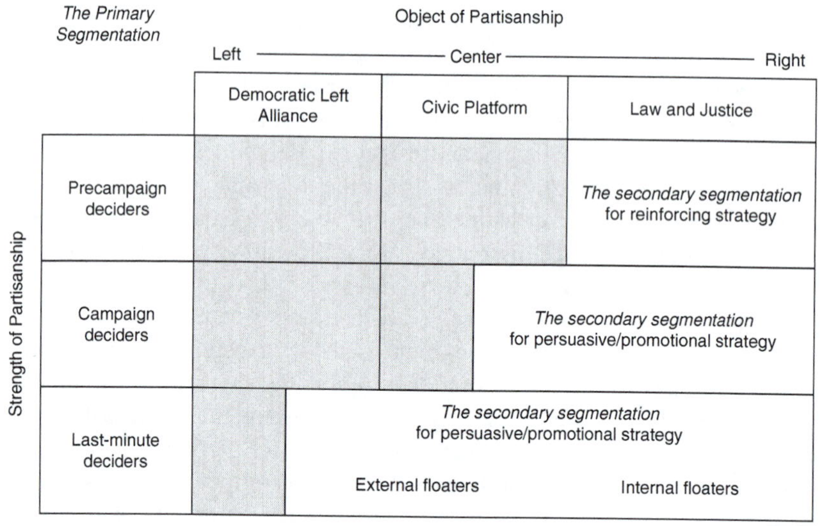

The Primary Segmentation		Object of Partisanship		
		Left ——————— Center ——————— Right		
		Democratic Left Alliance	Civic Platform	Law and Justice
Precampaign deciders				The secondary segmentation for reinforcing strategy
Campaign deciders				The secondary segmentation for persuasive/promotional strategy
Last-minute deciders			The secondary segmentation for persuasive/promotional strategy	
			External floaters	Internal floaters

(vertical axis label: Strength of Partisanship)

Electoral Segmentation: A Summary

The logic of the whole two-stage electoral marketplace segmentation is presented using the examples of three Polish political parties in Figure 3.4.

Figure 3.4 presents sample segmentation of the electoral marketplace from the perspective of the right-wing party Law and Justice (L&J) in the context of two parties competing against it: the left-wing Democratic Left Alliance (DLA) and the center-right Liberal Conservative. The goal of the primary segmentation is an a priori division of voters based on the party they support (identification object), the power of this support, and the certainty of making decisions (identification potency). The strategy allows for an initial division of the voting market and selecting those electoral segments that are worth focusing on during the campaign (target segments) and those that are out of reach.

The example presented in Figure 3.4 suggests that, if supported by these criteria, the campaign of Law and Justice should skip five electoral segments. First of all, it should not include strong partisans (precampaign deciders) for both DLA and Liberal Conservative. These voters are impervious to any political appeals coming from other parties than their own, which means that any attempt to win them is likely to fall through. Secondly, the probability that L&J will win DLA's weak supporters as well as voters split between supporting DLA and CP is low. They are voters who are more open to information and campaign appeals, but the parties they could consider supporting as a result of such information campaigns are too remote ideologically from the right side of the political scene. The fifth segment that is out of reach for L&J marketers is last-minute deciders, who are willing to support "a party," but it has to be a left-wing one. They can then be treated as politically left internal floaters.

In the case of the other segments, marketers from L&J should get to know their structure and characteristics better by conducting the secondary segmentation. The goal of getting to know these voters, to simplify a bit, is to develop a campaign strengthening its "own" electorate (precampaign deciders for L&J) and a persuasion-promotional campaign focused on winning "new and available" voters (campaign deciders willing to support L&J or CP and external and politically right internal floating last-minute deciders). The details of these strategies and positive and negative appeals created within them depend on the results of the second stage of segmentation.

Campaign workers should remember, however, that each election is very specific and it determines the division of voters relative to the time they spend making up their mind. What is most important from the marketing perspective, however, is the ability to influence grouped citizens. Precise voting market segmentation is the first step toward achieving that goal. Segmentation then leads to the next step in marketing actions—positioning candidates or parties in particular target segments.

Positioning of the Party and Candidate

After identifying voting segments, one needs to define the candidate's position in each of them in the multilevel process of positioning. It is a process of establishing and managing the images, perceptions, and associations that the voter applies to a political object (candidate or party) based on the values and beliefs associated with it. It refers to creating the optimal location in the minds of existing and potential (target) voters so that they think of the object in the "right way" (Keller 1999). Every candidate has some sort of position— whether intended or not—based upon voters' perceptions, which, in turn, may or may not reflect reality. Positioning on the voting market is then based on the psychological process of developing a candidate's or party's cognitive representation in voters' minds. As in mainstream marketing, where the position of a particular brand's product is represented by the product's positioning in customers' minds relative to competitors' products, in voting marketing the position of particular candidates is represented by their position relative to other competitive candidates participating in the election.

Positioning consists of "planning" in the voter's consciousness a clear and desired place for a particular candidate relative to the competitive candidates (Kotler and Kotler 1999). It is the deliberate, proactive, iterative process of defining, modifying, and monitoring voters' perceptions of candidates or parties (see Kalafatis, Tsogas, and Blankson 2000). Positioning is based on a combination of cognition and affect (Mahajan and Wind 2002; Smith 2005). Cognition depends on logical arguments in favor of a candidate. It focuses on policies, problems, solutions, values, or benefits sought by voters. Then affect is related to emotions, feelings, or drives associated with a candidate. That is why positioning usually focuses on creating an image of the candidate (*image and emotional positioning*) and developing his or her clear position on economic and social issues (*positioning via policies on issues*). However, these elements may and should be used jointly, because only their mutual fit allows the development of a coherent and efficient campaign strategy.

According to Richard M. Johnson (1971), the starting point for positioning is the answers to three simple questions:

1. How are various political candidates perceived by voters with respect to their strengths, weaknesses, similarities, and dissimilarities?
2. What are voters' expectations from candidates?
3. How should the answers to the first two questions be integrated to modify a candidate's image, thus maximizing his or her chances of being elected?

From the position of a political marketer, each of these questions translates into a separate technical problem, respectively:

1. To construct a space of a voting situation following the geometric representation of voters' perceptions of candidates;
2. To locate in this space the so-called voters' ideal point, also called the point of maximum preference, corresponding to such a candidate that best meets voters' expectations;
3. To construct a model that predicts voting preferences while introducing a new or modified image of the candidate.

Although a number of different approaches and methodologies for consumers and political brand positioning are possible (e.g., factor and cluster analyses), the method used most often is multidimensional scaling (MDS) techniques.

While MDS techniques can operate on a variety of types of data (e.g., similarities, dissimilarities, distances, or proximities), they have a common set of objectives. They are to produce a representation of the relationships between objects (e.g., brands), and/or between variables (e.g., brand attributes), and/or between evaluators of the objects or variables (e.g., voters or consumers) (Hooley 1980). MDS techniques seek to represent these relationships in the geometrical relations among points in the spatial configuration (R. Shepard 1961; Wilkes 1977). According to Peter Doyle (1975), a spatial representation has a number of practical advantages. First, the attributes most significant to consumers can be portrayed. Second, brands may be evaluated along with these attribute dimensions, and their relative strengths and weaknesses may be considered. Third, the extent of competition between brands can be seen together with the nature of their similarities and differences. Fourth, preferred positions in the perceptual space may be suggested, and opportunities for new brands and promotional strategy may be communicated.

In political objects' positioning, it is important to define the number and names of particular dimensions (or factors), which will help candidates understand voter preferences better—that is, to specify the criteria of candidates' perception and judgment. For candidate and party positioning on the electoral market, the obtained spaces were most often two-dimensional, with the following attributes:

- liberal—conservative vs. anti—pro administration; U.S. presidential election in 1968 (Johnson 1971);
- Republican (pro-Nixon) vs. Democratic (pro-McGovern); U.S. presidential election in 1972 (Shikiar 1976);
- liberal—conservative vs. passive—active leadership; U.S. presidential election in 2000 (Fiedler and Maxwell 2000);
- values (nostalgia for communist Poland and anticlericalism—negating communist Poland and support for the social role of the Catholic Church) vs. interests (liberal—prosocial); Polish parliamentary election in 1997 (Żukowski 1997);
- left—right vs. libertarian—authoritarian; UK general election in 2005 (Smith 2005);
- favorability vs. familiarity; UK general election in 2005 (Baines et al. 2005).

However, the results were also more complex. In research on the perception of twenty prominent American politicians conducted in 1971, Richard Sherman and Lee Ross (1972) obtained seven dimensions: (1) hawk-dove, (2) power within party, (3) acceptability as presidential candidate, (4) representativeness and lack of prejudice, (5) liberal-conservative within party, (6) attractiveness, and (7) Wallace (a single presidential candidate). In turn,

Joseph Forgas, Carolyn Kagan, and Dieter Frey (1977), in cross-cultural research on cognitive representation of political personalities conducted in Great Britain and West Germany, defined the following three-dimensional spaces: in the British sample, political potency vs. evaluation vs. intelligence, and in the German sample, conservatism vs. evaluation vs. political potency. In a study conducted four weeks before the first free election in Hungary in 1990, Forgas and his colleagues (1995) concluded there were the following dimensions: evaluation vs. conservatism vs. rural-urban. Then, in a study conducted in Moscow during a constitutional crisis in Russia in 1993 among members of political parties and movements, Viktor Petrenko, Olga Mitina, and Ruth Brown (1995) identified four dimensions by which Russian political parties could be described: (1) support versus opposition to President Boris Yeltsin's reform; (2) market versus planned socialist economy; (3) support for the rights of the individual versus support for an indivisible Russia protecting Russians; and (4) support for communist ideals and a new USSR versus opposition to communism and the USSR.

Frequently a brand space is assumed to be adequate to account for important aspects of the consumers' or voters' perceptions. However, it may also include the differences in their preferences. They are taken into account by considering each respondent's "ideal brand" or "ideal candidate" to have unique location in the common brand space, and by recognizing that different respondents may weight dimensions uniquely (Johnson 1971). Including such a point of maximum preference in a spatial configuration of political brands also provides information about the relationships between the actual political object and the ideal one. The closer a given candidate (or party) gets to such a point, the more preferred the candidate or party is. Such a map of preferences can also be of very practical use, since it allows a campaign to precisely define the strategy of repositioning a given brand to bring it closer to voters' expectations.

Candidates' Positioning: The 2005 Polish Presidential Election

Wojciech Cwalina and Andrzej Falkowski (2008b) conducted empirical research in Poland concerning the perception and differentiation of Polish politicians in the context of the presidential election in 2005. The research was based on the procedure of a continued verbal association task developed by Lorand Szalay and James Deese (1978, see also Szalay and Bryson 1973). Subjects were asked to generate as many response words (associations) as they could in one minute for six political objects: four Polish presidential candidates—Andrzej Lepper (leader of the populist, agrarian party Self Defense), Włodzimierz Cimoszewicz (candidate of the left-wing Democratic

Left Alliance; he withdrew from the elections during the campaign), Lech Kaczyński (candidate of the right-wing Law and Justice party; he won in the election and is the current president of Poland), and Donald Tusk (leader of the liberal conservative party Civic Platform)—plus Aleksander Kwaśniewski (left-wing politician, not running and stepping down after two terms) and a prototypical, "ideal" Polish presidential candidate (IC).

Using a continued verbal association task for political objects seems to be the most valid method for meeting the structure and judgment of political as well as consumer brands criteria (Keller 1993). Furthermore, it allows one to calculate intra-object dominance scores and an inter-object associative affinity index and their application for positioning politicians. Data collection by the continued association task requires preparation prior to analysis. Its result is a list, for each stimulus object (e.g., consumer brand, candidate), of associations and their dominance scores. Szalay and Deese (1978) assumed that the power of the recalled association is proportional to the sequence in which it is mentioned. If it is recalled as first, then it is more characteristic (it creates a stronger and more accessible node in memory) for a given object than if it is recalled as second, third, or the following. The fundamental problems relate then to the characteristic of this diminishing function of the power of association. Based on a number of studies, Szalay and Deese determined that the scores for the following associations should be assigned in the following way: 6 to the first response produced by a subject, 5 to the second response, 4 to the third response, 3 to the fourth through seventh responses, 2 to the eighth and ninth response, and 1 to each subsequent response. Dominance scores for common responses for each of the objects are then summed across subjects.

The next step in the data analysis is calculating inter-object associative affinity indexes for each pair of the objects. Affinity refers to the degree to which persons see relations of any sort between any two stimuli and is thus analogous to the meaning of similarity. Kleine and Kernan (1988), developing the operationalization model proposed by Szalay and Deese (1978), suggested that the affinity index is the amount of overlap between two response lists (i.e., the number of meaning elements two objects have in common). Calculation of this index involves then summing dominance scores across overlapping elements and stimuli (objects). This total score is then divided by the sum of the total dominance scores of the objects being compared. The resulting index value is the proportion of the combined total dominance scores accounted for by the affinity relations. The index has a theoretic range of zero to one and increases in value as inter-object affinity increases.

After the stage of generating associations for six political objects, the subjects filled out a questionnaire including questions about their sociodemo-

Table 3.1

Associations and Dominance Scores for Lech Kaczyński

Associations for Lech Kaczyński	Dominance scores
Characteristic sayings	84
Not good-looking	77
Unprofessional	52
Honest	43
Believing Christian	41
Twin	38
Ill-mannered	37
Intolerant	36
"Duck"*	19
Disagreeable	19
Backward	18
Bossy	14
Conservative	12
Obstinate	12
Full of complexes	12
Fierce	12
Envious	11
Spud	10
Superiority complex	10
Revengeful	10
Speech impediment	10
Nervous	9
Introvert	9
Huffy	8
Total dominance score	926

*The nickname related to the politician's surname: the Polish *kaczka* means "duck" in English.

graphic profile (gender, age, education, place of living, occupation), ideological self-identification (left-wing, center, right-wing), and the degree of their interest in politics (from very interested to not interested at all). They were also asked to specify the moment of making their political decision (before the campaign, during the campaign, or at the last minute) and specify the candidate they voted for during the first round of presidential elections in 2005 and in the second round (Kaczyński vs. Tusk vs. nonvoting).

The positioning of these six political objects was performed separately for two a priori established voters' segments: those with and without higher education.

On the basis of the associations generated by the respondents for each of the six political objects, dominance scores were calculated first, separately for the characteristics mentioned for each of them. Table 3.1 presents a sample

Figure 3.5 **Positioning of Politicians Among Voters With Higher Education**

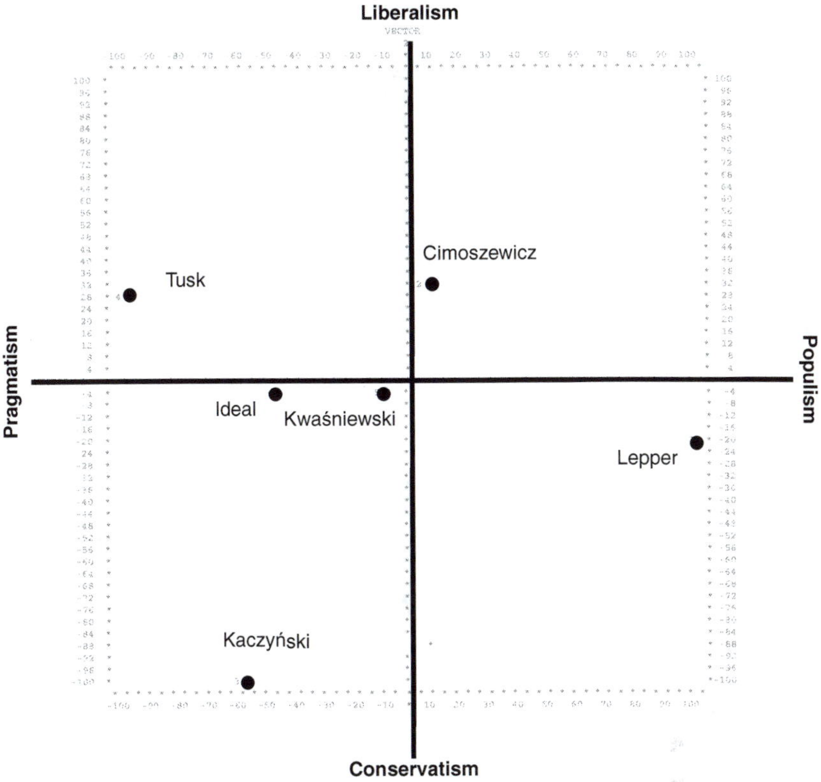

list of associations together with their dominance scores for Lech Kaczyński among voters with higher education.

The next step was to calculate inter-object associative affinity indexes for each object pair following the procedure developed by Kleine and Kernan (1988). The affinity indexes for each pair of stimulus politicians among voters with higher and lower education separately were the input data for the multidimensional scaling program MINISSA.

In both groups two-dimensional spaces were obtained and they are presented by Figures 3.5 and 3.6.

As expected, perceptual maps of the Polish presidential election market in 2005 among voters with and without higher education were different. It means that each of these groups perceived the political scene and the actors there in different categories. These results are mainly related to the complexity of these categories resulting, for instance, from the knowledge and the set of

Figure 3.6   **Positioning of Politicians Among Voters With Lower Education**

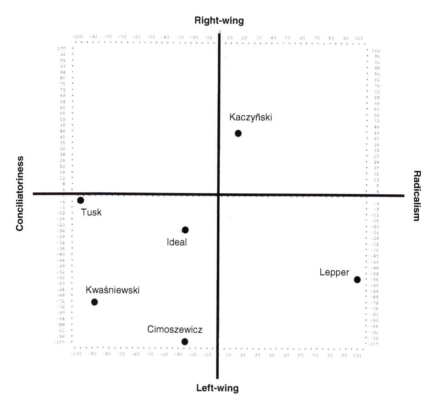

concepts that voters with different levels of education possess as well as their socioeconomic status (see Baines et al. 2003; Conover and Feldman 1984).

In the case of voters with higher education, the perception of particular candidates and preferences toward them (the distance from the ideal candidate) were determined by latent dimensions, which can be defined as liberalism (economic and social/moral) versus conservatism (attachment to tradition and religious values) and pragmatism versus populism. The ideal candidate was perceived as a rather liberal and pragmatic politician.

Voters with lower education understood the election scene in more general and less precise categories: left-wing versus right-wing (postcommunism resentment) and conciliatoriness versus radicalism. It seems that in this case the dimensions reflected to a large extent media frames related to covering political events and not a more detailed analysis of the meaning of these descriptive categories (see Lau and Schlesinger 2005). In this group the ideal candidate was defined as a rather left-wing and conciliatory politician.

Using the MDS technique for the positioning of politicians in the Polish presidential elections in 2005 provides important directions about developing political strategies for particular real candidates. From this perspective their goal should be such repositioning that would bring them closer to the point corresponding to the ideal candidate. Then, depending on the voter segment (with or without higher education), the point of maximum preference would be defined differently.

The analysis of associations on which the inter-candidate associative affinity index is based shows that the index does not include their valence, since common features may be both positive (and only positive when a real politician is compared with an ideal candidate) and negative. In this way the results of positioning reflect certain perceptual latent dimensions that are common for all the politicians but do not reflect signs of particular attributes associated with images of particular politicians. Marketing strategies developed on the basis of this, by operating in these dimensions, do not allow one to manage a politician's image more precisely by highlighting positive features (shared with the ideal candidate) and eliminating unwanted associations (decreasing dissimilarity with the ideal candidate). It seems necessary therefore to develop and supplement positioning based on inter-candidate associative affinity and with other elements also including the valence of particular associations. Such a development is possible based on Amos Tversky's contrast model of similarity (1977). According to him, a similarity between two objects does not depend only on their *common features*, but also on *distinctive features*, which are characteristics only for each of the compared objects. Therefore, this similarity increases with addition of common features and/or deletion of distinctive features (i.e., features that belong to one object but not to the other).

An ideal candidate (IC) is characterized exclusively by positive features. From the marketing perspective, the ID's image is a model and standard of comparison for each of the real politicians (RCs) running in the election. Therefore, their strategic goal is to form their image in such a way that it overlaps the most with the ideal candidate. In this case common features are always positive and it is those that are crucial for forming voter preferences. In turn, the area defining the differences between the ideal and real politicians may include both positive and negative features. They reduce the similarity between these two objects. However, in this case positive and negative features perform different functions when building a candidate's image. Negative features are always unfavorable and reduce the probability of voting for a particular politician, whereas positive features, as peripheral characteristics of his or her image, seem to enrich it. For the voter they can constitute additional reasons to support the politician. The contrast model of similarity shows then that in order to increase one's similarity to the ideal candidate, each real politician should try to broaden the area they share by addition of common features and/or by reducing the area including distinctive features by, above all, removing certain negative associations. The following formula expresses the similarity formed in such a way (Tversky 1977):

$$s(RC,IC) = F(RC \cap IC, RC - IC, IC - RC)$$

The similarity of RC to ideal candidate IC is a function F of three arguments: $RC \cap IC$, the features that are common to both RC and IC; $RC—IC$, the features that belong to RC but not to IC; $IC—RC$, the features that belong to IC but not to RC.

According to the contrast model of similarity, we can predict that the larger the distance between real and ideal candidates, the more negative features and the fewer positive features are associated with the first RCs. To test this hypothesis, all the associations generated by the respondents were divided into positive and negative ones, separately for each subject and each politician. Then, the means of both types of features and an indicator of general positive associations/positivity of associations was calculated for each of the candidates by dividing the average number of positive associations by the average number of negative associations. If the value of the indicator is higher than 1, it means a positive perception of a politician; if it is lower than 1, it means a negative perception; and if it is equal to 1, it is neutral. Then the correlation between these indicators and the distances of particular politicians from the ideal candidate were calculated, based on the results of MDS. The analysis was performed across all subjects. The obtained Spearman's rho correlation coefficient equaled -0.86 ($p < 0.01$). As predicted, its value and sign suggest that the higher voter's positive association with the candidate as related to negative associations, the shorter the distance between the real candidate and ideal candidate will be. Furthermore, negative associations increase this distance significantly (rho = 0.66, $p < 0.05$), and positive ones bring those objects closer to each other (rho = -0.93, $p < 0.001$).

It obtained results confirms the fact that political branding cannot be limited to searching for general similarity dimensions between a particular candidate's image and an ideal candidate; it has to be developed by more detailed valence association analyses on which the image is based.

The contrast model of similarity shows that particular political candidates can be compared not only against the ideal candidate but also against each other. In this way, negative associations related to one politician can simultaneously reduce preferences toward him and strengthen the support for his rival.

Table 3.2

Predictors of Voting Decision: Kaczyński vs. Tusk

	Model 1	Model 2
Gender (woman)	.09 (.08)	.18b (.08)
Age	−.04 (.28)	−.12 (.26)
Education (higher)	.20b (.10)	.10 (.12)
Interest in politics	−.05 (.11)	−.03 (.10)
Left-wing ideological self-identification	.54c (.19)	.57c (.17)
Center ideological self-identification	.56c (.11)	.51c (.10)
Precampaign decision	−.24a (.11)	−.17a (.11)
Last-minute decision	−.25 (.14)	−.15 (.14)
Kaczyński—positive associations		−.83b (.37)
Kaczyński—negative associations		.41b (.20)
Tusk—positive associations		.31a (.20)
Tusk—negative associations		−.15 (.48)
χ^2 (df_{model1} = 7; df_{model2} = 11)	47.52; $p < .001$	55.20; $p < .001$
pseudo-R2	.60	.65

Note: Coefficients are logit estimates. Bolded coefficients are significant at: [a]$p = 0.1$; [b]$p < 0.05$; [c]$p < 0.01$. Standard errors appear in parentheses.

It means that a political candidate's image should be referred to (at least) two standards of comparison: the ideal candidate and the main competitor.

Hierarchical logit regression was performed to test this hypothesis. The dependent variable was the support during the second round of the presidential election in Poland in 2005 for Kaczyński versus Tusk (0 vs 1). Before the analysis was conducted, all the independent variables were rescaled on a 0–1 range and some of them were introduced to the equation as dummy variables (see Cohen 1968). In the first model, only control variables were introduced: gender (0—man, 1—woman), age, education (0—lower, 1—higher), interest in politics, left-wing ideological self-identification (1—left-wing, 0—the others), centrist ideological self-identification (1—centrist, 0—the others), precampaign voting decision (1—precampaign, 0—the others), and last-minute voting decision (1—last minute, 0—the others). The following variables were introduced in the second step: positive and negative associations related to Kaczyński and Tusk. The obtained results are presented in Table 3.2.

Introducing positive and negative associations indexes for Kaczyński and Tusk increased significantly the accounted-for variance of the respondents' voting decisions. With both models, important predictors of voting for Tusk were to have left-wing and centrist voters' ideological self-identifications and to make a decision in the course of the campaign, but not in the very last moment before it was finished. Furthermore, after adding the variables related to the associations with Tusk and Kaczyński, the important predictor of preferences for Tusk, which was higher education, became insignificant, while what did become significant was the voters' gender. He was given more support by women. The associations related to both politicians also had significant influence on the voting. The support for Tusk was increasing as positive associations with him were increasing and negative associations with Kaczyński were increasing. But negative associations with Kaczyński would decrease when he evoked positive reactions of the voters.

This analysis supplemented, to some extent, the results of positioning candidates based on the inter-candidate associative affinity index and contrast model of similarity that are presented above. It provides directions about planning marketing strategies based on both the voters' characteristics and their way of understanding the election scene and the perception of politicians' image. These conclusions are valid for both positive and negative campaigns, whose goal is to weaken the image of the competitor.

Triangulation Model in Candidate Positioning

In the 1970s and 1980s, Robert M. Worcester developed a triangulation model in voter research and market positioning, under the general title of "political triangle" (see Worcester and Baines 2004; Worcester and Mortimore 2005). Its goal is to find a position of the candidate that will be particularly attractive to floating voters. Since the number of undecided voters is constantly growing and its importance for the results of political elections is becoming higher and higher, Worcester sought a way of controlling this segment of the voting market. The theoretical foundations of triangulation for positioning a particular candidate or party also have other practical implications for message development and policy development in political marketing research. The distinction between message development and policy development refers to the distinction between *how* to communicate a party's or candidate's message and *what* to communicate.

The concept of triangulation is very vividly described by Dick Morris (1997), President Clinton's chief strategist in the mid-1990s. For him triangulation referred to the process of positioning Clinton and his policies between but above the existing positions of the Republicans and Democrats. Robert Worcester and Paul Baines (2004) present Morris's concept of triangulation as an introduction to their own position on that subject. The central tenet of the political positioning problem is the creation of a consistent image that is centered on a single theme, with strongly tied-in underlying issues, and with other political parties or candidates attempting to undermine credibility and consistency. This image comprises both message development and policy development components of a particular party and its leader. The develop-

Figure 3.7 **Triangulation Model in Candidate and Party Positioning**

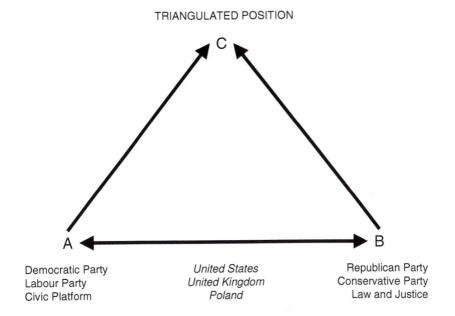

TRIANGULATED POSITION

| Democratic Party
Labour Party
Civic Platform | *United States*
United Kingdom
Poland | Republican Party
Conservative Party
Law and Justice |

ment and maintenance of an emotional and intellectual connection with the electorate are the principal objectives of the positioning process.

In 1996 Morris advised Clinton that the best course of action would be to triangulate, or create a third position, not just between the old positions of the two parties (Republican and Democrat) but above them as well, and identify a new course that would accommodate the needs of the Republican appeal but do it in a unique way. The concept of triangulation can be illustrated as in Figure 3.7.

The concept of triangulation consists then of combining the best elements of both parties in such a way that both parties' traditional voters can support it. Such an approach is particularly clever since this kind of policy proposition allows a party to appeal to the maximum number of voters along the continuum of Democratic Party—Republican Party in the United States, Labour Party—Conservative Party in the United Kingdom, or Law and Justice—Civic Platform in Poland. According to the logic of triangulation, voters most susceptible to information policy occupy middle ground between the competing parties—that is, those voters who might float between electorates.

According to Worcester and Baines (2004), the Morris model of triangulation is principally concerned with policy development rather than message development and originates from the U.S. context. Therefore, the authors make two assumptions about positioning according to the concept of triangulation, showing the fundamental role of marketing research in developing an efficient voting strategy:

1. Policy development processes best employ market research techniques to determine the acceptability of policy scenarios among voters in voter-oriented political campaigns.
2. Message development processes best employ market research techniques to determine the acceptability of how preselected policies are communicated to voters in voter-oriented political campaigns with specific reference to the medium employed.

Although Morris's concept boils down in fact to positioning politicians according to the method of triangulation for policy development, the concept of triangulation also concerns message development—that is, *how* to communicate.

Message Development and Management of Its Ambiguity

Compared to policy development, message development according to the concept of triangulation is a more tactical, communicational task and largely considered from a marketing perspective. Particularly interesting research in this area concerns the ambiguity of messages related to a candidate's or party's policies on the issues.

According to the assumptions of the rational voter theory, the foundation of defining a particular politician's or party's image is the message in which she defines her stand on issues. However, political candidates do not always form their views clearly and unambiguously and do not always have clear views on issues. What is more, they may use consciously an "ambiguity strategy" to avoid expressing clear views (Alesina and Cukierman 1990; Downs 1957; Page 1976; Shepsle 1972). This strategy allows them to increase the number of voters to whom the message appeals because the supporters of different solutions may interpret it as support for their own stands or—at least—as relatively close to their own views (Aragonès and Postlewaite 2002; Dacey 1979). An unambiguous message usually leads to a clear polarization of the electorate. The supporters of the view expressed there (e.g., "When I get the power I will abolish abortion") strengthen their support for the politician who expresses this view whereas the opponents strengthen their opposition. Undecided voters, who do not have an opinion on a particular subject, demonstrate an escapist tendency, fearing the candidate's radicalism. With an ambiguous

Figure 3.8 **A Man and a Sitting Woman as Ambiguous Figures**

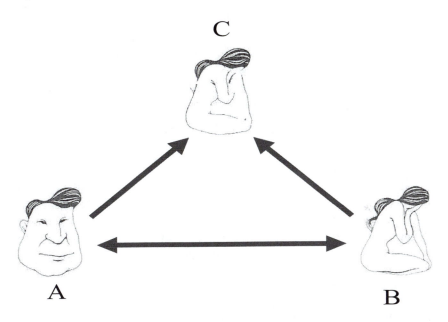

message (e.g., "When I get the power I will handle the issue of abortion") and no extra information about the politician, she may avoid polarizing the electorate and discouraging any of the sides, which would lead to her losing their support (Carmines and Gopoian 1981).

The problem of presenting a candidate's own views on some issues is related very closely to the concept of triangulation. In the context of Figure 3.7, unambiguous messages polarize the electorate strongly and are located either on the left at point A or on the right at point B. Ambiguous messages are in a triangulated position at point C. Metaphorically, this situation is presented in Figure 3.8. At point A there is a picture that is unambiguously read as the face of a man, at point B everybody can see a sitting woman, whereas at point C there is an ambiguous image that can be read as the face of a man from point A and as a sitting woman from point B.

The efficiency of ambiguity strategies is facilitated particularly by those issues on which voters are much divided (Bavelas et al. 1988). According to Larry Bartels (1986), it is also very important that such a message reaches various groups of the electorate and not only one, relatively homogeneous group because if voters have appropriate resources (e.g., knowledge, group support, and the opinion of the leader) they have a tendency to reject candidates whose views and stands they do not recognize with certainty. The efficiency of ambiguous messages is also facilitated by either scattered or differentiated opinions about particular issues (Campbell 1983).

Besides, according to the emphasis allocation theory of candidate ambiguity presented by Benjamin I. Page (1976), candidates strategically select unclear messages to divert the voters' attention from particularly controversial political problems and make them focus on issues or goals on which there is more agreement (e.g., integrity, development, and economic growth). In other words, politicians will try to convince the voter that they are honest and that they will ensure their country's economic development rather than state that they have a particular plan for improving the condition of the health-care system. They consciously present their position as ambiguous and do not make much effort to develop it. On the other hand, they do not usually have enough resources that would help them discuss their views in a precise and detailed way. As Page notes, voters are not interested in such detailed messages either, because analyzing and understanding them would require a lot of effort. Therefore, the strategy of ambiguous communication may also be the consequence of some factors that a candidate is not able to consciously control.

The ambiguity of the candidate's position is not always then the result of planned action. It may actually result from his lack of opinion on a particular subject (Huckfeldt et al. 1998). It is also influenced by such variables as voting environment and ways of reporting the campaign by the media, particularly if they focus on candidates' images, without paying much attention to their political programs or stands on issues (Conover and Feldman 1989).

When a candidate's position is not clearly defined, voters may infer a candidate's image using the information they have about him or such hints as his partisanship or religion (Feldman and Conover 1983; Kuklinski and Hurley 1996; Rahn 1993). Besides, voters may also "define" a politician's views following their affective attitude toward him (Ottati, Fishbein, and Middlestatd 1988). Edward Carmines and J. David Gopoian (1981) suggest that voters' reactions are both a function of their preferences toward problems and their assessment of the candidates. Therefore, if a politician focuses on an issue that is expressed in an ambiguous way but one on which voters are not divided, then he uses voting reinforcement. Thanks to this strategy, he develops his positive image and strengthens his support not only among his electorate but also those who are supportive of him.

The ambiguity of the message is present in many politicians' messages in various forms (Cwalina and Koniak 2007). The methods that are most often used are the following: (1) using general statements that include usually irrelevant content or that do not specify anything (e.g., "The situation of the health service must be improved") and (2) presenting various points of view without supporting any of them clearly (e.g., "The situation of the health service can be definitely improved by privatizing it or by imposing higher taxes on citizens"). The first type of ambiguity may be defined as semantic ambiguity whereas the second one as argument ambiguity. Both cases give voters much room for interpretation. The voters' decision whether to support a politician depends to a large extent on their beliefs, their sympathy toward the politician, the politician's image, and the voters' overall evaluation of the politician.

Experimental research on the reception of unambiguous and ambiguous messages was conducted by Wojciech Cwalina and Paweł Koniak (2007). The main research problem was to show how ambiguous messages influence voters' attitudes toward both the information the politician presents and toward the politician herself. Subjects were assigned into one of three groups that were presented, respectively, (1) a message including two-sided arguments and supporting a fictitious issue of introducing a fixed number of permanent seats for women in the parliament, (2) a message including two-sided arguments which was against such a solution, or (3) an ambiguous message—including only "for" or "against" arguments, without clarifying the final position of the sender. Each of the messages consisted of one argument for ("Women, who constitute half of the society, are not represented proportionately in the parliament and thus they become a kind of minority") and one against ("Such disproportions should be eliminated in a natural way and not by granting special privileges or even rights to women"). In the "for" and "against" messages, the final position of the source was presented directly ("I am for (against) introducing a guaranteed number of seats for women in the parliament"). In order to control the influence of the presented arguments, the ambiguous message was presented in one of the two versions—for/against or against/for. The conducted analyses did not show any difference between the sequences of the presentation so the two versions were combined.

In all the groups, before the stimulus material was presented, subjects were asked to express their own views on the issue of introducing a guaranteed number of seats for women in the parliament. The subjects could then be divided into two groups: "against" and "for." Each of them agreed with a politician who presented a similar view and disagreed with one whose view was different.

The results of the research on perceived consistency of views are presented in Figure 3.9. The results clearly show that messages consistent with the subjects' views were perceived by them as significantly closer to their own views than messages inconsistent with their views. Furthermore, both those "for" and "against" perceived ambiguous messages as similar to their views.

Figure 3.9   **Voters' Agreement With Politician's View Expressed in Politician's Message**

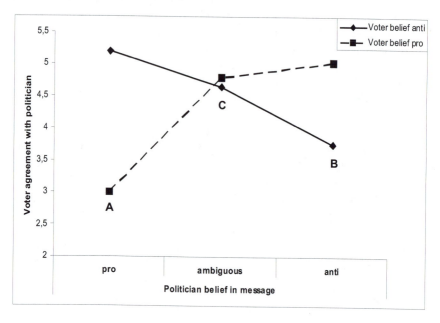

The results seem to a large extent compatible with the strategy suggested by the triangulation model. Both those against parity in the parliament and those supporting it who perceive the message as inconsistent with their own beliefs clearly reject the message and the candidate expressing it (respectively, points A and B in Figure 3.9). Both groups, however, have a positive attitude toward the ambiguous message (point C). Comparing Figure 3.7, 3.8, and 3.9, one can see that point A, B, and C correspond to one another. In this way, the strategy of managing ambiguity in voting messages supplements the concept of triangulation in positioning as far as message development is concerned. If unambiguous messages lead to the electorate's polarization and thus limit the number of the candidate's potential voters, then using ambiguous message may contribute to overcoming voters' division.

Party Positioning Based on Slogans

Despite the fact that political marketers most often try to position candidates and parties in target voter segments based on their image and stands on issues, an important supplement to adapting a candidate or a party to the voters' needs may also be positioned based on the slogans they create. It is obvious that making the correct choice of a campaign slogan is extremely important for building a coherent image of a political party. In other words, developing the best slogans for a particular party allows political marketers to find the best position for it.

According to Muzafer Sherif (1937, 450), a slogan is "a phrase, a short sentence, a headline, a dictum, which, intentionally or unintentionally, amounts to an appeal to the person who is exposed to it to buy some article, to revive or strengthen an already well-established stereotype, to accept a new idea, or to undertake some action." Slogans directly imply a value judgment. Usually the effective slogan is the one that appeals to a particular appetite, need, or other demand with a short, simple expression whose features—such as rhythm, alliteration, or punning—make its recurrence or repetition easy. But none of these features is enough in itself to make a slogan effective. This does not mean that these shortcuts necessarily express the true and objective proposal for the solution of some problems or a promise (voting, for example) that will be fulfilled.

A broader definition of the slogan is proposed by Kochan:

> Slogans are short messages, which constitute a closed entirety, either stand out from an advertising or a propaganda text, or exist by themselves, are characterized by a brief, often poetic form. Slogans have a certain meaning (information or promise and an encouragement to take action), which is most often implicit and uses largely emotional and paralinguistic means. Slogans contain "perlocutory aspirations"; that is, the intention to provoke actions pertinent to the direction set by the message carried by them, implementing those intentions only in the primary situation context and on the grounds of accepting the postulated by its common emotional identifications and expectations. (2002, 74–75)

From the marketing perspective, a slogan, name, and logo are the important elements that go into making integrated brand identity. These three components together can and should be used in union to provide the full positioning message. The primary use of a slogan is to summarize the brand's message and to provide continuity from one advertising execution to another in campaigns (Reece, Vanden Bergh, and Li 1994). However, the slogan should not be treated as something that does not change. Many companies change advertising slogans to improve marketing strategy and financial performance. Such changes might be influenced by changing demographics, changes in consumer values, competitive pressures, the firm's desire to reposition a product, or trouble with the previous slogan sending the wrong message. Lynette Knowles Mathur and Ike Mathur's (1995) research demonstrates that there may be positive market-value effects associated with announcements of advertising slogan changes, making investors show more interest in the shares of a given company.

In political marketing, changing party slogans every election is very common and reflects the attempt to be politically updated. Such slogans are supposed to embody a political platform that is best fitted both to the specific pattern of a country's political culture and to the needs of the voters at a particular moment in time. Besides, new slogans arise or become effective particularly when the situation people face is unstable or indefinite and demands a short epitomizing expression. According to Sherif (1937), slogans become especially effective at critical periods, such as wars or revolutions. Examples of such slogans are "Liberty, Fraternity, and Equality" of the French Revolution (one of the most important slogans in world history), "All Power to the Soviets" of the Communist Revolution in Russia; "He Kept Us Out of War" (the slogan of U.S. president Woodrow Wilson seeking reelection during World War I), and "No Freedom Without Solidarity" (the slogan of the Solidarity movement reflecting its attempt to restore democracy in Poland at the beginning of the 1980s).

Craig Varoga (1999, 69) stresses that politics is one of the few activities where a half-century-old slogan can be dusted off to imply youth and innovation—a tendency that Varoga calls "recycling an old campaign slogan." This is illustrated by several candidates running for reelection in several U.S. offices over the years using the slogan "compassionate conservatives." And it is not only old slogans from the same country that are adapted in this way but also more or less literal references to foreign slogans. A case in point is the slogan of the Polish party known as the Labor Union from 1997—"You Deserve More." Although the authorities of the party denied that they had copied the slogan, it was very similar to the slogan of the British Labour Party from 1992—"Britain deserves better."

Another marketing goal set for slogans is reducing any incongruity in the brand image. Therefore, the slogan is an important element of the "image platform" (Manzer, Ireland, and Van Auken 1980). Its goal is to broaden and supplement the contents carried by other elements of the message and recapitulate or summarize the essence of the message. Besides, it should make the receiver focus on a given message and make the brand's message stand out from the competitors' messages. According to Bonnie Reece (1984), slogans serve mainly to facilitate the storage in memory by consumers of a brand name and some pieces of information that identify and position that brand. The results of Kevin Pryor and Roderick Brodie's (1998) research suggest that a brand extension is rated as more similar to an existing family-branded product if the advertising slogan refers to attributes that the brand extension shares with existing products. It seems that a slogan may not only perform the function of primes or memory cues in the context analyzed by Pryor and Brodie, but also serve to activate a memory of a given brand and associations connected with it at the moment a purchasing or voting decision is made.

In the case of the political market, slogans must constitute the political brand essence also due to the "cognitive misery" of the voters (Fiske and Taylor 2008; Nisbett and Ross 1980). People do not usually think rationally or carefully, but instead take cognitive shortcuts when making inferences and forming judgments. These shortcuts include using schemes, scripts, stereotypes, and other simplifying perceptual tactics in place of careful thought (Cwalina, Falkowski, and Newman 2008). And because, as Sherif (1937) stresses, many people do not stop to investigate platforms, politicians try to catch them by slogans. However, not every slogan stands an equal chance of being remembered—no matter whether it is trustworthy or not (see Oehler 1944). Its memorability depends to a large extent on its linguistic construction, but also on factors independent of its creator, including age and gender of the consumers (voters), their media habits or interest in a given category of products. It should be stressed that remembering a slogan and associating it with a given brand is not a guarantee that it will influence consumer or voter behavior in a planned way. In addition to the mnemonics value, a slogan should be perceived as fitting a given brand, increasing its integrity, and developing positive attitudes toward it.

The goal of slogans is to remind people not only of the brand, but also the brand positioning—the brand promise. Branding efforts should avoid competing for the same value proposition as another firm; instead, they should have their own unique position on a given local market. Slogans, therefore, should stem from the company's unique positioning statement. As such, they should try to identify a single clarifying message that makes the brand stand apart.

However, in addition to the slogan fitting the image of a given party, politicians should consider the level of fit to competing parties and the level of the competing slogan fit to the image of the target party. Although a party's slogan may fit its image, the similarity between it and a competitor's slogan may prove of little importance if a number of features of this slogan are shared with the image of competing parties. In such a case, a slogan does not distinguish a party well from other parties.

Therefore, one of the most important factors influencing a brand's or party's marketing success is developing a slogan that will reflect appropriately the essence of the promotional message and, simultaneously, stand in contrast to the messages of competing brands or parties. From the strategic point of view then, it is important to position parties on the basis of their slogans as part of voting campaign development.

Table 3.3

Slogans Used in Polish Parliamentary Elections, 1990–2003

1. "For Poland to be Poland"—League of Polish Families (2001)
2. "Close to people's problems"—Polish Peasants' Party (2001)
3. "A good today—a better tomorrow"—Democratic Left Alliance (1997)
4. "A wise choice—a better life"—Labor Union (1997)
5. "Normal people. Normal state"—Civic Platform (2001)
6. "They have already been here. They have cheated us. They have to leave."
   —Self Defense of the Republic of Poland (2001)
7. "State, justice, law"—Law and Justice (2001)
8. "Poland needs a good host"—Polish Peasants' Party (1993)
9. "Let us restore normality. Let us win the future."—Democratic Left Alliance (2001)
10. "Together we can change a lot."—Civic Platform (2001)
11. "Together we can win Poland."—League of Polish Families (2001)
12. "Things do not have to be the same."—Democratic Left Alliance (1993)
13. "Everybody's talking, but we know how to do it."—Democratic Union (1993)
14. "You deserve more."—Labor Union (1997)
15. "No slogans, just facts."—Liberal Democratic Congress (1993)

The methodology of positioning a party on the basis of its slogans was proposed by Wojciech Cwalina and Andrzej Falkowski (in press). It allows capturing the specificity of a political party's perception in the context of the slogans it uses. The authors conducted a study on the evaluation of fifteen slogans used by various political parties in Polish parliamentary elections between 1990 and 2003. The task of the subjects was to evaluate each of the slogans on the basis of its fit to a given political party. The analyzed slogans are presented in Table 3.3.

In order to "fit" slogans to particular political parties, a single-factor variance analysis was conducted with repeated measures for each of the parties. For instance, the degree of adapting slogans to the image of the Polish Peasants' Party (PPP) is presented by Figure 3.10.

The results suggest that there are important differences between the fit of particular slogans as best reflecting PPP's image. The slogan that is best fitted to PPP's image is its own slogan: "Poland needs a good host." The evaluations of its fit are not considerably different only for the following slogans: "For Poland to be Poland" (s1), "Close to people's problems" (s2), and "Together we can win Poland" (s11). The worst rated slogans included "No slogans, just facts" (s15) and "Everybody's talking, but we know how to do it" (s13), which liberal parties—the Liberal Democratic Congress and the Democratic Union—used during the elections.

The degree of slogan fit to a party's image seems to influence its evaluation by the voters. The better the fit, the more distinct a given party is from others. It should be stressed that the position of a given party defined by its slogan also depends on the perception of the slogans of election rivals.

Figure 3.10   **Differences in Election Slogan Fit to Image of the Polish Peasants' Party**

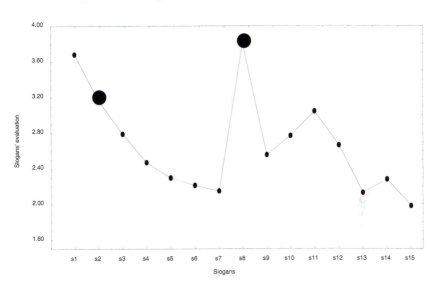

Various perception psychology analyses suggest that the way of perceiving a given stimulus depends on its context (Bransford 1979; Neisser 1967). Amos Tversky's contrast model of similarity (1977) suggests that the best position of a given party defined by its slogan depends not only on its best fit to the image of the party, but also on minimizing the fit of other slogans to its image. The position of a given party is then most salient when it is associated with its slogan and not associated with the slogans of competing parties. Only when these two conditions are met is one able to define to the level to which a given party stands out from competition.

The results of the research allow Cwalina and Falkowski to define the position of a given party expressed by slogans according to contrast model of similarity. The calculation procedure developed for this purpose assumes that one should deduct the mean degree of a competition slogans' fit to party image from the mean degree a party's "own" slogans' fit to its image. One then obtains a party's positioning indicator expressed by slogans. The greater the difference, the more distinct and unique will be the party's position.

The positioning indicator is expressed by the following formula:

$$P_K = \frac{\sum_{i-1}^{n} \eta_{S_{iK}K}}{N} - \frac{\sum_{j=1}^{m} \sum_{i=1}^{n} \eta_{S_{iL_j}K}}{\sum_{j=1}^{m} N_j}$$

Figure 3.11   Party Positioning Indicators Defined by the Party's Own and Competitors' Slogans

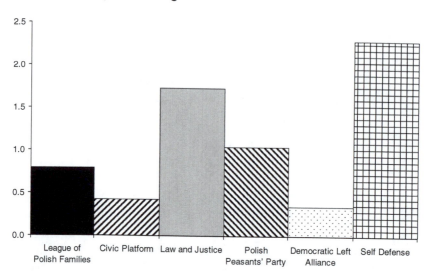

where P_K is party's position K; S_{iK} is slogan $S_i(I = 1, ...\ n)$, belonging to party K; $\eta_{S_{iK}K}$ is degree of fit of S_i party's slogan K to its image; S_{iLj} is slogan $S_i(I = 1, ...\ n)$ belonging to party L_j (j=1,...,m); $\eta_{S_{iLj}K}$ is level of fit of S_i party's slogan L_j to the image of party K; N is number of slogans belonging to party K; N_j is number of slogans belonging to parties different than K.

Figure 3.11 presents calculated indicators of the degree of slogan fit for the six analyzed parties.

It clearly suggests that the following parties have the best positions: Self Defense and L&J. The slogans of these parties make them stand out from competing parties and help voters to distinguish them from others. The worst positions are held by CP and DLA, whose slogans hardly distinguish them from other parties. They are the least distinctive.

The positioning indicator presented here may not be enough to completely understand the position of a party expressed by its slogans. Another step is then to define to what degree a party's "own" slogans are perceived as not only fitted to itself, but also fitted to competing parties. The best position of a given party depends then not only on making its slogans most fitted to the party's image, but also on making them least fitted to the images of the competing parties. The position of a given party is distinct when a given slogan is associated with the party that created it and not with competing parties. The calculation procedure in this case consisted of deducting the mean level of the slogans' fit to competing parties from the mean level of fit of a party's own slogans to its image. This positioning indicator can be expressed by the following formula:

$$P'_K = \frac{\sum\limits_{s=1}^{n} \eta_{S_{iK}K}}{N} - \frac{\sum\limits_{i=1}^{n}\sum\limits_{j=1}^{m} \eta_{S_{iK}L_j}}{N \times M};$$

where $\eta_{S_{iK}L_j}$ is the degree of fit of S_i party's slogan K to party's image L_j $(i = 1,...,m)$; N is number of slogans belonging to party K; M is number of slogans belonging to parties different than K.

Figure 3.12 presents such positioning indicators for the six analyzed parties.

According to this indicator, the best positions are again best occupied by L&J and Self Defense. These two parties clearly distinguish themselves from competitors on the basis of their slogans. They are fitted to their image and are characteristic only for these parties. The weakest positions are held by DLA and LPF. These parties are not well distinguished from their competitors. For DLA the negative value of the difference points even to a better fit of its slogans to competing parties than to itself. And since there is no relevant concord between the two indicators, despite a positive tendency in the relationship between them, the positioning of a party based on slogans should be analyzed separately for each of the two indicators.

The results presented above prove that a slogan as an element of image is an important factor in brand identity. It is an open question, however, to what degree slogan recognition for a party is accurate and to what degree it

Figure 3.12   **Positioning Indicators Based on the Fit of a Party's Own Slogans to Its Image and Images of Competing Parties**

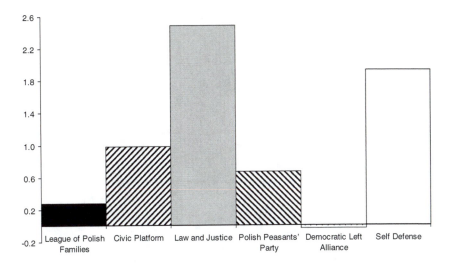

can be learned through increased promotional activity of a given party fighting for voters. Some slogans are particularly easily recognizable due to the cultural specificity of the content they express and their associations with a given party's program (e.g., PPP as a good host or Self Defense emphasizing the need for radical changes among the ruling elites). More general slogans that can be defined as supracultural lead to more recognition problems for the subjects, as was the case with CP. Most likely these recognition problems are caused by the authors of the slogans referring to a conceptual category that is too broad. Referring to certain values at an overly general level in slogans (for instance to such notions as "Poland, a better life, normal/ordinary people") leads to some confusion, loss of recognition, and a poor position of a party in voters' minds and does not bring them closer to a given party.

Voter segmentation and candidate or party positioning combined represent the process in which political strategists determine who their most influential supporters are, determine how they can be reached, and develop a detailed plan to determine how best to develop the candidate's campaign message. Despite various sociopolitical conditions in a particular country, the processes have the same foundation, logic behind them, and goal. Their results may significantly increase the probability of election success.

4

Candidate Image

It is no accident that the sphere of political activity has been called "the political stage" and the politicians "actors." They perform a certain play in front of their audience (voters) in order to win support, which bestows power on them. Such a collective performance is based upon images reflecting dreams of a better standard of living, intended to evoke strong feelings and steer away from the rational control of reality (see Le Bon 2002/1895). Paul Ekman (1992) claims that every politician who gains power and who has the ability to speak in public and a good television image has a communicational predisposition to be a natural liar. However, to quote Francisco Goya's series of graphics—*The Sleep of Reason Produces Monsters*—spontaneity is thus eliminated, critical thinking "switched off," and an individual's original psychological acts are replaced with somebody else's feelings, thoughts, and desires (Fromm 1965). Consequently, as Bruce Newman (1999b, 1999c) puts it in the titles of his publications, politics enters the "age of manufactured images." Analyzing presidential elections in the 1980s in the United States, Martin P. Wattenberg (1991) announced the beginning of a new era in voting politics, referring to it as "candidate-centered politics." It is characterized by the electorate's attention shifts from political parties to specific candidates running for various offices and, particularly, for president. The shift is accompanied by the growing importance of a candidate's individual characteristics of which makes up her image.

Each candidate running for any state office surrounds herself with an image-creation specialist, strategists planning her campaign, public opinion pollsters, and so on (Butler and Kavanagh 1992; Kinsey 1999; Newman 1999c; Plasser, Scheucher, and Senft 1999). Only when properly "packaged" does a candidate stand a chance of election success. The challenge to the political marketer is the ability to connect a politician's words, actions, and

Figure 4.1   **Stanisław Tymiński During the Polish Presidential Campaign, 1990**

Source: Gazeta Wyborcza, November 27, 2008.

vision into a realistic transformation of the electorate's dreams and aspirations. That transformation takes the form of an image of the politician in the minds of the citizens, one that is carefully developed and fine-tuned over a long period of time (Newman 1999b). But people in countries around the world are longing for change. This puts pressure on the successful leader to constantly respond to the people by altering an image that may have been fixed in the people's minds (Newman 1999d). Using James McGregor Burns's (1978) terminology, contemporary politicians exercise leadership *by* opinion rather than leadership *of* opinion (see Chapter 1 for Henneberg's differentiation between market-driving and market-driven strategies in political marketing, and delegate-oriented and trustee-oriented leadership; Sigelman, Sigelman, and Walkosz 1992).

An example supporting Newman's thesis on manufacturing a political leader is the case of Stanisław Tymiński's presidential campaign in 1990 in Poland (see Figure 4.1).

It was the first free and fully professional campaign in democratic Poland that used television and other media in order to gain political support (see Cwalina 2008a; Cwalina and Falkowski 2006). Although it did not lead to Tymiński's victory, it was a huge success for its authors. From the beginning, Tymiński's aides cooperated closely with the advertising agency Golik &

Dąbrowski. Together they set the campaign plan and decided what his image should be. Tymiński was running for the Polish presidency as a newcomer from abroad, completely unknown to the electorate. As a rich businessman and citizen of three countries (Poland, Canada, and Peru), he was a successful man who managed to avoid the dangers and traps of the capitalist world on his own. In his election program, he stressed that Poland should follow its own, national way in the world. Although he perceived and showed the threats of capitalism, by using his own story, he claimed that these dangers could be avoided by Poles' creating a modern market economy. A completely new element that could not be found in other candidates' election strategies was the motif of an outsider that Tymiński was characterized by. His message was targeted at people dissatisfied with the ruling politicians who had no chance to influence them. Tymiński's most emphasized attribute was his "foreignness." Building his image as an "external" candidate who was able to see the divisions in the Solidarity union and the people's embitterment with market reforms helped him gain support among many social strata.

The need for constant modifying a politician's image depending on current voters' needs and the current political situation also puts a tremendous amount of power in the hands of marketers who are trained at repositioning brands and their images in response to competitive forces. For example, Tony Blair of the United Kingdom remanufactured his image and the image of his party by referring to it as "New Labor"; Gerhard Schroeder in Germany came up with the catchy phrase "The Third Way," which successfully positioned his party for victory in a recent election. The same is true in the United States, where Bill Clinton's campaign theme in the 1992 election, "It's the Economy, Stupid," helped to position him as the candidate who would help the middle class succeed economically. Similarly, in his successful 1996 campaign, President Clinton used the theme "Bridge to the 21st Century" to manufacture an image of himself as the candidate who would lead the American people into the next millennium (Newman 1999c).

To truly understand the role of image manufacturing in politics around the world today, we need to look back at the first use of modern marketing techniques by Franklin D. Roosevelt in the United States (see Newman 1999d). The main thrust of his efforts was creating an image of a physically strong leader. During Roosevelt's presidential campaign, imagery management convinced voters that he could walk, when in fact he was disabled by polio. Using a technique that took him many years to master, he would lean on the muscular arm of his son and use a cane in the other hand to give the illusion that he was walking, when in fact he was not. At the time, Americans knew that Roosevelt had contracted polio, but many did not know that the disease had disabled him. In close to 50,000 pictures of Roosevelt at his summer home in New York, only two show him sitting in a wheel chair (see Figure 4.2). To convince the American people

132

Figure 4.2 **President Franklin D. Roosevelt, his dog Fala, and Ruthie Bie—a friend's granddaughter—at Hill Top Cottage in Hyde Park, New York, 1940**

Source: Courtesy of the Franklin D. Roosevelt Presidential Library and Museum, Hyde Park, New York.

that he was not crippled, Roosevelt had the braces on his legs painted black and always wore black pants that went down to his shoes so the braces were hidden. Elaborate schemes were devised for every public appearance he made, with the Secret Service building ramps to enable him to drive up in his car to the podium. Careful attention to details included decisions such as the placement of his chair and, most importantly, how he would ascend and descend from the podium. It was not until Roosevelt's last speech to Congress after the Yalta Conference, the first time he gave a speech to Congress sitting down, that he admitted wearing ten pounds of steel to keep him supported while he was standing. This effort to hide his disability certainly would never have worked in today's television era, but it does demonstrate that polishing political images is not new.

Roosevelt was also a master of his personal image. He had a terrible relationship with his wife, and it was believed he was in love with his personal secretary. After Eleanor Roosevelt found love letters in Franklin's suitcase when he returned from a trip, she and Franklin were never intimate again. But the president did have a terrific relationship with the press, and several secrets, including the estranged relationship with his wife and his disability, were kept from the American people. Despite their estrangement, Franklin and Eleanor forged a political alliance that kept her traveling all over the country to push his New Deal programs. In her travels, Eleanor served as the eyes and ears of the president, continually monitoring public opinion and perceptions of Franklin's programs. Today, Eleanor's efforts have been replaced by sophisticated polling techniques that allow a president to carry out that same monitoring function (Newman 1999d).

Candidate Image Structure

A citizen's image of a politician consists of the person's subjective understanding of things, or what that person likes and dislikes about the politician. Similar to brand images (see Chapter 1), political images do not exist apart from the political objects (or the surrounding symbolism) that affect a person's feelings and attitudes about the politician. The term "candidate image" means creating a particular type of representation for a particular purpose (e.g., voting, governing, negotiating), which, by evoking associations, provides the object with additional values (e.g., sociodemographical, psychological, ethnic, or ethical) and thus contributes to the emotional reception of the object (Cwalina, Falkowski, and Kaid 2000; Cwalina, Falkowski, and Newman 2008; Falkowski and Cwalina 1999). The values through which the constructed object is enriched may never be reflected in his "real" features—it is enough if they have a certain meaning for the receiver. However, in order for such an image to be reliable and for the candidate to be efficient in his actions, he needs a balanced personality and oratorical skills. In sum, a politician's image consists of how people perceive him based on his characteristics, leadership potential, and surrounding messages that are conveyed through the mass media and by word of mouth in everyday communication with friends and family (Newman 1999c). A candidate's image is also affected by endorsements of highly visible people in the country who support him (e.g., Bruce Springsteen participating in John Kerry's and Barack Obama's campaign meetings in 2004 and 2008; Barbra Streisand and Warren Beatty promoting Bill Clinton during campaign rallies in 1992).

In the current era of politics focused on a candidate, creating a politician's positive image becomes the fundamental element of an election campaign (see Chapter 3). European political consultants studied at the beginning of 1998 by Fritz Plasser, Christian Scheucher, and Christian Senft (1999) stated unequivocally that it is a very important factor influencing a candidate's chances of success. In fact, it is even more important than the candidate's ability to use the media or cope with particular political issues.

Although creating a positive image is neither a simple nor an easy task, one may easily find many clues on how to achieve it. Studies conducted by social psychologists, political scientists, marketers, and academics working on communication provide a great amount of valuable data that can be very use-ful in devising better and more targeted actions by image-creation specialists (see Cwalina, Falkowski, and Newman 2008). The structure of the complete candidate image is presented in Figure 4.3.

The most important issue in creating any image is selecting those features that will lay the foundations for further actions. Such characteristics include personality features that can refer to voters' beliefs about human nature (especially integrity and competence) or be a consequence of social demand in a given moment of time and particular sociopolitical situations when the campaign is conducted. They are the core around which peripheral features are placed. They are less relevant for the voters but important for the realism of the candidate's image. The image has to present a candidate who is psycho-logically coherent and does not include contradictions that would make him "weird" or "implausible." Therefore, not all the peripheral features have to be positive. Even the best politicians have some (small) sins on their conscience. It can then be said that completing the image with some peripheral features leads to the creation of a candidate's "human face."

Another stage in creating the image is "translating" the characteristics into behaviors that illustrate them or are perceived as if they did. Above all, these are nonverbal behaviors (see, e.g., Sullivan and Masters 1988). They include both static characteristics, such as facial expressions or clothing, and dynamic characteristics, such as behavior at a meeting, home, work, or some unexpected event (Bucy and Newhagen 1999; Druckman 2003).

Figure 4.3   **Candidate Image Structure**

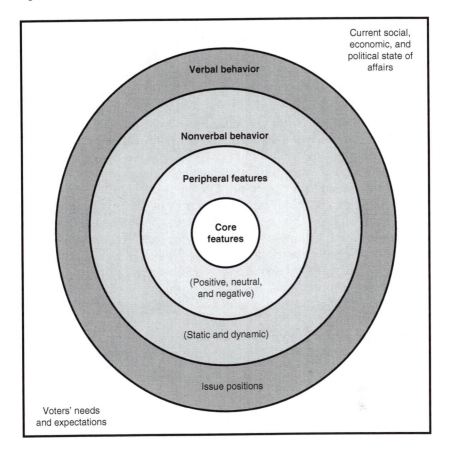

Such behaviors should be completed by an appropriate "soundtrack." The candidate has to say something! He must present his own views, proposed reforms, or solutions to difficult political problems. Margaret Scammell (1996), though acknowledging the role of issues in election campaigning, sees their importance not in their intrinsic merit but in their ability to affect the overall image of a candidate's credibility and competence. This assumption is also supported by the results of analyses conducted by Marvin Schoenwald (1987). Combining issues with candidate imagery via correlational analyses, he found, for example, that an improved voter perception on the devotes-time-to-education attribute could translate into a better reading on caring about children, caring about state problems, and being generally more human. David Peterson (2005) claims that in addition to the direct impact on vote choice, issues also matter because they determine how voters perceive candidate character traits. The more certain a voter is about a candidate's policy positions, the more that the voter uses those positions to inform her perceptions of the candidate's personality. This relation, in turn, produces sizable differences in whom the voter is likely to support.

The results of experimental research also confirm the importance of candidate image and stand on issues in the forming of voter support. Thomas Budesheim and Stephen DePaola (1994) in two studies investigated the effects of image and issue information on evaluations of political candidates. Results demonstrated that subjects' evaluations were less influenced by their agreement with candidates' issue positions when image information was presented than when it was not. In other words, presentation of image information reduced subjects' reliance on issue agreement.

From this perspective, neglecting program proposals by a candidate and focusing only on image may lead to marketing myopia (Levitt 1960). Issues perform a twofold function—on the one hand, they influence directly the support offered to a particular candidate (whose views the voter embraces); on the other hand, they have also an indirect influence by bolstering particular features of the candidate's image.

Politicians should also bear in mind that all these image creation activities take place in particular sociopolitical and economical conditions. That is why getting feedback from voters is so important. A constant monitoring of the image's perception is important for maintaining it, regardless of the political campaign.

Ideal Political Leader

All citizens want their country to be ruled by the best or an almost ideal political leader. However, the following questions arise: What is this "ideal"? What features should the ideal leader have?

Studies on social perception demonstrate that in voters' minds, an "ideal politician" is a prototype, an example of the category of people professionally dealing with politics (Kinder 1986; see also Cantor and Mischel 1979; Falkowski 1995; Fiske and Neuberg 1990). Such a cognitive schema is a reference point for people when passing judgments on candidates running for a certain office or when making voting decisions.

S. Mark Pancer, Steven Brown, and Cathy Barr (1999) conducted a study designed to determine the key dimensions along which individuals judge the personalities of political figures in three countries: the United Kingdom, Canada, and the United States. The results indicated that common key evaluation dimensions were (1) integrity (honest, caring, straightforward, responsible);

(2) competence (intelligent, hardworking, committed, sense of purpose); and (3) charisma (charming, good-looking, charismatic). However, these three components were less useful in judgment of the less salient or foreign leaders than in evaluation of most salient leaders in their respective countries (e.g., Bill Clinton and George H.W. Bush in the United States, Margaret Thatcher and John Major in the United Kingdom, and Brian Mulroney in Canada).

Then, according to Mark Leary (1996), five features are extremely important for a political leader to possess: (1) competency, (2) the ability to evoke sympathy, (3) morality, (4) power, and (5) the ability to embarrass others. Possession of all these attributes contributes to the leader's charisma and improves his chances for electoral success.

Competency is the key element used to select a candidate for a "political job." However, in this sphere it is more difficult to clearly state what the candidate should be about. Is a competent politician one who has been educated as a political scientist? Maybe an economist or a lawyer? Or maybe a psychologist or a journalist? Should competency relate to the ability to manage others, solve problems, negotiate? Or, rather, does competency pertain to knowledge and experience in business, international relations, and legislation? It seems that "political competency" is made up of all these traits, in certain proportions. The goal is to win the respect of others—to be professional, effective, and successful.

The ability to evoke people's sympathy seems to be one of the most fundamental elements of social relations. Respect for others, humility while in contact with others, and the ability to maintain one's authority are indicators of social attractiveness. Provoking sympathy, or in other words being liked, guarantees social and professional successes, and it is the foundation for well-being and satisfaction with life.

According to Leary (1996), a charismatic leader should also be moral and his behavior should be immaculate. Although we are not saints ourselves, we want our politicians to be as "saintly" as possible. Problems with morality were the reason for many spectacular political falls, such as Richard Nixon's resignation from the presidency after Watergate (Winter and Carlson 1988). Nevertheless, in some cases, politicians managed to get away with scandals, such as Bill Clinton's affair with Monica Lewinsky, which, however, left a flaw on Clinton's image and weakened people's trust in him (see, e.g., Ahluwalia 2000; Benoit 1999). In some cases it is possible to repair one's reputation by admitting one's guilt.

Another characteristic of an ideal leader mentioned by Leary (1996) is power. Such a politician should be calm, firm, and composed. A charismatic leader can carry through every action she plans. The power of politics is best visible during situations of crisis or stress, including a war, terrorist threat, or financial crisis. Bertram H. Raven (1990, 1999; Gold and Raven 1992) in his power/interaction model of interpersonal influence distinguishes six bases of power, resources that an influencing agent can utilize in changing the belief, attitudes, or behavior of a target: reward, coercion, legitimacy, expertise, reference, and information. Reward power stems from the leader's ability to grant some reward to the target. Coercive power involves threat of punishment. Legitimacy power is based on social norms (e.g., formal legitimate position, reciprocity norm, responsibility norm, or equity norm), such that the target feels an obligation to comply with the request by the agent. In expert power, the target trusts in the superior knowledge or ability of the influencing agent. Reference power is based on the target's identification with the leader, and informational power (or persuasion) is based on the information or logical argument that the agent can present to the target. Wielding or exercising any of these forms of power, according to Raven (1990), results from various features of both the agent and the target person and is situationally conditioned. Besides, particular forms of power have different consequences, both for developing "subordinates'" loyalty and for maintaining the changes brought about by the influence. For example, for reward and coercion, maintenance of the change would be socially dependent; especially if it depends on surveillance by the influencing agent. However, the changed behavior resulting from information would be maintained without continued social dependence on leaders (Raven 1999).

Such attributes demonstrate the charismatic character of the leader and bring her closer to a successful election. However, Leary stresses that a leader must not only be competent, kind, moral, strong, and dominant, but also incorporate these characteristics into the repertoire of self-presented behaviors that create her image, which is not necessarily compatible with reality.

Another study on the characteristics of leaders was conducted by Martin P. Wattenberg (1991). After analyzing the personality features of all the candidates running for the U.S. presidency between 1952 and 1988, he found that a candidate's personal attributes can be divided into five general categories: (1) integrity—associated with the candidate's trustworthiness and incorporating comments concerning honesty, sincerity, and any reference to corruption in government; (2) reliability—a candidate being dependable, strong, decisive, aggressive, stable, or the reverse of these; (3) competence—refers to a candidate's past experience, ability as a statesman, comprehension of political issues, realism, and intelligence; (4) charisma—a candidate's leadership abilities, dignity, humbleness, patriotism, and ability to get along and communicate with people; and (5) personal aspects of the candidate—appearance, age, religion, wealth, former occupation, family, and so on. The results obtained by Wattenberg demonstrate that in seven cases out of ten, the candidate who got higher ratings in public opinion polls regarding the previously mentioned personality categories won. Only three times was a less valued candidate able to win: Kennedy versus Nixon in 1960, Carter versus Ford in 1976, and Reagan versus Carter in 1980. According to the study, the best-rated president, chosen two times (in 1952 and in 1956), was Dwight D. Eisenhower.

Another way of "discovering" what characteristics voters desire in a candidate is by simply asking them. In a poll conducted by Centrum Badania Opinii Społecznej (The Public Opinion Research Center 1997) before the Polish parliamentary elections in March 1997, adult Poles were asked about the most valued characteristics of a good politician. The task of each respondent was to select five such characteristics from a list. The respondents stated that the most valued characteristics of a politician are honesty (47 percent of respondents), credibility (46 percent), intelligence (43 percent), understanding the problems of "ordinary people" (39 percent), competence (36 percent), and acting for the good of Poland (35 percent).

To a large extent, these characteristics are compatible with the results obtained by Wirthlin Worldwide in a survey conducted before the 1996 U.S. presidential elections. The American respondents stated that the most important features of a good president are honesty and trustworthiness, high ethical standards and moral values, a clear vision of where to lead the country, sincerity, decisiveness, concern about "people like me," strength, and the ability to accomplish his plans for the country (Wirthlin 1996). The authors of the report summed up their results by stating that both Bill Clinton and Bob Dole, as candidates for president, had to constantly develop their public images, including all the features mentioned previously as well as unselected ones. Only then could they sufficiently count on voters' support in order to win. What is required of a candidate for president is not necessarily the possession of the desired features, but that he displays them in public and gives the impression that he possesses them. To use the language of marketing, a candidate must create a proper image of himself.

In studies conducted during the presidential elections in Poland in 1995 and 2000, Wojciech Cwalina and Andrzej Falkowski (2000, 2005, 2006; Cwalina, Falkowski, and Newman 2008) checked the conformity of the features mentioned in answers to open-ended questions about presidential candidates Aleksander Kwaśniewski (in 1995 and 2000), Lech Wałęsa (in 1995), Andrzej Olechowski (in 2000), and Marian Krzaklewski (in 2000), with the features of "an ideal president." The task of the respondents was to write down the features that an ideal president should have and those that each individual candidate was characterized by. The questions were open-ended, so the respondents were free as to the number of characteristics they could list. All of the characteristics they wrote down were counted and categorized according to their

Table 4.1

Comparison of Features Attributed to Ideal President and Main Candidates in Presidential Elections in Poland, 1995
(percentage of indications)

Feature	Ideal President	Aleksander Kwaśniewski	Lech Wałęsa
Honesty, credibility	80.3	15.8	49.3
Competence, professionalism	47.3	17.2	10.8
Education	37.4	7.4	0.0
Appearance, attractiveness	33.5	25.6	0.0
Intelligence	33.0	25.1	0.0
Efficiency	31.0	9.9	6.4
Power	29.6	29.6	24.1
Openness to people and world	26.6	11.3	5.9
Clarity, eloquence	17.2	24.1	3.5
Wisdom, reason	13.3	12.3	1.5
Activity	11.3	13.8	1.0
Calmness, self-control	11.3	9.4	0.5
Conscientiousness, reliability	9.9	0.0	1.0
Authority, charisma	7.9	2.5	10.3
Caring for others and the country	6.9	0.0	3.0
Responsibility	6.7	2.0	5.2
Seriousness	5.9	7.4	0.5
Independence, objectivity	5.4	1.0	0.0
Fairness	4.9	0.0	0.0
Being a Catholic believer	4.4	0.0	6.4
Being known abroad	3.0	0.0	15.8
Friendliness	0.5	6.9	3.0

Source: Cwalina and Falkowski (2006, 332).

content similarity and number of the same characteristics being mentioned. The results obtained for an ideal president and for the candidates participating in the presidential elections in 1995 are presented in Table 4.1.

An analysis of the features presented in the table demonstrates the importance of creating the candidates' image and evaluating it to match the prototype of an ideal president. The key features that an ideal president should be characterized by include honesty and credibility, competencies and professionalism, education, appearance and attractiveness, intelligence, efficiency, power and determination, and being open to people and the world. Aleksander Kwaśniewski's image was based on power and determination, appearance and attractiveness, intelligence and clarity, and eloquence. The dominant features of Lech Wałęsa's image included honesty and credibility, and power and determination.

The results of the studies conducted during the presidential election campaign in Poland in 2000 are presented in Table 4.2.

Table 4.2

Comparison of Features Attributed to Ideal President and Main Candidates in Presidential Elections in Poland, 2000
(percentage of indications)

Feature	Ideal President	Aleksander Kwaśniewski	Andrzej Olechowski	Marian Krzaklewski
Honesty, credibility	89.6	30.6	32.8	34.8
Appearance, attractiveness	36.7	8.9	10.9	4.8
Education	32.2	3.2	21.3	28.7
Competence, professionalism	24.2	28.2	12.6	3.9
Intelligence	23.1	8.1	10.3	2.6
Caring about others and the country	21.2	18.6	5.8	20.0
Power	19.7	21.0	29.3	10.0
Openness to people and the world	19.7	27.4	21.3	2.6
Responsibility	18.6	4.0	4.0	1.3
Independence, objectivity	18.2	11.3	7.5	0.9
Efficiency	16.3	4.8	1.2	3.5
Fairness	14.8	4.0	1.2	1.3
Clarity, eloquence	13.6	11.3	8.1	1.7
Activity	13.3	4.0	5.6	0.9
Conscientiousness, reliability	12.9	5.7	5.2	1.7
Wisdom, reason	8.7	8.1	15.5	2.6
Being a Catholic believer	7.2	0.0	1.7	29.1
Seriousness	5.3	7.3	9.2	0.9
Calmness, self-control	3.8	16.1	9.2	0.9
Being known abroad	3.0	1.6	1.2	0.0
Friendliness	2.7	16.9	12.1	2.2
Authority, charisma	1.5	4.8	12.1	0.9

Source: Cwalina and Falkowski (2006, 332).

In the year 2000, an ideal president was characterized by honesty and credibility, appearance and attractiveness, education, competencies and professionalism, intelligence, care for others and the country, power and determination, and openness to people and the world. Aleksander Kwaśniewski's image included features such as honesty and credibility, professionalism and competencies, openness to people and the world, power, and determination. His main opponent in the presidential fight, Andrzej Olechowski, was characterized by honesty and credibility, power and determination, education, and openness to people and the world. The most important features for Marian Krzaklewski's image included honesty and credibility, being a believer (Catholic), education, and care for others and the country.

In both presidential elections, one can notice the discrepancy between Poles' expectations of an "ideal candidate" and the images of particular politicians. Apart from a qualitative analysis of the features forming a politician's image, a quantitative analysis between the profiles of an ideal president and candidates was conducted. The results suggest that the structure of the category "ideal president" in 1995 and 2000 differed considerably from all the candidates competing for the presidency in the elections. The results suggested that none of the candidates was close to achieving the image that was attributed to the ideal. From a marketing perspective, it meant that the campaigns of all the candidates were unsuccessful in meeting voters' needs.

Another conclusion derived from the research was connected with the dynamics of images change (repositioning). The images of both an ideal politician and the candidates were characterized by internal changeability. This means that in time, the perception of the features of the same object underwent significant changes (the percentage of their indications changed). The most characteristic shift relative to the changes in the image of an ideal candidate over five years (1995–2000) concerned appearance and attractiveness moving from fourth to second position. Also, important shifts were observed in the following categories: care of the country (increasing from 7 percent in 1995 to 21 percent in 2000), responsibility (7 percent to 19 percent), and independence (5 percent to 18 percent). On the other hand, some features of an ideal president became less important. In 1995, 47 percent of the respondents stressed the role of competencies whereas five years later it was only 24 percent. A similar situation could be observed with efficiency (decreasing from 31 percent to 16 percent), and intelligence (from 33 percent to 23 percent). A comparison of the importance of particular features of an ideal president in different years is presented in Figure 4.4.

A high dynamics of change is also represented by the perception of Aleksander Kwaśniewski's image. In 1995 he was not well-known as a presidential challenger. In 2000 he was running for reelection as a well-recognized politician. His image ratings went down considerably (from 25.6 percent to 8.9 percent), which resulted from his neglecting the effort to stay and look fit. The worse ratings concerned such areas as intelligence (25.1 percent and 8.1 percent) and eloquence (24.1 percent and 11.3 percent). An important issue was also voters' taking into account the president's education. In 1995, 7.4 percent believed that he had a higher education, whereas in 2000 it was only 3.2 percent. These results are interestingly from the perspective of the Supreme Court's considering voters' protests after the election when he gave untrue information about his education. However, there were also some positive changes about the politicians' image. Compared to 1995, in 2000 he was perceived as more honest (15.8 percent and 30.6 percent), open to people and the world (11.3 percent and 27.4 percent), friendly (6.9 percent and 16.9 percent), and caring about others and the country (0 percent and 18.6 percent). Comparisons between particular features of Aleksander Kwaśniewski are presented in Figure 4.5.

Figure 4.4   **Changes in Image of an "Ideal Polish Politician," 1995–2000**

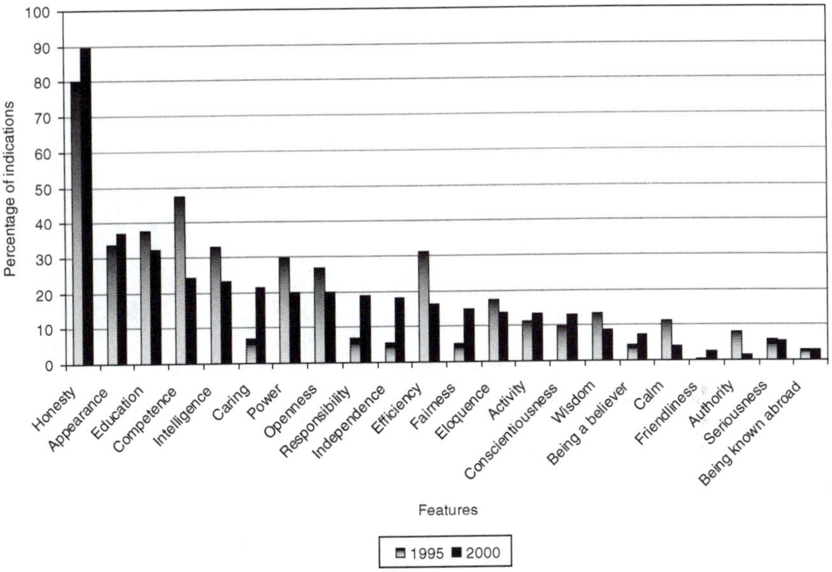

Source: Cwalina and Falkowski (2005, 184).

It can be stated that the results of the research suggest that the politicians' running for the Polish presidency between 1995 and 2000 did not meet, despite the efforts of marketing experts, the categories of an ideal politician defined by the voters. The prototype of an ideal president is a dynamic category. In time, the relevance of particular attributes changes, and so does voters' selection of particular attributes as relevant for an ideal president.

The "ideal president" concept is further developed in the superman/everyman model of image formation and candidate selection proposed by John Sullivan and colleagues (1990). The model assumes that when comparing candidates, voters make use of intuitions about human nature. Therefore, they may expect that candidates for president should be supermen or superwomen who are able to rise above the limitations imposed by human nature. If none of the candidates meet these requirements, then the voters will support the one who has the smallest deficit, hoping that once elected, he or she will grow while in office. This way of evaluating candidates may be defined as the superman model of image formation and candidate selection. On the other hand, voters may accept the assumptions about human nature, yet choose the candidate who is the most typical. For instance, Ronald Reagan's presidency (called the "Teflon presidency") may have evoked a conviction on the part of some voters that they should support him because

Figure 4.5   **Changes in Image of Aleksander Kwaśniewski, 1995–2000**

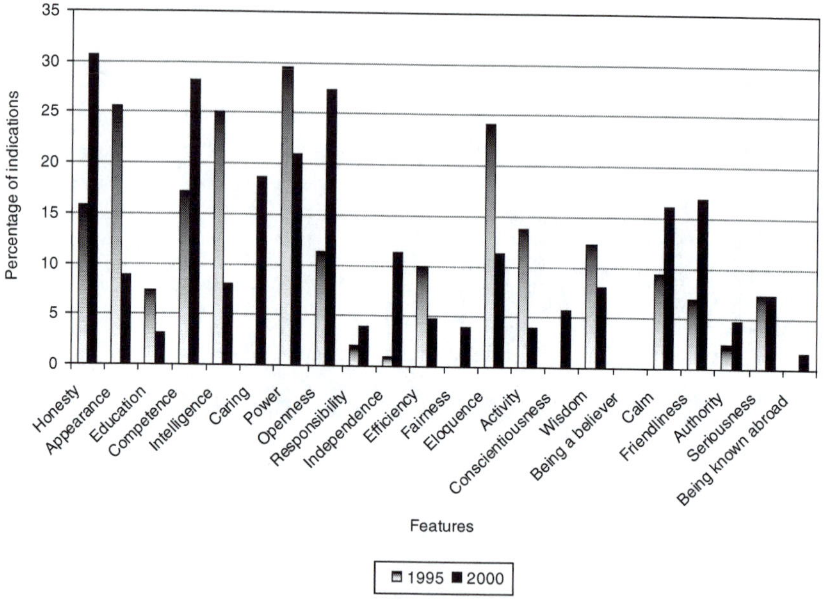

Source: Cwalina and Falkowski (2005, 185).

he personified "a next-door neighbor." He was not the best and most intelligent, but rather, the most typical. This model of candidate evaluation may be defined as the everyman model of image formation and candidate selection. The model assumes that candidates who are perceived as worse than or much better than the majority of people are rejected by voters. The first are discarded for obvious reasons, and the latter because they are too different from "everyman." Such people are usually considered overintellectualized and thus neither understood nor liked.

Sullivan and his colleagues tested the candidate selection models during the presidential elections in the United States in 1984 (Ronald Reagan versus Walter Mondale). The results they obtained demonstrate that voters want their presidents to be trustworthy, lack egotistical tendencies, and have control over events in the country, to the maximum extent possible. In addition, most citizens placed the incumbent, Reagan, into a modified version of the everyman model. People liked him and supported him because they perceived him as being at least as good as the majority of Americans. Mondale, on the other hand, as a challenger, was measured against the superman model. If he came out well in this comparison, voters reported a positive emotional attitude toward him. However, such a situation occurred quite rarely, and

Reagan won the election. The results pointing to the superman model though are consistent with the hypothesis put forward by Kinder (1986) that people compare candidates to their prototype concept of an ideal president.

The results of the studies presented here seem to bear out the hypothesis that when electing candidates for public office, people vote for those who, according to their opinions, are closest to the ideal—the candidates whose image better matches the ideal attributes of a head of state. The research on social perception proves that an ideal politician is a certain prototype in voters' minds, a model of the category of people dealing professionally with politics. However, a politician's image, as well as the ideal to which it can be referred, is not stable. It changes over time and according to the political situation in the country as well as being a result of marketing strategies in which political advertising plays an important role. Therefore, an important challenge for image-creation specialists is their ability to "package" their candidates in order to accommodate them to the voters' current dream, and then monitor their performance. Therefore, the first step in all political campaigns is to determine voters' expectations toward candidates and then to create an image of a politician as is desired by society (see Chapter 3). It may be an exaggeration, but we can say that what really counts is not the content, but the form, not the candidate's name and competencies, but the public mask (or persona) that the candidate assumes. To push this reality even further, we could venture to say that each of us is a potential political superman.

Integrity and Competence: Core Features of Candidate Image

The results of many studies about the fundamental categories on the basis of which judgments of other people are formed prove that they include two dimensions, namely morality (or integrity) and ability (or competence) (e.g., Fiske, Cuddy, and Glick 2006; Peeters 1992; Reeder and Brewer 1979; Wojciszke 1994, 1997, 2005). The defining attributes of the first dimension include characteristics such as frankness, helpfulness, reliability, and honesty. In the case of the second, they are persistence, hard work, and qualifications.

The ability categories are usually more important for their "owner" (self-profitable traits), whereas the morality aspect is more important for those who perceive it (other-profitable traits) (Wojciszke 2005). Furthermore, as Guido Peeters (1992) emphasizes, only the morality dimension is a typical evaluative dimension of other people. It reflects people's tendency to approach those of whom they have a positive opinion and to avoid those whose moral qualifications are questionable. The traits that are positive for others do not change their value even in a negative context. For instance, an honest friend will under any circumstances be better than a dishonest one. The practical characteristics (competencies and abilities), in turn, do not provoke an instant reaction of approaching or avoiding their owner. This reaction does not depend upon a larger evaluative context in which they occur. For instance, an intelligent enemy is worse than a dumb one. Therefore, the evaluative value related to social (morality) characteristics is absolute, while the value of ability characteristics is relative and contextual.

Glenn Reeder and Marilynn Brewer (1979) have argued that people perceive different relations between dispositions and behaviors depending on the nature of the dimension that underlies the attribute to be judged. Perceived relationships between dispositions and behaviors are called implicational schemata. The researchers propose that an individual with a moral disposition is behaviorally restricted whereas an individual with an immoral disposition is not. Moral people behave in moral, not immoral ways, though immoral people can behave both in immoral and moral ways, because the latter are socially demanded and rewarded. The opposite directional tendency applies to ability-related dimensions. Everybody can behave in incompetent ways, but only capable persons can behave in smart ways. In this way, the judgment in the ability-related dimensions promotes a more sympathetic and understanding approach to another person. In other words, the evaluative picture of the world is much more positive when ability and not morality schemata are created.

Furthermore, inferences of morality traits are based on the perceived person's goals and on how they relate to moral norms and the well-being of other people. Whereas a negative morality is inferred when a perceived person breaks the norms or harms others, a positive morality is attributed when the person maintains the norms or benefits others. Inferences of competence, however, are based on something different—on the efficiency of goal attainment. Low competence is inferred when the perceived person fails to reach a goal, and high competence is inferred when the goal achievement is efficient and successful (Wojciszke 2005). The moral contents of an actor's goal and the efficiency of its attainment are orthogonal. Both moral and immoral actions can be successful, indicating competence, but both types of goals can also remain unattained, thus showing the actor's incompetence. This suggests the possibility of classifying actions into four types (Wojciszke 1994). The first type of action is *virtuous success*, where the action goal is moral and successfully achieved (e.g., successfully helping a friend in math); the second is *virtuous failure*, where the actor aims at a moral goal but fails to achieve it (failing to help the friend); the third is *sinful success*, where the goal is immoral and successfully achieved (e.g., undetected cheating in an exam); and the fourth is *sinful failure*, where the actor fails to achieve an intended immoral goal (being caught cheating in an exam). Bogdan Wojciszke (1994) shows that the same behavioral acts can be construed in two ways, though not at the same time by the same person.

The dimensions of morality and competence appear regularly in voting polls and in academic analyses of the relation between a politician's image and voters' support, for instance in the studies by Leary (1996), Wattenberg (1991), Pancer, Brown, and Barr (1999), and Cwalina and Falkowski (2000, 2005, 2006) discussed above. Donald Kinder and David Sears (1987) determined that integrity and competence are two separate and fundamental dimensions of their perception that positively influence voters' behavior toward political leaders. The results of the research conducted by Jeffery Mondak and Robert Huckfeldt (2006) reveal that voter's attitudes regarding candidate competence and integrity are highly accessible to them and strongly influence their assessments of politicians. Furthermore, competence and integrity may help to unite that which partisanship and ideology divide, and they matter the most when voters with strong and consistent political views are called on to evaluate candidates with strong and consistent political affiliations.

Shanto Iyengar, Donald Kinder, Mark Peters, and Jon Krosnick (1984) stress that competence, integrity, and general performance represent correlated but distinct dimensions of presidential evaluation. According to them, Americans no doubt recognize that performance on any particular problem reflects the president's competence imperfectly. Performance is always determined in part by forces beyond even the most competent president's control (e.g., international economy, Congress, and television news coverage). Thus, how well presidents deal with problems such as unemployment and rising prices has little to do with their personal integrity, a point with which most citizens would no doubt agree. Iyengar and his colleagues also demonstrate that television news programs help define standards by which presidents are evaluated. This effect is greater for evaluations of presidents' general performance than for judgments of their competence and integrity, and it is more pronounced among novices than among experts.

Spiro Kiousis, Philemon Bantimaroudis, and Hyun Ban (1999) conducted two experiments to investigate how media emphasis on certain political candidates' attributes (personality and qualification traits) would influence public perception of those politicians. Their findings suggest that people's impressions of candidates' personality traits (their corruption level) mirror media portrayals of those traits. Meanwhile, perceptions of candidates' qualifications (their education level) do not appear to conform to media depictions of those qualifications. Media emphasis on candidate qualifications seems to make a candidate more appealing, whereas media convergence on personality traits does not. Therefore, candidate personality traits have a stronger impact on attribute-to-attribute salience (second-level agenda-setting), but candidate qualifications seem to wield greater influence overall on judgments of politicians.

The importance of politicians' integrity and competence for the political support they receive has been the subject of complex analyses by Jeffery J. Mondak (1995b, 1995c; McCurley and Mondak 1995). He used broad definitions of competence and integrity: competence includes any indicator of effectiveness, or capacity of the incumbent to get the job done, while integrity refers to a moral sense of right and wrong. The goal of the voter is to identify the best candidate from those running for an office. The quality of the candidates refers to the nonpolitical traits that can be traced in their behavior, including integrity and competence. From this perspective, an electoral system functions as a filtration mechanism in that voters strive to maximize the quality of their elected representatives. Candidates who do not meet these criteria remain, like sediment, at the very bottom. In order to verify these assumptions, Mondak conducted content analysis of the written descriptions of the U.S. House members that appear in the 1972–1994 volumes of the *Almanac of American Politics*. All words and phrases that spoke of a House member's competence or integrity were recorded. A two-step procedure was then used to derive numerical scores for these words and phrases. First, the judges evaluated every phrase on a scale from 0 (poor quality) to 3 (excellent quality), and whether each term primarily concerned a House member's competence or integrity. Then, for each of the described politicians, they calculated the mean of the phrases from his or her description and converted the score to the 0–1 scale. Then the results were juxtaposed with the judgments of the same candidates made by American voters in National Election Studies (NES) from 1976 to 1992. The results of these analyses are presented by Figure 4.6.

The results show that American congressmen do not treat service in the House as a stepping stone, and thus the collective quality of the House does not converge toward mediocrity over time. The highest degree of collective quality was found among those people who remained in the House for at least seven consecutive terms. The politicians running for higher office were—on average—less moral than those who remained in the House of Representatives. Thus, strategic retirement from reelection seemed to be related to their morality (scandals) rather than competencies. Their competencies were on a level similar to those still holding office but their honesty was lower.

Mondak's analysis also demonstrates that quality and integrity evaluations exert a strong direct effect both on the general evaluation (the NES feeling thermometer) and on the vote choice. Competence, in contrast, affects only the vote. Furthermore, challengers receive additional votes per dollar when they oppose low-quality rather than high-quality incumbents. Consequently,

Figure 4.6 **Competence and Integrity of House Members, 1969–1981**

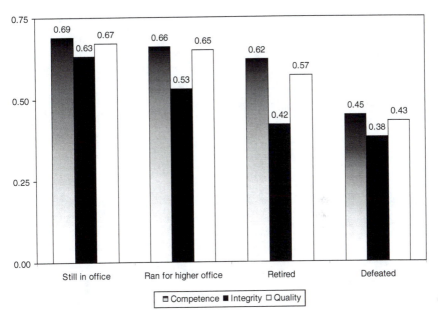

Source: Based on Mondak (1995b).

according to Mondak (1995b), the electoral system functions not only to weed out the worst incumbents, but also to preserve the best.

As far as the importance of morality and competence in forming the image of political candidates and voting intention are concerned, experimental research was conducted by Wojciech Cwalina and Andrzej Falkowski (2007). Before the experiment, the subjects were randomly divided into four groups. Each group was presented with one of the four versions of a fictitious character, a Polish parliament candidate named Tomasz Zakrzewski, prepared for the purpose of the study. His name and surname were chosen on purpose, so that the subjects would not have any associations with a particular public person, which would guarantee that their subjective judgment would be based on the curriculum vitae only. Descriptions of the candidate were developed with focus being put on the two dimensions of perceiving and judging others: competency and morality. Each of these variables had two levels: positive or negative. Four versions of Zakrzewski's biography were developed, presenting him as incompetent and immoral, competent and immoral, incompetent and moral, and competent and moral.

In order to verify empirically the causal relations among the judgments of

Figure 4.7 **Candidates' Morality and Competence in Forming of Voter Preferences**

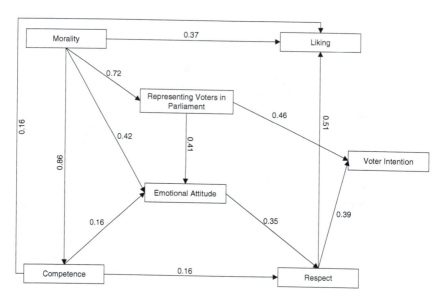

competence, morality, liking and respect, declared intention to support the politician in parliamentary elections, voters' predictions whether he would represent them well in the parliament, and the general emotional attitude toward him, a structural equation analysis was performed on all subjects jointly (discrepancy function estimated by maximum likelihood method). Its results are presented in Figure 4.7.

The results meet the statistical goodness-of-fit requirements [$\chi^2(7) = 9,454, p > 0.2$, GFI = 0.983; Gamma = 0.996]. The causal relations in Figure 4. 7 present a complex model of forming voter decisions. Voter intention is directly influenced by respect and the voters' idea about how a politician is going to represent them in the parliament. In both cases, positive judgments in these areas increase support. Evaluation of competence influences respect whereas evaluation of morality influences liking. However, competence has also a direct, positive influence on the emotional attitude toward a politician. Positive evaluation of morality helps the evaluation of competence. Besides, if a candidate is considered moral, then the voters' global evaluation is more positive and they are convinced that he is going to represent their interests in the parliament well. However, a positive evaluation of his competences influences only the general attitude toward him. It should be stressed that this global attitude also influences the respect toward him. The results of this analysis clearly show that support intention for a given candidate is determined *directly* by the respect that voters feel for him and their belief that he can represent voters' interests and, *indirectly*, by their judgment of his competence (two causal chains: by respect and by global evaluation and respect) and morality (also two causal chains: by evaluation of the representation of their interests and by global evaluation and respect).

In sum, voters can recognize very well whether a candidate is moral and competent, and their evaluation in these dimensions is going to influence not only whether they like and respect the candidate but also whether they will support him in the elections. Voters thus function as a filtering mechanism whose goal is to maximize the quality of their representatives.

Both politicians and—above all—marketing specialists seem to be fully aware of the functioning of this mechanism. Therefore, their efforts to present a candidate's image as honest and competent are quite often efficient. Sometimes, in order to win support, it is enough to make people believe that a politician has particular traits without necessarily having them. In other words, the key element here is a successful image that voters are going to find attractive.

Nevertheless, some politicians manage to get away with scandal, and in some cases it is possible to repair their image by admitting their guilt. A series of studies on the consequences of a politician's public confession conducted by Bernard Weiner, Sandra Graham, Orli Peter, and Mary Zmuidinas (1991) prove that this strategy is successful only in certain cases. Confession is to a politician's benefit when it is obvious that she has done something wrong. In other words, if evidence of her guilt is clear, it is better to admit it and ask for forgiveness than to deny it. However, even in this situation it is not really possible to wholly recover the lost image. Admitting guilt also has positive consequences when it is not certain who is responsible for the wrongdoing. This strategy may also be successful if a politician is only accused of misconduct; it is better to anticipate the attack than to desperately defend oneself. It is better to admit something spontaneously than to be condemned. Admitting guilt is also more efficient for repairing one's image when the charges concern character and not actions. It is easier to justify weaknesses of character than improper behavior and the damage done because of it.

According to William Benoit (1995, 2006a, 2006b; Benoit and McHale 1999), threats to a politician's image have two critical components: the accused is held responsible for an act, and the act is portrayed as offensive. Therefore, all the activities aimed at restoration of image should be organized around them. In his image repair theory, Benoit distinguishes five main strategies and twelve detailed tactics that politicians (or companies) may adopt to avoid the negative consequences of their actions. Their characteristics are presented in Table 4.3.

Table 4.3

Image Repair Strategies and Tactics

Strategies and tactics	Key characteristics
Denial	
Simple denial	The act did not take place.
Shifting the blame	Someone else did (caused) a particular act.
Evasion of responsibility	
Provocation	The act was a response to someone else's action—that is, a justified reaction to a provocation.
Defeasibility	The person had no information or ability to control some important elements of the situation.
Accident	The act happened by accident; the person did not have full control over it and the situation.
Good intentions	The person had good intentions.
Reduction of offensiveness	
Bolstering	The person stresses positive things or actions undertaken in the past.
Minimization	The act did not have such serious consequences as are sometimes presented.
Differentiation	The act was less harmful than other similar actions.
Transcendence	There were more important, "higher" reasons or values justifying the act. The act is put in a more favorable or broader context.
Attacking the accuser	The person reduces the credibility of the accuser.
Compensation	The person compensates those who were wronged.
Corrective action	The person plans to solve the problem by restoring things to their former state. The person promises to undertake actions that will prevent such things from happening in the future.
Mortification	The person apologizes, admits guilt, and pleads for forgiveness.

Source: Based on Benoit and McHale (1999, 267).

Peter Smudde and Jeffrey Courtright (2008) conducted a meta-analysis of 308 cases in which businesses, companies, and so on used the image repair strategies discussed by Benoit. Their results are presented in Figure 4.8.

The strategy used most often for image restoration was the reduction of offensiveness (almost 51 percent of all the cases), and the least often used strategy was corrective action (almost 8 percent). Of course, the fact that a particular strategy is used most often does not necessarily mean that it is most efficient. Its efficiency depends mainly on the bad deed that a politician has committed, the circumstances (e.g., media coverage, competition on the market), and the group whose opinions the politician wants to influence. Furthermore, these strategies can also be used to various degrees, which is confirmed by the analyses conducted by Benoit for Bill Clinton's August 17,

Figure 4.8   **Frequency of Using Image Repair Strategies**

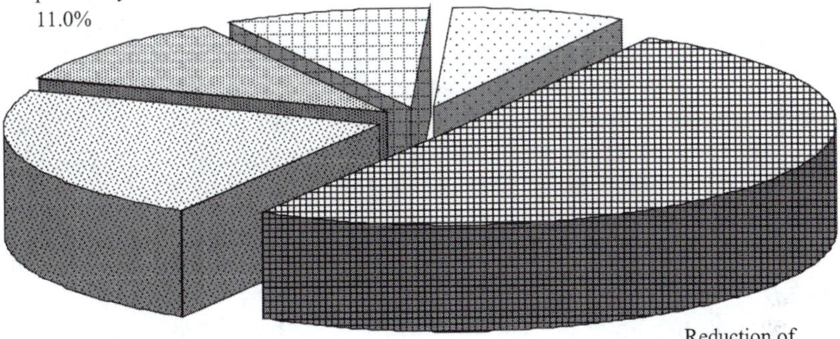

Source: Based on Smudde and Courtright (2008).

1998, apologia speech about his relations with Monica Lewinsky (Benoit 1999) and George W. Bush's April 13, 2004, press conference dedicated to the war in Iraq (Benoit 2006a). However, planning corrective actions well in advance and then realizing them may significantly help politicians restore their good name and—at least to some extent—win the voters' forgiveness.

The Importance of Advertising in Forming Politicians' Images

The dynamics of change in the image of a politician is certainly modified by political advertising. Televised political advertising is a tool of political marketing that has been successfully used since the beginning of the 1950s to create an image of politicians running for various state offices (Diamond and Bates 1992). It uses a certain image of the candidate to convey what voters may achieve if they vote for a particular person. To create a certain image of a politician, political consultants rely, frequently unconsciously, on the principles of social perception, discovered and developed within the field of social psychology (see, e.g., Fiske and Taylor 2008).

A detailed study on the importance of such advertising in forming a politician's image in voters' minds was presented by Lynda Kaid and Mike Chanslor

(1995), who theorized that perceiving and evaluating candidates for political offices are characterized by dimensionality. However, from the position of creating a candidate's image, the dimensions that are used by voters are not always favorable. If citizens "test" a given politician on his morality and his conscience is not clear, then his chance of election success becomes smaller. If, however, he manages to draw attention to, for instance, his competencies, his chance of winning may grow. Televised political advertising often performs the function of a spotlight that focuses on the desired features of the candidate, diverting people's attention from his weaknesses. It thus directs voters' attention and changes the dimensions according to which the candidate is perceived and evaluated (Cwalina and Falkowski 2000).

Kaid and Chanslor (1995) proposed a model of the influence of political advertising on changes in the perception of a candidate's image and its influence on voting behavior. The empirical research verifying this model was conducted during the presidential campaigns in the United States in 1988 and 1992, when George H.W. Bush ran first against Michael Dukakis and then against Bill Clinton. In order to measure the candidates' image, Kaid and Chanslor used a twelve-scale semantic differential in which every scale had seven points. The test procedure consisted of a pretest and posttest, between which randomly chosen advertising spots of both politicians were presented. Every subject evaluated each of the candidates twice—before and after watching the spots. In order to distinguish the dimensions according to which the candidates were perceived, the factor analysis was applied separately to each candidate and separately to each pretest and posttest. The results for the presidential candidates in 1992 are presented in Figure 4.9.

Analyzing the results of their tests, Kaid and Chanslor concluded that for each candidate, the spots caused a change in the structure of the perception of the image by the subjects. The dimensions of Bush's images became condensed. The reconfiguration of his image consisted mainly in the elimination of the demeanor/style factor. On the other hand, the changes in perceiving Clinton were much bigger. The spots made the first two factors obtained in the pretest (achievements and credibility) melt into one. In addition, a new factor appeared concerning the style of Clinton's behavior. Furthermore, the correlation between the results of the evaluation of the image in the posttest and the probability of voting for a given candidate was $r = 0.86$ ($p < 0.01$) for Bush and $r = 0.73$ ($p < 0.01$) for Clinton. Unfortunately, Kaid and Chanslor (1995) made no attempt to analyze the connection between the evaluation of the politicians' images and the voting intention before the spots were presented. Therefore, we cannot state whether the spots, apart from reconfiguring the image of both candidates, also influenced the changes in the support given to them.

Figure 4.9   **Dimensions of Bush and Clinton Images Before and After Viewing Spots**

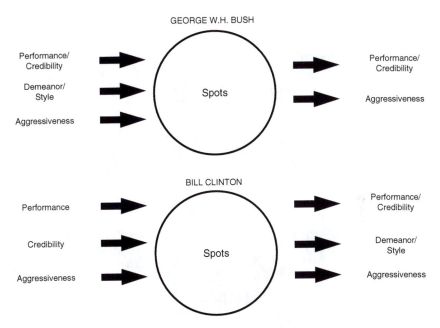

Source: Based on Kaid and Chanslor (1995).

Studies of the influence of political advertising on changes in voters' perceptions of candidates were also conducted by Wojciech Cwalina and Andrzej Falkowski in Poland during the presidential elections in 1995, when incumbent Lech Wałęsa fought against Aleksander Kwaśniewski, and in 2000 when incumbent Kwaśniewski fought against Andrzej Olechowski (Cwalina and Falkowski 2000, 2003, 2006; Cwalina, Falkowski, and Kaid 2000, 2005; Falkowski and Cwalina 1999). The experimental procedure was analogous to that used in Kaid and Chanslor's studies with one exception. Namely, Kaid and Chanslor's (1995) model concerned perception and changes in perception of a candidate's image by all subjects, no matter whether they were supporters of one candidate or the other. Such an analysis prevents the possibility of tracing the reconfiguration of a given candidate's image among people supporting him as well as those supporting the other candidate. Psychological knowledge about social perception also supports the division of voters into electorates; voters pay attention to certain aspects of a candidate they like and to other characteristics of a candidate they dislike. It can be assumed then that every voter perceives every candidate differently, depending on whether

Figure 4.10 Lech Wałęsa's Electorate: Change in Kwaśniewski's and Wałęsa's Images Before and After Viewing Spots

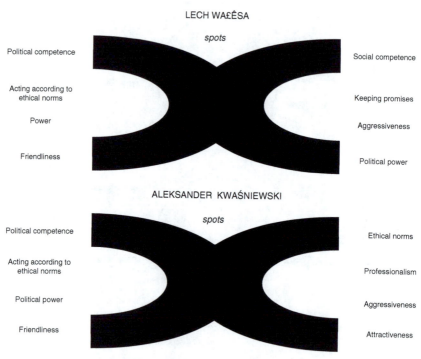

Source: Based on Cwalina and Falkowski (2000).

or not the voter supports the candidate. The image of the same candidate is thus different, depending on the predisposition or the party identification of voters (see Chapter 3).

In order to identify the dimensions according to which Aleksander Kwaśniewski and Lech Wałęsa were perceived, the exploratory factor analysis with orthogonal rotation was used. Eight such analyses were conducted, four for each candidate among his own and his opponent's supporters, before and after exposure of the spots. A general conclusion that can be drawn is that political advertising causes a reconfiguration, among supporters as well as opponents, of dimensions according to which presidential candidates are perceived (see Figures 4.10 and 4.11).

In the case of Wałęsa's supporters, the number of his perceptual dimensions did not change. However, the spots did cause changes in their content. Before the subjects saw the spots, Wałęsa was evaluated according to four criteria: political competence, acting according to ethical norms, power, and friendli-

Figure 4.11 **Aleksander Kwaśniewski's Electorate: Change in Kwaśniewski's and Wałęsa's Images Before and After Viewing Spots**

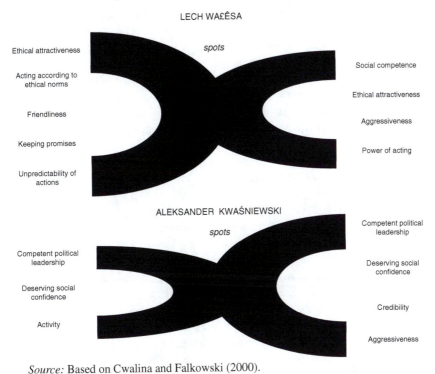

LECH WAŁĘSA

spots

Ethical attractiveness

Acting according to ethical norms

Friendliness

Keeping promises

Unpredictability of actions

Social competence

Ethical attractiveness

Aggressiveness

Power of acting

ALEKSANDER KWAŚNIEWSKI

spots

Competent political leadership

Deserving social confidence

Activity

Competent political leadership

Deserving social confidence

Credibility

Aggressiveness

Source: Based on Cwalina and Falkowski (2000).

ness. After the subjects watched the spots of both candidates, two totally new dimensions emerged: keeping promises and aggressiveness. Another two dimensions were converted: political competence into social competence and power into political power. Two factors, on the other hand, fell away: acting according to ethical norms and friendliness.

The perception of Kwaśniewski's image by his opponents was also subject to considerable changes. Before the viewing of the spots, he was perceived through the perspective of five factors: acting according to ethical norms, political competence, social attractiveness, keeping promises, and aggressiveness. After the spots were presented, only one dimension did not change: aggressiveness. Acting according to ethical norms lost its element of activity and converted into more declarative ethical norms. Attractiveness lost its social aspect, and political competency converted into professionalism of behavior. The dimension of keeping promises fell apart completely, which, normally, lets a politician "breathe a sigh of relief." Neutralizing this latter factor can be perceived as Kwaśniewski's Machiavellian success while in the enemy camp. It is worthwhile to notice that the dimension of keeping promises came up after presenting the spots evaluating Wałęsa.

Among Aleksander Kwaśniewski's supporters, the influence of spots on the perception of the candidates was also very conspicuous. The number of dimensions according to which Wałęsa was perceived decreased from five to four after the spots were viewed. The factor of ethical attractiveness was the only element that remained constant. Acting according to ethical norms, friendliness, keeping promises, and unpredictability of actions converted into social competence, aggressiveness, and power of actions. An opposite trend could be observed in the case of Kwaśniewski's image perception. His image was developed progressing from three to four dimensions. Two dimensions remained unchanged. After the spots were presented, the independent factor of activity was eliminated, whereas two new dimensions appeared: credibility and aggressiveness.

Among Lech Wałęsa's supporters, both politicians, in a number of cases, were evaluated according to the same criteria, which made a direct comparison easier. On the other hand, Aleksander Kwaśniewski's supporters evaluated their candidate according to totally different dimensions other than those applied to Wałęsa. Therefore, they had no chance to evaluate the politicians according to the same categories. Consequently, we can venture to say that Kwaśniewski's voters were constantly reassured in their preferences by their candidate, whereas Wałęsa's supporters were constantly put to the test, which may have led to a potentially high decisional uncertainty. Kwaśniewski's image was attractive for the people supporting him and, simultaneously, competitive to Wałęsa's image among the supporters of the incumbent. It seems that the objective of Kwaśniewski's advertising was met, whereas the promotional materials of his competitor proved to be less effective.

Summing up the analyses concerning the directing of perceptual dimensions, it can be said that making use of the laws of social perception, in light of which voters perceive politicians, makes citizens unaware of marketing manipulations. Political advertising shows voters what they should concentrate on. It tells them about the virtues of a given candidate, leaving out completely or blurring his faults. Therefore, the promoted politician is perceived in consciously idealized and thus false categories. In the majority of cases, voters are not aware of this manipulation and submit to the candidates' persuasion.

The Role of Emotion in Politics

Models of voting behaviors consider emotions as a separate element not only influencing voters' behaviors, but also shaping the way of perceiving a candidate's agenda and receiving political information broadcast by the media (see Abelson et al. 1982; Cwalina, Falkowski, and Newman 2008). Therefore, forming a candidate image is a process oriented mainly at evoking the most positive emotions in voters.

Martin P. Wattenberg (1987) found that around one-third of voters do not know anything about particular politicians despite having strong emotions toward them. In addition, empirical researchers of voting behavior discovered that the emotional attitude toward candidates or political parties is a very good predictor of voters' decisions. Bernice Lott, Albert Lott, and Renee Saris (1993), for instance, stated that in the U.S. presidential elections in 1988 a preference for a candidate correlated significantly with the emotions toward him on the level of $r = 0.68$ for George Bush and $r = 0.60$ for Michael Dukakis. Kulwant Singh and colleagues (1995), using the multiple regression equation to analyze the attitude of voters immediately before parliamentary elections in Singapore in 1988, obtained a voting intention prediction based on emotions toward a party and its candidates on the level of $R^2 = 0.36$ ($p < 0.001$). In the research conducted by Wojciech Cwalina and Andrzej Falkowski (1999; Cwalina, Falkowski, and Kaid 2000) in Poland in 1995 during presidential elections, the coefficient correlation between emotional attitude toward candidates and voting intention was $r = 0.85$ ($p < 0.001$), which points to a very strong link between affection and voting behavior.

Another group of analyses concentrated on the importance of the affective attitude toward candidates and evaluations of their views and features for citizens' voting behaviors (Holbrook et al. 2001; Rahn, Krosnick, and Breuning 1994). Two types of processes were considered here that might characterize a voter making a decision: derivation and rationalization. Derivation is defined as a process in which voting decisions are the consequence of an individual evaluation of information about candidates and their features. In this way, the choice is based on analyzing the available "implications." ("I know what features would make me support a candidate. I know what features will prevent me from supporting a candidate. What prevails, it determines my positive or negative evaluation of the candidate. Based on that, I vote.")

Rationalization assumes that choosing a candidate is based on this general evaluation. But the "implications" of this evaluation are hardly retrievable from memory (hardly available). In this way, the choice is based on the generalized impression that can be justified only after the event and often occurs "creatively." ("I know that I support and like the candidate. Why? I may have to think for a while . . .").

In order to determine which decision processes, derivation or rationalization, are more characteristic for a voter, Wendy Rahn, Jon Krosnick, and Marijke Breuning (1994) conducted a study during the governor elections in

Ohio in 1990. The research consisted of two parts: the first part was conducted a month before the elections and the other was conducted a week preceding the elections. The task of the subjects was to define their general attitudes toward candidates and write down what they liked and disliked about particular candidates. Using multiple regression analysis, the researchers established that voters make their decisions on which candidate to support based on whether or not they liked him. Asked to justify their choice, they started "combing" their memory and often simply made up some arguments. In this way, the research supported rationalization as a dominant process for voting decisions. However, the results of other analyses from the National Election Study from 1972 to 1996 proved less categorical (Holbrook et al. 2001). It turned out that wondering before making their final decision on whom to support caused many voters to thoroughly analyze the available information.

Partial explanation of these contradictory results is provided by the results of two experiments conducted by Wojciech Cwalina (2008b). The first experiment compared the process of impression formation (rationalization versus derivation) with regard to well-known politicians who had either positive or negative emotional evaluation (Lech Kaczyński and Donald Tusk), and the second experiment focused on forming impressions of a likable though fictitious politician. The results prove that evaluations of a likable politician (both known and unknown) are based mainly on rationalization, which is online information processing. On the other hand, when a politician is well-known but has negative emotional evaluation, the process of forming impressions ceases to exist.

Nevertheless, as Elliot Aronson, Timothy Wilson, and Robin Akert (1994) metaphorically suggest, today people vote with their hearts more than with their minds.

5

Dissemination of the Campaign Message

Direct Campaign and Debates

In every democratic system, political parties and candidates face a fundamental problem: how to communicate with voters and influence them so that they accept the candidates' leadership. Such communication may be based on direct or indirect human communication, for instance via media. The intention of such communication is to persuade voters to embrace the politician's views, which, in the area of political marketing, may be achieved through voting rallies, debates, information programs, or political advertising. Constructing a desirable image of politicians and designing their communication related to particular issues is the first step in bringing them closer to election success (see Chapter 3). The key element that should be included in a political campaign is to choose the media and decide how a politician will be presented by them (see, e.g., Newman 1994; Scammell 1999; Wring 1997). The most influential media are definitely mass media (television, radio, the Internet). However, ways of presenting politicians to their potential voters are not limited to the use of mass media (see Chapter 2). Also important and—in lower-level or local campaigns—even most important is personalized, direct forms of winning voter support (Lilleker 2005; Ross 1999).

The direct political campaign focuses most often on managing candidates' meetings with voters and managing volunteers' work. In both areas psychological mechanisms of social influence are commonly used, both directly and via social networks.

Meetings With Voters and Candidates' Appearances

Direct meetings with voters are the oldest historical form of winning support by candidates. Since the French Revolution and the introduction of rules of choosing legislative and executive authorities, leaders have had to fight for citizens' support. One of its leaders, Maximilien Robespierre, is considered the first "alchemist of the revolution's public opinion," who changed the rules of direct democracy into the secrets of ruling over masses. The idea of ruling the "voting crowd" to win and maintain its support was developed in the nineteenth century by Gustave Le Bon in his still timely study titled *The Crowd: A Study of the Popular Mind* (2002/1895). According to Le Bon, the voting crowd is a mass appointed to choose representatives to particular bodies of executive or legislative power. It belongs to the category of heterogeneous masses characterized by failure to reason any more, a lack of criticism, irritability, gullibility, and simplicity of feelings. The crowd gives in to the speeches of its leaders, who keep saying the same thing over and over, offering unconfirmed truth, surrounding themselves with prestige and counting on the effect of contagion—both emotions and opinions.

The key to control the crowd is the politician's prestige. A politician who has prestige can impose it on the crowd without any discussion. Neither talent nor skills can, according to Le Bon, replace personal prestige. However, it should be supported by flattering the crowd and indulging in its wishes. A politician should fawn on every member of the crowd, making most improbable promises. The politician should be able to appeal to the crowd's lower instincts and claim to give more to the crowd than other politicians. Le Bon also offers some hints about the political program that the politician should present to the voters. It is not supposed to be unambiguous, since rivals can instantly take advantage of it. It should be full of promises. According to the author, voters do not really care whether the politicians they elect actually do fulfill these promises.

The cynical and humiliating opinion about voters presented by Le Bon was reflected in the marketing effort undertaken by Adolf Hitler and Joseph Goebbels in Germany. They both scorned public opinion and cynically praised lies and manipulation as the best (because efficient) ways of winning voters (see, e.g., Irving 1996; O'Shaughnessy 2004).

Electoral Conventions

The primary function of the contemporary convention is to generate an image of the candidate and the party that can be taken into the remaining months of the campaign. According to Thomas M. Holbrook (1996), it is important that conventions provide the parties with a stage from which they can dominate not only news about the campaign but also news in general for a period of several days. The ability to dominate the flow of information is expected to work to the advantage of the party holding the convention, assuming that it is able to generate positive information (the 1968 Democratic National Convention in Chicago was an exception; see McGinniss 1969). The anticipated consequence of the convention period is a "bump" in public support for the party, but the main limit on the influence of conventions is the news media's editorial and interpretive discretion (see Chapter 2).

Besides offering a party opportunities to present its candidates and their image to the public, the convention also provides the opportunity to do this in a relatively uncontested format. Unlike the information in a debate, which involves at least two politicians sharing the stage and challenging each other, the information generated by the convention is almost one-sided.

James Campbell, Lynn Cherry, and Kenneth Wink (1992) distinguish two main functions of American party conventions: the deliberative function and the rally function. The deliberative function refers to the elaboration of the election platform and the presentation of the candidate and his stands on issues. Over the years, the national party conventions have lost many of whatever deliberative functions they once had. Although they still write platforms, officially bestow the party nomination on a previously determined nominee, and provide an audience for the announcement of the vice presidential nominee, conventions have not served as a forum in which the presidential nomination is actually decided for some time. The rally function is intended to provide impetus and set the tone for the election campaign—to arouse a convention bump.

There are several possible reasons why candidates might benefit directly from their conventions, but three of them appear most important (Campbell, Cherry, and Wink 1992). First, the convention may help to heal internal party divisions. Supporters of candidates who did not win the party's nomination may feel uncomfortable immediately casting their support for the nominated candidate whom they had opposed just a short time ago. They may resent that candidate. Many may initially indicate indecision about their general election vote decision. For a time, some may even indicate a decision to vote for the opposition party. While some of the wounds of internal party battles may heal with time alone, the convention may speed the process. Conventions allow factional leaders to come together in a show of unity, sending the message that differences with the opposing party outweigh any differences remaining within. As a result, though some disgruntled and disappointed partisans may sit out the election or even bolt to the opposition, the convention encourages many who might have contemplated these options to return to the fold.

Second, national conventions may also give an extra push to their nominee's bandwagon. The official investing of a candidate as the party's standard-bearer may draw less attentive voters to declare their support. Once nominated, a candidate may also gain greater respect from the more wary partisans who had held off from committing themselves to any candidate.

Third, the convention bump may also reflect the generally favorable publicity for the party generated by its convention. Certainly, conventions focus a good deal of media attention on the party. Moreover, most of this attention is likely to be favorable to the party. Convention speakers and the usually warm to enthusiastic receptions they receive from the delegates create positive images of the party.

In order to define the intensity of the influence of national party conventions on voters' opinions, Campbell, Cherry, and Wink (1992) analyzed the data drawn from the results of trial-heat polls conducted by the Gallup Poll and the Harris organizations in the seven elections from 1964 to 1988. They found that, in most cases, conventions continue to fulfill their rally function for the political parties and their presidential candidates. Presidential candidates typically increase their poll standings following their party's convention. On average it was 6.3 percent, although greater for the Republican Party (7.9 percent) than for the Democratic Party (4.8 percent). The greatest increase in support was observed for Richard Nixon in 1968 (from 46.8 percent to 60.8 percent). Only one case analyzed by Campbell and his colleagues in this period worked to the disadvantage of the candidate: in 1971 Democratic candidate George McGovern's standing fell from 41.3 percent to 39.3 percent. Furthermore, the effects of conventions are not strictly short-lived; the convention bump is not merely a "convention blip." In most cases, the effects of the convention carry well into the campaign. The way a candidate comes out of the convention is of some real consequence to the ultimate election outcome. The results also show that the convention effects are somewhat larger when a party has been divided during the nomination campaign but manages to hold a conciliatory convention.

Moreover, the convention effects are more substantial for the first convention in a campaign (on average 8.2 percent) than for the second one (4.4 percent). Whether because the out-party traditionally holds its convention first or because the first convention reaches voters when they are more impressionable, on average, presidential candidates nominated during the first convention of a campaign receive about twice the boost in the polls that candidates nominated in the second convention receive. According to Holbrook (1996), the first convention affords a party a good opportunity to effectively transmit its message for three reasons. There is a large pool of undecided voters who need information to make their voting decision. The information is relatively scarce at this point in the campaign, and the voters generally have less information about the challenging party, which is the first to hold its convention.

These results confirm and supplement the analyses conducted by Daron Shaw (1999), who studied various presidential campaign events (debates, speeches, candidate mistakes, and conventions) from 1952 to 1992. He found that national party conventions were the most influential campaign events for both Republican and Democratic candidates. Their effect was almost always positive and large, averaging 7.4 percent, and there was little decay in the change effected by the conventions. Republican conventions were slightly more successful than their Democratic counterparts, producing 7.8 percent bounce compared to a 6.9 percent bounce for the Democrats.

Rallies and Meetings

Current debates in studies of election campaign management focus on the extent to which the process has evolved, becoming more centrally orchestrated and professional. The normative account is that election campaigns focus on news management and elevate the status of party leaders. Mediatized pseudo-events have replaced direct interaction with the voter. However, at the level of local campaigning, one may see a more disparate set of individually tailored campaigns focusing on issues relevant to constituencies. In this local context, according to Darren Lilleker (2005), at times central office interventions could be problematic. For example, visits by party leaders are not always useful. On a practical level they may cause local resources to be diverted in order to collect the visitors and escort them to the event, which often involves high security; it is the local team that has to find locations for helicopters to land, plan routes, and organize photo opportunities, and so on (see Barrett and Peake 2007; Eshbaugh-Soha and Peake 2006). The campaign is one that local voters will respond to, which means designing constituency-specific campaign messages and styles. Furthermore, the communication in local campaigns is highly interpersonal. Whether face-to-face or via direct mail, the message will be locally focused and will promote the service orientation of the candidate within the constituency.

S. Mark Pancer and his collaborators (1992) observe that political candidates face a dilemma. In order to build a reputation within the party, it would be best for a candidate to demonstrate loyalty for the party by supporting the party's policies. Such a strategy, however, may adversely affect impressions of the candidate's integrity and honesty in the eyes of the public, especially with regard to unpopular policies. Similarly, the candidate who attempts to gain public support by saying what the electorate wants to hear risks being perceived as weak. These observations are confirmed by the results of the experiment Pancer and his colleagues conducted. It was designed to assess the impact of political partisanship and audience support on the impressions of political figures. Research participants read a speech that has supposedly been given by a member of the Canadian parliament. In all conditions, this was the same pro-environmental speech. This position was portrayed as being either supportive of or hostile toward the politician's party. The results indicated that perceptions of a politician were affected by both partisanship and audience support. When she gave a nonpartisan speech, she was perceived as having greater integrity than when she gave a partisan speech. Audience support influenced perceptions of her strength. If the politician spoke to a hostile audience, she was perceived as stronger than if she spoke to a supportive audience.

From this perspective, direct meetings of candidates with voters are of particular importance. Keith Sanders and Lynda Kaid (1981) conducted research on voters who went to political rallies held by Gerald Ford, Fred Harris, Jimmy Carter, and George Wallace while they were campaigning in southern Illinois before the Illinois primary election in 1976. The political rallies attracted a large percentage of people who were not members of the featured candidate's party. Most of them were still making up their minds. People attend rallies for a variety of reasons, which can be summarized as a need for cognitive orientation and reinforcement. Those who attend rallies arrive with a generally positive attitude toward the candidate, and, while there, they change their attitudes in a positive direction, regardless of party affiliations. This change takes place largely among those who arrive with the least favorable attitudes. While these attitudinal changes do not persist, rally-goers do perceive themselves as paying particular attention to news about the rally and as increasing their interpersonal communication about the candidates. About half say that their vote was influenced by rally attendance. In addition, Lynda Kaid and Robert Hirsch (1973), in a study of attendees at a rally for Democratic presidential contender Edmund Muskie in 1972 at Southern Illinois University found that the manner in which the audience viewed the image of the candidate before and at the time of the rally differed from the way in which they viewed his image in the follow-up. There was a significant positive shift in image perception, but although its effect persisted, the characteristics of the image differed after a two- to three-week period. As Kaid and Hirsch (1973, 51) conclude, "A single appearance by a political candidate can result in a favorable shift in his image, and that shift can persist over time."

In addition to *whom* politicians speak during a meeting and *what* they talk about, the *way* they speak is also very important for their evaluation. Harold Zullow and Martin Seligman (1990; Zullow et al. 1988) hypothesize that, other things being equal, American voters will choose presidents who are optimistic and do not ruminate over bad events. In other words, the explanatory style of candidates directly influences the voters' choices. Explanatory style refers to the optimism or pessimism with which people explain the causes of bad events. It has three dimensions: stable–unstable (the cause can be seen as one that will either persist or go away); specific–global (the cause can be present in many areas of policy and functioning or in only one); and internal–external (the cause can be located in oneself and one's group, or in others and their situation). Then, rumination is the tendency to dwell on analyzing problems.

Zullow and Seligman (1990; see Zullow et al. 1988) content analyzed the twenty nomination acceptance speeches given at the Democratic and Republican conventions of 1948 to 1984. They used the nomination acceptance speech because it is a standard setting in which candidates outline their goals for the country and their view of the country's condition. It is also a speech that affects many voters because it receives a wide national audience, not only in newspapers but also, since 1948, on television. The researchers found that the candidates higher in pessimistic rumination lost nine of ten elections. The 1968 election was the exception. In that election, Humphrey was only slightly lower in pessimistic rumination than Nixon. Humphrey, however, began his campaign after the Chicago riots with a deficit of 16.2 percent in the polls, and during the period between the conventions and election, he pared that gap to 0.8 percent. Furthermore, candidates leading in the polls who were much less pessimistically ruminative than their underdog challengers retained and even increased their lead to win landslide victories. Examples of this tendency were Eisenhower's victories over Stevenson in 1952 and 1956 (Eisenhower was much lower in pessimistic rumination than Stevenson and won two landslide victories), Johnson's victory over Goldwater in 1964, Nixon's over McGovern in 1972, and Reagan's over Mondale in 1984.

Moreover, underdog challengers who were much less pessimistically ruminative than the leader cut into the leader's margin and upset the leader in the general election. Examples of this were Truman's upset of Dewey in 1948, in which Truman started out behind by 13 percent and won by 4.5 percent; Kennedy's upset of Nixon in 1960, in which Kennedy started out 6.5 percent behind and yet eked out a victory; and Reagan's upset of Carter, in which he started out 1.2 percent behind and won by 10.6 percent. Underdog challengers who were close in level of pessimistic rumination to the leading candidate tended to gain support and nearly upset the leader, examples being Humphrey's gains in support in 1968, starting out 16.2 percent behind and finishing 0.8 percent behind, and Ford's gains in 1976, with Ford closing in from 20 percent behind to 2 percent behind.

Subsequent analyses conducted by Zullow and Seligman (1990) included the period from 1990 to 1984. They found that the candidates higher in pessimistic rumination lost eighteen of twenty-two elections. In addition to the elections mentioned above, their win–lose predictions failed to predict correctly the three Franklin D. Roosevelt reelections. The authors conclude that "twentieth-century [American] candidates who ruminate pessimistically in their acceptance speeches tend to lose the election" (Zullow and Seligman

1990, 59). Furthermore, they propose that the explanatory style of candidates may influence voters in a two-stage process. Voters who decide early may base their decision on criteria known by the end of the conventions, such as party affiliation, ideology, and the economic record of the current administration. Voters who decide late may arrive at a decision based more on emotional responses such as feelings of hope. These two mechanisms derive their impact on the voter not necessarily through true personality characteristics of the candidates, but from their appearances. Zullow and Seligman note, however, that in some situations ruminations about problems in the inaugural address may predict presidential greatness and intellectual brilliance (e.g., Franklin Roosevelt). When a crisis occurs, voters may prefer a more realistic approach from their leaders.

Electoral Debates

Electoral debates conducted during presidential campaigns have become an inseparable part of political campaigns all over the world. They are traditional campaign events in the United States, but also have become an important component of electoral contests in Australia, Canada, Croatia, France, Germany, Greece, Holland, Israel, New Zealand, South Korea, Sweden, Poland, and Ukraine. Debates are the only time during the campaign when tens of millions of potential voters focus on the candidates simultaneously, see them stand side by side, listen to them responding to similar questions, and watch their body language as they react to each other's answers. During debates, candidates are engaged in the classic act of persuasion—trying their best to persuade potential voters, either undecided voters or opponents, to change those potential voters' minds and support the candidates. In addition, the media spend a considerable amount of time and energy analyzing the candidates' debate performances. Therefore, the public is saturated with debate news for the hours and days following debates. The news media's "instant analysis," presented immediately after the debate and continuing over the next days, has become a part of the folkways of debates. The instant analysis appears across network news, cable news networks, radio, and the Internet. The media present spokespeople for each candidate, interviews with undecided voters, and analyses of who "won" or who "lost" the debate.

William Benoit (2000, 21) believes that political debates are important for three main reasons. First, they give viewers an opportunity to see the principal contenders running for office, meeting eye to eye, and treating the same topics. In this way, voters have the opportunity to compare the candidates in a relatively extended period of time in a political debate. Second, viewers can obtain a somewhat less contrived impression of the candidates from debates than from other forms of campaign messages. While candidates prepare for debates, they cannot anticipate every question from the panelists, moderators, or audience members or every remark from an opponent. Thus, voters may obtain a somewhat more spontaneous and accurate view of the candidates in debates. Third, political debates attract the largest audience of any campaign message form. The large size of the audience means that the candidates' opportunity for influence from these campaign messages is substantial. For instance, the second presidential campaign in 2008 between John McCain and Barack Obama, according to the data from Nielsen Media Research, was watched by 63.2 million people, and the debate between Jimmy Carter and Ronald Reagan in 1980 was watched by 80.6 million (www.debates.org). Besides, Stephen Coleman (2000) notes that televised debates help candidates to equalize access to the mass media, force rivals to know each other's positions, and have an educational impact on citizens.

Modern research on debates shows that debates during live broadcasts do allow viewers to learn about important issues and—above all—get to know the candidates' opinions about important economic and social problems in the country as well as foreign policy (see Hellweg, Pfau, and Brydon 1992). Analyzing the amount of candidate information held by the general public, as articulated through open-ended candidate evaluation questions asked in the biennial National Election Study (NES)—conducted from 1976 to 1996 before and after presidential debates—Thomas M. Holbrook (1999) noted that major events such as debates do stimulate information acquisition among the mass public. Generally speaking, respondents interviewed after a debate were able to retrieve more information about the presidential candidates than those interviewed before the debate, all else held constant. In addition, the context in which information is presented affects the degree to which it is acquired. The evidence overwhelmingly indicates that the most important debate, at least in terms of information acquisition, is the first debate. Impact of information also depends upon the subject of the information. Following virtually every debate, respondents were more likely to have learned something about the lesser-known of the candidates than about the better-known candidate. Besides, those who are most directly exposed to political information are most likely to benefit from the information. Uninformed and disengaged voters—those who could potentially benefit the most from campaign information—are not sufficiently exposed to the political messages and therefore do not gain as much information from the campaign as do the politically engaged. In this way, presidential debates can lead to a widening knowledge gap, which is also supported by the analyses of James B. Lemert (1993). Debates further inform the already informed without adding new people to their number.

Direct confrontation also allows assessing the skills and the efficiency of the candidates based on their argumentation. As a result, it develops the perceptions and images of the competing sides in the viewers' minds, helping them to appreciate which of the candidates does better in the debate (Druckman 2003; Powell and Wanzenried 1993). What also helps to develop this image are polls conducted during and after debates, showing the "winner" or the "loser." This immediate feedback was administered using a technology first displayed during the televised debates of 1992. For those events, the cable television news network CNN showed viewers continuous and real-time responses of focus-group members who were watching the debate in an auditorium and used hand-held response dials to record their changing impressions of the event. This computer-based technology thus provided TV viewers with real-time and public-opinion poll data.

However, analyzing debates becomes more complicated if one takes into consideration not only the effect of these debates but their structure, defined by a previously prepared scenario. The Lincoln-Douglas format,[1] often considered an ideal format, is characterized as a debate consisting of (1) a confrontation, (2) in equal and adequate time, (3) of matched contestants, (4) on a stated proposition, (5) to gain an audience decision (Auer 1962).

In light of these criteria, the modern TV debate is similar to a "joint press conference," to use Jamieson and Birdsell's phrase (1988, 6), rather than a classical debate. There is hardly any direct confrontation in a television debate; instead, the candidates answer the questions asked by a third-party moderator, usually the journalist conducting the debate. Besides, Ronald Milavsky and Jian-Hua Zhu (1996) claim that candidates often do not offer clear answers about particular issues. What is more, the short time the candidates have to answer a multitude of questions, forcing them to think very quickly, might lead to distorted opinions that are not necessarily congruent with the candidates' intentions.

One element of the classical debate has not been changed: equal and adequate time for the competing sides. It seems very important for the viewers to be able to evaluate the candidates participating in a debate. The importance of this element was appreciated by Greek philosophers, who claimed that if equal speakers had the same amount of time while presenting their points about particular issues, then the audience would be able to tell truth from falsehood and draw their own conclusions about the presented issues (Milavsky and Zhu 1996).

Certainly, the equal amount of time given to candidates during a debate allows viewers to evaluate in an objective way the candidates' positions on particular issues and exemplifies the right to a free expression of thoughts guaranteed in the First Amendment of the U.S. Constitution. In interpreting this provision, Justice Oliver Wendell Holmes of the Supreme Court used the analogy of the "marketplace" when considering the need for ideas to be freely disseminated in the community. By this he meant a free circulation of ideas from which people could pick those that seemed most likely to be true (Ward and Cook 1992, 23).

Undoubtedly, such a provision facilitates democratic processes, which, in the context of political debates, take place when voters are presented with various concepts and can reject, after critical evaluation, those that they consider unacceptable. However, although political debates help to limit a selective presentation of the candidate used in political advertising, arriving at objective conclusions may not always be possible. Based on his research into the ways that voters perceive candidates participating in debates, Steven Chaffee (1978) concludes that it is not possible to discover their "real" image and their "real" stance on various issues. However, such perception allows voters to distinguish better and better between the candidates' stances on particular issues.

According to Bruce Newman's model of political marketing (1994: see chapter 1, figure 1.9), debates represent mainly environmental influences on the marketing campaign. They are connected then with the course of the marketing campaign, where particular strategies of influencing voters are precisely defined. If the main goal of these campaigns is to make voters believe that this is the best candidate, then the following question should be posed: "Do debates influence the development of such beliefs?" Researchers often focus on the importance of debates in forming voter preferences during the political campaign. Some studies help predict exactly the influence of TV debates on the different rankings candidates are going to get from viewers. Most such studies were conducted in the United States, and this chapter presents the results directly related to the influence of debates on forming voter preferences. Particular emphasis will be put on forming judgments about candidates in voters' minds relative to the problems they present as well as their (perceived) image.

The Influence of Debates on Voter Behavior

Studies related to political debates may focus on the general aspect, showing their influence on candidate evaluation without taking into consideration particular characteristics of the voter. For instance, Božo Skoko (2005) writes that as many as 18 percent of Croatian voters changed their opinion about presidential candidates in 2005 election after the televised debates. Changes in voter preferences after political debates were also discussed by Krzysztof Pankowski (1997) in the context of the Polish presidential elections in 1995. He determined that the support for Aleksander Kwaśniewski among the viewers of political debates increased by 8 percent net—he won 10 percent of new supporters but lost, at the same time, 2 percent. But the support for Lech Wałęsa did not increase—he won and lost 4 percent of the viewers. The support for the politicians among those who did not watch the debates did not change at all.

More detailed analyses have also been conducted, examining those individual elements of voters that may lead them to modify their attitude toward candidates while watching debates. These studies refer to the voter's individual characteristics, including, for instance, party identification or partisanship.

Debates and Candidate Evaluation

Thomas Holbrook (1996) presented data related to the dynamics of changes in candidate evaluation influenced by watching political debates. He analyzed the beliefs of voters in pre-election polls about the "winner," "loser," or "drawer" of the debate. Table 5.1 presents the percentage distribution, according to the viewers, of the results of candidates' "fight" during debates in 1984, 1988, and 1992.

Most of the data shows the advantage of the Democrat, Republican, or independent candidate. As the table shows, in some cases the viewers clearly saw the winner. The percentage difference is clear and considerable then. For instance, in the first debate in 1984, 61 percent of the respondents considered Walter Mondale the winner, whereas the percentage for Ronald Reagan, running for reelection, was only 26 percent. However, in the first presidential debate in the presidential election in 1988, there was no clear "winner." Both candidates were, to a similar degree, perceived as winners (Michael Dukakis—41 percent, George Bush—43 percent).

Figure 5.1 presents the direct influence of American presidential debates in 1984, 1988, and 1992 on the support for candidates, as discussed in Holbrook's studies. (In 1984 and 1988 the leading candidate was Republican—Reagan over Mondale, and Bush over Dukakis, respectively—and in 1992, Democratic—Clinton over Bush.)

The figure presents the changes in percentage-point advantage of the leading candidate (Republican in 1984 and 1988, and Democratic in 1992) the week before and the week following the day of the debate. One should also note the relation between the perception of a candidate as winning the debate and the support for the candidate in the polls—that is, the results presented in Table 5.1 compared to the results presented in Figure 5.1. The data in the figure show that immediately after the debates there was a relatively high increase in support for the "winner" and decrease of support for the "loser." However, after a few days the levels of support go back to the state before the debate.

Table 5.1

The "Winner" of the Debates According to the Viewers (in percent)

	Democrat	Republican	Neither/tie	Independent
1984				
First debate (Walter Mondale, Dem. vs. Ronald Reagan, Rep.)	61	26	13	—
Second debate (Walter Mondale, Dem. vs. Ronald Reagan, Rep.)	33	45	22	—
Vice presidential debate (Geraldine Ferraro, Dem. vs. George Bush, Rep.)	34	48	18	—
1988				
First debate (Michael Dukakis, Dem. vs. George Bush, Rep.)	41	43	16	—
Second debate (Michael Dukakis, Dem. vs. George Bush, Rep.)	28	51	21	—
Vice presidential debate (Lloyd Bentsen, Dem. vs. Dan Quayle, Rep.)	55	29	16	—
1992				
First debate (Bill Clinton, Dem. vs. George Bush, Rep. vs. Ross Perot, Indep.)	35	19	8	38
Second debate* (Bill Clinton, Dem. vs. George Bush, Rep. vs. Ross Perot, Indep.)	54	25	—	20
Third debate* (Bill Clinton, Dem. vs. George Bush, Rep. vs. Ross Perot, Indep.)	36	21	—	26
Vice presidential debate* (Al Gore, Dem. vs. Dan Quayle, Rep. vs. James Stockdale, Indep.)	50	32	—	7

*The percentages for these debates were taken from postdebate surveys, which did not report the percentage who thought the debate was a tie; thus the percentages do not add up to 100.

Source: CBS News/*New York Times* surveys.

Figure 5.1   **The Impact of Presidential Debates on Leading Candidate Support, 1984–1992**

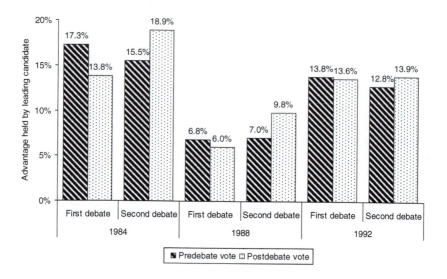

Source: Based on data from Holbrook (1996).

The data presented here suggest that debates do lead to changes in the support for a candidate measured in polls, usually about 3 percent. For instance, in 1984, after the first presidential debate, the support for Reagan decreased from 17.3 percent to 13.8 percent. In some other cases, however, debates do not lead to any changes in preferences, particularly if the "fight" is, according to the viewers, close. The first debate in 1988 and the two debates in 1992 led to a hardly observable fluctuation in support for the candidates, about 1 percent.

Analyzing such data allowed Holbrook to statistically define the relation between the results of the candidates' competition during debates and the support given to them by their voters. The author used regression analysis, where the independent variable (X) was the percentage difference in the viewers' perception of the "winner" (the percentage of viewers stating that the Republican candidate "won" minus the percentage of the viewers stating that the "winner" was the Democratic candidate). The dependent variable (Y) was the change in the support for the Republican candidate. The resulting regression equation has the form

$$Y = 0.866 + 0.097X$$

The multiple correlation coefficient turned out to be too high ($R^2 = 0.75$), which means that the evaluation of debates accounted for 75 percent of the variance in poll results. If a candidate turns out to be better than the opponent, he gets more percentage points in the polls. The regression equation suggests that a 0.87 percent increase or decrease in specifying the "winner" of a debate by the viewers translates only into a 0.097 percent increase or decrease in his support in the projected poll results studying the support for a given candidate. It should be stressed that the relation defined on the basis of empirical research clearly demonstrates small importance of debates for the support for a candidate. If a candidate wins an election debate by a clear majority of votes, it may be considered a decisive victory. However, this is often mere perception, having little to do with reality. We can demonstrate it using a hypothetical example where 70 percent of viewers believe that candidate A has won a debate, 20 percent of viewers believe that candidate B has won it, whereas the other 10 percent of voters think the debate was a draw. In this case, candidate A, following the viewers' judgment, has a 50 percent advantage over candidate B. Such a decisive victory—much higher than the actual ones (see Table 5.1)—would have translated only into a 5.7 percent increase in support for candidate A. One may want to replace the data in the equation to arrive at the following results: $5.7 = 0.866 + (0.097) \times 50$.

Observing political campaigns may show relatively small and, above all, impermanent influence of political debates on the support for the candidates, which is proven by Holbrook's analyses.

Debates and the Evaluation of the Candidates in the Context of Voters' Characteristics

Some external factors influencing the interpretation of the results of a debate include the characteristics of the voters themselves. Although campaign debates provide a lot of multidimensional information allowing voters to evaluate the candidates very comprehensively, not all these characteristics get noticed by the voters. People's perceptions are very selective; voters filter out only the information that is useful for them. Evaluating TV debates, voters cannot break away from their experience and knowledge of the political situation and the "fighting" candidates. Various voters prefer different political options and will perceive the same candidate differently, depending on whether they support him or not. This is what causes the difficulty of determining whether the candidates can convince voters of their views during political debates. The most important variable modifying candidate evaluation seems to be predebate vote choice. It makes voters evaluate the debate as if "their" candidate has won. Besides, the results of the experiment conducted by Rene Ziegler, Frederike

Arnold, and Michael Diehl (2007)—in the context of the 2002 German election TV debate between chancellor candidates Gerhard Schroeder and Edmund Stoiber—point to the pervasive effect of participants' predebate preferences not only on their evaluations of candidates, but also on their thoughts about politicians' statements and positions. Additionally, salience of political candidates' characteristics is comparatively low in the written modality (transcript of the debate). However, in the audiovisual and the audio (radio) mode, these analyses suggest that statement-related and issue-related thoughts mediated the effect of politician preference on position agreement.

Lee Sigelman and Carol Sigelman (1984) analyzed data obtained from a *CBS News/New York Times* election survey conducted shortly after the Carter-Reagan debate on October 28, 1980. They found that 86.2 percent of the Carter voters and 96.1 percent of the Reagan voters thought their candidate won the debate. In the case of undecided voters, 56.7 percent of them were convinced that Carter won, and 43.3 percent believed that it was Reagan. However, in this group liberal ideology pushed respondents toward the view that Carter had won, while conservatism led respondents to see Reagan as a winner. These results indicate that knowing a voter's prior candidate preference is almost equivalent to knowing whom he or she would declare the winner of a presidential debate. Such preferences function as a powerful cognitive screen.

An important supplement to the conclusions presented above is the results of Thorsten Faas and Jürgen Maier's (2004) analyses based on the data from the 2002 German election study, which includes pre- and postelection (face-to-face) interviews with about 2,000 respondents from the old Länder and about 1,000 respondents from the new Länder.[2] The interviews concerned the reactions of voters to televised chancellor candidates' debates between Gerhard Schroeder and Edmund Stoiber. The results suggest that even though the perceptions of the candidates' debate performances depend to a large extent on already existing party identifications, debates nonetheless do affect vote intentions. If an interviewee's favorite candidate was seen as the winner of the contest, vote intentions were moderately reinforced. In contrast, if the preferred candidate was seen as the loser of the discussion, the probability of voting for that candidate considerably decreased. The largest debate effects overall appeared for voters without party identification. Winning (or losing) a debate easily increases (or decreases) the vote share of the candidate's party by 20 percent to 30 percent in this group.

Sidney Kraus and Dennis Davis (1981) discuss three groups of voters for whom debates perform different functions. The first group includes citizens moderately interested in the campaign and having their interest sparked by campaign events. For them debates are the source of knowledge about the candidates and the current social, economic, and political problems in the country. What they learn from debates may be very useful to them throughout the rest of the campaign. Another group of individuals is those who can be described as seekers of political information. They already have a relatively good knowledge of the country's political situation and the campaign and they use debates to get to know the candidates better. This knowledge does not seem to influence their choice, but may increase or decrease their certainty during voting. The third group of citizens includes those for whom debates provide little more than a reinforcing function. They are strong supporters of a particular political option and the course of the debate only confirms the decision they have already taken.

Such a division of the viewers of political debates refers to the problems of voter market segmentation. It shows, above all, that political debates—being part of environmental influence—are closely related to the marketing campaign, whose goal is to adapt the message and influence the specificity of particular voter groups (see the discussion of segmentation in Chapter 3).

Including the element of previous preferences toward political candidates might demystify the myth about John F. Kennedy's smashing defeat of Richard Nixon during debates in 1960. The research into the influence of these debates was conducted by Kurt Lang and Gladys Engel Land (see Hilgard 1962). Ninety-five inhabitants of New York City participated in the study and they were asked three times to express their support for these politicians: before the first debate, immediately after it, and, finally, after the last (fourth) debate. Although the sample was not representative, the distribution of preferences that could be observed was consistent with that from the national poll. The results showed that after the first debate ten voters out of ninety-five (10.5 percent) began to support Kennedy, whereas Nixon lost only three of his supporters (3.5 percent). A more detailed analysis showed that Kennedy gained more in terms of a positive impression than actual votes. These changes referred mainly to undecided voters who, even before the debates, were inclined to support a particular politician. After the fourth debate the number of Nixon's supporters was exactly the same as before the debates. The support for Kennedy increased only in the group of undecided voters. Detailed results of the changes in voter preferences related to the 1960 debates are presented in Table 5.2.

Such a distribution of debates' results was caused by the influence of the medium of television. It was confirmed by the results of the repeated analysis of the first Kennedy-Nixon debate focusing on the medium (TV vs. radio) conducted by James N. Druckman (2003). He found that television viewers were significantly more likely to think Kennedy won the debate than audio listeners. According to him, the results are the first clear empirical evidence consistent with the widespread assertion of disagreement between viewers and listeners in the first Kennedy-Nixon debate. The television images have

Table 5.2

Changes in Voter Decisions Caused by Political Debates Between John F. Kennedy and Richard M. Nixon, 1960 (in percent)

	Decided to vote for Kennedy	Undecided	Decided to vote for Nixon
Before first debate	39	28	33
After first debate	49.5	21	29.5
After fourth debate	55	12.5	32.5

Source: Adapted from Hilgard (1962).

an independent effect on individuals' political judgments: they elevate the importance of perceived personality factors, which can in turn alter overall evaluations.

It is obvious then that a correct and detailed analysis of the influence of political debates on voters' choices needs to take into account the voters' political preferences and dispositions developed before they watch TV debates. Such detailed analyses, including the voters' individual variables, were presented by Thomas Holbrook (1996). In his analyses he used the results of the polls conducted by *CBS News* and the *New York Times* during the presidential elections in 1984, 1988, and 1992—before and after television debates. The analyses allowed controlling the variables related to the attitude of the viewers toward the candidates before watching the debates. The variables included (1) party identification (Democrat, Republican, independent), (2) vote intention for a particular candidate before watching debates, (3) ideological orientation (liberal, moderate, conservative), (4) attitude toward a candidate (positive, undecided, negative), and (5) the evaluation of the president's service (approve vs. disapprove). The variables defined the general attitude of the voters toward each candidate and could influence both their evaluation of the debate and their vote intentions after watching the debate. Logistic regression analysis was used where the dependent variable was the intention of voting for a particular candidate and the independent variables were the characteristics of the voter mentioned above and the evaluation of the candidates participating in debates. According to Holbrook, introducing the evaluation of candidates in political debates as an independent variable while including, at the same time, the voters' characteristics should be a reliable test of the actual influence of debates on vote intentions.

The results he obtained showed that voters' political preferences and dispositions are strongly connected to the intention of voting for a particular candidate after watching debates. A particularly strong variable explaining this intention was the voter's prior preference before watching debates. The evaluation of the candidates in debates turned out to be a variable influencing vote intention. One could state, then, that watching television debates influences the support for a candidate, independent of voters' particular political characteristics.

Holbrook conducted an additional study in order to determine the influence of two variables (the influence of prior preference for a particular candidate and the evaluation of candidates' performance in a debate) on vote intention after watching the debate. He excluded from the analysis the influences of the other independent variables. The results were presented as the probability of voting Republican, which is presented in Figure 5.2.

The results show that the leading candidate had a stable position among his electorate whereas the electorate of the other candidate swung in its voter preferences. Naturally, the stronger candidate won the election: in 1984 it was Ronald Reagan and in 1988 it was George H.W. Bush. This regularity was particularly visible during the first debate in 1984. The voters who in their first vote intention favored Walter Mondale and stated that he had "won" the debate changed their preferences only to a very small degree. Only 7 percent of them would have voted for Reagan and 75 percent would have been willing to change their voting decisions. The Republican Party electorate, on the other hand, proved very stable, hardly sensitive to the influence of debates. The probability of voting for Reagan among those members of his electorate who admitted Mondale's victory was very stable—81 percent would not have changed their decision. Naturally, the probability increased among the voters having positive impressions about Reagan's performance—99 percent of them would have made the same decision they made before.

A particularly striking example of the influence of political debates on changes in vote intentions for a weaker candidate was the results of the second debate in 1988. The supporters of Dukakis who thought that he had won the debate were certain of their decisions to support him (only 3 percent of the voters would have changed their vote decision). However, his supporters who admitted Bush's victory decided to change their voting preferences (93 percent of the voters would have changed their decisions about whom to support; see Figure 5.2).

The observed changes in predicted voting decisions in the 1984 and 1988 debates point to comparatively little stability of the candidates who score worse in polls and a strong influence of debates on the changes in his support. On the other hand, they also point to comparatively high stability of the leading candidate's electorate and the debates' much smaller influence on the changes in his support. This influence is also modified by a voter's belonging to a particular electorate. Using detailed analysis that includes voters' individual characteristics, politicians may define more precisely the importance of debates for voter behavior than if analysis is performed on a more general

Figure 5.2 **Debate Performance Assessments and Probability of Voting for Republican Candidate**

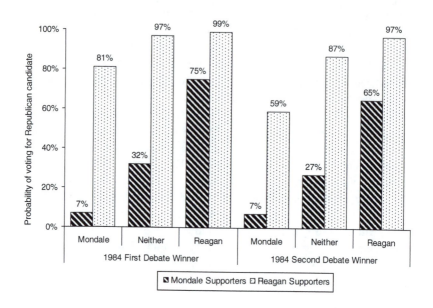

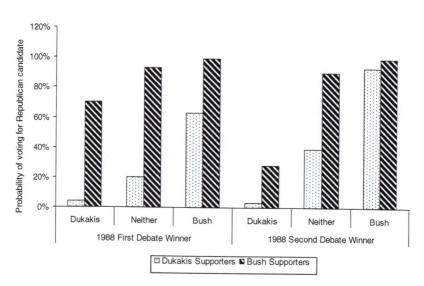

Source: Based on data from Holbrook (1996).

level, where political preferences and dispositions of various electorates are not taken into account.

Candidate Image and Stands on Issues

The influence of debates on forming voter preferences may also depend upon a number of more subtle characteristics. The key role is played here by candidates' focus on presenting their image or/and stands on the country's sociopolitical issues. William Benoit and his colleagues (see Benoit and Sheafer 2006), analyzing every American presidential debate (1960 and 1976 to 2004), found that these debates emphasized policy more than characters (75 percent to 25 percent). Furthermore, they were more positive than negative, with 57 percent acclaims, 35 percent attacks, and 8 percent defenses. There were differences between the discourse of incumbents and challengers: incumbents acclaimed more (64 percent to 51 percent), attacked less (25 percent to 44 percent), and defended more (12 percent to 6 percent) than challengers. In addition, incumbents were far more likely to acclaim their own record than to attack their opponents' record (72 percent to 28 percent); conversely, challengers used the past much more to attack than acclaim (82 percent to 18 percent); both incumbents and challengers devoted more remarks to the incumbents' record in office. Similarly, in the five Israeli debates (from 1984 to 1999), policy was more common than characters: 77 percent to 23 percent (Benoit and Sheafer 2006).

The Concept of Limited Influence of Political Information

Research into the importance of political debates on voting decisions that include candidate image and their stands on the disputed issues was presented by Steven Chaffee (1978) in the context of a limited effects model of political communication. According to this concept, broadly understood political communication (including meetings, political advertising, information programs, and debates) may only reinforce decisions that have already been made but it cannot change them. This finding resulted from research conducted in the 1960s about the importance of debates for voting behavior. This research emphasized the characteristic motivation of the supporters of a particular candidate, who wanted to reinforce their conviction about the support for him and find arguments against the opponents. However, the research conducted during presidential elections in the 1970s demonstrated something completely different. Almost 90 percent of the voters claimed that learning the candidates' stances on particular issues was very useful. More than 70 percent believed that what referred to the perception of his image was equally important.

Chaffee decided to find out then to what degree this concept was valid and proposed a model of voter behavior presented in Figure 5.3.

An analysis of causal relations between particular elements of the presented model shows the influence of candidates' political and social dispositions on the cognitive representation of the voting situation and voter decision. The two fundamental variables defined in voters before the launch of a political campaign are their party identification and their socioeconomic status. They constitute the voter's internal context, in light of which perceived political events are later interpreted. The other two variables of the model are specific to political campaigns, but they occur before debates. One of them refers to the perceived ideological difference between the candidate and the voter in the following dimension: liberal versus conservative. The other one corresponds to voter intention for a particular politician. The final two variables of the model refer to the difference between the images of two candidates perceived by the voter and to the difference between their stands on issues in relation to the voter's views. All these elements of the model have a cause-and-effect on the voter decision taken on Election Day.

Chaffee verified his model using the data from the U.S. presidential election in 1976, when Gerald Ford and Jimmy Carter were competing. An important component of this study was the division of voters into three groups, relative to the frequency of their watching debates: (1) regular viewers, watching all debates, (2) occasional viewers, watching some debates, (3) nonviewers, those who watched only a fragment of a particular debate. In order to verify the model, Chaffee used regression analysis.

Stability of Voting

According to the concept of limited influence of political information, the more the voters watch debates, the more stable their behavior and the more predictable their voting decision will be. The concept corresponds to the segmentation of the voting market into decided voters, who follow carefully the course of the campaign, and undecided voters, who are not interested in the voting situation and do not watch debates. Although undecided voters are more sensitive to voting communication, it does not in fact influence them, since they are not interested in the campaign. However, even occasional contact with political information—watching fragments of debates, for example—should have important influence on voter behavior in the segment of undecided voters. Chaffee did not find out anything like this. The best final decision prediction of the support for a particular candidate based on the intentions expressed before debates was for voters who watched them occasionally, whereas the worst one was for regular viewers.

Figure 5.3   **Chaffee's Model of Voter Behavior**

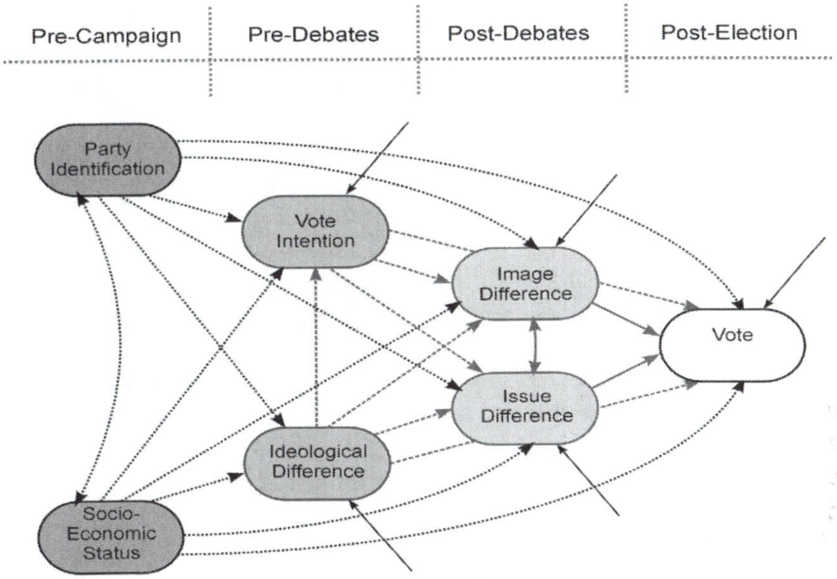

Source: Adapted from Chaffee (1978).

The result is not then consistent with the concept of limited influence of political information. It is intuitively obvious that the best prediction is for viewers watching debates very occasionally, because in this group the forming of a candidate image and specifying the candidate's stand on various issues while watching the programs does not really take place. However, one should also expect a good prediction of the final choice based on the primary preferences in viewers watching debates regularly, because they took their voting decision a long time ago. The result recorded here suggests high importance of mediator variables related to debates (image and issues) that modify the relation between vote intention and the final choice. One could suspect then that watching debates influences the choice of the candidate based on image and stands on issues in voters watching debates regularly. Decided voters are not then insensitive to the influence of political information during voting campaigns.

Party Identification

The concept of limited influence of political information stresses the importance of party identification for voting decisions. The variable should be the strongest predictor of the final choice because the party that the voters belong to "tells" them how they should vote. Debates should then have no importance for the citizens identifying strongly with a particular party. Party identification influences strongly vote intentions in all the studied groups. However, its influences decrease considerably after voters watch debates. As in the voting stability analysis, here the influence of debates also decreases considerably the relation between party identification and the final choice. It is another argument against the concept of limited influence of political information and points to the importance of debates for the final support given to politicians. In voters regularly watching debates, their party identification defines very clearly their vote intention. Decided voters follow very carefully the course of the campaign and know exactly whom they are going to vote for. However, debates weaken considerably the party identification variable as a predictor for the final choice.

If such elements of the debate as image and issues weaken the relation between vote intention and party affiliation or the final choice, then one may assume that they may also modify considerably the final support for politicians. These two aspects of debates may be defined as *image voting* and *issue voting*.

Candidate Image in Debates

The results of Chaffee's analysis show that image has the greatest influence on nonviewers and becomes less the more people watch debates. It is quite a paradoxical situation because one would expect a reverse effect, namely that image should have the greatest impact on regular viewers. However, one may suspect that for regular viewers image is strongly shaped by such political characteristics as party identification, socioeconomic status, and the perceived ideological difference between the candidates. This assumption has been partly confirmed, because one variable, which is the perceived ideological difference between the candidates, influences significantly the perception of a candidate image by regular viewers. However, it has no influence on occasional viewers and nonviewers.

Analysis of the perception of the image and the importance of debates for its forming is then consistent with the concept of limited influence of political information. The image of a candidate is already formed before debates in those voters participating actively in the campaign. Therefore, debates have little influence on the forming of the image in voters' minds.

Issues Presented by the Candidates in Debates

According to the concept of limited influence of political information, the issues discussed in debates should have no influence on voters' decision about whom to vote for. Although debates may provide the viewer with information about the politician's stands on issues, this information is assimilated into the voter's already developed attitude. In other words, before watching debates, the voters know very well the stands of the candidates. Therefore, they adapt what they learn to already developed beliefs. This phenomenon is defined in psychological literature as biased assimilation (Lord, Ross, and Lepper 1979). Through such biased assimilation even a random set of outcomes or events can appear to lend support for an entrenched position, and both sides in a given debate can have their positions bolstered by the same set of data.

In Chaffee's research, issues were defined in the following way. Each voter participating in the research defined his or her own stand and the stand of each candidate on a five-position scale regarding the following issues: (1) government action to increase employment, (2) changes in the tax system so that high-income people pay more, (3) government spending for defense and military, and (4) legalized abortions. Then the difference between the voter's stand and the perceived stand of each of the candidates on those issues was calculated. The analysis demonstrated that issues included in debates influenced significantly the voters' decision in regular viewers. They had no importance, though, in occasional viewers and nonviewers.

The research presented here that tested the concept of limited influence of political information points out the importance of candidates' image and their stands on issues discussed in debates for forming voter decisions. However, the influence of debates is different on different voter groups. Viewers watching the campaign events regularly are sensitive to the fact that issues and debates do influence their choice. Occasional viewers depend on the choices of the party with which they identify. Nonviewers do not participate in campaign events. Therefore, quite understandably, their vote intention before watching debates has the greatest influence on their final choice.

The research also represents a very interesting methodology of analyzing the influence of political debates. It shows systematically and in detail the importance of particular variables in forming voter decisions, according to the division of voter dispositions (internal context) and the political events (debates: external context). These variables may then become the foundation of preparing a marketing strategy for the political campaign.

Chaffee's research is limited only to one presidential election in 1976. Certainly analyzing various debates in various political elections may achieve a better and more detailed picture of the problems of image and issues in political debates. Jian-Hua Zhu, Ronald Milavsky, and Rhaul Biswas (1994) used another methodology for the field, concentrating only on the image and political issues. Using the example of U.S. presidential elections from 1960 to 1988 and their own research from 1992, they show the tendencies that can be observed in the analysis of debates in the area of image forming and issues taken up by the candidates.

The Image and Issues and Democratic Processes

In the introduction to this chapter, we noted that debates allow the voter to evaluate the candidates' presented stands and that they therefore facilitate democratic processes. Their structure helps to eliminate selectivity in presenting a candidate, something that is very typical for political advertising. However, it is not possible to remove from debates the candidates' images and limit the whole process to presenting stands on issues only. Zhu, Milavsky, and Biswas (1994) observe that according to the classic theory of democracy, a televised debate contributes positively to the democratic process when it increases the electorate's rational decision-making by informing it about issues and where the candidates stand on them. On the other hand, debates may influence these processes in a negative way when during debates the voters mainly develop the images of the competing sides in their minds, not focusing so much on following the stands presented by the candidates (see Druckman 2003). This perspective leads to two general concepts related to the importance of issues and image development during debates.

According to the first concept, represented by the *issue-only* school, televised debates of politicians influence only changes in voters' stands on particular issues but do not play any role in forming their image. The main reason why debates do not lead to changes in a politician's image is that while watching debates viewers evaluate candidates mainly on the basis of their political dispositions—for instance, party affiliation. Debates may only reinforce already developed images but cannot change them (see, e.g., Powell and Wanzenried 1993). It confirms then to some extent the results of the analyses conducted by Chaffee, where, following the concept of limited influence of political information, he noticed, on the one hand, the importance of perceived ideological difference between the candidates for the perception of the politicians' image and, on the other hand, no importance of the candidate image for predicting the final voter decision in voters watching debates regularly.

The second concept represented by the *image-only* school maintains that television debates are crucial for forming politicians' image and do not contribute too much to a better understanding of their stands on issues. This concept is supported by the specificity of the medium, which, although it does get some verbal messages across, transmits mainly visual information (Druckman 2003; Ziegler, Arnold, and Diehl 2007). The medium requires much less information-processing capacity from viewers than do the printed words in newspapers and magazines. Visual information from television debates is better remembered and understood than verbal content (see, e.g., Graber 1990; Mackiewicz and Cwalina 1999). This quality of television is well understood by debate organizers, who underline on purpose their visual character. Well-prepared candidates use very well the technology offered by television in order to present their nonverbal behavior, including, for instance, eye contact, a smile, or the clothes they wear. Such behavior translates into a positive image of a candidate in the viewers' eyes.

These completely different concepts were precisely discussed by Zhu, Milavski, and Biswas (1994), who analyzed a few dozen studies on the changes in the perceptions of issues and candidate image by voters in the U.S. presidential debates from 1960 to 1988. The authors, however, had serious reservations about these studies, because the majority of them focused either on issues or image; only three studies included both of these variables. Besides, most of the studies included no control conditions, which would have made it possible to compare the behavior of voters watching debates with that of those who did not watch them as well as the behavior of the voters after watching them. The validity of such results, which would have had the character of planned experiments, would also have to be checked by comparing them against an external criterion, the result of a study conducted during the natural and unforced process of watching these television programs. All these limitations were included in Zhu, Milavski, and Biswas's analyses of the first presidential debate in 1992 between George Bush, Bill Clinton, and Ross Perot.

The voters participating in the study filled out the same questionnaire twice—before and after watching debates (pretest/posttest). The questionnaire related mainly to the country's economic and social issues, the image of the candidates, and voter preferences. Subjects were divided into three groups, the first of which watched the debate only under experimental conditions (*experimental viewers*), directly after it was shown on television.[3] The second group watched the debate "live" in natural conditions, in their homes (*natural viewers*). The third group, the control, consisted of people who did not watch the debate (*nonviewers*).

The problems that the country faced were included in a list of twenty-four most likely subjects that were raised in the debates[4] (e.g., supporting full and active participation of African-Americans in American social and economic life, or advocating a government program to retain workers who became unemployed). Subjects were to state whether a particular candidate was for, was against, or had no opinion about each of the presented issues. It was possible then to gauge the degree of accuracy related to the knowledge viewers had about the candidates' stands on the discussed issues. The candidates' image was measured on a few dozen seven-degree scales including these five characteristics or personality features: competence, potency, integrity, charisma, and communication skills.

The authors sought to answer the question whether debates had a stronger influence on developing the candidates' image than on understanding their stands on particular issues or whether it was issues that were better understood whereas the image remained unchanged. The results of the regression analysis proved that debates had a much stronger influence on differentiating between the candidates based on their stands on issues. Debates had much less influence on the changes in the perceptions of their images. Figure 5.4 presents the differences in understanding the stands of each of the candidates on economic and social issues between the experimental viewers and natural viewers.

The results of the research show that viewers watching the debate had a significantly better understanding of the problems than those not watching. The experimental viewers were by 34 percent better in understanding George Bush's stands on social and economic issues. They also understood Bill Clinton's (by 25 percent) and Ross Perot's (by 39 percent) stands better. The conditions under which the study was conducted did not lead to significant differences. The observed increase in understanding turned out to be very similar both under natural and experimental conditions. One should note the relatively small improvement in the voters' understanding of Clinton's stand. In both research groups it was the lowest compared to the other candidates. One may suspect then that before the debate subjects had much knowledge about the candidate. Figure 5.5 presents viewers' and nonviewers' knowledge about each candidate's stands on problems before and after watching the debate. Clinton's stand is best known in all the groups.

The results presented in this figure emphasize one more important issue. The knowledge acquired during watching debates got balanced out for all the candidates (i.e., created so-called convergence structure). After the viewers watched the debate, their level of knowledge became not only significantly higher but also balanced out.

But the influence of debates for the perception of candidates' image turned out to be significantly smaller than for knowledge about the candidates' issue. It turned out to be significant only for Perot in experimental conditions for such features as integrity, charisma, and communication skills. No significant differences were found for the other two features, competence and potency. The characteristics for these two features are that they are developed in voters' minds throughout the whole political campaign and cannot be changed after a ninety-minute political debate. The fact that no differences were found in the perceptions of Clinton's and Bush's image as a result of the debates points out the perceptions' high stability and their forming during a campaign lasting over a year. It is understandable then that some changes were observed in Perot's

Figure 5.4   **The Influence of Debates on Voters' Knowledge About Candidates' Stands on Issues Among Voters Watching the Debate in Experimental and Natural Conditions**

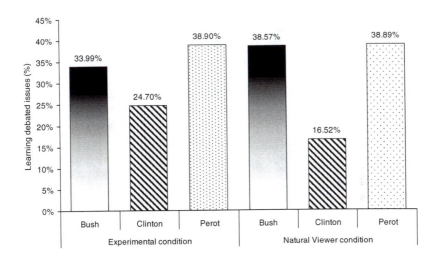

Source: Based on data from Zhu, Milavsky, and Biswas (1994).

image because he appeared much later on the political scene. One should remember, however, that when viewers were watching debates in "natural" conditions, they did not change their perception of any of the personality features in any of the candidates.

Following the research, one may state that debates change the candidates' image to a very small extent if the candidates are well known. Some changes may occur only when the candidate is not well known and only in the dimensions with such easily noticeable features as charisma or communication. But the features that the viewer may predict based on the politician's actions (e.g., competency) are not likely to change under the influence of debates.

However, the full picture of the influence of debates on issues and image is revealed only when we define separately the influence of verbal and visual elements in a televised presentation (visuals with sound) and the influence of the candidates' verbal statements only in an audio/radio presentation (sound without visuals). In this context there is a group of personality features creating the politician's TV personality (*media-savvy person*) and attracting the viewers' attention and interest.

An analysis of political debates where the verbal elements (radio) were separated from verbal-visual ones (television) was conducted by James M.

Figure 5.5   **Changes in Voters' Knowledge About Candidates' Stands on Issues Among Voters Watching the Debate in Experimental Versus Control Conditions**

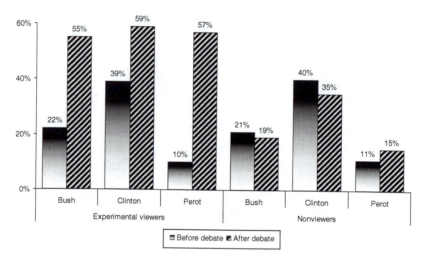

Source: Adapted from Zhu, Milavsky, and Biswas (1994).

Druckman (2003). He decided to check, among other things, how television images during a presidential debate affected the criteria on which citizens base their candidate evaluations—that is, the relative impact of image and issues. He used the famous first debate between John F. Kennedy and Richard Nixon, because according to many researchers this debate was the quintessential example of the power of television images. The experiment carried out was quite simple in design: some participants listened to an audio version of the debate while others watched a televised version.

As Druckman stresses, the relative importance of the personality and the issues presented by the candidates for overall comparative evaluations may be controlled by ways of presenting the debate. Let us assume that voters see one candidate as superior when it comes to personality and another candidate as preferable when it comes to the issues. If voters watch the debate on television, then personality performs a more important function and the viewers might prefer a more media-savvy person. Television viewers have access to visual imagery and nonverbal cues that often play an important role in shaping personality evaluations of others. Television introduced a more image-based political environment that accentuates a candidate's personal qualities. However, if the voters listen to the presentation on the radio, they may tend to prefer a candidate with a better-received set of issues, because personality will weigh less in their overall evaluations. Therefore, one could assume that television viewers will be significantly more likely than audio listeners to use personality criteria when evaluating the candidates.

Druckman conducted a study in which he randomly assigned some participants to watch and listen to the debate (television) and others to listen to the audio (radio) version. The dependent variable was the subjects' response to the question of which candidate won the debate, measured on a seven-point scale with higher scores indicating a leaning toward Nixon. The independent variables included perceptions of the candidates' personality traits (leadership effectiveness, integrity, and empathy) and perceptions of the candidates' issue positions. The regression analysis used by the author gave a result clearly showing the significant influence of such personality traits as integrity and the very small influence of issue agreement on the evaluation of a candidate in a televised debate. Quite the opposite results were achieved for a radio debate: the issue agreement variable was important for the evaluation of the candidates whereas such personality traits as leadership effectiveness, integrity, and empathy were less important. Figure 5.6 shows the power of predicting the candidate's evaluation on the basis of unstandardized regression coefficients (b) for integrity and issue variables in a televised and radio situation.

The result supports the hypothesis: issue agreement remains a significant factor for audio listeners but not for television viewers. On the contrary, integrity plays a significantly more important role for viewers than for listeners. Druckman's study is then empirical evidence supporting the view that the medium can prime alternative standards of evaluation (see Chapter 2). Television primes its audience to rely more on its perceptions of candidate image (e.g., integrity), whereas radio primes an increasing reliance on issues. Television images elevate the importance of perceived personality factors, which in turn alter overall evaluations. The research conducted is consistent with the general assumption that television supposedly enabled Kennedy to win due to his superior image even though he was not necessarily better on the issues. In fact, the ostensible difference in appearance led many to conclude that television viewers of the debate thought Kennedy won while radio listeners, who did not see the candidates, favored Nixon.

In this context, the results of the research by Miles Patterson and his colleagues (1992) are also important. They conducted two experiments related to the second presidential debate between Ronald Reagan and Walter Mondale during the campaign in 1984. Their student subjects were divided into four experimental groups. The first group was presented with a full audio-visual version of the debate, as it was in reality; the second group was introduced only to the visual aspect of the debate; the third group heard only the audio;

and the fourth group was presented with a word-for-word transcript of the politicians' statements. Then the subjects evaluated Reagan and Mondale using a semantic differential consisting of eleven scales. These evaluations were summed up so the final results were indicators of positive attitude toward each of the candidates. In addition, subjects were asked to specify the winner of each debate.

The variance analysis conducted showed clearly that in all the experimental groups Reagan scored much better than Mondale (see Figure 5.7). The results suggest that the Republican was perceived in a more significantly favorable way than the Democrat in the visual context than in the audio-visual and audio contexts. Reagan also got more positive scores than Mondale from the subjects who only read the transcript of the debate as compared to the subjects who could only hear the candidates. However, Patterson and his colleagues did not find that the method of presentation had any influence on the subjects' naming the winner of the debate (66 percent of subjects thought it was Reagan, 13 percent thought it was Mondale, and 21 percent were not certain).

The goal of the second study conducted by the same authors was to answer the question why Reagan was perceived more favorably than his opponent during the visual presentation of the politicians. It turned out that the key factor in this case was the subjects' perception that Reagan was more physically attractive and had more facial expression during the debates. In fact, Mondale moved his head, blinked, and changed the direction of his gaze less often than Reagan.

The results of Patterson and his colleagues' research are consistent with the results of Druckman's research: the behavior and self-presentation of the candidates modify significantly their perception by the viewers. Some politicians simply create a better impression than others. The research does not specify, however, the influence of such formed images of politicians on the voters' preferences toward them.

The Influence of Televised Debates on Voter Preferences

Debates create an unforgettable chance during a campaign to evaluate simultaneously all the candidates. It should be stressed, however, that although the goal of debates is the most comprehensive evaluation of the candidates without any exposure biases, the actual practice of debates is somewhat different. The interfering factors may be related to the campaign's external environment, including factors such as the media coverage following the debate.

Kim Fridkin with her colleagues (2007) conducted an extensive study whose goal was to analyze the influence of the third and final presidential debate in 2004 between President George W. Bush and Senator John Kerry on

Figure 5.6   **Evaluations of Debate Winner on the Basis of Integrity and Issue Agreement in Radio and Television Conditions**

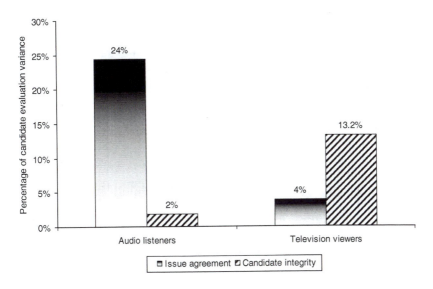

Source: Based on data from Druckman (2003).

the voters and the direct coverage of the debate on *NBC News* and the CNN website. The research design included a telephone public opinion survey of citizens in the Phoenix metropolitan area (1,466 respondents interviewed within twelve hours following the debate), a content analysis of the debate and the news media's "instant analysis" immediately following the debate (*NBC News* and CNN.com), and a controlled experiment with six conditions. In condition 1, subjects watched the presidential debate. In condition 2, subjects watched the debate and then watched the *NBC News* coverage for twenty minutes following the debate. In condition 3, subjects watched the debate and then were given Internet access to CNN.com for twenty minutes to read the news analysis of the debate. Condition 4 was the control condition where subjects were not exposed to the debate nor media coverage of the debate. Instead, subjects had the option of watching episodes from the television show *Friends* or the Red Sox/Yankees playoff game. In condition 5, subjects watched either *Friends* or the baseball game, and then watched the twenty-minute *NBC News* analysis of the debate. Finally, in condition 6, subjects watched *Friends* or the baseball game and then logged onto CNN.com to read postdebate coverage. In each of the six conditions of the experiment, subjects answered a pretest questionnaire upon their arrival and then

Figure 5.7   **Attitude Ratings Toward Reagan and Mondale in Various Debate Presentation Conditions**

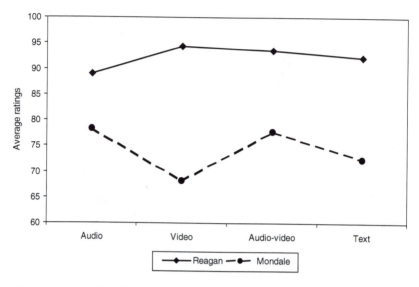

Source: Adapted from Patterson et al. (1992).

completed a posttest questionnaire at the end of the experiment. The questionnaires included measures assessing subjects' attitudes toward the candidates, their views about the candidates' personal traits, and their opinions about the candidates' positions on issues. Subjects also answered questions about the tenor of the debate and questions about their vote preference.

Overall, content analysis of the debate revealed similarities in the tenor and substance of the candidates' comments: both candidates preferred to highlight their own personality strengths instead of attacking their opponent's personal weaknesses. News coverage of the debate, however, tended to be less uniform and balanced. Content analysis of the "instant analysis" on *NBC News* with Tom Brokaw and CNN.com revealed that these two news organizations presented distinctly different slants in their coverage immediately following the debate. In particular, the instant analysis on *NBC News* portrayed Bush more positively, while CNN.com's instant analysis was more favorable toward Kerry.

Furthermore, experiment results suggested that voters' attitudes were influenced by the arguments presented directly by the candidates during the debate as well as by the media's instant analyses of the candidates' debate performances. Fridkin and her colleagues found that citizens were often persuaded by the candidates' messages regarding their personal traits, policy performance, and overall performance. However, the impact of the candidates' messages was often altered by the media's instant analyses. The debate and the NBC analysis produced the most favorable trait and affective assessments of Bush, while the debate and CNN.com analysis generated the most negative views of Bush. The impact of the debate and the instant analysis had the opposite effect on evaluations of Kerry. In particular, people exposed to the debate and to the CNN.com instant analysis developed the most positive trait and affective evaluations of Kerry, while people exposed to the debate and the NBC analysis exhibited the most negative trait and affective evaluations of Kerry.

In addition, the debate, as well as particular media coverage of the debate, influenced how citizens "framed" the outcome of the debate—who won. Forty-eight percent of the people watching only the debate thought Kerry had won, while less than one-quarter (24 percent) of subjects thought Bush had won. However, people who viewed the debate followed immediately by the *NBC News* analysis saw the debate outcome much differently. In particular, the proportion of people saying that Bush had won the debate was more than double in this condition, with half of all subjects declaring Bush the winner. In contrast, less than 20 percent of the people exposed to the debate and NBC interpretation of the debate thought that Kerry had won.

In one of the experiments (Experiment 3) conducted by Steven Fein, George Goethals, and Matthew Kugler (2007), participants were informed that they would receive continuous real-time feedback about their group's average opinion in the form of a line graph superimposed over a debate videotape (a ten-minute segment consisting of excerpts of the second 1984 presidential debate between Reagan and Mondale). In fact, the feedback they received was false and preprogrammed to indicate that Reagan or Mondale was gaining in support over the other depending on the experimental condition. Researchers found that participants who saw a graph suggesting that their peers thought Reagan won the debate rated Reagan's performance more than 15 points better than Mondale's, whereas they rated Reagan's performance more than 20 points worse than Mondale's if they saw a graph suggesting that their peers believed Mondale performed better, resulting in a net difference of about 36 points. As Fein, Goethals, and Kugler state, these results, which were striking in their breadth and magnitude, suggest that the practice of presenting TV viewers with continuous focus-group data (or, as can be expected in upcoming elections, the practice of seeing others' real-time reactions on the Internet as people watch the debate) constitutes a powerful source of social influence information.

William L. Benoit with his colleagues compared the content of presidential debates from 1980 to 1992 (Benoit, Stein, and Hansen 2004), the content of U.S. Senate debates from 1998 to 2004 (Benoit and Davis 2007), and newspaper coverage of these debates. In both cases they found that newspapers overrepresented candidates' attacks compared to debates (presidential elections: 50 percent to 31 percent; Senate: 48 percent to 29 percent) and underrepresented candidates' acclaims—that is, themes that portray the candidate in a favorable light (41 percent to 61 percent and 39 percent to 60 percent). Besides, news stories reported on character more often than this topic occurred in debates (31 percent to 26 percent and 43 percent to 29 percent) and less frequently about issues (69 percent to 74 percent and 57 percent to 71 percent). In the case of presidential debates, the researchers also found that the typical newspaper story reports about 11 percent of the themes in a debate. Benoit, Stein, and Hansen conclude that clearly newspapers perform a gatekeeping function, reporting only a small part of what is actually said in debates. The information available to voters who watch debates is significantly different from the information available to voters who read debates in newspapers. Nonviewers who rely on newspaper accounts of debates receive a highly filtered version of events.

Some newspapers, including, for instance, the German *Die Zeit* (August 22, 2002), go even a step further, publishing observation questionnaires that voters may use to evaluate particular candidates and then generalize their evaluations by the "won-drew-lost" verdict (see Figure 5.8). Definitely, such a situation is closely related to the process of the campaign and may distort or even completely change the voters' evaluation of the candidate that has already been established after their watching the debate.

The Importance of Political Debates in Democratic Processes

The presented results of debates suggest that debates do facilitate democratic processes because they contribute to a better understanding and differentiating between candidates' stands on socioeconomic issues. However, that does not mean that debates cannot perform their functions better. William Benoit (2000) proposes six specific suggestions for improving the format of presidential debates:

1. Debates should focus on a single topic.
2. Debates should feature as topics the issues most important to voters.
3. Debates should encourage clashes between the candidates.
4. Questions, when they are used, should come from voters, not journalists.
5. Candidates should be permitted to question each other.
6. Debates should have a limited number of participants.

Figure 5.8   **How to Watch Debates: "The Duel"**

According to Benoit, these suggestions do not need to be implemented all together, which is important because candidates and their campaign advisers may well resist some suggestions more than others. But these changes would probably improve the quality of presidential debates. Debates ought to inform the voters, treat topics that matter to voters, highlight the differences between candidates, and encourage clashes on issues of policy and character.

Volunteers and Canvassing

Political candidates and their program of appearances and meetings with voters are an important component of the campaign, but each campaign needs people who will work in the election committee and in the field as well. It needs volunteers. These people must form a cooperative, focused working unit, develop and implement complex campaign projects, and analyze and react to a fast-changing environment.

Gregory Lebel (1999) distinguishes three crucial categories of volunteers. The first group consists of highly skilled, politically savvy party stalwarts. They usually form the finance committee, the steering committee, and the "kitchen cabinet." The finance committee is composed of individuals who are committed to raising campaign funds for the candidate. The steering committee is populated by individuals whose medium is political influence. Men and women whose opinions are respected in the community ("opinion leaders") are targets of these volunteers. The "kitchen cabinet" is made up of the candidate's closest and most trusted advisers.

The second set of volunteers is those who fill key positions within the campaign staff. These volunteers most often are drawn from the ranks of party regulars and staffers from earlier campaigns. For example, county, precinct, and district organizers, as well as finance and legal staff, are drawn from these ranks.

The third level of volunteers consists of those people whose specific high-level political experience is minimal or nonexistent. They perform the role of canvassers, phone bank callers, and letter and email writers in the campaign. These rank-and-file volunteers bring to any campaign a level of enthusiasm that is to be shared with the voters they meet directly. The few existing studies on the efficiency of door-to-door or telephone electoral canvassing suggest that it does not significantly increase support for candidates in national elections or increase voter turnout (see Adams and Smith 1980; Bartell and Bouxsein 1973; Gerber and Green 2001; Kramer 1970/1971; McAllister 1985). However, William Swinyard and Kenneth Coney (1978, 47) believe that "candidates in low-level races can not only benefit greatly from advertising, but also further increase their advertising returns with a canvassing campaign."

Lebel (1999) emphasizes, however, that if volunteers' work is to be successful, it has to be very precisely planned, based on well-thought-out recruitment of volunteers of all types, and professionally managed. Ongoing recruitment, careful scheduling and management, and regular assessment of volunteers will help move the campaign toward its short-term objectives and its long-term goal—success at the polls on Election Day. However, these activities have to be supported by impersonal, indirect, or mediated tools of the marketing permanent campaign.

Campaign Influence Through Social Networks

One of the campaign volunteers' tasks is to influence citizens through persons whose opinions are respected in the community—opinion leaders. Bibb Latané (1981) defines social impact as any influence on individual feelings, thoughts, or behavior that is exerted by the real, implied, or imagined presence or actions of others. In a seminal study, Leon Festinger, Stanley Schachter, and Kurt Back (1950) interviewed 100 residents of Westgate, a housing project constructed for married World War II veterans enrolled at MIT, about their attitudes toward a proposed tenant council. Couples were randomly assigned to the nine identical courtyards composing Westgate, so there were neither differences in environmental circumstances nor any chance of selective migration. The power of social influence processes to create group standards is shown by the relative homogeneity of attitudes within courts (only 38 percent of residents deviated from the modal attitude pattern of their court) with heterogeneity of opinion among courts (with 78 percent of the residents deviating from the modal pattern of the project as a whole). Within courts, Festinger and his collaborators found that those people who lived in corner houses or isolated apartments had less social contact with other residents and were more likely to deviate from the majority opinion than those who lived in more central locations.

The contemporary studies also show the importance of public opinion leaders and social networks. Charles Pattie and Ron Johnston (1999, 2000) analyzed data from the British Election Study 1992 cross-section survey and found that the more support a party had in a polling district in 1987, the more likely it was to make new converts there in 1992. Voters were influenced to some extent by the dominant political view in their immediate locality, and statistically significant numbers changed their vote accordingly. For instance, respondents who switched to the Conservatives in 1992 lived in polling districts where on average about 40 percent of voters had supported this party. Respondents who did not switch to the Conservatives, however, lived in less Conservative areas: on average only 31 percent of voters there had voted for the party in 1987 (for comparable results in Honduran parliamentary elections, see Canache, Mondak, Conroy 1994). Furthermore, among respondents who had not previously voted for a party, switching to the party became more likely as the number of discussants supporting that party rose. But people talked politics predominantly to their "nearest and dearest" (family, friends, and workmates) and much less so to more casual acquaintances (members of church or voluntary organizations). Politically important social networks relied then on preexisting relationships of kin and friendship with some admixture from the workplace. Pattie and Johnston (2000) sum up these results by the title of their article: "People who talk together vote together."

Robert Huckfeldt and his collaborators (1995) state that the construction of a citizen's social network serves as a filter on the macro environmental flow of political information (e.g., from mass media). In this way, the consequences of the larger environment of opinion depend on the existence of microenvironments that expose citizens to surrounding opinion distributions. At the beginning of an election campaign, many individuals are uncertain about their preferred candidates. As they formulate preferences in response to the campaign, their newly constructed opinions produce implications for other citizens. The conversion of any single individual to a particular candidate's cause is not only important as a single unit of social influence. It is also important in terms of the enhancement and attenuation effects that it creates throughout the networks of relationships within which each individual is embedded, quite literally transforming entire patterns of social influence. According to Robert Huckfeldt, Paul Johnson, and John Sprague (2002), the logic of social influence creates a bias in favor of majority sentiment, thereby making it difficult for disagreement to be sustained. Indeed, to the extent that networks of communication and influence constitute closed social cells, characterized by high rates of interaction within the network but very little interaction beyond the network, one would expect to see an absence of disagreement among and between associates. Hence, the survival of disagreement depends on the permeability of networks created by weak social ties and the bridging of structural holes. At the same time, these ties lead to the dissemination of new information, and they bring together individuals who hold politically divergent preferences, thereby sustaining patterns of interaction that produce political disagreement. Thus, the political influence of a particular discussion partner depends in a very fundamental way on the larger social network within which the individuals are located.

Moreover, citizens communicate more frequently with those whom they judge to be politically expert. This asymmetrical quality of communication, in which citizens rely heavily on locally defined experts, increases the effectiveness of communication as well as the influence of politically expert citizens (Huckfeldt 2001). In business and marketing, the idea that a small group of influential opinion leaders may accelerate or block the adoption of a product is central to a large number of studies (see Rogers 1995). The opinion leaders play a key role in the flow of information because of existing social capital or because these leaders span "structural holes"—they have relationships that allow them to form bridges between groups that would otherwise have no contact (see Roch 2005). They gain influence not only because they have contacts with members outside of the group, but also because they possess contacts that other group members lack. These contacts provide opinion leaders with unique access to potentially valuable information. The opinion leadership is not simply tied to a set of characteristics but also depends on the nature of the social environment in which the opinion leader is embedded. An individual with extensive contacts who is an opinion leader in one group may not be an opinion leader in a second group in which other individuals possess similar contacts.

Notes

1. The Lincoln-Douglas debates of 1858 were a series of seven debates between Abraham Lincoln, the Republican candidate for Senate in Illinois, and incumbent Senator Stephen Douglas, the Democratic Party candidate. The debates previewed the issues that Lincoln would face in the aftermath of his victory in the 1860 presidential election. The main issue discussed in all seven debates was slavery. The debates were held in seven towns in the state of Illinois: Ottawa on August 21, Freeport on August 27, Jonesboro on September 15, Charleston on September 18, Galesburg on October 7, Quincy on October 13, and Alton on October 15.

2. Lands which have been included to the Federal Republic of Germany as a result of its integrating with the German Democratic Republic, October 13, 1990.

3. The respondents were 185 undergraduate students enrolled in introductory courses in communication and public speaking. The first session (pretest) was held between October 7 and 9, two to four days before the debate. The posttest took place either on Sunday evening, October 11, right after the debate aired, or throughout the following day. According to their appointment made before the pretest, fifty-three students came to the posttest on October 11. Upon arrival, they were asked to watch the ninety-minute telecast of the first presidential debate. This is the first time students became aware that the presidential debate was involved in the study. Right after the debate, they answered the posttest questionnaire, which was identical to the pretest. This group of fifty-three was called "experimental viewers." When the remaining 132 students arrived the next day, they were first asked a series of filter questions to determine whether they had watched the debate on TV. Almost half of them ($n = 65$) had watched or listened to the debate ("natural viewers"), whereas the other half ($n = 67$) had neither watched the debate nor been exposed to news about it ("nonviewers").

4. After consulting various election news reports, researchers compiled a list of twenty-four "most likely to be debated" items for both pre- and posttests. These items asked the respondent to indicate whether a candidate supported, opposed, or had no position on twenty-four specific policy issues. The same twenty-four items were asked for Bush, Clinton, and Perot, respectively.

6

Dissemination of the Campaign Message

Mediated Campaign

Mediated (indirect) marketing becomes a second information channel for the candidate. Instead of the person-to-person channel used with a direct marketing approach, this channel makes use of electronic and printed media outlets such as television, radio, newspapers, magazines, direct mail, the Internet (e.g., email, websites, blogs), campaign literature (e.g., flyers, brochures, fact sheets), posters, billboards, and any other form of promotion that is available.

In every campaign most resources are spent on television political advertising (see, e.g., Kaid 1999b; Wisconsin Advertising Project 2008), making this promotion tool the most noticeable representation of a political campaign. Ken Goldstein and Paul Freedman (2002) reported that overall in the year 2000, just under one million (970,410) political television advertisements were aired in the top seventy-five U.S. markets. At the presidential level, almost 300,000 spots were broadcast in 2000. Comparing 1996 and 2000, there was a full 82 percent increase in the number of ads aired in the presidential race, from 162,160 to 293,942 spots.

However, many cheaper tools are also used in political campaigns, supplementing and strengthening TV advertising messages. They include buttons, T-shirts, and bumper stickers. According to Charles Case (1992), bumper stickers and car signs provide opportunities to interject the voter's own values and opinions into the environment of mass-mediated messages and proclaim a unique personal identity through symbols and statements representing individual interests or affiliations. This medium differs from other more institutionalized ones because it affords the person in the street a way of participating in the national discourse (see Bloch 2000).

Printed Campaign Materials

Another relatively cheap way of communicating with voters is so-called campaign literature. Campaign literature in the form of flyers, brochures, fact sheets, and letters is a ubiquitous feature on the electoral landscape in every country. It is funded by political parties, political action committees, private individuals, and candidates. According to Karen King (2002), using written campaign literature as a way to gain votes is particularly important for candidates for local political office because they, unlike their counterparts seeking state and national offices, seldom have the resources to barrage the voting public with radio and TV spots. In addition, written materials have the advantage of being portable in that they can physically be passed from one community member to another, thus increasing the number of opportunities they have to make an impression. Distributing written materials is also a way for local candidates to utilize volunteer labor in their quest to gain votes, because although it takes professionals to produce a TV commercial, it does not take much skill to hang a flyer on a doorknob. The information candidates include in campaign literature, as well as how it is presented, can reveal their perception of the criteria citizens use when deciding for whom to vote. King examined 288 pieces of campaign literature distributed by candidates for city council seats in eleven Ohio counties in November 1997, and she found that the candidates perceive potential voters as susceptible to both intellectual and emotional campaign messages. The candidates who were represented by these pieces of campaign literature created an image of themselves as experienced, competent, and well-informed members of the community. Thus, they appeared to think that voters would be swayed by appeals to their intellectual capacity for making rational judgments based on concrete qualifications. On the other hand, descriptions of candidates' family units and photographs of them with family members were very powerful emotional symbols. The reason for inclusion of family images may be that candidates feel it is necessary to tie into voter biases, perhaps unconsciously, by showing that they are not representatives of nontraditional family arrangements.

Using pictures in printed promotional materials—especially flyers and billboards—is supported by the mechanisms of visual persuasion. Paul Messaris (1997) outlines three major roles that a visual image can play in an ad. First, it can elicit emotions by simulating the appearance of a real person or object. Second, it can serve as photographic proof that something really did happen. Third, it can establish an implicit link between the object being promoted and some other images (e.g., endorsers, a child's portrait).

In political campaigns it is important to consider not only *what* is in the picture but also *the way* it was photographed. Dolf Zillmann, Christopher Harris, and Karla Schweitzer (1993) found that the angle and perspective from which people are photographed are relevant to the way they are going to be evaluated. The worst impressions are evoked by photographs taken from a very close distance and front. Politicians are more likely to evoke positive

Figure 6.1   **Examples of Political Parties' Logos**

attitudes if they are portrayed from a further distance, from a side angle, and from the bottom. These rules, as the authors state, do not necessarily hold for people who are very well known in the society. Such persons are known "from all angles."

Also some formal features of a leaflet or billboard can generate a positive attitude and emotion toward the candidate they present. A picture or heading is often included in a marketing communication as a device for capturing the reader's attention, the net result being that the customer is more likely to consider claims contained within the communication. The selection of a particular attention grabber is commonly guided by creative strategy whereas its placement within the communication is determined by artistic rules of balance. In a series of experiments in a consumer behavior context, Chris Janiszewski (1990a, 1990b) created four versions of a perfume ad by locating the brand name (Shalimar Guerlain) to the left or right of either the model's face or the slogan. The brand name was placed so that it would be in a peripheral visual field whether the viewer was focused on the model's face or on the slogan. Janiszewski found that the brand name was preferred when placed to the right of the pictorial information (model's face) or to the left of the verbal information (slogan). Thus, if the goal of the communication is to have the reader comprehend and recall precisely a set of verbal information, it would be best

Figure 6.2   **Spatial Layout of Elements in a Leaflet: A Candidate, Slogan, and Party's Logo**

to place pictorial attention grabbers (e.g., a photograph) to the right of verbal claims and verbal attention grabbers to the left of verbal claims. In each case, the attention-grabbing material would be sent to the appropriate hemisphere of the brain during the reading of the verbal claims and would be less likely to interfere with cooperative processing and accurate comprehension.

In political marketing the graphic or verbal logos are also crucial for visual differentiation between candidates or parties. Examples of graphic logos of different parties are presented in Figure 6.1. Due to the specificity of the human brain's processing of verbal and graphic information, political marketers who want to develop a leaflet or billboard should consider what graphic layout or form to use depending on whether the goal is to draw attention to the candidate's party affiliation (logo), slogan, or recognition (see Figure 6.2).

In addition to visual tools, political campaigns also use other, indirect ways of communicating with voters, including direct mail, telemarketing, or short message service (SMS) (see Mylona 2008; Newman 1994; O'Shaughnessy 1988; Prete 2007; Sherman 1999; Steen 1999). They focus mainly on providing target segments of an electorate with promotional materials (test and visual ones). They are used mainly as an efficient fund-raising and communications tool.

Television Political Advertising

The fast development of television, which began in the 1950s, opened new possibilities for influencing citizens' political preferences (see Chapter 2). Since the first political advertisement was broadcast by Dwight D. Eisenhower when he was running for president, this particular form of voting communication has become the dominant element of all political promotion strategies (Diamond and Bates 1992). Until the 1960s, the central role was played by so-called hard-sell advertising, based on multiple repetitions of the persuasive message in order to force it into the minds of potential voters. After this period, marketers turned to soft-sell advertising, whose main purpose was to influence by an emotional message. Claiming that people assume strong attitudes toward political problems, Tony Schwartz maintained that the purpose of advertising is to smooth and direct the voter's already existing feelings by associating them with specific values and created images (Schwartz 1973).

At present, television political advertising is used in practically all the world's democracies, in all election campaigns for all political offices, from the presidency to the local school council (see, e.g., Kaid and Holtz-Bacha 1995, 2006). The American model of conducting political campaigns in the media was soon adopted in other democratic systems (see, e.g., Baines 2005; Ingram and Lees-Marshment 2002; Plasser, Scheucher, and Senft 1999). The defining characteristics of modern political advertising are control of the message and use of mass communication channels for message distribution. As a marketing tool in politics, political advertising's greatest advantage is its ability to completely control the message conveyed to the public (see Kaid 1999b). The only limitation of using television in political promotion, apart from some legal regulations, is the financial resources needed for purchasing TV time and producing the commercial.

Contemporary analyses concerning TV political advertising include two basic areas of research (Kaid 1999b):

1. analysis of the form and content of persuasive messages—types of content, relationships between the presentation of image and issues, negative appeals, and formal features of ads, such as length, production techniques, and the structural features of the message (see, e.g., Cwalina, Falkowski, and Rożnowski 1999; Kaid and Holtz-Bacha 1995, 2006; Kaid and Johnston 1991).
2. analysis of the widely understood influence of advertising on voter behavior—selective exposure, processing and remembering information presented in advertisements, contextual influence of alternative

sources of political information (press, radio, TV news, the Internet, etc.), and direct or indirect influence of political advertising on voter preferences and behavior.

Ronald Faber (1992) adds a third research area that is characteristic of political advertising receivers, which includes their demographics, party identifications, and their cognitive and emotional involvement in elections (see Chapter 3).

Distinguishing those research areas may be somewhat artificial since any analyses of political promotional messages boil down to determining whether advertisements influence voting preferences or not. Therefore, from the point of view of a political marketing campaign, the most important influence is the effectiveness of advertising and its mechanism of influencing voters.

The Influence of Political Advertising on the Voter's Level of Knowledge

Measuring the knowledge gained by voters while watching advertisements is done in many different ways: from identifying a candidate's name to asking viewers a simple question of what it is they have learned from the ads and casual recalling of presented problems (*free recall*). Darrell West (1994) investigated the advertising and news environment during the 1992 U.S. Senate campaign in California. Especially, he was interested in how people used campaign media (ads, newspaper, and local TV news) in evaluating candidates. West found that, in general, advertising had a stronger effect on voters' recognition of candidates than the local television news or newspapers, both in the primaries and general election. Seeing ads for most of the candidates was associated with recognizing those individuals.

West also carried out a wider analysis of television advertising from 1972 to 1990, using panel and cross-sectional public opinion surveys data (West 1994/1995). He found that even after controlling for factors such as respondents' partisanship, education, race, age, and gender, ads still had a significant impact on citizen learning about candidates' issue positions. For example, seeing Richard Nixon's ads in 1972 made viewers more likely to see him as wishing to uphold commitments made to other nations. The same phenomenon occurred in the 1988 nominating process. During that year, exposure to ads moved people closer to the issue positions of Michael Dukakis (the military), Albert Gore (unfair competition from Japan), and George H.W. Bush (deficit reduction).

The relationship between watching political advertisements and knowledge about candidates and their issue positions was also investigated by Charles

Atkin and Gary Heald (1976). They conducted telephone interviews with mid-Michigan voters during the last weeks of the 1974 congressional campaign and found that frequency of viewing ads correlated positively and significantly with learning of candidate names and issue stands ($r = 0,34$).

Richard Faber and M. Claire Storey (1984) analyzed the level of remembering various types of information (issues, image, mudslinging, and mentions of scenery or actions presented in ads) from political ads during the 1982 gubernatorial election in Texas. A large majority of the respondents (about 84 percent) recalled having seen television commercials for candidates, but only slightly over half (55 percent) could recall everything from these spots. Furthermore, voters recalled more information from their preferred candidate's ads than from the opponent's spots. Faber and Storey also found a significant association between respondents' perceptions of the helpfulness of ads in making decisions and recalling issues and image information from the ads and the number of items recalled from the nonpreferred candidate's commercial.

However, information gains or learning from ads do not have to translate directly into changes of preferences for candidates or even their assessments.

The Influence of Political Ads on Processing of Candidate Image Information

Nowadays the image of politicians taking part in voting campaigns is the most popular subject of research and analysis concerning campaign communication (e.g., Garramone 1983, 1984; Kaid and Holtz-Bacha 2006; Kern 1989). The existing studies conducted in many countries clearly confirm that political advertisements influence voters' image of the candidate and may lead to a reconfiguration of the structure of image attributes (see Chapter 4). An example of this type of research is represented by the studies on the influence of television political advertisements on politicians' image conducted by Wojciech Cwalina, Andrzej Falkowski, and Lynda Lee Kaid (2000; see also Falkowski and Cwalina 1999). These researchers propose a sequential model of the influence of spots on voters' behavior (see Figure 6.3). The model includes four causally connected components, which allow predictions of citizens' voting behavior: (1) cognitive-affective elements (candidate image); (2) general feelings toward the candidate; (3) intention for whom to vote; (4) decision for whom to vote.

The model was empirically tested during the 1995 and 2000 presidential elections in Poland, the 1995 presidential elections in France, the 2004 presidential election in the United States, and the 1994 parliamentary elections in Germany (Cwalina and Falkowski 1999, 2003, 2005; Cwalina, Falkowski, and Kaid 2000, 2005; Falkowski and Cwalina 1999).

Figure 6.3   **Sequential Model of the Influence of Spots on Voters' Behavior**

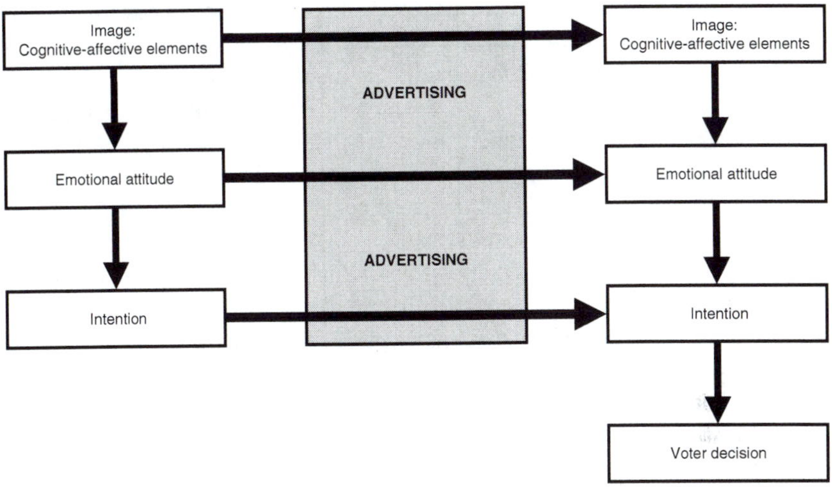

Source: Falkowski and Cwalina (1999, 228).

From the marketing point of view, it is important to determine two things: (1) what general processes lay the foundations of the influence of advertising on forming voting preferences, and (2) what attributes politicians need to be "enriched by" in order for their image to have a better influence on positive attitudes toward them. For this purpose, two types of analyses were conducted in the 2000 presidential elections in Poland and the United States (Cwalina, Falkowski, and Kaid 2005):

1. With reference to the empirical test for the processes assumed in the sequential model, structural equation modeling (SEM) was used, defining causal relationships between cognitive elements of the politician's image, affective elements, and voting intention. The specificity of the cause relationship obtained by the structural equation methodology allows some practical suggestions regarding the general strategy that should be used in electoral campaigns. In this case, the SEM method of extraction generalized least squares (GLS) was used, where analyzed data were correlations.

2. In order to generate more detailed practical suggestions of what attributes of a politician's image influence positive attitudes toward the politician, multiple regression analyses were conducted.

The research conducted during the 2000 presidential elections in Poland and the United States used the same experimental design. The experiment consisted of three stages. At the first stage an experimental group completed anonymously a research questionnaire (pretest). Then they watched four political advertisements. The presented advertisements were chosen at random from the advertisements that each of the candidates used in his television campaign. Subjects were exposed to two advertisements of each of the candidates in an alternating sequence—Aleksander Kwaśniewski's (incumbent) and Andrzej Olechowski's (challenger) in the Polish contest, and George Bush's and Al Gore's in the U.S. election. After the subjects had watched the spots, the experimenter handed out research questionnaires (posttests) concerning the demographic attributes of the subjects and items measuring their perceptions of the candidates' image (the semantic differential with twelve bipolar scales), emotional attitudes toward the candidates (the standard feelings thermometer), and voting intention (for details, see Cwalina, Falkowski, and Kaid 2005).

In order to simplify data structure from the semantic differential and to distinguish perception dimensions of the candidates' image, four principal component analyses were conducted for each politician. In each case, a two-factor solution was obtained. In Poland, with reference to Kwaśniewski, two factors accounted for 53.6 percent of total variance. Factor 1, "leader's abilities" (42.5 percent of variance), included such attributes as *qualified, open to the world, believable, successful, sophisticated, calm, unaggressive, strong,* and *friendly.* Factor 2, "morality" (11.1 percent of variance), consisted of *honest, attractive, active, Catholic,* and *sincere.* In the case of Olechowski, the factors explained 52.4 percent of total variance. Factor 1, "leader's abilities" (42.3 percent of variance), consisted of the following attributes: *qualified, open to the world, believable, successful, attractive, strong,* and *active.* Factor 2, "sociability" (10.1 percent), consisted of the following attributes: *honest, sophisticated, calm, unaggressive, Catholic,* and *friendly.*

In the United States, with reference to Bush two factors accounted for 69.3 percent of total variance. Factor 1, "leader's abilities" (55.5 percent), included attributes such as *qualified, sophisticated, honest, believable, successful, attractive, friendly, sincere, strong,* and *active.* Factor 2, "calm" (13.8 percent), consisted of *unaggressive* and *calm.* In the case of Gore, the factors explained 61.7 percent of total variance. Their structure was the same as in the case of Bush. Those factors were again defined as "leader's abilities" (51.2 percent) and "calm" (10.5 percent).

The results of structural equation analysis for each of the candidates among his supporters are shown in Figure 6.4 (Polish candidates) and 6.5 (U.S. candidates). The partition of the sample into two partisan groups was based on declared voting intention.

Figure 6.4   **Structural Equation Models: Polish Presidential Election, 2000**

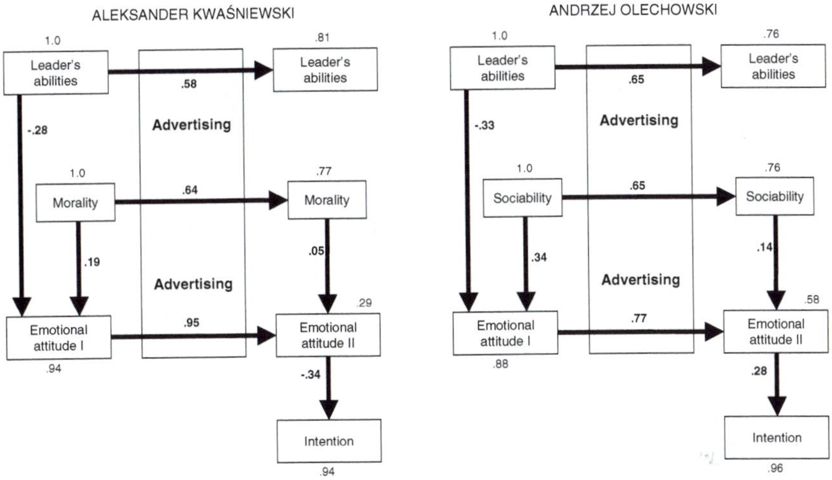

Source: Cwalina, Falkowski, and Kaid (2005, 27).

The SEM models for Polish candidates present specific arrangements of causal relationships obtained empirically, connecting image with affects and voting intentions for particular candidates. Despite slight differences in the parameters of the paths, the model explains in a similar way the voting behavior of Kwaśniewski's and Olechowski's supporters. For the two candidates, initial emotional attitude toward them depends on their evaluation by the voters in the two dimensions of the image: leader's abilities and morality for Kwaśniewski and leader's abilities and sociability for Olechowski. However, political advertising leads to the loss of the influence of the candidates' leadership abilities on the final forming of voting intentions. It turns out that a positive attitude toward them depends only on the "soft" characteristics of their image. Therefore, it seems that political advertising draws voters' attention to the social and moral virtues of politicians, pushing the importance of their competencies and professional preparation for performing the function of a president to the background.

The SEM models obtained for both U.S. candidates are similar, but they are different from those in Polish case. Emotional attitudes toward Bush and Gore depend entirely on their perceived leadership abilities, both before and after the subjects' exposure to the candidates' advertisements. Besides, the advertisements create changes both in the assessment of these abilities and in emotional attitudes. They also modify the assessment of Bush and Gore in relation to the *calm* dimension. However, the change does not translate into either emotions for these candidates or intentions of supporting them in the

Figure 6.5   **Structural Equation Models: U.S. Presidential Election, 2000**

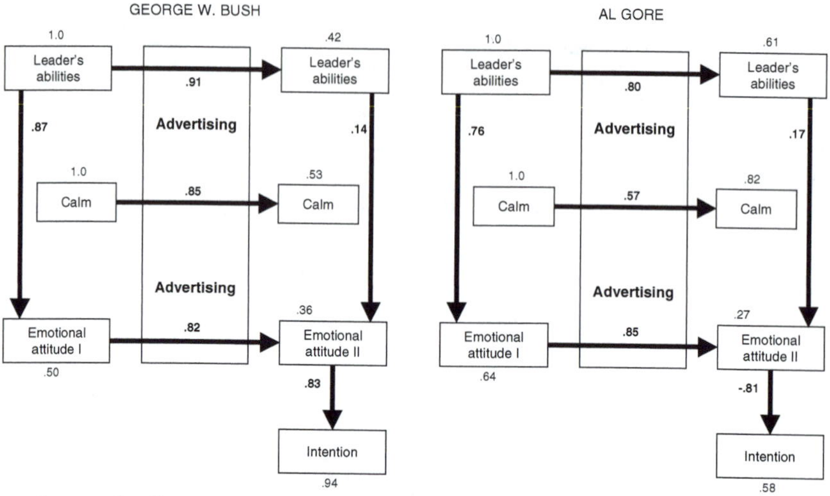

Source: Cwalina, Falkowski, and Kaid (2005, 29).

elections (for other variants of the sequential model of the influence of spots on voters' behavior, see Cwalina 2000; Cwalina, Falkowski, and Kaid 2005).

From the marketing point of view, it is important to determine what attributes politicians need to be "enriched by" in order for their image to have a better influence on positive attitudes toward them. One method that distinguishes important attributes in a politician's image is multiple regression analysis. The dependent variable here is emotional attitude toward the candidate, whereas the independent variables are particular scales of the semantic differential—attributes of the image. Therefore, eight regressions were conducted for each of the countries: for feelings toward each candidate among his supporters and opponents, before and after viewing the spots. Their results for the Polish candidates are presented in Table 6.1.

In Kwaśniewski's electorate the mean values of R^2 (averaged from pre-test and post-test) for "own" candidate (Kwaśniewski) and the opponent (Olechowski) are 0.38 and 0.52, respectively, while in Olechowski's electorate, they are 0.66 for the appraisal of Kwaśniewski's image and 0.53 for Olechowski's. In both electorates the percentage of the explained variance is smaller for "own" candidate than for the "strange" one, possibly implying that the affective attitude toward "own" candidate is to a lesser degree dependent on his image and to a larger degree on the other candidate's attributes (e.g., political program, party affiliation, system of values). The "strange" candidate is monitored more carefully, mainly in order to find his negative attributes

Table 6.1

The Adjectives Accounting for the Variance of the Thermometer of Feelings Toward Candidates: The Polish Presidential Election, 2000

Candidate's supporters	Target	Attributes (pretest)	Beta (standard error)	Attributes (posttest)	Beta (standard error)
Kwaśniewski	Kwaśniewski	Attractive	−.50 (.13)	Attractive	−.30 (.14)
		Aggressive	−.40 (.14)	Successful	−.34 (.16)
		$R^2 = 0.43$		$R^2 = 0.33$	
	Olechowski	Honest	.52 (.12)	Friendly	.48 (.18)
		Successful	−.45 (.14)	Sincere	.36 (.15)
		Catholic	−.32 (.12)		
		Attractive	−.26 (.12)		
		$R^2 = 0.55$		$R^2 = 0.49$	
Olechowski	Kwaśniewski	Attractive	−.48 (.16)	Qualified	−.42 (.19)
		Friendly	.59 (.23)	Passive	−.33 (.16)
		Honest	.46 (.19)		
		Believable	.50 (.21)		
		$R^2 = 0.62$		$R^2 = 0.70$	
	Olechowski	Strong	−.76 (.25)	Honest	.75 (.18)
		Passive	−.56 (.24)	Passive	−1.07 (.33)
				Successful	−.56 (.24)
		$R^2 = 0.39$		$R^2 = 0.66$	

Source: Cwalina, Falkowski, and Kaid (2005, 30).
Note: All parameters are significant at the level $p < 0.05$.

or attributes that discredit him as a potential president. In both electorates a strong polarization of attitudes toward individual candidates can be seen. However, the spots did very little for the relation between candidate's image and emotional attitude. The R^2 values are, in fact, similar before and after showing the spots.

The percentage of the explained variance in the thermometer of feelings by differential adjectives is relatively high, which points to the possibility of controlling affective attitude toward candidates by proper emphasis on the candidate's relevant attributes (see Table 6.1). It appears to be a reconfiguration of the politicians' images under the influence of their spots. The set of significant adjectives explaining the temperature of feelings toward a given candidate is different after the exposure. It seems clear that after the subjects watch the spots, the images of the candidates change within the overall cognitive behavior, which links all the components of the model: image, feeling, and intention. In other words, after watching the spots the voter is sensitive to different adjectives. We can "warm up" or "cool down" the feeling toward the candidate by manipulating selected characteristics of the candidates' images in a promotional advertising strategy (see also Cwalina, Falkowski, and Kaid 2000).

The results of regression analyses for the U.S. candidates are presented in Table 6.2. R^2 values are very different before and after showing the spots, which points to different efficiency of advertising campaigns in the two electorates. It seems that in Bush's electorate the spots did not influence his supporters' sensitivity to the image of their candidate. R^2 values before and after showing the spots are comparable for Bush (0.55 and 0.43, respectively) and Gore (0.24 and 0.38, respectively). In Gore's electorate, on the other hand, his spots turned out to be a success: they did weaken sensitivity of Gore's supporters to the image of the opposing candidate, which points to the decrease of R^2 value from 0.56 to 0.32. At the same time, the spots increased considerably the sensitivity of voters to the image of their own candidate, which is expressed by a considerable increase in R^2 value from 0.28 to 0.57.

In the analysis of both the Polish and the American research, after the advertisements were screened, the reconfiguration in the perception of both candidates' images also changed. The attributes-adjectives that were significant for the affective perception of both Gore and Bush changed. The exception here is Gore, who, among his electorate, retained the same feature—that is, sophisticated—regardless of the advertisements, which had an important influence on emotional attitude toward him (see Table 6.2). This also points to the qualitative changes in the perception of the politicians' images under the influence of their advertisements.

Taking into account these results, we conclude that even slight changes in the attribute weights or even a significant change in only one of the attribute's weights may elicit a complete reconfiguration of the candidate's image. The change of image relies not so much on the exchange of particular attributes as on the exchange of the whole attribute configuration.

The Influence of Political Ads on Processing of Party Image and Issue Information

The results of the research by Cwalina, Falkowski, and Kaid (2005) point out explicitly that political advertising significantly influences the selection and processing of information concerning political candidates. It also influences changes in the perception of their images, leading to its reconfiguration. However, the crucial question is whether political advertising has an impact on the ways the presented stands on issues are perceived. It is obvious that political advertising deals with issues related to the candidate or party program.

Table 6.2

The Adjectives Accounting for the Variance of the Thermometer of Feelings Toward Candidates: The U.S. Presidential Election, 2000

Candidate's supporters	Target	Attributes (pretest)	Beta (standard error)	Attributes (posttest)	Beta (standard error)
Bush	Bush	Honest	.45 (.12)	Friendly	.53 (.11)
		Sincere	.39 (.12)	Aggressive	.35 (.11)
		$R^2 = 0.55$		$R^2 = 0.43$	
	Gore	Qualified	.49 (.12)	Strong	.39 (.12)
				Qualified	.37 (.12)
		$R^2 = 0.24$		$R^2 = 0.38$	
Gore	Bush	Qualified	.75 (.13)	Believable	.57 (.16)
		$R^2 = 0.56$		$R^2 = 0.32$	
	Gore	Sophisticated	.52 (.16)	Sophisticated	.75 (.12)
		$R^2 = 0.28$		$R^2 = 0.57$	

Source: Cwalina, Falkowski, and Kaid (2005, 32).
Note: All parameters are significant at the level $p < 0.05$.

It covers themes related to ideological programs, the economy, international relations, environmental protection, health, poverty, ethnic minorities, crime, morality, and so on.

The issue elements in political ads are related to a strategy based on rational or logical argumentation for a candidate (see Cwalina, Falkowski, and Newman 2008). Some of the research directly concerns the relative importance of the image and the issues for voter behavior. Teresa Harrison and her collaborators (1991) showed that female voters' preferences were shaped most of all by politicians' images; the issues were not very important. On the other hand, male voters' behavior depended on politicians' programs; the images were not that significant. A slightly different view was presented by Victor Ottati, Martin Fishbein, and Susan Middlestadt (1988), who maintained that the voter's understanding of issues is shallow and superficial. According to this view, the candidate's personal characteristics and party affiliation outweigh specific issues in shaping the voter's choice (see Chapter 4).

Therefore, in order to obtain a more complete view of the whole process, it seems necessary to include another variable in the sequential model of voting behavior (see Figure 6.3 on page 209) to define the perception of a given political candidate's or party's advertisements in terms of its issue versus image appeals. In the former model, advertisements constituted the mediating variable,

Figure 6.6   **The Extended Sequential Model of the Influence of Spots on Voters' Behavior**

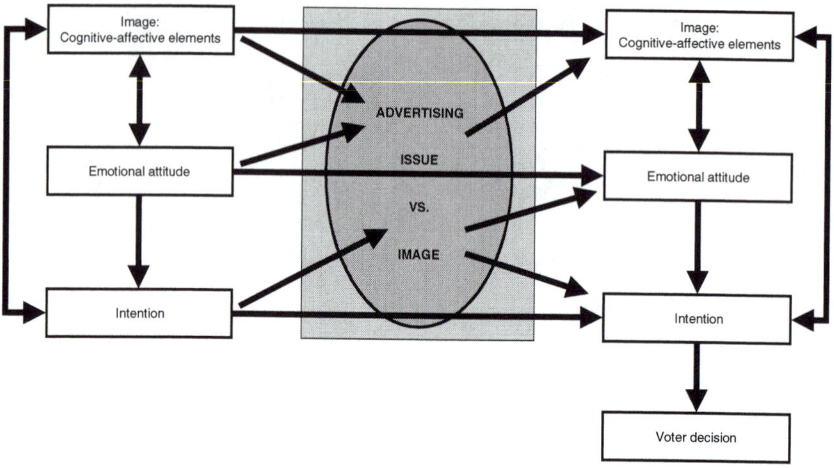

Source: Adapted from Cwalina and Falkowski (2008a, 109).

without, however, measuring its direct influence on image and emotional feeling toward the party or candidate. The influence of advertisements was measured directly, by a reconfiguration of the structure of features that make up candidate image, and changes in emotional feelings. However, if the analysis of perceived advertisements was conducted according to their contents, researchers could then introduce the variable of advertising perception. Thus, Wojciech Cwalina and Andrzej Falkowski (2008a) proposed the extended sequential model of the influence of spots on voters' behavior (see Figure 6.6).

The extended sequential model assumes that before being presented with an advertisement, voters have particular political preferences (Vote 1) and know whether they are going to participate in elections and which party they are going to support. These initial voting preferences are shaped by the voter's general emotional attitude measured by the thermometer of feelings and the voter's perception and evaluation of the image of that party, either as positive or negative. The voter's general emotional attitude toward a party and the perception of its image influence each other, creating a positive feedback, which is illustrated by the arrows connecting image and emotional attitude in Figure 6.6. The more positive the evaluation of the image, the warmer the attitude toward a party, and vice versa. The key element of the model is that the influence of viewing advertisements on voter behavior depends on their contents: whether the message of the advertisement concentrates more on presenting a party's issues or image. Therefore, this aspect of voting advertising is the mediating variable. The perception whether an ad is focused on issues or image is conditioned both by the first evaluation of the party's image, emotions toward it, and voting support intentions. The issue versus image advertising strategy perceived by the voters shapes the final perception of a party's image, emotional attitude toward it, and voting support intention. Besides, the final voting support intention is also conditioned by the evaluation of the image and emotional attitude. Before and after the viewing of the ads, the image perception and emotional attitude create a positive feedback. It should also be stressed that the evaluation of the image, emotional attitude, and voting intention developed before watching the ads has an important influence on the final level of these variables.

Cwalina and Falkowski conducted an empirical test of this extended sequential model of the influence of spots on voters' behavior in reference to advertisements of Polish political parties broadcast before the first elections to the European Parliament in Poland in 2004 (2008a; see also Cwalina, Falkowski, and Koniak 2006). The research methodology was the same as in the research described above, and the analysis concerned the influence of the advertising of two parties: the Civic Platform (CP) and the League of Polish Families (LPF). The posttest questionnaire included an item concerning whether an ad focuses more on presenting the issues (program) or image of a given party. Lower values correspond to the respondents' belief that advertising strengthened the image, whereas higher values suggest that it focused on the presentation of the program. The image of each party was expressed through one variable (the mean of all the thirteen ratings of a given party of the scales of semantic differential). The higher the indicator, the more positive the evaluation (perception) of a given party's image is.

The left panel of Figure 6.7 presents the empirical structural equation model for the CP, and the right panel, the LPF. The arrows represent relevant statistical relations between particular elements of the model. A statistically standardized parameter of the path is marked above each of them.

According to the assumptions of the extended sequential model of voter behavior, the initial intention of voting for CP is related to the general emotional attitude toward that party. Emotional attitude and evaluation of the image strengthen each other, through positive feedback. It should also be stressed that the evaluation of CP's image influences voting intention support for this party only indirectly, through emotional attitude.

The perceived content of advertisements expressed through the mediating variable of perceptions is not important for the forming of voting preferences for CP. In the left panel of Figure 6.7 there are no arrows connecting such elements of the model as vote, image, and emotional feeling, with the vari-

Figure 6.7   **Polish Parliamentary Election's 2004 Election Structural Equation Model: Civic Platform and League of Polish Families**

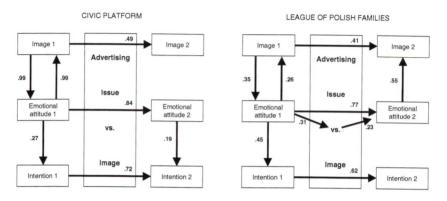

Source: Adapted from Cwalina and Falkowski (2008a, 114–115).

able of advertising. One may then say that any influence on the changes in the perception of CP, emotional attitude toward the party, and voting support intention for the party should be attributed to advertising as a whole—in its content and formal (structure) aspects rather than its issue versus image appeal. The key factor marking the support for CP is emotional attitude toward the party after viewing the ads. The image of the party seems completely separated from both intentions and emotional attitude. Preferences for CP are then quite stable, so their change under the influence of campaign communication (television political advertising) is quite unlikely.

The influence of political advertising on the forming of voter behaviors is completely different in the case of the LPF compared to that of the CP, though the initial voting intention of this party depends on the same configuration of image evaluation and emotional attitude (see Figure 6.7). The initial support for the LPF was directly influenced only by the emotional attitude toward that party. This, in turn, enters a positive and mutually strengthening relationship with image perception. In this way the perception of LPF's image influences only indirectly—through emotions—voting intention for this party. In this structure of causal relations between the variables there is no difference between the voting situation of the LPF and the CP.

However, there are differences in the important influence of the advertising perception variable. The general emotional attitude expressed by the variable emotional attitude *1* influences the perception of LPF ads as more issue-oriented, which is illustrated by the positive value of the path's parameter that combines these two variables, on the border of significance (0.34,

$p = 0.06$). Such issue-oriented perception of the advertisements increases people's positive attitude toward that party after viewing them, which is in turn expressed by the significant path connecting the advertisement perception variable with emotional attitude 2 (0.23, $p < 0.01$). This emotional attitude influences the final perception of its image. However, both image evaluation and emotional attitude have no important influence on the support for the LPF. It is dependent only on voters' initial declaration of voting for that party. It should then be stated that the content aspect of LPF's advertisements has an important influence in the forming of the final emotional attitude toward that party. However, the final support preference for LPF is relatively independent of the party's promotional activities. The results of the analysis demonstrate then that the supporters of this party have fixed voting preferences resistant to any advertising effort.

The analysis of the influence of Polish political parties' strategies in the European Parliament campaign on citizens' voting behavior suggests, above all, that the messages used by the parties were not successful. Although in the case of the LPF the advertisements introduced some changes in emotional attitude, they did not influence the support for this party. The support was closely related to the voters' initial declaration. The same was true with the CP. The final voting decision was the result of a decision taken before and emotional attitude, and the spots had neither emotional nor voting influence on the viewers.

The Influence of Political Ads on Attitude Certainty

The research results by Cwalina, Falkowski, and Kaid (2005) and Cwalina and Falkowski (2008a) point out explicitly that political advertising influences significantly the selection and processing of information concerning political candidates and parties. It also mediates, to some extent, the influence of their stands on issues. Most importantly, however, political ads influence changes in the perception of the candidate's image or political parties, resulting in their reconfiguration. The methodology of the evaluation of the advertise-ments' influence upon the candidate's image, based on multiple regression analysis, helps to capture the changes in the perception of the image linking it to the emotional attitude toward the competing politicians. However, it does not clarify whether these feelings really change under the influence of advertisements. In other words, these results do not reveal a lot about the ef-fectiveness of political advertising on strengthening the political views of a given candidate's supporters and simultaneous weakening of positive attitudes (or their certainty) toward the candidate's opponents. In other words, they do not prove that political ads may lead to an increase of polarization in voters' attitude (Lord, Ross, and Lepper 1979). From the point of view of an effective political advertising campaign, this type of information is fundamental for both the appropriate designing of advertisements and for the monitoring of their influence upon voters.

An attempt to analyze the influence of advertising from this angle was proposed by Cwalina, Falkowski, and Kaid (2000; see also Cwalina 2000; Falkowski and Cwalina 1999). Attitude certainty may be operationalized as a difference in voters' attitudes toward competing candidates measured by the feeling thermometer (see Chapter 3). When the difference is large (one is liked and the other one is not), it may reflect voters' certainty in relation to their preferences. If, on the other hand, the attitude toward both politicians is similar, this suggests uncertainty. Effective political advertising should, therefore, stimulate increase of certainty concerning the support for its sponsor, while simultaneously increasing uncertainty in relation to support for rival candidates.

Cwalina, Falkowski and Kaid (2000) conducted an analysis of the change of general affective attitude toward the candidates based on the psychological signal detection theory (see, e.g., Green and Swets 1966; Falkowski 1995; McNicol 1972). The main emphasis in this theory is put on distinguishing between the notion of sensitivity, defined by the d' value, concerning the sensory aspect of the subject, and the notion of the threshold of the reaction-β. The d' value is the difference between the statistical mean of the distribution of the sensory effects of two states of things expressed in the units of standard deviation, corresponding to the difficulty of recognizing a given signal: big values of d' point to the easy way of distinguishing (big difference between the means of statistical distributions S_1 and S_2); small d' values, on the other hand, point to a big difficulty (small difference between the means of these distributions). The β value then, also called the credibility index, or decisional threshold, located in a given point of the decisional axis, depends upon the behavioral variables controlling the behavior of the observer in the detection experiment (among others the instruction, the matrix of payments).

It is possible to interpret the elements of the methodology of studying political preferences within the signal detection theory. In the first place, the data on the feelings thermometer should be taken into consideration, where the analysis of the closeness of this data allows for defining the degree of the polarization of voters' attitudes. If the data from the feelings thermometers are presented in the form of normal statistical distributions (e.g., Gaussian distributions), then the degree of attitudes certainty in relation to particular candidates is easily noticed. For supporters of any given party or candidate X, there will be two such distributions, corresponding to X and to the competing party or candidate, Y, respectively. The analysis of voting preferences in a given electorate should then be conducted with regard to the overlapping of these distributions. Thus, the more they overlap (big uncertainty interval), the more similar emotional attitude to X and Y the voters of this electorate represent (even though they opt for a given candidate) and thus the more susceptible they might be to the influence of advertising. The small polarization of attitudes occurring then allows them to be classified as to the segment of undecided voters. When the overlapping of this distribution is small (small interval of uncertainty), there is a strong polarization of attitudes (i.e., strongly decided voters). So the size of the interval of uncertainty is then defined by the X and Y distinguishing parameters, which is the d' value. It can then be said that the efficiency of the influence of advertising on changing the voters' attitudes is inversely proportional to the d' indicator. This indicator is calculated from the formula

$$d' = \frac{Ms_1 - Ms_2}{\sigma_{1-2}} = \frac{Ms_1 - Ms_2}{\sqrt{\sigma_1^2 + \sigma_2^2 - 2r\sigma_1\sigma_2}}$$

where d' = the index of the polarization of attitudes in a given electorate; Ms_1, Ms_2 = means of the distributions of two states of things S_1 and S_2 (candidates);

σ_{1-2} = standard deviation of the difference between two distributions;

σ_1, σ_2 = standard deviation of the S_1 and S_2 distributions; and

$2r\sigma_1\sigma_2$ = covariance of the distributions.

If d' does not change significantly after watching advertisements or remains on a similar level in the pretest and posttest, it means that the advertisements do not influence voters' attitudes toward the candidates.

Cwalina, Falkowski, and Kaid (2000) conducted an empirical verification of these assumptions using data from three experiments carried out during the 1995 presidential elections in Poland (Lech Wałęsa vs. Aleksander Kwaśniewski) and France (Jacques Chirac vs. Lionel Jospin), and the 1994 German parliamentary election (candidates for chancellor Helmut Kohl vs. Rudolf Scharping). The distribution of feelings toward individual candidates in their electorates before and after the ads' exposure is presented in Figures 6.8, 6.9, and 6.10.

The attitude polarization indices for Poland, France, and Germany calculated from the formula are presented in Table 6.3 (see page 225).

In the Polish presidential campaign, the advertisements caused the voters from both electorates to become less certain of their voting preferences (decrease in the d' value). In France, the advertisements had no influence whatsoever on Jospin's electorate (d' remained on the same level) and strengthened

Figure 6.8   **Feelings Temperature Distributions: The Polish Presidential Election, 1995**

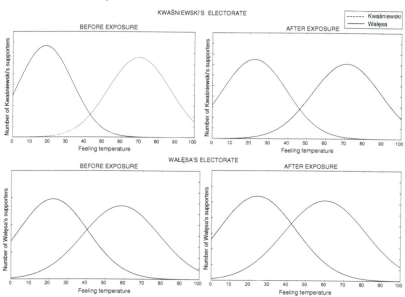

Source: Cwalina and Falkowski (1999).

the attitudes of Chirac's supporters. In Germany, the advertising strengthened the attitudes of Scharping's voters (an increase in the d' value) and polarized the attitudes of Kohl's electorate (a decrease in the d' value).

Summing up, the research results presented in this section of the chapter concerning the influence of political advertising on shaping the perceptions of candidates' image and shaping voting preferences toward them allow distinguishing three types of influence:

1. Advertisements strengthen the already existing voting preferences. The supporters of a given candidate consolidate themselves in their support for their candidate, whereas the opponents consolidate themselves in their opposition. In other words, the polarization of voting convictions increases. Political ads also can be connected with a certain reconfiguration of the candidates' image in the minds of their electorates. In the presented studies, such a situation occurred among Jacques Chirac's and Rudolf Scharping's electorates in France and Germany, respectively.

2. Advertisements weaken the already existing voting preferences and, in extreme cases, may even cause their change. We encounter here the influence that leads to the increase in uncertainty of voters about whom to support. This increase is usually accompanied by a recon-

Figure 6.9   **Feelings Temperature Distributions: The French Presidential Election, 1995**

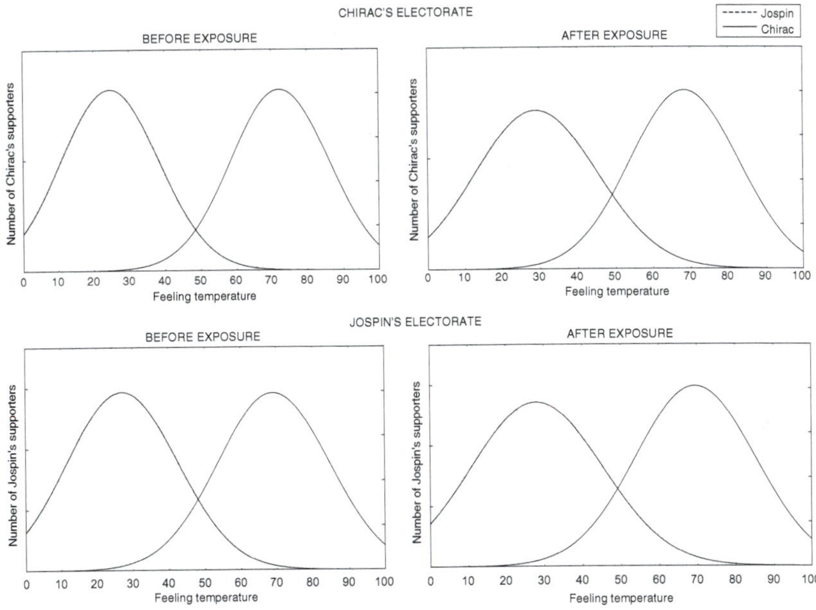

Source: Cwalina (2000).

figuration of the candidate's image. After the voters watch the advertisements, certain features of the candidates, other than the ones the voters perceived as important before, become relevant. So the voters must reconsider arguments for a given decision. This type of influence was observed among the electorates of Aleksander Kwaśniewski and Lech Wałęsa in Poland and Helmut Kohl in Germany.

3. Advertisements neither weaken nor strengthen political preferences, but they lead to the reconfiguration of the candidate's image in voters' minds. This type of influence can be called cognitive influence because, as a result of it, the argumentation of the earlier made decision does change, but the direction and certainty with which it was made do not change. From the point of view of political marketing and, thus, from the point of view of shaping political preferences, this type of promotional influence during a presidential or parliamentary campaign can be treated as inefficient. But leading to the change of a politician's image can be treated as the first step in the strategy preparing the candidate for the fight for power. It is also a kind of influence that can be said to contribute to creating public relations. Such influence of advertising can be observed in the case of Lionel Jospin's electorate in France.

Figure 6.10 **Feelings Temperature Distributions: The German Parliamentary Election, 1994**

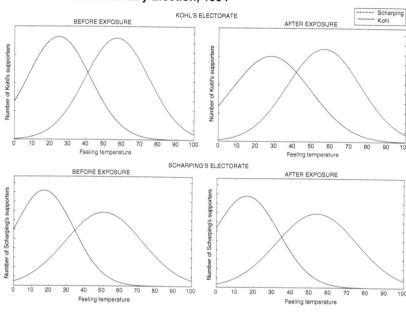

Source: Cwalina (2000).

These results and conclusion also point to differences in effectiveness of political advertising. The differences depend on the candidates themselves and their political advisers, but also on the specificity of individual countries (see Cwalina, Falkowski, and Newman 2008; Cwalina, Falkowski, Newman, and Verčič 2004; Kaid and Holtz-Bacha 2006).

Negative Television Advertising

Negative advertising was utilized in the first political campaign where television as a channel of communicating with voters was used, in the 1952 Eisenhower-Stevenson race (Kaid and Johnston 1991). Several commercials from the "Eisenhower Answers America" series overtly attacked the Democrats, although Stevenson was not usually mentioned by name. Negative political advertising serves a number of campaign functions. It creates awareness about candidates and their issue positions, helps voters in setting issue priorities on their political agenda, and increases interest in the campaign by stimulating interpersonal and public discussion of it and by generating media coverage. Ads increase voters' evaluation of the sponsoring candidate while decreasing it for the targeted candidate, and they ensure that voter evaluations

Table 6.3

Indices of the Attitude Among Candidates' Electorates in the Pretest and Posttest for Poland, France, and Germany

				Electorate		
Country	Pretest	Posttest	Change	Pretest	Posttest	Change
Poland	Kwaśniewski's			Wałęsa's		
d′	2.00	1.75	↓	1.30	1.15	↓
France	Jospin's			Chirac's		
d′	2.02	2.02	0	1.57	1.71	↑
Germany	Scharping's			Kohl's		
d′	1.68	1.79	↑	1.60	1.56	↓

Source: Cwalina, Falkowski, and Kaid (2000, 136).

Note: All changes in *d′* value are statistically not significant (Fisher's Z test). It shows only some tendencies of change in electorates' polarization from pretest to posttest.

of the candidates become polarized and thus the electoral choice becomes simpler (Johnson-Cartee and Copeland 1991). Moreover, Pamela Homer and Rajeev Batra (1994) in their experimental study found that negative political communications are more successful in damaging overall voter attitudes toward the targeted candidate than positive communications are in raising such attitudes.

Richard Lau (1985) believes that the psychological principles behind the effectiveness of negative communications consist in the fact that negative information is figural against a positive background (the figure-ground hypothesis) and that people are more strongly motivated to avoid costs than to approach gains (the cost orientation hypothesis). The first phenomenon is defined as perceptual explanation for negativity. According to this assumption, we like our jobs, our neighborhoods, and the people around us, and it is against this positive background that negative information may stand out due to its relative infrequency. It may work as a simple perceptual contrast because it is unexpected and therefore more credible, more informative. The other mechanism Lau points out is a motivational explanation for negativity. It is related to the survival of species: it is more adaptive to avoid life-threatening costs than to approach pleasurable gains. John Skowronski and Donal Carlson (1989) point to yet another mechanism that may lay the foundation of negative campaigns' effectiveness: greater diagnosticity of negative (than positive) information in person impression formation. The extreme or negative behaviors are generally perceived as more diagnostic than are moderate or positive behaviors and, in consequence, have more influence on the process of impression or attitude formation.

Since the first negative advertising spot was broadcast by Eisenhower's staff, this way of appealing to voters has become one of the most frequently used marketing methods. Its goal is to undermine or even destroy the image of the rival and—by contrast—strengthen voters' perception of the candidate's own image. Lynda Lee Kaid and Anne Johnston (1991) conducted a content analysis of 830 American television spots from eight presidential campaigns from 1960 to 1988. They found that 29 percent of all ads contained some negative appeals. However, there were frequent fluctuations in their frequency, depending on particular presidential campaigns. Most occurrences of negative communication were observed in 1964 (40 percent); then their number dropped in the 1970s to about 25 percent and eventually grew in the 1980s to about 35 percent. During the 1992 and 1996 campaigns, they made up more than half of the total advertising content (Kaid 1999b). As noted by Richard Lau, Lee Sigelman, and Ivy Brown Rovner (2007), 83 percent and 89 percent, respectively, of the ads sponsored by the Democratic and Republican Congressional Campaign Committees in 2004 were negative. The researchers from the Wisconsin Advertising Project (2008) found that during the one week of September 28–October 4, 2008, nearly 100 percent of John McCain's campaign advertisements were negative and 34 percent of Barack Obama's. Comparing this presidential election to 2004, the researchers indicate that both the McCain and Obama campaigns aired more negative advertisements than did their counterparts. In all of 2004, 64 percent of George W. Bush's ads were negative, while (to October 4) 73 percent of McCain's ads were negative. Similarly, 34 percent of all Kerry ads were negative while 61 percent of Obama's were.

Many more cases of "going negative," as Stephen Ansolabehere and Shanto Iyengar (1995) define it, are related to both candidates and their political consultants being convinced that negative ads are effective and that they bring particular profits to the sponsor. However, the results of meta-analysis of 111 studies on negative political advertising conducted by Lau, Sigelman, and Rovner (2007) clearly disprove this view. They found that existing empirical results do not bear out the idea that negative campaigning is an effective means of winning votes and bolstering a candidate's own image relative to that of an opponent, even though it tends to be more memorable and stimulate knowledge about the campaign. It should be emphasized, however, that although negative ads are memorable, these memories are often inaccurate (Geer and Geer 2003). Furthermore, Lau and his collaborators also stated that the bulk of the evidence points to a modest tendency for negative campaigns to undermine positive affect for the candidates they target. Furthermore, there is no reliable evidence that negative campaigning depresses voter turnout, though it does lead to slightly lower feelings of political efficacy, trust in government, and possibly overall public mood.

Although Lau's analysis contradicts conventional wisdom, in some circumstances negative campaigns have an advantage over positive ones. It is probably easier for candidates and their consultants to fine-tune attacks than positive messages and, therefore, to focus on what is more controllable and new. Furthermore, negative campaigning is also used in a tactical manner. Lee Sigelman and Emmett Buell (2003) analyzed the statements of the presidential and vice presidential candidates in the 1960 through 2000 campaigns. They found that in runaway races the side that trailed could be counted on to wage an especially negative campaign and that the vice presidential candidate of the leading ticket could be counted on to play an unusually aggressive role, although candidates adjusted their strategies according to the ebb and flow of a campaign (see Sigelman and Shiraev 2002).

Ronald Faber, Albert Timms, and Kay Schmitt (1990) assume that using negative advertising during political elections is driven by three major goals:

1. Negative appeals may simply give a voter a reason not to vote for the target candidate. As a result, voters choose based on whom they do not want to be elected ("negative vote" or "protest vote").
2. Negative appeals make voters compare the candidates, making the sponsor look better by comparison. As a result, the sponsoring candidate gains positive support.
3. Negative appeals may polarize voters. The existing attitudes of supporters of the sponsoring candidate strengthen and increase the likelihood of voting.

These goals may be achieved by using different types of negative advertising. Karen Johnson-Cartee and Gary Copeland (1991) identify three main modes of negative appeal: (1) the direct attack, (2) the direct comparison ad, and (3) the implied comparison ad. The authors found that direct attack decreases the targeted candidate's evaluation and voting preference scores significantly. The direct comparison ad features the candidate as well as the opponent and contrasts their records, their experience, and their issue positions. Johnson-Cartee and Copeland found that this mode produced the greatest decrease in the targeted candidate's evaluation and voting preference scores. Finally, the implied comparison ad does not make specific references to the targeted candidate and may not feature the sponsoring candidate until the very end. These ads present in some detail the sponsoring candidate's position, record, or other characteristic that has become important during the course of the campaign, without mentioning the opponent. According to the findings of Johnson-Cartee and Copeland, such ads decrease the targeted evaluation and voting preference score significantly while increasing the respective scores of the sponsoring candidate. Moreover, negative ads may be focused on the opponent's issue positions and/or image. Ads emphasizing the former comment on the political record, the voting record, issue positions, and the criminal record of the rival candidate, while the latter type comment on the rival's medical history, personal life, religion, sex life, family members, and so on.

The crucial thing is that competing political campaigns should be evaluated in tandem because of synergies between them. The results of two experiments conducted by David Houston, Kelly Doan, and David Roskos-Ewoldsen (1999) give support to this view. They found that competing positive campaigns produced relatively high evaluations of both candidates, whereas competing negative campaigns produced relatively low evaluations (see also Ansolabehere, Iyengar, and Simon 1995).

From this perspective, negative advertising can be considered efficient only in three cases, when it increases support for the sponsor candidate and, simultaneously, lowers or keeps at the same level the support for the target candidate, and when it does not change the support for the sponsor but lowers it for the target candidate. However, six possible effects of using negative advertising are still left: three of which preserve the status quo (support for both candidates simultaneously lowers, increases, or does not change) and three related to a backlash effect (target gains or loses support and sponsor loses or, if target gains support, the voting situation does not change (Faber, Tims, and Schmitt 1990). From this perspective, without taking into account the content of the advertising and its target audience, the probability of a negative campaign's success is 30 percent. An important element here is also the medium in which negative advertising appears—for example, a billboard (Merritt 1984) or the Web (Jagoda and Nyhan 1999; Klotz 1998)—and the context in which it is presented.

The results of an experiment conducted by Lynda Lee Kaid, Mike Chanslor, and Mark Hovind (1992) show that some types of political commercials are more likely to increase vote likelihood when placed in specific types of television programming. The negative ad was more effective in the context of news coverage than when placed in a drama or situation comedy. In comparison, the positive image ad was more effective in the comedy context than in news coverage and drama surrounding. But ad context did not have influence in the case of issue advertising.

Response to Negative Advertising

An important factor conditioning the efficiency of negative advertising is that attack is usually followed by counterattack. Brian Roddy and Gina Garramone

(1988) conducted an experiment to determine the relative effectiveness of different types of negative political advertising appeals and of various strategies for responding to the appeals. They created six fictional commercials featuring two fictional Congress candidates. The target of the attack ad was pictured in both his own and the attacker's ad. Two attack spots were created, one featuring an issue appeal (attack on the targeted candidate's positions on crime and the environment), the other an image appeal (the target was accused of being indecisive, inconsistent, and unethical). Negative response commercials corresponding to each of the attack ads were then created (negative issue response and negative image response). They featured counterattack. Positive response (issue and image) ads were also created. Their claims ignored the attacking ad and described the target in a positive way. These spots were presented to subjects in four treatment conditions: issue attack/negative issue response; issue attack/positive issue response; image attack/negative image response; and image attack/positive image response. The results obtained by Roddy and Garramone show that when attack ads are followed by a response from the target, issue ads were more effective than image attack ads. Viewers of an issue commercial demonstrated a significantly more positive evaluation of the attacker's ad and character, and significantly less likelihood of voting for the target, than did viewers of an image ad. The findings for response strategies were more complex. Viewers evaluated the positive response spot more favorably than the negative response spot. But the negative response ad was more effective in discouraging voting for the attacking candidate. It may prove that although the negative response ad itself may be liked less, it may be still effective in creating a backlash against the attacker (see Chapter 4 on image repair strategies). Thus, the implication for campaign planners is that it may be wiser to address an opponent's weaknesses on issues than to attack the opponent's character. Furthermore, if the criterion for evaluating the effectiveness of negative ads is the effect of vote intention, then it appears that a negative response to an attack may be more advisable than a positive one.

Third-Party Negative Advertising

A more and more common phenomenon during political campaigns is the emergence of negative advertising not sponsored by the candidate (so-called third-party advertising). Third-party election advertising is political advertising in any medium during an election period with the purpose of promoting or opposing, directly or indirectly, a registered political party or the election of a registered candidate. These ads are sponsored by various "independent" voter or pressure groups (e.g., Swift Boat Veterans for Truth's ad against John Kerry or the anti-Bush ad produced by the National Air Traffic Controllers

Association [NATCA] in the 2004 U.S. presidential campaign). Research on the effectiveness of such negative advertising was conducted by Gina Garramone (1985). More precisely, her experiment explored the roles of sponsor and rebuttal (refuting the attack within one's own ad or ignore it) in negative political advertising. A 1982 political commercial targeted against Montana senator John Melcher by the National Conservative Political Action Committee (NCPAC) was used as the stimulus. The video-only sponsor identification tag was removed from the original spot. Two corresponding sponsor identification tags consisting of lettering and an announcer's voice-over were created. The first read "Paid for by the Williams for Senate Committee" and the second "Paid for by the National Conservative Political Action Committee. Not authorized by any candidate or candidate's committee." The newscast containing the NCPAC-sponsored ad was used in the rebuttal manipulation. For the "no rebuttal" condition, subject viewed only this newscast. For the "rebuttal" condition, an actual rebuttal ad that aired in Montana was exposed.

The experiment results showed that both sponsor and rebuttal factors determined the impact of the negative ad on perceptions of the candidates and vote intentions. Independent sponsorship was more effective than candidate sponsorship, resulting in greater intended effects against the targeted candidate and in reduced backlash effects against the opponent. Rebuttal by the targeted candidate increased backlash against the opponent, but failed to influence perceptions of the target. According to Garramone, campaign media planners may draw some implications from these results. The intended effects of negative political ad are increased by the use of an independent sponsor, while backlash effects against the opponent are decreased. The author concludes that "the direct implication for campaign planners is to leave the 'dirty work' to the independent organizations" (Garramone 1985, 158). The results also confirm the tactical way of using negative campaigns proposed by Sigelman and Buell (2003).

Formal Features of Negative Advertising

The effectiveness of a negative appeal depends also on the technology used to make a spot. In 1996 Lynda Lee Kaid (1997) conducted experimental research on the perception of advertising spots that distorted the physical image of the candidate during the presidential campaign in the United States, where Bill Clinton and Bob Dole were competing for the presidency. It is relatively easy to distort an image in political advertising using modern computer technology by, for instance, slow motion, superimposing of images, top, bottom, and front shots. Kaid selected a few television spots from the presidential elections in which a visual distortion of the content describing the candidate was used. As a rule, such spots only appear in a negative campaign whose task is to reduce the appeal of the candidate among the voters. In total, as many as 70 percent of the spots distorted the image of the candidate. Clinton's voting spots were focused on criticizing his rival, and in 84 percent of the cases they presented a distorted picture of Dole, whereas Dole's campaign presented a distorted voice of his rival in half of its spots.

In order to determine the influence of the distorted image of the candidate on people's evaluation of him and their voting preferences, Kaid selected four experimental groups. The first two groups watched, in sequence, two original negative spots of Dole and Clinton where a distorted picture was used. Dole's spot used complex computer graphics that distorted Clinton's picture by a superimposition of words consisting of big red letters. They expressed the criticism of Clinton's attitude toward taxes. The spot also presented a cutting from a publication suggesting that it was published in a newspaper, presenting arguments for increasing taxes. The spot also showed a growing red arrow illustrating how quickly taxes were rising. Clinton's spot presented his rival moving in slow motion among the elderly and children against a background showing a polluted environment. The spot was black and white in order to increase the viewers' negative impressions. The second and third group watched the same two spots. However, the distortion was completely removed from them. In Dole's spot the red color of the letters distorting Clinton's picture was removed and the arguments for increasing taxes were no longer presented as press cuttings. The size of the red arrow presenting growing taxes remained the same during the whole presentation of the spot. In Clinton's spot, the picture presenting Dole remained but the colors of the landscape were restored. The same verbal expression, distorted or not, was preserved in each of the candidate's spots. The influence of advertising using distortion on the evaluation of the candidate and subjects' intention about voting for him is presented in Figure 6.11.

The evaluation was the mean of twelve seven-point scales of semantic differential, developed in order to measure the candidate's image, and the intention was measured on one seven-point scale. The higher the number, the more positive the picture of the candidate or the greater the intention. The differences in the evaluation of the candidates connected with watching the distorted spots and the spots from which the distortion was removed are relevant and clearly demonstrate the negative influence of distorted stimuli in advertising on the evaluation of the rival and subjects' voting intentions. Distorted advertising not only decreases the rival's chances, but also increases the chances of the candidates whose campaign prepared these spots. In the case of spots prepared by Dole, the differences in candidates' evaluation while watching the original message, distorted message, and message from which the distortions

Figure 6.11   **The Effect of Distorted Stimuli in the Ads Presented by the Dole Campaign on Candidate Image and Vote Intention**

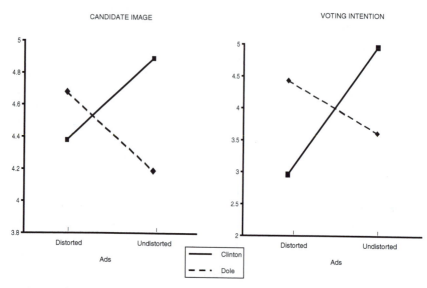

Source: Based on data presented by Kaid (1997).

were removed turned out to be significant. They clearly showed the negative influence of distorted stimuli on the candidates' evaluation and the intention of voting for him. Besides, such advertising not only lowered the chances of the rival, but also increased the chances of the voter's sponsor—Bob Dole. With Bill Clinton's advertising, the results turned out to be less unequivocal. The technological distortions used in the Clinton ads had selective impact on the attitudes toward both candidates. After the distortions were removed, the image of Clinton was perceived the same as with the distortions and the probability of voting for him lowered. But the image of Dole attacked in the spots was perceived in a more positive way. The probability of voting for him was on a similar level as in the case of the distorted advertising.

However, the results of research conducted by Ansolabehere and Iyengar (1995) and Faber, Tims, and Schmitt (1990) confirm that negative ads are more likely to cause target-partisans to strengthen support for the target candidate and source-partisans to strengthen support for the ad sponsor. In this way, they rather contribute to increasing the electorate's polarization than bringing about changes in voting decisions (see Chapter 3). Besides, Houston, Doan, and Roskos-Ewoldsen (1999) found that a candidate sharing a voter's ideology was denigrated for using a negative campaign only when the opponent

Figure 6.12   **A Frame From the "Daisy Girl" Spot**

Source: www.nysun.com/arts/museum-of-the-moving-image-offers-a-history/85684.
Note: This frame is from the online edition of the *New York Sun* (nysun.com). S. James
Snyder, "Museum of the Moving Image Offers a History of Politics on TV," September
12, 2008.

was also negative, whereas the opposing ideology candidate was bolstered
by using a positive campaign only when the shared ideology candidate was
also positive (see also Budesheim, Houston, and DePaola 1996; Houston
and Doan 1999).

Fear Appeal

A specific use of negative advertising is fear appeal. Probably the best-known
piece of political advertising is the spot titled "Daisy Girl" made by Tony
Schwartz for Lyndon Johnson and the Democratic Party in 1964 (see Figure
6.12). Although the spot was broadcast only once by NBC, it actually determined the result of the presidential election in the United States.

"Daisy Girl" was targeted at the Republican Party candidate, Barry Goldwater. It presented a small girl counting down while tearing daisy petals. Her
countdown was gradually taken over by an off-screen voice counting down
before the launch of a nuclear missile, followed by an explosion and the sight

of the mushroom cloud of an atomic bomb. Johnson's voice suggested that such a course of events might follow in the United States if his opponent, Goldwater, rose to power (Diamond and Bates 1992). At the end of the spot there was text reading "On November 3 vote for President Johnson." It should be noted that "Daisy Girl" manages perfectly the time sequence of the three elements conditioning the effectiveness of the fear appeal.

John Tanner, James Hunt, and David Eppright (1991) developed the protection motivation model, which provides a clear prescription for how to develop messages (especially fear appeals) that can influence adaptive behavior. According to this theory, with fear advertising the following sequence of presenting information should be followed: (1) presenting the threat, (2) identifying the cause of the threat, and (3) showing ways of neutralizing or removing the threat. Such a sequence influences changes in behavior, which is confirmed by the authors' results of their research on using various types of protection against AIDS. Besides, only these advertising appeals that arouse an appropriate amount of emotional tension can be successful in achieving desired attitudinal changes (Wheatley and Oshikawa 1970). The results of classical research on fear-arousing communications conducted by Irving Janis and Seymour Feshbach (1953) revealed that high fear produces less conformity to the recommendations of the communication and less protection against later counterpersuasion, despite inspiring more worry. The high fear communication inspires more avoidance because of its gruesome content.

In "Daisy Girl" the sequence of presentation follows exactly the sequence described in the model of fear advertising. First, it presents a threat, represented here by the atomic explosion. Then it shows the cause of this threat, namely the Republican Party candidate Barry Goldwater, whose radical stance on nuclear armament was well known. Finally, it presents a simple way of eliminating the threat, by choosing Lyndon Johnson for president.

The results of the influence of negative TV advertising on voter preferences suggest that it is very seldom consistent with the intentions of the sender of such messages. To be efficient, such spots need to meet a number of criteria:

1. Negative advertising should be addressed to a candidate's own voters or/and undecided voters. Only in those groups can candidates' increase their position and increase polarization among all voters. The reactions of the supporters of the attacked candidate toward the sponsor are usually negative. One should also remember that if they can influence the mass media, their opinions will be publicized. In consequence, they will be another source of pressure exerted on the voters not connected with any of the candidates.

2. The influence of other sources of political information (particularly television and press) modifies the influence of negative advertising. Those who are most susceptible are citizens carefully following the development of political events. That is why decisions about attacking the rival by negative political advertising should be accompanied by increased public relations efforts, whose goal should be to ensure at least neutrality in the comments about the campaign.

3. When more than two candidates run in the election, using negative advertising seems particularly risky (Merritt 1984), because the "third" candidate may benefit the most from "defaming" others.

4. Using negative advertising is not recommended for representatives of parties enjoying little support in society or those for which support is decreasing. As negative advertising unites the electorate of the one under attack, chances for election success drop considerably in this case.

5. Negative advertising should focus on highlighting mistakes and issue weaknesses of the rival rather than attack the rival's character or ethical stands. And the problem attacks should relate to issues that are important for the voters.

6. It is less profitable to initiate attack than respond to it from the position of the attacked. Besides, the reaction should be positive rather than negative—that is, it should focus on a reliable and actual presentation of the attacked candidate's stand rather than an "eye for an eye" response. It may lead to escalation of voting battles and discourage citizens from participating in the election (see Austin and Pinkleton 1995; Pinkleton, Um, and Austin 2002).

7. Negative advertising should be produced with state-of-the-art TV technology and techniques (e.g., computer graphics). These methods are very expensive and require employing professionals, but they will increase the ad's effectiveness.

8. Negative spots should be broadcast in the context of TV information programs. Only such an environment may influence their better reception and effectiveness.

9. The best way to influence voters by negative advertising is to broadcast them under the name of an independent organization whose logo is not associated with one of the competing parties.

10. Negative spots should be broadcast in the middle stage of the campaign. Its beginning and end should include positive messages about the candidate's voting platform (Diamond and Bates 1992).

11. Negative advertising should be varied. The results of analyses conducted in the field of psychology of learning show clearly that

negative reinforcements very quickly stop exerting any motivational influence on the individual.

Radio Political Advertising

In the first half of the twentieth century the dominant role among the media was played by the radio. One of its most important characteristics was its ability to provide its listeners with a kind of accompaniment to their everyday chores (Blumler and Madge 1967). Besides, radio programs create and then maintain a certain psychological mood and provide people with subjects of their everyday conversations.

Since its very beginning, the radio has been exposed to pressures of political elites and ruling groups (see Pandora 1998). Franklin D. Roosevelt is believed to be the first politician to have discovered the propaganda power of this medium for democratic systems. In 1933 he inaugurated a series of programs that became known as "fireside chats." A total of eight programs were broadcast at irregular intervals (the first took place on March 12, 1933—the last one on September 6, 1936). According to David Michael Ryfe (1999), their main goal was to evoke a sense of unity among Americans and mobilize them around Roosevelt's socioeconomic program (the New Deal). Ryfe believes that these programs were an example of so-called media events, whose goal was to attract listeners' attention. They were prepared in advance, although they were broadcast "live" (see Dayan and Katz 1992). Such programs, reaching most U.S. citizens, allowed the president to create and then maintain his own image. Roosevelt resembled a salesman there, offering his citizens an attractive vision of the country.

Soon the radio became, following voting rallies, leaflets, and the press, yet another channel of communicating with the voters. However, research on its persuasive power shows that its influence on voting behavior is minimum (see, e.g., Atkin and Heald 1976; Garramone and Atkin 1986). But radio is used not only as a channel of disseminating voting advertisements. It also provides information, and that is why politicians eagerly accept invitations to political commentary and information programs. Radio is another opportunity for them to present their political views and opinions. Martin Harrison (1992) found that during the British parliamentary elections in 1992, of all its information about the campaign, Radio 4 dedicated 35.7 percent of the Conservatives, 31.4 percent to the representatives of the Labour Party, and only 23.2 percent of them to Liberal Democrats. The politicians who were most often heard on the radio were the leaders of these parties, namely John Major (125 appearances), Neil Kinnock (120), and Paddy Ashdown (120).

It seems then that the radio as a channel of political persuasion is not particularly efficient. It may, however, contribute indirectly to forming citizens' voting or even ideological preferences, as is the case with Rush Limbaugh in the United States or the Catholic Radio Maryja in Poland. From the perspective of political marketing, no channel of disseminating voting information should be rejected.

Campaigning on the Internet

Philip N. Howard (2006) argues that the hypermedia campaign has succeeded the mass media campaign, such that the 1988 campaign was the beginning of an important transition in the organization of political information in the United States. Between the 1988 and 2004 presidential campaign seasons, the political Internet emerged as a critical component of U.S. campaign strategies. The proportion of people using the Internet to collect news or to research policy alternatives increased significantly as the technology diffused. From inside candidate and issue campaigns, the Internet and related tools allowed a number of campaigns to make significant advances in fund-raising, volunteer coordination, logistics, intelligence on voters, and opposition research. This new channel for mass communication provided the political parties and candidates with new means to reach the voters. Further, it was expected that this could be done at low, or at least reasonable, monetary costs and without the interference of news media. The Web also opened a new, fast, direct channel for two-way communication between the parties and the electorate (e.g., Gibson and Ward 1998; Margolis, Resnick, and Wolfe 1999).

Howard (2006) quotes American survey results that reveal that citizens increasingly use information technologies such as the Internet to learn about political campaigns, follow the news, and engage in political activities by volunteering, donating funds, or researching public policy options. However, as Göran Djupsund and Tom Carlson (2003) note, it seems that the group of Internet users consists in particular of citizens who are already interested in or connected to politics. Thus, this would enhance the reinforcing rather than the mobilizing effect of politics on the Internet. In other words, the Internet will strengthen existing patterns of political participation more than it will encourage those who are currently marginalized from the political system to participate in political discourse.

These survey data also show that, at least at the national level, almost every political campaign fielded by major party candidates and most minor party candidates must now have a website. Some websites provide merely a basic statement of a candidate's political ideas, but increasingly websites offer interactive ways of participating and also serve as internal logistical tools for campaign operations. However, although the proportion of political candidates for elected office producing a campaign website has grown significantly over the last election seasons, still the prevailing source of information concerning election is television news programs and newspapers (Howard 2006). This is related, among other things, to the specificity of using these media. As to newspapers, radio, and television, the uninterested voter is, more or less directly, often by chance or accident, exposed to messages concerning politics or a particular party. Hence, in a way, the voter has to be active in order to avoid these messages. The situation regarding the Internet, however, is quite the opposite. The passive, but wired voter does not even have to be aware of the existence of party sites and other political sites. In fact, voters have to take active measures in order to expose themselves to messages conveyed by the parties and candidates (see Djupsund and Carlson 2003). Howard (2006, 32) goes as far as to say that "the production of political campaigns through Internet technologies is a process of tailoring content not for mass consumption but for private consumption." Thus, it is more similar to direct marketing than to marketing strategies that use mass media (e.g., television, radio, the press), an example of which is the so-called email electioneering—sending a candidate's promotional materials via email.

Candidates' Websites

Eric Klinenberg and Andrew Perrin (1996) claim that a well-designed candidate website should perform six basic functions: (1) supporting campaign organization, networking, and fund-raising (distributing campaign literature, organizing volunteers in local communities); (2) increasing political education and presenting political "substance" (position papers, speeches, quotes, pictures, and video); (3) building a community, providing a space for supporters to communicate with the candidate and the campaign staff; (4) offering cyber-celebration, providing space for discussing the candidate's sophistication with technology and commitment to a high-tech society; (5) providing hyperlinks to other sites; and (6) allowing the campaign to be interactive. The first two categories are essentially functions of a traditional, offline political campaign translated into cyberspace, whereas the next two categories refer to activities whose immediate goal is online. Then, links to other websites allow campaigns to connect their visitors to related political sites for coalition-building, education, mobilization, or comparison with political competitors. The interactivity refers to the ability of visitors to provide information to the campaigns or their websites and to receive meaningful responses.

Steven Schneider and Kirsten Foot (2002) demonstrated that presidential campaign sites in the 2000 U.S. elections provided online structure for a variety of both online and offline political actions, including information-gathering and persuasion, political education, political talk, voter mobilization, and campaign participation. Their analysis indicates that all or nearly all presidential campaign sites provided online structure facilitating information-gathering and persuasion and campaign participation. Fewer sites facilitated political education, political talk, or voter mobilization.

Jennifer Stromer-Galley (2000) argues that there are fundamentally two types of interactivity. The first is computer- or network-mediated human interaction. Two or more people use the channels provided by, for example, the Internet as accessed by a computer or a television-top device, such as WebTV, to communicate with each other. The communication can occur in real time or can occur in a time delay, as long as there is a response to the original message. People respond to each other in a communicative exchange facilitated through the Internet. The second kind of interactivity concerns engagement with the medium itself. People can manipulate the medium to provide information or perform functions that are commanded by the users. The channel of communication provides the feedback either between two machines or between some technological device and a person. For example, a hyperlink on a website changes the content presented based on the user's mouse-click. Jennifer Stromer-Galley and Kirsten Foot (2002) empirically tested whether U.S. citizens identify and distinguish between the media and human interaction components of the Internet and how they understand the role of the Internet in political campaigns and the role they themselves can play in the campaign process by utilizing the interactive features of Internet applications. Data for this study were collected through a series of thirteen focus groups with U.S. citizens in New Hampshire in January 2000, two weeks prior to the presidential primary elections. Thanks to a laptop computer, access to an Internet service provider, and an image projection system, each group was shown at least two presidential candidate sites, one from each major party. Participants in the focus groups were directed to the home page of a candidate site and then asked to comment and reflect on what they saw. They were then encouraged to navigate the website collectively, discussing the site as they explored it.

Stromer-Galley and Foot found that even without direct questions regarding interactivity, participants distinguished between the capacity to interact with a website by navigating its spaces as their interests dictated and the possibility of interacting with other people through a website. The participants viewed the Internet as offering potential for political participation, but, at the same time, they were skeptical whether candidates would be willing or able to use the human interactive capacity of this new medium to the fullest extent. For these citizens, media-interactivity was understood in relation to the levels of control websites provided to users. Control in the focus group interactions referred primarily to participants' ability to navigate, to look in greater depth at political information they were interested in, or to change the configuration of the websites. They did not discuss at length the media-interactive components such as click-polls or audio and video as media-interaction. These elements were referred to not in terms of interactivity, but more often as ways that users could get more information or get more involved in the campaign. In summary, these results suggest that in light of political campaign communication, citizens view the Internet as giving them greater control in seeking political information and increased contact with the campaign. However, citizens are aware of the obstacles campaigns face if they incorporate features on their campaign websites that enable genuine interaction between candidates or campaign staff and citizens.

S. Shyam Sundar, Sriram Kalyanaraman, and Justin Brown (2003) conducted an experiment designed to investigate a website's interactivity effects on the impression formation of political candidates. The researchers designed a website to serve as the campaign website for a fictitious political candidate. All participants were exposed to one of three conditions, each with identical content but a different level of website interactivity. In the low-interactivity condition, the website did not have any hyperlinks. Participants were able to read a brief biography of the candidate and his platform stances on education, economy, crime, and civil rights by scrolling down the screen. Each major policy area was broken into subissues. Underneath each subissue was a brief paragraph indicating a policy position. In the medium-interactivity condition, the initial page of the website gave a brief biography of the candidate along with links to four main policy issues. In the high-interactivity condition, the initial page featured a brief biography and links indicating four policy areas. On selection of a particular hyperlink, participants were led to another page (with the relevant heading), which simply consisted of links listing the three subissues of the selected policy area and a link back to the initial page. By clicking on one of the three subissues, participants were led to a subsequent page (with the relevant heading) describing the policy position of the selected subissue, followed by a link back to the previous layer of the site at the bottom of the page. The results of Sundar, Kalyanaraman, and Brown's experiment suggest that although participants in the three interactivity conditions did not perceive differences in the informativeness of content on the website, and although they did not show differential memory for content, they differed significantly in their perceptions of the level of interactivity of the experimental website. Furthermore, the results indicate that the interactivity of the website had an influence on participants' impression formation of the candidate as well as their levels of agreement with the candidate's positions on policy issues. Moderate interactivity seemed to enhance the candidate's appeal as well as character, but high interactivity seemed to detract from it. Similarly, the level of voter agreement with the candidate's position on policy issues was enhanced with moderate interactivity but not with high interactivity.

In analyses of the websites of Finnish political parties and their candidates during the first round of the 2000 presidential election campaign, Djupsund and Carlson (2003) obtained less optimistic results. They found that the websites were only partially interactive. Thus, all sites featured email addresses. Still, there was no guarantee that the candidates would reply to the messages. Furthermore, none of the candidates offered the voters opportunities to real-time chats. According to the authors, these results suggest that the candidates did not exploit the interactive Web features that could have activated the voters. Rather, the websites resembled traditional campaign brochures that inform readers about the candidates' issue priorities and their personal characteristics. The websites predominantly disseminated information downward, from the candidates to the voters. Moreover, very few voters considered the websites important as an information source when deciding how to vote. In seeking political information, the voters relied on traditional media—the press and, especially, television. In conclusion, Djupsund and Carlson state that the Finnish parties in the 2000 presidential election campaign gained rather little from "getting wired." They did not really manage to reach new voters, nor was internal party activity or party cohesion promoted. "In many ways the sites seem to have functioned as modern versions of the partisan press of days gone by" (48).

This observation has been confirmed by the results of Harold J. Jansen's analyses (2004). In his study, he focused on the websites created by candidates from Alberta and British Columbia during the 2001 Canadian provincial elections. He found that, essentially, candidate websites were digital versions of campaign brochures. Many candidates did try to use their sites to solicit donations, volunteers, and lawn signs, which suggests an attempt to broaden the uses of campaign websites. But there was little evidence that candidates took advantage of the defining characteristics that set the Internet as a medium apart from traditional media: multimedia, interactivity, and linking. According to Jansen, these results tend to reinforce the argument that the Internet represents "politics as usual" (see also Stromer-Galley 2000).

Soonyoung Cho and William Benoit (2005) content-analyzed the websites of six Democratic presidential candidates—John Kerry, Howard Dean, John Edwards, Wesley Clark, Dennis Kucinich, and Al Sharpton—during the 2004 primary campaign (from December 2003 to February 2004). Examining the candidates' news releases on their websites, the researchers found that, as in other media, these candidates used acclaims (themes that portray the candidate in a favorable light) more frequently than attacks (70 percent and 29 percent, respectively). Defenses (attempt to repair the candidate's reputation) were rarely employed and used only by Kerry. Candidates focused most on policy (55 percent), followed by character (34 percent), and campaign-related topics (10 percent). Unlike in the 2000 primaries, the Democratic primary candidates in 2004 attacked each other less often than they attacked President Bush and the Republican administration. Cho and Benoit also noted that the impact of news releases posted on websites might be greater than we might imagine because of their potential influence on news coverage. However, as Spiro Kiousis and Arlana Shields (2008) state, how an issue is discussed or framed by candidates on their websites not only sways media, voters, donors, and other constituencies, but also might influence the way in which competing candidates discuss issues in their own campaign communications.

To sum up, we may agree with Rachel Gibson (2004) that while political Web campaigning might not yet be effective in influencing the majority or even a significant minority of voters, this is largely a problem relating to access rather than to the content of sites. Once voters view the contents of a campaign-specific site, they generally appear to respond positively to the messages received. A complicating factor here, however, is that the requirement of finding the website, although it may raise a barrier to reaching a mass audience, also might be vital to creating a sense of ownership and control among users once they arrive at the site, which may in turn be responsible for creating the more positive responses reported above. Thus, the challenge for Web campaigners is to find a way to address this paradox such that the "push" aspect of the medium becomes more ubiquitous in drawing voters in, but not so invasive as to make viewing the Internet message an entirely passive experience.

Blogs

While other forms of online involvement, such as campaign donation and volunteer recruiting, already existed in campaign websites, the year 2004 saw the use of additional tools for possible involvement with voters. In this election year, campaigns—and scholars—discovered blogs. In particular, Howard Dean's presidential campaign made strategic use of blogs, encouraging people to write up their thoughts on politics within the informational architecture provided by the Dean campaign. The Dean campaign also took advantage of MeetUp.com's technology, which allowed community groups to easily form, discuss online, and then meet in person to continue discussion.

Campaign blogs may be written by the candidates themselves, by a ghostwriter, or by an identified member of the campaign staff. Some campaign blogs invite comments from readers as a form of two-way communication, while others provide one-way communication from the campaign to prospective voters.

Andrew Paul Williams and his collaborators (2005) employed a quantitative content analysis to evaluate the content of the front pages of candidate websites and blog posts during the 2004 campaign in order to identify the blogging and hyperlinking strategies used by the two presidential candidates—George W. Bush and John Kerry. They found that the two campaigns used the Internet in similar ways, mainly as a platform to discuss many of the same issues. The issues discussed on websites, though, were significantly different from issues discussed in blog posts, which indicates that the campaigns used these online communication tools in a different manner. In terms of hyperlinking and fund-raising, websites tended to link internally and frequently offered promotional and revenue-generating materials, while blog posts frequently linked externally and were less likely to solicit donations or otherwise engage in fund-raising. In summing up their results, the authors hypothesize that the lack of correlation between the candidates' blog posts and Web pages is perhaps due to lack of an integrated, congruent political marketing strategy (see also Jankowski et al. 2005).

Kaye Trammell (2007) used content analysis to investigate the use of blogs by both major party candidates during the 2004 general election cycle and the strategic targeting of messages to young people. In this study he specifically examined how frequently each campaign posted messages targeted to young people and which campaign posted more messages. The blog post was the unit of analysis. Trammell found that only 8 percent of the total combined campaign blog sample was explicitly targeted to young voters. The Bush campaign clearly showed a more explicit attempt to reach out to young voters via blogs. Although Bush published fewer posts than Kerry (496 vs. 694, respectively) during the study period, he published more than twice as many items targeted to young voters. Bush's campaign blog targeted more of its posts to young people (15.5 percent) than Kerry's (4.2 percent), although the issues discussed causes concern that campaigns are not giving young people information on the issues most relevant to young voters. For example, Bush mentioned the reinstatement of the draft in one post as a rebuttal attempting to dispel a rumor that he supported a military draft. Kerry published one post attacking what he called Bush's "failure" regarding Pell Grant college funding for qualifying students. Instead, issue statements appeared to be hastily repurposed to ambiguously introduce general issues in a way that only nominally related to young people.

Moreover, a number of the youth-targeted posts published by the Bush campaign were not even written by the official campaign bloggers. Rather, these were "dispatches" submitted from supporters on the ground who wanted to share their story and excitement about the campaign with others. The explicit personal references to young voters appear consistent with Bush's overall blog strategy. Both campaigns actively used the young adult children of the candidates to hit the campaign trail. For the Republicans, Barbara and Jenna Bush wrote a blog segment called "Barbara and Jenna's Journal," where they gave first-person accounts of campaign rallies they attended across the nation and on college campuses. The Democrats posted similar reports (written in the third person) of campaign rallies attended by Kerry's two daughters, Vanessa and Alex, Andre Heinz (Kerry's stepson), and vice presidential candidate John Edwards's daughter, Cate.

During that same 2004 campaign season, Trammell and his collaborators (2006) content-analyzed the website front pages and blog posts of the ten Democratic presidential primary candidates. They found that campaign blogs promoted interactivity more through text than technology. Regarding technology, all blogs promoted the perception of involvement through the presence of the comment feature; four blogs also included trackback. The prevalence of hyperlinks within a post has been overstated. The message strategy in blog posts focused predominantly on the campaign message. However, inviting participation did develop as a major strategy. Furthermore, personal presence and a conversational style of writing in blog posts provided examples of text-based interactivity. Considering the newness of blogging, the authors found that campaign blogs moved with trepidation in garnering the power of the hyperlink. The primary hyperlink destination from blog posts brought readers back into the candidate's website.

Overall, these research findings suggest that campaign blogs are not meant to be one-shot communication messages tasked with conveying the entirety of a candidate's platform, qualifications, and issue stance. Rather, it appears that blogs make use of subtler opportunities to build relationships over time through personal anecdotes, interaction, and issue discourse.

Online Advertising

The Internet is also a communication channel through which political candidates' or parties' advertisements are distributed. They may have the form of advertising banners, which are put on pages of frequently visited services, including, for instance, YouTube.

Advertising banners as tools of political advertising were used for the first time in the United States in the 1998 election campaigns for senators and governors. That year three companies dealing with online marketing consulting and studies of Internet use, Westhill Partners, Turtleback Interactive, and DecisionTree, in collaboration with the *New York Times* Electronic Media

Company, conducted an analysis of the online banner campaign of Peter Vallone, the Democratic candidate for governor in the state of New York. The authors of the model of the research and the report were Karen Jagoda from Turtleback Interactive and Nick Nyhan from DecisionTree (Jagoda and Nyhan 1999). Their research, called *E-Voter 98*, was focused on the influence of Peter Vallone's banners targeted at George Pataki, the Republican governor who was running for reelection. Vallone's banners, which included negative slogans about the achievements and program of his rival, were put on the *New York Times* webpage toward the end of October 1998. They were part of the media mix developed for this campaign by the consulting company Gould Communication Group. The research was conducted between October 17 and November 3 (the day of the election) in the form of a mail survey sent out to registered voters in the state of New York. It was answered by 1,335 respondents, 729 of whom had at least once seen Vallone's advertising banner (the expose group). The other 606 respondents had never been exposed to the banner (the control group). The main objectives of *E-Voter 98* were to

1. quantify the attitudinal impact of Vallone for Governor online banner advertising;
2. determine if the mere presence of the online advertising had any impact on favorability ratings and unaided and aided awareness; and
3. provide the first set of empirical research data on the topic of online political advertising and its attitudinal impact on people who were exposed to it.

The obtained results suggest that Pataki's favorability rating stood at 42 percent among the exposed group, compared with 49 percent among the control group. None of the exposed group clicked on the banner, serving as evidence that the mere presence of the banners and their negative anti-Pataki message had an impact on people even when they did not click on the banner ad. Furthermore, the banners sponsored by Vallone had a significant unfavorable impact on the attitudes of the undecided and independent voters toward the target candidate. The banners had a strong influence also on people who used the Web often.

Despite the fact that Vallone's negative banners had a negative influence on the evaluation of his rival, they did not develop a more positive image of their sponsor. Eventually, Peter Vallone lost decisively the fight for the governor's seat in New York State to George Pataki.

In recent years we have seen the rise of mass collaboration and information-sharing tools, loosely termed "Web 2.0" (Madden and Fox 2006). Among the ten most popular websites in the world, four sites can be regarded as Web 2.0 platforms (Carlson and Strandberg 2007): YouTube (a site where people upload, tag, share, and comment on videos); Myspace and Orkut (social networking and community sites); and Wikipedia (the online user-collaborative encyclopedia). The use and role of YouTube in the 2006 elections eventually led commentators to speak of "the YouTube elections" (Lizza 2006). YouTube is a website that enables users to upload, tag, watch, share, and comment on videos online free of charge. It is no surprise, then, that candidates, as well as their supporters, turned to YouTube in order to reach out to voters. YouTube offers candidates free advertising and is seen as one more venue for bypassing the media filter in order to directly connect with voters. However, when uploading campaign videos on YouTube (mostly to reshow spot ads already broadcast on television), candidates and supporters ceded control over their messages as viewers could freely comment on the videos on the site and share links to the commented-on videos in various online networks. In addition, YouTube became an uncontrolled channel for negative campaigning as videos showing candidates' gaffes were uploaded, commented on, and publicly spread (Carlson and Strandberg 2007). Nevertheless, such service is also a way for candidates (particularly less known ones) to gain recognition on the voting market.

Emilienne Ireland (2009) states that, in the early days of the Web, political campaigns typically had little or no Internet strategy. Political marketers viewed the Internet as a fulfillment device or an e-commerce tool, incapable of persuasion. However, the recent hypermedia campaigns, especially the 2008 U.S. presidential campaign, unfolded the full range of many-to-many communications, fund-raising, and volunteering opportunities. In consequence, the innovations of Web 2.0 have made politicians more accountable, campaigns more interactive, and the public more engaged.

7

Postelection Marketing

Maintaining and Enhancing Relationships With Voters

In Chapter 1, political marketing is defined as a process of exchanges and establishing, maintaining, and enhancing relationships between objects in the political marketplace (politicians, political parties, voters, interest groups, institutions), whose goal is to identify and satisfy their needs and develop political leadership (see also Cwalina, Falkowski, and Newman 2009). The goal of political marketing, then, is not only to attract citizens, but also to build relationships with them so that the goals of the relationship are achieved. In this respect political marketing is close to relationship marketing (see, e.g., Grönroos 1994, 1996; Harris and Rees 2000; Henneberg 2006a, 2006b). Its integral element is the promise concept, on which, to a large extent, the election campaign message is based. However, the responsibilities of marketing do not only, or predominantly, include giving promises and thus persuading voters as passive counterparts in the political marketplace to act in a given way. Fulfilling promises that have been given is equally important as a means of achieving citizens' satisfaction and maintaining their support. If promises are not kept, the evolving relationship between a candidate or political party and voters cannot be maintained and enhanced. Thus, the second key element in political marketing is trust. On the one hand, trust is related to the voter's believing in the politician's or party's trustworthiness, which results from expertise and reliability. On the other hand, trust is also related to a behavior that reflects reliance on the other partner.

Therefore, whereas mainstream marketers help a company stay on the market by controlling consumers' postsales behaviors, political marketers must develop a stable relationship based on mutual trust as well as keeping the promises made during the election campaign. Most of the activities related to political life occur between successive elections. Therefore, it seems obvious that in order to rule efficiently and have a realistic chance of being reelected, politicians should take care of their image after the election or, to be more precise, between elections. William Nordhaus (1975) even claims that parties that do not look beyond the next election follow what Theodore Levitt (1960) defined as "marketing myopia."

The analyses of a society's postelection satisfaction as well as its formation and maintenance come from various behavioral approaches whose main advantage is their empirical nature. Based on the methodology used for these studies, politicians can develop strategies for maintaining postelection satisfaction and use marketing tools during the relatively long periods between political campaigns. This chapter discusses the factors influencing the popularity of politicians as well as the problems of voters' trust in the ruling politicians, which is the key factor allowing politicians to maintain the positions they currently hold. This chapter will also discuss the strategy of manipulating information in the press during nonelection periods, based, among others, on Daniel Kahneman and Amos Tverski's (1979) psychological prospect theory.

Institutional Popularity of Politicians

It is obvious that most important politicians have the highest chance of getting reelected. Therefore, frequent opinion polls showing current trends in the support for politicians and parties have become an inseparable part of the political landscape. The results of such polls allow politicians to learn about the opinions and feelings of the society about them; however, in most cases the polls are descriptive, which does not allow politicians to understand exactly the reasons for their growing or diminishing popularity. Therefore, the press presents various analyses whose goal is to specify the root causes of such events. Quite often the analyses are based on the intuition of journalists and professionals from various fields analyzing political behaviors. Increased unemployment, economic crises, and broken election promises are the most common examples explaining politicians' diminishing popularity. However, quite often it is very difficult to validate such statements. They can be verified only from a longer perspective after several sociopolitical changes have taken place.

We may pose the question then whether there are any methods that can objectively determine the reasons for the successes or failures of those in power and whether there are any rules controlling the public perception of politicians as far as their popularity is concerned. In order to solve the problem, intuitive perceptions about either positive or negative evaluations of politicians need to be converted into principles developed by the behavioral sciences.

Research into the reasons for politicians' popularity was conducted by Glenn R. Parker (1977). The goal of his research was to show how social and economic factors in a particular country as well as international events influence the rankings of those wielding power. Although his research is already of a historical nature since it analyzes congressmen's popularity between 1939 and 1974, the methodology he used represents a quantitative approach to political research, which is characteristic for the behavioral sciences. Therefore, this chapter will first present social and economic factors and then the procedure describing their usefulness and validity for predicting politicians' popularity.

Determinants of Congressmen's Popularity

Using the existing analyses of social behavior, Parker (1977) focused on four fundamental variables that might influence the popularity of politicians: (1) the coalition of minorities, (2) the rally around the flag, (3) the economic slump, and (4) war.

The *coalition of minorities* refers to the decrease in support for the ruling president, which is a regular trend. The value of this variable is measured in different time periods, starting from the first days in office. The term "coalition of minorities" might be misleading here; Parker believes that the decrease in support for the ruling president results from the higher and higher numbers of his opponents—that is, initial supporters who eventually "leave" him. It is they who create the minority, which, in time, becomes stronger and stronger. This observed trend is the inevitable consequence of citizens' disappointment caused by their exaggerated expectations developed during the presidential campaign that are not met in reality. Growing dissatisfaction with the ruling of those in office leads to electoral disappointment among the growing number of the president's opponents.

The *rally around the flag* refers to citizens' patriotism, which, according to the author, should be closely related to politicians' popularity. It corresponds to voters' reactions to critical events on the national and international scene, uniting citizens around national symbols, the most obvious of which in the United States is the American flag. However, their influence decreases over time. One such event that evoked strong patriotism and strongly united U.S. citizens was the terrorist attack of Muslim extremists on New York and Washington on September 11, 2001. Figure 7.1 shows U.S. president George Bush at the site of the World Trade Center and the rescue teams on the ashes with an American flag.

The *economic slump* is based on the reasonable assumption that the valuation of those ruling a particular country is closely related to economic conditions and standards of living there. If citizens' subjective and objective economic condition is worse compared to the period when the politicians be-

Figure 7.1   **President Bush and Rescue Teams on the Ashes of the World Trade Center**

Source: www.photolibrary.fema.gov/photodata/original/3905.jpg; www.photolibrary. fema.gov/photodata/original/3969.jpg.

Note: These photos from the website are provided as a public service by the U.S. Federal Emergency Management Agency.

gan serving their term, then citizens' natural reaction is disapproval. This may sometimes lead to politicians trying to pass false or manipulated information to citizens. Such an attempt by the British Labour Party was discussed by Danny Dorling and his colleagues (2002). They analyzed a set of statistical indicators for each of the 641 parliamentary constituencies in England, Wales, and Scotland, published in the months leading up to the 2001 British general election on the Labour Party's website. These indicators referred to such areas as economic stability and making work pay, cutting crime, standards in schools, pensioners, and rebuilding the National Health Service. The researchers determined that in many cases these indicators were subject—as they put it—to "political statistical manipulation" (476). The rationale underlying the website was an attempt to show that things had gotten better since Labour was elected in 1997, in all areas for all social issues. Besides, as the authors state, it is fair to say that nothing presented on the Labour Party website was untrue in the strict sense of the word. Rather, the way in which the statistics had been put together (mixing and matching years and areas to present the best possible picture of improvement) was disingenuous overall.

In Parker's analysis the economic slump corresponds to the differences between the percentage of the unemployed when politicians began their term of office and the percentage in their subsequent years of ruling.

The war factor is specific to superpowers shaping the world's economic policy and often engaging in military conflicts all over the world. John Mueller's (1973) analysis shows that war depresses a U.S. president's popularity if it was started during his term. Such was the case with Lyndon Johnson during the war in Vietnam in the 1960s and also with the first Gulf War, which led to a decrease in George Bush's popularity. This factor is not very important though for the popularity of the president when he has to manage a military conflict provoked by his predecessor. The U.S. Congress is also perceived as responsible, at least to some extent, for a state of war because Congress must finally approve it. However, its decisions are also to some extent justified (which is not the case with the president) since some of the current lawmakers might have been influenced by their predecessors.

These principal variables often included in studies of politicians' popularity were supplemented by Parker by the following dimensions: the popularity of the current president in office and the president's emotional attitude toward the office, perceived by voters in positive-negative categories. The results of Parker's initial analyses (1977) showed that Franklin Roosevelt, Harry Truman, and John Kennedy were classified as "positive" whereas Dwight Eisenhower, Lyndon Johnson, and Richard Nixon as "negative." The popularity of Congress was also diminishing while the "positively" evaluated presidents were in office. Such presidents demonstrated high political activity. The relation between Congress's lack of popularity and the president's positive affective attitude and his high activity (*positive-active president*) must be the result of the strong political conflicts between the White House and Congress.

Parker also included in his study as a potential predictor of politicians' popularity Congress's legislative support of the president as perceived by voters. Voters expect that Congress will offer legislative support for the president. Various conflicts between Congress and the president may create a negative picture of Congress and contribute to its unpopularity. Various conflicts between them may create a negative picture of Congress and contribute to its unpopularity.

We may suppose then that the factors mentioned by Parker (1977) may influence, to a smaller or larger degree, the popularity of congressmen. However, what is also important for the discussion here is the definition of popularity. If, as Parker says, it is closely connected to voters' satisfaction, then the popularity of the politicians sitting in Congress may be defined by polls exploring voters' satisfaction with their activity (or the lack of it). The results of such research show a lot of variety over the years. It is worthwhile to focus though on cases when the variety was the greatest. The analysis of politicians' popularity between 1939 and 1974 presented by Parker shows that the first such case was observed in 1953, when, under Dwight Eisenhower, a ceasefire was signed with Korea. A second such case happened in 1965, when Lyndon Johnson was in office. What particularly distinguished him on the political scene was Congress's very high support for his legislative initiatives. Some 70 percent of the 450 legislative proposals presented by Johnson were approved by Congress.

In order to determine which of the variables discussed above influence significantly congressmen's popularity, Parker used a number of models of multivariate regression analysis. The final result determined three important predictors that accounted for 62 percent of congressional unpopularity: economic slump, positive-active presidential character, and rally-around-the-flag.

The sources of voters' satisfaction with congressmen's activity include economic growth, no critical domestic or international events evoking citizens' patriotism, and electing an inactive president treating his office with reserve. An active president often provokes political conflicts, which does not help Congress's popularity. The factor of war, quite unexpectedly, turned out to be least related to popularity, although in the United States it is Congress who, by Constitution, declares war. Voters do not seem to remember this fact very well, because the media emphasize the president's special role in such problems, as commander in chief and an important player on the international scene. This approach is also the result of historical evidence, always showing the president's personal involvement in such conflicts.

A politician's popularity does contribute to voters' willingness (or the lack of it) to support the politician in the next parliamentary or presidential election. However, this factor seems quite superficial and results from an innate feeling of the voter that can be called "trust." The question of voting satisfaction should then be extended to politicians. Their popularity would then be only one of the many factors influencing the electorate's choice. This problem was taken up by Parker (1989; Parker and Parker 1993) in his subsequent, more advanced analyses.

Voters' Trust in Politicians

The concept of trust in the area of voting behavior is difficult to define although everybody *implicitly* realizes what it means. Richard F. Fenno (1978) discusses this concept in a very vivid way. When the voters trust a member of parliament, they are willing to admit, "I am willing to put myself in your hand temporarily; I know you will have opportunities to hurt me, although I may not know when these opportunities occur; I assume, and I will continue to assume until it is proven otherwise—that you will not hurt me; for the time being, then I'm not going to worry about your behavior" (Fenno 1978, 56). Fenno states that the voter's trust is something that a politician must create with difficulty and then care for. It requires a lot of effort and time and cannot be developed within a few days or even the whole political campaign. This process takes several years and is developed between campaigns too. Winning the voters' trust and then maintaining it is the basic challenge for all politicians since it may be the key to their reelection; voters who no longer trust "their" congressman will vote for somebody else. The emergence of an attractive competitor may result in more and more floating voters.

The goal of Parker's other study (1989) was a quantitative illustration of direct and indirect relations linking constituent trust to political electoral support. Constituent trust is defined as the level of confidence that constituents have in their elected representative. The measure of constituent trust was derived by Parker from the data of the University of Michigan's National Election Survey from 1978, 1980, and 1984, in which respondents in open-ended questions mentioned some elements of trust as something liked or disliked about their representative. Distrusting responses referred to the incumbent's pursuit of self-interest, lack of integrity or principles, untrustworthiness, dishonesty, or lack of independence from political bosses or parties. Constituent trust was reflected in responses that mentioned the opposite of these traits (e.g., honesty, integrity). The constituted trust index was operationalized by subtracting the number of distrusting responses from the number of trusting responses. The frequency of high trust responses (78 percent) on this measure suggests that constituents maintain fairly high levels of confidence in their congressmen.

In order to determine the validity of this indicator, Parker checked its relation to other variables that should be associated with constituent trust: the perceived helpfulness of the respondent's congressman and the extent to which the respondent agrees with the votes cast by the congressman. The results clearly confirmed the prediction. There were substantial positive correlations between constituent trust and perception of helpfulness and voting agreement.

Parker (1989) assumed that constituent trust influences voting in congressional elections in at least two major ways: indirectly, by influencing the increase in a congressman's popularity, and directly, as influencing the intention to vote for him. The causal relation between trust and popularity was based on the assumption that a voter's trust in a congressman, which she values a lot, is the foundation of her evaluation. Politicians enjoying a lot of trust from their voters have many positive evaluations, contributing to their popularity, whereas the lack of such trust influences negatively their evaluation, contributing to their unpopularity. Popularity then has direct influence on voting in an election. This feature is then understood as a mediating mechanism that translates politicians' perceived activity into the scope of support for them. Congressmen act in such a way, then, as to increase their popularity by generating and increasing higher voter support, thus taking care of their voting "safety." Popularity was operationalized here by a standard feeling thermometer question.

The direct influence of constituent trust on voting support is based on the assumption that such trust makes voters look for the politician's successor, as a result of which a politician loses the support of some of the electorate. Definitely such a model of voting behavior would not be complete if other variables influencing voting behavior were not included. Parker supplemented it, therefore, by congruence in party identification between voter and congressman, the congressman's perceived attention to the district, and personal contact with the incumbent.

The attractiveness and popularity of politicians should then increase according to the number of the voter's meetings with them, participation in political rallies, watching them often in the media, and receiving letters from them. We should then assume that popularity might be gained in the same way by politicians' caring about their voters. This care is demonstrated through their regularly informing their electorate about all the activities of the government, gathering opinions from their constituency, and representing them in Congress. Such an activity often requires the politicians' personal contact with their electorate.

The characteristics of the model's particular elements suggest clearly a complex structure of causal relationship between them, which is presented in Figure 7.2.

Analyses demonstrated that the model has a good fit to empirical data and explains 56 percent of variance of electoral support for the congressman. The different sizes of arrows in Figure 7.2 mean the strength of the influence between the variables. The thicker the arrow, the stronger the influence, which corresponds to a higher value of path coefficient. A dashed line arrow connecting personal contact with a politician with trust in him means that there is no causal relation between them.

The relations show that the influence of personal contact on trust is indirect and is achieved by a politician's caring about his voters (perceived attention to district). This indirect path shows the importance of postelection political activity for keeping the voters. It means that a congressman who does not forget about his voters stands a high chance of maintaining their support, which will have a direct influence on his support during the next political election. It also turns out that congruence in party identification is an important element

Figure 7.2   **Trust in Politicians and Their Popularity in Parker's Model of Voting Behavior**

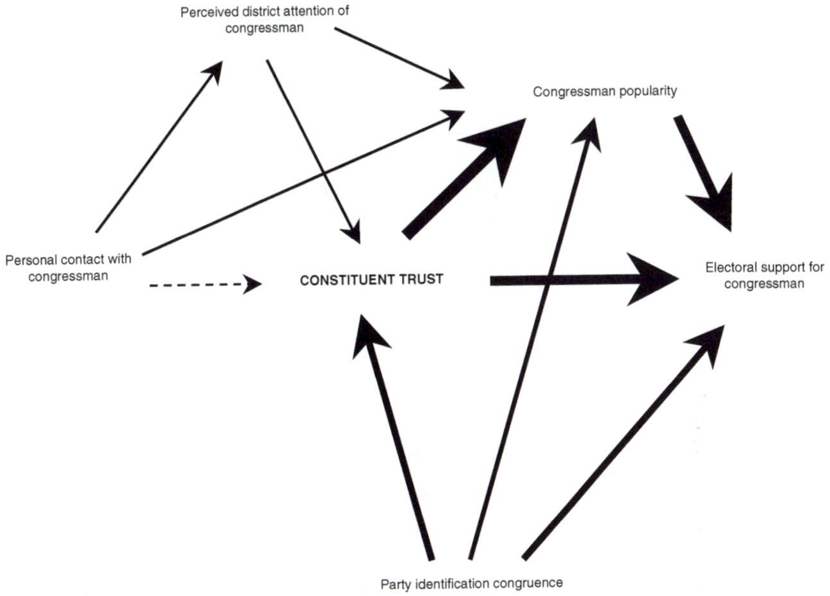

Source: Based on Parker (1989).

forming constituent trust, which, in consequence, influences the politician's popularity. However, the direct relation between congruence and incumbent popularity is much weaker than the direct one—mainly trust. It is another argument supporting the assumption adopted by Parker that it is rather trust that determines popularity. It is natural, then, that a congressman representing an opposition party will evoke voters' high distrust.

We may wonder then if a politician from another party has really little chance of getting the voters' support. Given the fact that the element of partisanship has been getting less and less importance in political elections over the years (see Chapter 3), a politician may think about developing an appropriate marketing strategy. The influence of party affiliation on the support for a politician during the election is negative, which is demonstrated by the negative coefficient of the path connecting congruence in party identification with strength for electoral support. It validates the need to undertake actions strengthening the support for a politician when emphasizing partisanship is not only the most important thing but sometimes not even recommendable. Such an approach puts into the background the role of party identification and expands the scope of the voting situation by other elements influencing trust.

The direct relation between trust and voting support shown by Parker (1989) suggests that this relation does play a crucial role in political elections.

The question arises then whether voters' trust is the only quality ascribed to politicians and influencing their support in elections. There are, after all, a number of other dimensions of candidate evaluation, including particular personal characteristics, leadership qualities, and experience, all of which also seem important to win support. The question was taken up by Parker (1989) in his subsequent analysis, which proved that among these variables constituent trust is the most important influence on electoral support.

There are several implications for marketing strategies related to Parker's research (1989). First of all, politicians should do their best to evoke voters' trust in them. However, it is not a relationship that can be developed during a political campaign, which is held a few weeks before election. It is a feature that a politician needs to develop for at least a few months. It means that political marketing should also be used between elections. The methodology presented here may then be used as a model of developing a method of monitoring voters' trust in a politician. The advantage that it offers is that this characteristic is not treated separately but is related to voters' political preferences or other elements, including those distinguished in the analyzed model (see Figure 7.2).

Another strategic consequence of the research presented here is that trust in a congressman is to some extent independent of the electorate's party affiliation. Trust is particularly important for politicians from opposition minority parties. A congressman from such a party should minimize in her voting strategy the role of partisanship because it may influence trust in a negative way. Stressing her party independence and encouraging the voters to vote for someone from outside the party system, she may in some cases prevent the drop in her own support caused by party identification.

The decreasing importance of party identification that has been observed in elections made researchers look for other voting behavior predictors. Sole trust in a candidate is not enough, though, since it has to be based on some external structures within which such a politician functions. If her political party is not such a point of reference, it may be a state's political system. Analyses including the importance of trust for political behavior were conducted by Suzanne L. Parker and Glenn R. Parker (1993) and also Virginia Chanley, Thomas Rudolph, and Wendy Rahn (2000).

Trust in Political Systems and Politicians

Parker and Parker (1993) analyzed thoroughly the internal structure of voter trust based on the former model of voting behavior (see Figure 7.2), supplementing their analysis by distinguishing between two types of trust: constituents' trust in their representative and political system trust. The researchers assumed that the two kinds of trust are mutually related; it is difficult to trust in politicians if one does not trust in the system that they represent. The researchers also modified the potential set of factors that may influence such trust, including, this time, personal and impersonal contact, economic outlook, tax waste, and socioeconomic status.

Personal contact with the representative is understood as direct meetings with congressmen (e.g., attending a meeting where he spoke), while *impersonal contact* refers to getting to know a politician through the media (e.g., radio, television, press, electronic mail). The more voters hear their congressman in the media, the more trust they should in him. This hypothesis was the foundation of introducing the variable of contact with politicians in Parker's previous research (1989); besides, it is further justified by the fact that in local (state) media in the United States the candidate is usually presented in a more positive way than in all-state media. Local media usually highlight the best features of candidates, thanks to which voters' trust in them may develop.

Economic outlook and tax waste refer to the financial situation and tax waste perceived by voters in their evaluations. Bad management of taxpayers' money refers to the whole country as well as the state of Florida, where the research was conducted. The perceived economic situation was divided into three areas: retrospective and prospective evaluations of the voters' financial position, and perceptions of "good times" in the country's future. Parker and Parker expected that a good financial position (the voters' own and the country's) and not wasting the taxpayers' money—as perceived by the voters—will be followed by a high level of trust in the congressman who represents them.

Since there are examples suggesting a relation between *socioeconomic status* and the level of voters' trust in contemporary literature, Parker and Parker assumed that the relation between these two variables is positive. They predicted then that the higher the status of the voters, the higher their trust of their own representative. The status variable was defined by two indicators of the research: the level of respondents' education and their income.

System trust was defined by the extent to which respondents harbor trusting feelings toward Congress, the executive branch, the Supreme Court, the Florida legislature, and the U.S. government in general. Then *constituents' trust in their U.S. representative* was measured in the same way as in Parker's research (1989), namely by open-ended questions referring to respondents' likes and dislikes about their U.S. House member.

The data in the analysis came from a statewide telephone survey of 989 Floridians eighteen years and older, who were interviewed between January 20

Figure 7.3   **Structural Model of Constituents' Trust in U.S. Representatives**

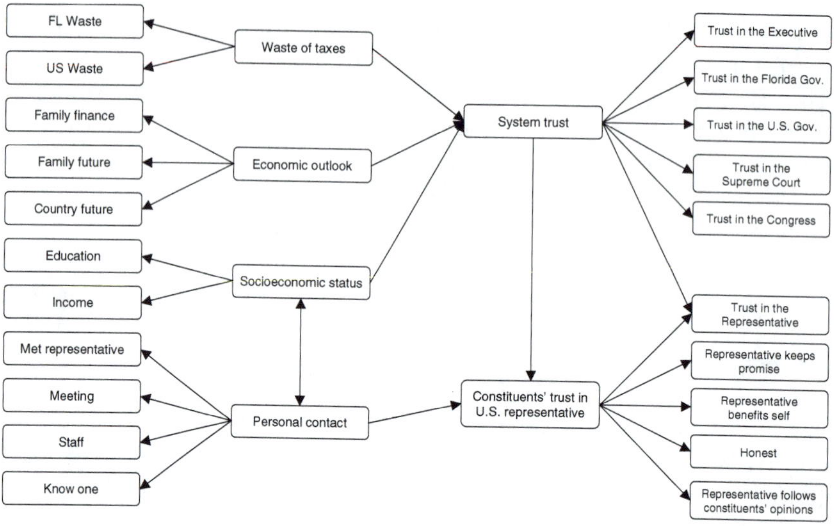

Source: Based on Parker and Parker (1993).

and February 29, 1988. In order to verify their predictions, Parker and Parker conducted confirmatory factor analysis. Their structural model of constituents' trust in U.S. representatives is presented in Figure 7.3.

The size of the arrows in Figure 7.3 represents the differences in the strength of the relations between the variables. The structure of the relations suggests that the efforts made by the congressman can only partly contribute to higher trust in him among the voters. This is illustrated by the path connecting personal contact with constituents' trust. This trust is to a large extent dependent on constituents system trust. In turn, system trust is dependent on a number of important factors that a single member of Congress cannot control: waste of taxes as perceived by voters, economic outlook, and the voter's socioeconomic status. The higher the conviction that taxes are wasted and the more negative the economic consequences (of constituents and the country), the less trust in the system. The consequence of this growing distrust is a drop in trust in constituents's U.S. representatives. Contrary to the predictions, people of lower socioeconomic status were characterized by higher trust in the system. A congressman will not then be able to fully control the element that is so important for political support—namely trust. Voting success does not only depend on the effort put into building trust, but also on a number of socioeconomic coincidences that a candidate cannot control directly and which contribute to developing constituents' trust in the whole political system. It should be emphasized here that the research by Parker and Parker was deliberately conducted in a period when no political elections were taking place so that political campaigns would not distort their results.

Trust in the political system is closely related to trust in government, which was the focus of the research conducted by Chanley, Rudolph, and Rahn (2000). They conducted a study on trust in the U.S. national government from 1980 to 1997. Their primary interest was to determine which factors are most responsible for causing the fluctuations in public trust in government. The authors applied path analysis, which showed that the key factor influencing the scope of trust in government is subjective perception of crime and political scandals. A lesser but nevertheless important influence was economic expectation. Obviously these criteria for evaluating the government do influence constituents' trust in members of Congress. However, they are beyond the members' control, which was demonstrated by Parker and Parker.

Following Chanley and her collaborators' study, we may pose the question whether a congressman may also control these variables, thus developing constituents' trust in him. It should be emphasized that the important variable influencing the level of trust was not the objective level of crime but its subjective perception. Such subjective perception is often formed by the media, just like political scandals, which also may be publicized by the media. Thus, an avoidance of scandal, skillful handling of the economy, and alleviation of public concern about crime each may help to restore public confidence in government.

Therefore, even those factors influencing constituents' trust in the political system and, indirectly, in the congressman, who at first glance he is not able to control, may in fact be controlled by him, at least to some extent. A particularly important role is played here by the media by priming particular problems, such as crime or political scandals. In this way these problems also become more important in voters' minds.

Timing of Political Events

It is obvious that in the period between the elections the popularity of politicians from both the ruling and the opposition party depends on a number of social, political, and economic events. The barometer of voters' feelings keeps fluctuating, following the positive or negative aspect of various events. Definitely, it is very difficult to control the nature of these events, which is often the result of coincidences not related to a politician's current activities. For instance, economic decisions of the former government may bring about changes only after a few years, resulting in a dramatic increase or decrease of unemployment.

However, politicians can undertake actions controlling voters' perceptions of both positive and negative events. Analyses dealing with time information management, whose goal is to minimize voters' disapproval and maximize their satisfaction with ruling politicians, were conducted within the frame of a *theory of politicians' timing of events*, presented by John Gibson (1999). It is based on well-developed and empirically validated psychological theories. Before presenting these theories as well as their practical implications for controlling time event presentation, we will analyze a particular example based on Gibson (1999, 471–472), showing the dilemma of a politician wondering when to inform voters about a certain political event.

The Conservative Member of Parliament for Newbury, Judith Chaplin, died suddenly in February, ten months after the common election. The then Conservative government of John Major had to make a difficult decision: when to announce a by-election. The problem was that at that time the prime minister and his government were very unpopular after their failure to meet their voting promises about improving the country's economic situation, the UK's departure from the European Exchange Rate Mechanism in 1992, which was to stabilize the value of European currencies, and the Conservative Party's ambiguous position toward ratification of the Maastricht treaty. (The treaty led to the creation of the euro currency, and created what is commonly referred to as the pillar structure of the European Union.) No wonder then those polls were very unfavorable for the prime minister and his party, constituting a serious threat to his position. In this situation the Conservative Party could expect the worst—losing the seat in Parliament after the by-election. However, the prime minister had trumps in his hand because he was responsible for setting the date of the by-election. The decision on the timing of the by-election lay with the prime minister because in Britain the decision on the choice of date on which to hold a by-election is, by convention, in the hands of the chief whip of the party that won the seat at the previous general election.

Prime Minister Major had two choices, one of which was to time the by-election together with the local government election, which takes place every year in May. However, this election could also be a failure for the party for the same reasons. This option was supported by the idea expressed by a well-known English political commentator, Philip Stephens, in the *Financial Times*: "The assumption is that it is better to get the bad news from both out of the way on the same day" (Gibson 1999, 472). The second option was to wait until late June in the hope that by then the government would be more popular given the chances that the economy would be more fully recovered from recession and conflicts over Maastricht would have had subsided. Major chose the first option—to hold the by-election on the same day as the local elections. As anticipated, the Conservatives did very poorly in both the local government elections and the by-election. They recorded their worst performance in local elections and lost the by-election to the Liberal Democratic Party. Although it seems that the option of holding two elections on the same day resulted in lots of losses for the ruling party, it will be shown later that according to prospect theory (Kahneman and Tversky 1979) it was the right action.

What type of political event is a by-election? In order to determine that, we could classify possible events influencing the popularity of the ruling politicians. Among all the events we can distinguish between recurring events and nonrecurring, one-off events that happen only once. Recurring events may be regular or irregular. An example of a regular recurring event is a monthly unemployment report from a government agency; an example of an irregular recurring event is a parliamentary by-election. These events can be divided according to their frequency; according to the level of control over them (controlled or uncontrolled events, the latter often being one-off events, such as an earthquake or energy crisis); or according to their predictability (predictable and unpredictable events). An example of an irregular and predictable event would be a visit of a head of another state, planned usually a few months ahead. Each event may then have a predictable character over a short period of time, as is the case with the by-election discussed above, or be unpredictable over a long period of time.

We can classify then the example of the by-election as recurring, irregular, and unpredictable over a long period of time. It becomes predictable and may be controlled over a shorter period of time only when it is known that there is a vacant seat in Parliament and decisions about timing the by-election have to be made.

Psychological Foundations of the Management of the Times of Events

The main goal of politicians, both incumbents and opposition, is to present (mainly in the media) social and political events in such a way that the political costs they incur are minimized and profits maximized. Efficient management in this field is based on psychological rules of learning, including memory and minimizing risk while making decisions.

Every general psychology manual and some psychological application handbooks present such basic learning processes as classical and instrumental conditioning and the rules of memory's functioning (e.g., Kosslyn and Rosenberg 2004; Roediger 2008). It seems that the first area that should be

Figure 7.4   **Forgetting Curve**

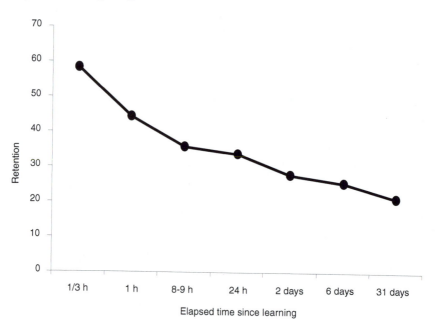

addressed, from the perspective of management of event presentation time, is the functioning of human memory.

The forgetting curve presented in Figure 7.4 represents a typical course of learning. It shows that knowledge gained at the beginning of the learning process is quite high, whereas after some time and after more knowledge has been gained, the level drops. In addition, a memory trace once formed is not lost, but its strength may decay. Studies of long-term retention show gradual but continuous forgetting. This phenomenon of the decreasing amount of knowledge in the human mind after it was learned is described as power function of forgetting (e.g., Kosslyn and Rosenberg 2004).

A theory explaining forgetting is the so-called interferential concept of forgetting, where two fundamental processes can be distinguished: retroactive and proactive interference. *Retroactive interference* consists in overlapping remembered stimuli with stimuli learned after. In other words, memory content is lost only when it is replaced by some other content. *Proactive interference* is a reverse process, where previously gained knowledge makes it difficult for someone to remember new information. From the perspective of management of political event presentation time, it is retroactive interference that is very important. The amount of presented information expunges from memory earlier preserved information. Presenting in the media events that are not favorable for the ruling politicians should then be preceded by favorable events, which, following the rule of interference, will make it more difficult to remember the unfavorable events.

Another psychological regularity refers to one of Jost's laws of forgetting and concerns material distribution or spacing effects of repetition on material's recall and recognition. Adolf Jost (see Roediger 2008; Woodworth and Schlosberg 1954) presented subjects with sequences of meaningless syllables to remember in two different configurations. He repeated them once thirty times during one day to one group and ten times within three days to the other. In both cases, on the following day after the thirty drills were completed, the sequence was repeated until a subject was able to repeat it without any errors. It turned out that with integrated repetition more repetitions were needed to remember the sequence again than with repetition distributed over time. In other words, Jost observed a very clear advantage of distributed over massed repetitions.

According to this law, in planning a presentation of events favorable for politicians, at the beginning they are presented in every TV news program, but later the frequency of such presentations is limited—they are presented only in a few TV news programs. A similar presentation of such events in other media, including newspapers or information magazines, is distributed in time because reruns of the same program over time are more efficient than accumulated presentations.

What is also important here is the place of this information in the whole information block. Research shows that people remember better the beginning and end of a sequence of elements rather than the middle part (see Kosslyn and Rosenberg 2004). This pattern is caused by the strong influence of retroactive and proactive interference on the middle part.

A more complex way of describing cognitive functioning is prospect theory developed by Daniel Kahneman and Amos Tversky (1979). They made a number of assumptions about how people judge gains and losses. Formulating these assumptions, they aimed at juxtaposing the concept of rationality to people's actual behavior under risk. In fact the rational implications of prospect theory depart considerably from the traditional model of maximizing subjective expected utility (SEU), described for the first time by Leonard Savage (1954). These assumptions are presented in Figure 7.5.

The shape of the value or utility function is different for gains and losses. Its characteristic feature is that the function is steeper for losses than for gains. It means that a loss is more painful than a gain is pleasurable. For instance, the impact of losing $1,000 will be stronger than the impact of gaining $1,000. Besides, the function is concave for gains; subsequent gains are accompanied by smaller and smaller utility gains. The function of value for losses is

Figure 7.5   **Gains and Losses According to Prospect Theory**

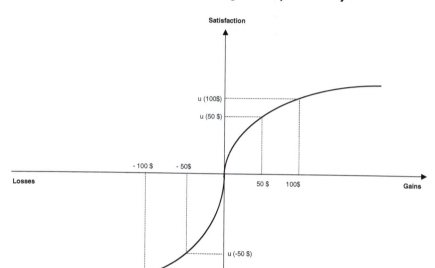

convex, which means that subsequent increases in losses are accompanied by smaller and smaller increases in disappointment (grief). The characteristics of the utility function can be illustrated in the following way. For gains, the subjective distance (difference) between the gain of $0 and $500 is greater than the difference between $500 and $1,000. So is the case with losses—the subjective distance (difference) between the loss of $0 and $500 is greater than the loss between $500 and $1,000. A loss of $1,000 subjectively seems to be smaller than two separate losses, each $500. Again, the gain of $1,000 is perceived to be smaller than two smaller gains, $500 each (see Figure 7.5). These fundamental principles of valuing have a lot of practical implications, the most interesting of which refers to mental accounting.

Richard Thaler (1980) formulated a number of rules of mental accounting resulting from the value function for gains and losses described in prospect theory. As far as the management of political events presentation time is concerned, two rules seem to be important: the rule of segregate gains and integrate losses.

The rule of segregate gains posits that our satisfaction with a few smaller gains is greater than with one greater gain that is the sum of those smaller gains. For instance, a customer who receives another product while buying something gets satisfaction with buying two products. Insurance companies offer discounts for accident-free driving and renewing the contract. In this way the customer feels satisfaction with two separate gains. According to the *rule of integrate losses*, we feel less disappointed with one big loss than with a loss consisting of smaller losses. For instance, selling life insurance, mishap insurance, and so on in packages makes customers more satisfied than if they bought these products separately. Also the payments made with credit cards are accumulated at the end of the month because the payment or loss seems to be smaller than a number of individual payments.

The rules resulting from perspective theory as well as the principles of learning and memory functioning are used (consciously or not) in developing marketing methods of controlling the time of presenting political, economic, and social events.

Theory and Practice Over Management of Political Events

John Gibson (1999) presents four hypotheses resulting from the psychological principles of managing the event presentation time that find practical application in politicians' political activity. These hypotheses, as rules of action, also may be used as foundations for developing marketing strategies used in postelection periods:

1. *Integrating events (packaging)*. Politicians, if they can, try to integrate all the negative information in one media presentation—that is, they present all the negative information at the same time.
2. *Separating events (splitting)*. Politicians, if this is technically possible, try to divide information about positive events into a number of independently presented pieces of news.

These two hypotheses clearly result from perspective theory. The example of the British by-election described above, in which the by-election was combined with the local Newbury constituency election, confirms the effect of a few (predicted) negative events integrated into one. The implications for politicians are the following: if two pieces of bad news appear at the same time, they are going to do less harm for the image of the party or politician than if they are presented separately. On the other hand, if good news is distributed over time—for instance, if each piece appears in a different edition of a newspaper—it will be more profitable for a party or politician than if they are presented together (see Figure 7.5).

3. *Attracting attention (highlighting)*. Politicians try to make sure that bad news is presented in a place or time when voters' attention is small. Good news is presented when voters' attention is the highest.

These hypotheses refer to structural characteristics of the media. Main TV news is broadcast in prime time, when viewers' attention is the highest. Newspaper readers also focus on front pages. Because TV time or the place of presenting a particular event in newspapers is limited by the number of competing events, politicians try to manage the viewer's or reader's attention. They present "bad" events together with attractive events, diverting the viewer's or reader's attention from the negative ones. "Good" events are presented against the backdrop of less interesting events. This rule is obviously connected with the rule of packaging events, because other pieces of competing news presented together with negative events make people focus less on the latter.

4. *Sequencing events (phasing)*. Politicians control the presentation of events by phasing in more positive information about them than negative information as the campaign is approaching. Besides, bad news precedes good news while being announced. This hypothesis is justified by the principles of memory and learning discussed above. It is also consistent with Nordhaus's (1975) classical analysis of the political business cycle. The specific case he examined was the behavior of a democratic government that faces choices between present and future state welfare—that is, the trade-off between inflation and unemployment. In this context, the typical political business cycle will run as follows: immediately after an election the winner will raise unemployment to some relatively high level in order to combat inflation. As elections approach, the unemployment rate will be lowered until, on election eve, the unemployment rate will be lowered to a purely myopic point.

In his article Gibson (1999) presents analyses of politicians' actual behaviors that confirm the hypothesis he formulated. Those cases refer to a by-election to the British parliament, National Health Service prescription charges, and the timing of changes in the official monetary discount rate.

By-Elections

The rules of packaging for negative events and splitting good ones resulting from prospect theory have practical application in the strategy of announcing the date of British by-elections. Politicians from the ruling party become less popular than those from the opposition party quite soon after winning an election. This happens because voters develop too high expectations during the political campaign and also because various negative economic events

Figure 7.6 **Packaging and Splitting British Parliamentary By-Elections**

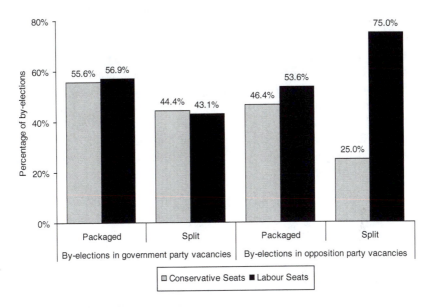

Source: Based on Gibson (1999).

occur. The fact that politicians cannot meet these expectations translates into their and their party losing popularity and voters getting more interested in the opposition party.

The case of the by-election to the British parliament in May 1993 described by Gibson is an example of combining two events that had negative resonance for the ruling party. Figure 7.6 shows figures presented by Gibson related to announcing such elections to the British parliament from 1955 to 1997.

The results clearly validate the hypotheses about packaging negative events and splitting positive ones in by-elections over a period of more than forty years. The Conservative Party during its periods in power used the strategy of packaging such political events in 55.6 percent of the total number of 136 elections, whereas as opposition it packaged the elections in 47.4 percent. These differences are even greater for the Labour Party. Out of the total number of 147 elections, 56 percent of the events were packaged when the party was in power compared to only 25 percent when it was in opposition. In the most recent of the observed years, fewer and fewer by-elections were conducted by the ruling parties because they suffered a lot of defeats during them. The Conservative Party, ruling between 1979 and 1997, conducted only thirty-four by-elections, usually integrating at least two of them at the same time.

The rule of packaging bad news and splitting good news finds its validation in setting British by-elections. It does not mean, of course, that politicians know perspective theory. Their actions seem to result from the rationale expressed by the chair of the Conservative Party, Norman Tebbitt, in 1986: "In early May we did poorly in the local elections and in the two more by-elections which were held on the same day to avoid two days of bad news rather than one" (Gibson 1999, 485). In this context, perspective theory should be treated as an intuitive way of describing politicians' behavior rather than a set of rules according to which politicians consciously plan the timing of good and bad news. But it may be used strategically for developing a plan of political actions.

National Health Service Prescription Charges

Every price rise or additional fee for public services is perceived in a negative way by voters. Sometimes, however, such actions are necessary to improve the working of various public institutions, including, for instance, the National Health Service, which offers services to all citizens in the United Kingdom. The Conservative government decided to subsidize this public institution by systematically raising the fees for issuing prescriptions well above the inflation level.

According to the rule of attracting attention, politicians should present news about price rises in the context of either positive or neutral information in order to divert citizens' attention from the negative event. Table 7.1 presents the exact day when each of the higher fees for issuing prescriptions was announced from 1990 to 1995. The timing of the announcement of increases on at least four of the five occasions took place when another unusually salient or important event that was bound to dominate the news was also occurring. Respectively, these were an opposition poll tax debate in the House of Commons at the height of its unpopularity; the release of the jobless figures when they showed their highest level for four years; the prime minister's talks with President Boris Yeltsin in Moscow; and the release of the government's "Strategy for Peace" proposals for Northern Ireland (see Table 7.1).

The third event, which was the return of detention centers, was certainly less important than the other events but it was featured on the front pages of the most widely read newspapers, which must have attracted readers' attention. Politicians were able to time the presentation of these events in such a way that the negative news concerning higher prescription fees could be presented simultaneously.

Table 7.1

Increase of Fees for Prescriptions Issued by National Health Service in Great Britain, 1990–1995

Date of increase	Size of increase compared to inflation rate	Other news events
March 1, 1990	8.9 (7.5)	Opposition poll Tax debate
February 13, 1992	7.5 (3.7)	Release of worst jobless figures for four years
March 3, 1993	13.3 (1.7)	Return of detention centers
February 7, 1994	10.0 (2.4)	John Major's meeting with Boris Yeltsin in Moscow
February 23,1995	10.5 (3.3)	Release of Northern Ireland peace proposals

Source: Based on Gibson (1999).

The pattern of introducing increases presented in Table 7.1 illustrates the rule of attracting attention (highlighting). Concentrating on the other event, the voter does not focus on the negative situation related to higher prescription fees. In this way politicians try to manage their electorate's disappointment and take care of their popularity. The amount and frequency of the increases also suggest using the rule of splitting events. It was much more profitable for the politicians to have one annual increase exceeding considerably the level of inflation than a few smaller increases introduced every few months. A rise is a negative event and integrating such moves is less painful for the society than splitting them, which is confirmed by perspective theory.

Interest Rate Changes in British Money Market

Each government is directly involved in financial policy related to interest rates, because controlling the money market allows it to control interest rates of mortgages. The government needs this kind of influence tool to achieve higher voter support, which could be observed on the British political scene. David Sanders (1991) proved that an important element influencing support for the Conservative government was its ability to manipulate interest rates in such a way that it led to economic optimism, which, in turn, translated into the government's popularity in the 1980s. The sensitivity of governments to the level of interest and lending rates in the economy, especially in the British context, because of their effect on mortgage lending rates, is a commonly accepted phenomenon. The rationality of this perception has been backed up by recent analyses of the determinants of party support in the United Kingdom, which found that the level of interest rates, through its effect on economic optimism, was the most important economic influence on public support for the Conservative governments during the 1980s (Sanders 1991).

Obviously interest rates as a reaction to inflation are regulated by the economic situation. However, the government or central bank (if it is autonomous) has some freedom in setting such interest rates independent of the market rules. One should of course take into account the economic consequences of such a proceeding, which in Britain was clearly used for political goals not related to the economy, mainly for controlling politicians' popularity. In the 1970s and 1980s, the Bank of England was controlled by the British government and advised it on financial policy (Goodhart 1989).

Many analysts of the money market in Great Britain expressed their disapproval of the government's financial policy, stressing that it was not related to the economy and that the interest rates that were introduced at that time were driven not by the market but by politicians' attempts to maintain power. Such activities led to some chaos on the money market, but also were controlled in order to avoid serious problems on the market. Detailed analyses of the Conservative government's reasons for using particular financial policies are presented by Charles Goodhart (1984) and Michael Moran (1986).

We might wonder then whether it is possible to prove that controlling interest rates is related to politicians' voting strategy. Figure 7.7 presents changes in interest rates under eleven governments in Great Britain.

The results show that almost every government cut down interest rates more often than it raised them. Between 1951 and 1992 the number of cuts was 142, whereas the number of rises was 70—half as many. What was paradoxical about the whole situation was that although the number of cuts was considerably higher, their average rate was only 0.49 percent, whereas the average rate of rise was 1.1 percent, which is twice as much.

This seemingly paradoxical government policy of controlling interest rates in the money market can be better understood in light of perspective theory. It is consistent with the rule of integrating negative events and splitting positives ones. Raising interest rates is not welcome by voters; therefore, it should not occur too often. However, each increase should be considerable (aggregating increases). But a reduction of interest rates is very welcome; therefore, there should be as many such events as possible (splitting reductions). Using such a strategy develops politicians' popularity.

We could suspect then that ruling politicians try to control interest rates during their term in office in order to maintain their popularity. Data related to the dynamics of the magnitude of the rate changes helps us to define yet another rule, namely the phasing aspect of the timing of interest rate changes. According to this rule, politicians control presentation of events by phasing in more positive news than negative news as the campaign approaches. This

Figure 7.7 **Number and Magnitude of Interest Rate Changes: British Governments, 1951–1992**

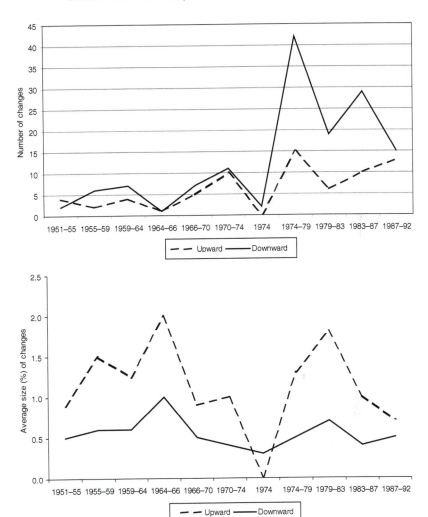

Source: Adapted on the basis of Gibson's data (1999).

rule is illustrated by Figure 7.8, presenting changes in the official lending rate during the first two years compared to the remainder of the period of office of successive governments.

We clearly can see that almost every government in the first years of its period in office made unpopular decisions about considerable increases in

Figure 7.8   **Changes in Official Lending Rate During First Two Years Compared to Remainder of Period of Office: Successive UK Governments**

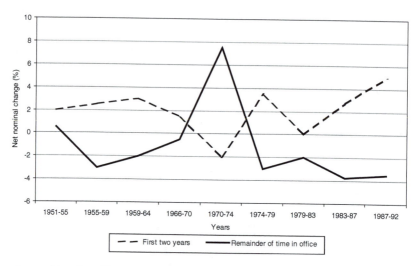

Source: Based on Gibson (1999).

interest rates, whereas in the remainder of the period in office, when the election campaign was approaching, the government often decided to reduce the rates. In summing up the difference between the increases and reductions of interest rates presented in Figure 7.8 for each government during the first two and the last two years then, the rules of phasing in the timing of changes in controlling the money market are obvious. In the first two years the sum is +18.25 and in the last two years it is –9.79.

In fact, it is not only the money market that can be used for controlling the popularity of the ruling party. Such control also can be exerted by such instruments of macroeconomic policy as inflation and unemployment to achieve political objectives by representative governments: to maximize their share of the vote at the next election (Nordhaus 1975). We might wonder, however, if everybody is susceptible to such activities, where a party's popularity is controlled by higher or lower unemployment or inflation. A study on the importance of such instruments of macroeconomic policy for the popularity of the government was conducted by Paul Mosley (1978), and his observation was that so-called floating voters were most sensitive to such a strategy because they are characterized by a pragmatic approach toward political reality. They constitute an important segment of the voting market that can be relatively easily influenced by various marketing strategies (see Chapter 3). These voters are absolute opposites of the voters firmly "frozen" into partisanship on behalf of one party or another (e.g., Conservative or Labour in the United Kingdom or Democratic or Republican in the United States), whom no economic improvement can convert. The growing number of floating voters who are sensitive to changes in economic variables considerably influences the results of various elections. Mosley, referring to psychological processes, noticed that voters do not take simple averages of economic variables over the last electoral period, but have a decaying "memory" of past events. On Election Day, the memory of recent events is more vivid and clearer than that of older events (see the forgetting curve in Figure 7.4). This is the result of using particular methods of controlling presentation timing of economic events, which is illustrated by the results presented in Figure 7.8.

Mosley tested his concept, which shows that voters' preferences will appear to change when and only when "trigger levels" of unemployment or inflation are crossed. Using various combinations of regression analysis, he demonstrated that such variables as unemployment crisis periods and inflationary crisis periods significantly explain the dependent variable: the governing party's lead over the principal opposition party.

We should note that cyclic fluctuations in unemployment and price inflation do not necessarily have to influence the government's popularity. We could put forward a hypothesis then proposing a completely different relation: a certain level of popularity influences the control of these economic variables. A government's low popularity and an approaching election force political actions aimed at reducing inflation or unemployment. Such causal relations, where the popularity of the government regulates various economic variables, could be observed in the British money market (see Figure 7.9).

Marketing-Oriented Parliament

The analyses of voters' trust in politicians and political systems conducted by Glenn Parker (1977, 1989; Parker and Parker 1993) clearly show that these two elements are important mechanisms regulating the support offered to politicians between particular elections. The issue related to the perception of the political system and, particularly, the government and its actions was also undertaken by Jennifer Lees-Marshment (2003). She postulated, within her concept of comprehensive political marketing (see Chapter 2), that it is not only parties that should adopt a marketing orientation in developing their activities on the political scene but also Parliament. Her proposal is presented in detail in Figure 7.9.

According to Lees-Marshment, the democratic system and parliamentary

Figure 7.9   **Marketing-Oriented Parliament**

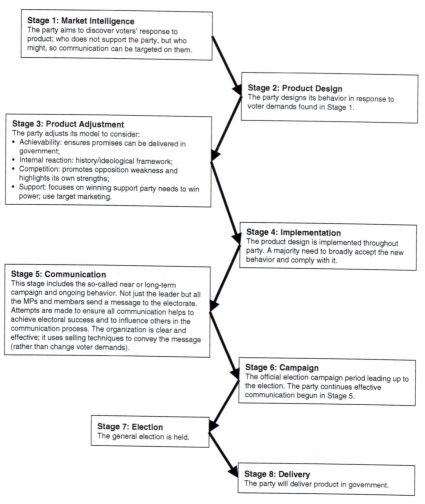

Stage 1: Market Intelligence
The party aims to discover voters' response to product; who does not support the party, but who might, so communication can be targeted on them.

Stage 2: Product Design
The party designs its behavior in response to voter demands found in Stage 1.

Stage 3: Product Adjustment
The party adjusts its model to consider:
- Achievability: ensures promises can be delivered in government;
- Internal reaction: history/ideological framework;
- Competition: promotes opposition weakness and highlights its own strengths;
- Support: focuses on winning support party needs to win power; use target marketing.

Stage 4: Implementation
The product design is implemented throughout party. A majority need to broadly accept the new behavior and comply with it.

Stage 5: Communication
This stage includes the so-called near or long-term campaign and ongoing behavior. Not just the leader but all the MPs and members send a message to the electorate. Attempts are made to ensure all communication helps to achieve electoral success and to influence others in the communication process. The organization is clear and effective; it uses selling techniques to convey the message (rather than change voter demands).

Stage 6: Campaign
The official election campaign period leading up to the election. The party continues effective communication begun in Stage 5.

Stage 7: Election
The general election is held.

Stage 8: Delivery
The party will deliver product in government.

Source: Adapted from Lees-Marshment (2003).

work can be perceived in a more positive way and fully understood by citizens only when they are thoroughly informed about those areas. Therefore, strategies of postelection marketing should not be limited to political parties and their leaders. They should be extended to Parliament, beyond party differences and divisions, in order to make citizens get more actively involved in democratic procedures, which should lead to their satisfaction with this participation as well as stronger democracy and more control over particular governments.

8

Political Marketing and Democracy

Politics may be defined, as is proposed by David Miller (1987), as a process whereby a group of people whose opinions or interests are initially divergent reach collective decisions that are generally regarded as binding on the group and enforced as common policy. Politics presupposes diversity of views, if not about ultimate aims, at least about the best means of achieving them. When people agree spontaneously on a course of action, or more importantly when they are able to reach unanimity simply through unconstrained discussion, they have no need to engage in politics. The goal of politics and politicians is then to try to satisfy needs and expectations of the people as well as their well-being and to constantly improve the quality of life.

Expansion of politics can be observed all over the world. According to Giovanni Sartori (1970), to some extent politics has gotten objectively bigger because the world is becoming more and more politicized—more participation, more mobilization, and in any case more state intervention in formerly nongovernmental spheres. In no small measure, however, politics is subjectively bigger in that people have shifted the focus of attention both toward the periphery of politics (in the context of governmental process) and toward its input side.

In his *Politics* (1995 [c. 350 B.C.E.]), Aristotle wrote that humans are created to live in the political state. Despite the many centuries that have since passed, this statement is still valid and has inspired many theoreticians and practitioners studying the life of people under many social systems. However, it has been modified many times in order to keep it up-to-date with the changing picture of humans shaping their conditions in life. In social psychology, the statement was popularized by Elliot Aronson (1992), who coined the notion of humans as *social animals*. Sociology, particularly the sociology of politics, treats individuals, to use Seymour M. Lipset's term (1981), as *homo politicus*. All these concepts point to the fact that people may fulfill their goals and desires only when they belong to a group, namely society. And because they belong to such a group, they must also obey the rules and standards that prevail there.

Democracy is currently the main form of people's organization of themselves within state structures in the world. Despite being often criticized, this system is spreading across the world and is becoming the final destination for many societies under authoritarian power (see Huntington 1991). A fundamental element of the idea of democracy is that the authorization to exercise state power must arise from collective decisions by the equal members of a society who are governed by that power. According to a deliberative conception of democracy, decisions are collective when they arise from arrangements of binding collective choice that establish conditions of free public reasoning among equals who are governed by the decisions (Dahl 2000). In the deliberative conception, then, citizens treat each other as equals not by giving equal consideration to all interests, but by offering justifications for the exercise of collective power framed in terms of considerations that can, roughly speaking, be acknowledged by all as reasons.

According to Dahl (2000), the idea of deliberative democracy has three main features. First, a requirement that justification of the exercise of collective power involves deliberation, understood as a presentation of reasons of an acceptable kind in support of proposals. Second, a mutual commitment on the part of citizens to accept and follow that requirement, thus treating political power as their collective power. Third, a framework of social and institutional arrangements that fosters free reasoning among equal citizens by providing favorable conditions for expression, association, and participation, and tying the exercise of public power to public reasoning, by establishing a framework ensuring the responsiveness and accountability of political power to it through regular competitive elections, conditions of publicity, legislative oversight, and so on.

No matter whether a particular democracy is candidate-, party leader-, party-, or government-oriented, in order to exist and develop, every modern democracy needs the following six institutions (Dahl 2000):

1. *Elected representatives.* They constitute the parliament elected by citizens and their major task is to control the government's decisions.
2. *Free, honest, and frequent elections.* People are neither forced to participate in such elections nor are they forced to elect a given person or political party.
3. *Freedom of speech.* Citizens have the right and absolute freedom to express their political views without fear of punishment. They can criticize their representatives, government, or system.

4. *Access to various sources of information.* Citizens have the right to seek political information from many different sources, independent of the government power or other monopolies present.
5. *Freedom of association.* Citizens, if they wish, should have a chance to establish independent associations and organizations, including political parties and interest groups.
6. *Inclusive citizenship.* This means that no adult having the citizenship of a given country may be deprived of the rights that others enjoy and that are essential for democratic institutions.

Students of political life are most interested in the first two democratic institutions mentioned by Dahl (2000): elected representatives and free, frequent, and honest elections. These two elements of democracy are the main areas in the research involving citizens' voting behaviors and ways of influencing these behaviors through political marketing (see also Cwalina, Falkowski, and Newman 2008). However, the idea of deliberative democracy and changes in modern societies clearly suggest that such a narrowing of political marketing's interest is outdated and requires modernization. Political marketing is not only limited to the activities taken up by politicians and political parties during elections. It can and should be used to establish, maintain, and enhance relationships between the governing and various social groups: "ordinary" citizens, nongovernmental organizations, interest groups and corporate lobbyists, the media, and other politicians and political parties. This can be achieved by a mutual exchange and fulfillment of promises, analogically to the stakeholder theory of the corporation (see, e.g., Donaldson and Preston 1995; Freeman and Evan 1990). Stakeholders are persons or groups with legitimate interests in procedural and substantive aspects of corporate activity. They are identified by their interests in the corporation, whether the corporation has any corresponding functional interests in them. The stakeholder management requires then simultaneous attention to the legitimate interests of all appropriate stakeholders, both in the establishment of organizational structures and general policies and in case-by-case decision-making.

The advanced model of political marketing presented here is an attempt to include the changes taking place in modern democracies and turning political marketing into political marketing science. It is an attempt to introduce a new logic for political marketing. According to what Stephen L. Vargo and Robert F. Lusch (2004) suggest, discarding the other political marketing models and approaches is not required. Their observations are to a large extent based on the studies of Bruce Newman (1994, 1999c), Wojciech Cwalina, Andrzej Falkowski, and Bruce Newman (2009), Stephen Henneberg and Nicholas O'Shaughnessy (2007; Henneberg 2008), Phil Harris (2001a, 2001b; Harris and Rees 2000; Lock and Harris 1996), Paul Baines (2005; Baines et al. 2002, 2003), Dominic Wring (1997, 1999), and many other scholars, and they try to refocus and broaden perspective through reorientation rather than reinvention.

The Advanced Model of Political Marketing: An Application

The presented advanced model of political marketing may find its application in various areas of modern social and economic life in democratic societies, including their cultural and political differences. Above all, it directly translates into ways of planning and managing political election campaigns. Depending on its level (local vs. national vs. regional), type (e.g., presidential vs. parliamentary elections), and system conditions (candidate-, party leader-, party-, or government-oriented), the advanced model of political marketing demonstrates regularities in campaign activity. It describes and suggests an empirically justified approach to message development and dissemination and the need and ways of building relationships between candidates and voters and, what is also important, between citizens and government and other democratic institutions local (e.g., parliament) and regional (e.g., the EU parliament). Its integral element is the promise concept, but not from the perspective of the promises one needs to make to influence citizens' behavior. Fulfilling promises that have been given is equally important as a means of achieving citizens' satisfaction and maintaining their support. If promises are not kept, the evolving relationship between politicians and citizens cannot be maintained and enhanced. This may lead to citizens withdrawing from political life, developing a cynical attitude toward both politicians and democratic institutions, and refusing to get involved in social activities (see Chapter 7). Furthermore, developing knowledge and reflection on political marketing may also benefit in improving communication with voters and the public, increasing the quality of governing and working of state institutions, and planning of responsible election campaigns.

As Patrick Butler, Neil Collins, and Martin Fellenz (2007) indicate, political expressions do not take the form only of voting behavior. It may well be that marketing analyses can identify, draw attention to, and substantially inform understanding of nonvoting behaviors as expressions of citizens' political activity (see also Dalton 2007). Many citizens think of politics as concerned with the legislature, parties, voting, and so on. But their politics is the everyday experience of government-run, publicly owned institutions. While some might perceive such matters as belonging to the realm of public administration, the condition of the local school and the length of the hospital queue are, fundamentally, political issues. The level, quality, and cost of public services are at the core of politics. Moreover, as Charles Lamb (1987) states, because government agencies are owned essentially by citizens, potential clients often have performance expectations that exceed their expectations for private organizations. Regardless of whether citizens use the services offered, they pay for these activities indirectly with their taxes. Public agencies have a much more comprehensive interrelationship with the general public than do their private sector counterparts. For this reason, the manner in which services are delivered becomes a central focus for analysis in political marketing. Thus, the advanced model of political marketing shares significant common ground with public sector management.

The advanced model of political marketing may also be useful for nonprofit organizations, interest groups, and corporate lobbyists. It may equip these groups with a set of strategies and tools, thanks to which they will be able to publicize their interests and influence government decisions. The model is particularly important in relation to human rights and environmental concerns. To face those issues and try to solve them, as Ian McAllister and Donley Studlar (1995) state, all political parties have to adapt to New Politics concerns. Although political change may occur at the mass level, this does not mean that it is automatically translated into change at the elite level. Government is unlikely to adopt a radical position toward many of the salient issues of today, for fear of marginalizing its actual supporters. However, if these supporters appear to be aware and concerned about a particular issue, then it would be wise for the government and political parties to take note when planning their policy proposals (see Freestone and McGoldrick 2007). The process of adaptation by which parties and/or governments change their outlooks to accommodate changes at the mass level may be very useful, for example by strategic public relations, agenda-building, issue-framing, and message dissemination proposed here in the advanced model of political marketing.

Many problems that politicians face are global in nature—terrorist threats, economic crises, epidemics (e.g., AIDS, influenza), the greenhouse effect, and more and more poverty areas. Meeting those challenges requires coordination on the local and very often supraregional level—not only by particular governments, but also by such international institutions as the United Nations and its agencies (e.g., UNICEF, WHO), the European Union, the International Monetary Fund, and the Organization for Security and Co-operation in Europe. However, all the activities undertaken in those areas are always exposed to the scrutiny of global public opinion. Therefore, the advanced model of political marketing may also turn out to be useful in planning communication adapted to particular target groups of the mass public; it may also improve the working of the decision-making institutions. It may help all these actors bridge perceptual differences and avoid conflict over policy decisions.

Political Marketing: Implications for Democracy

It is undeniable that current social and cultural changes have led to the development of an information society, where information has become its fundamental resource and where processing information has become an important source of the society's gross national product. In a truly democratic manner, each member of society has the right to inform others and to be informed. The new forms of social and political life in the information society can increase people's access to democracy and administration procedures. We must then be able to transform information into knowledge, which is the task of media education (Toffler and Toffler 1994).

Information technology, which is already a key element of society's life, can be considered advantageous as it facilitates the development of cognitive structures through which people learn how to transform information into knowledge. We have to remember, however, that the world of "virtual reality" is being constructed with information. Information creates a new category of market products that can be sold to create profits. Therefore, people might be tempted to use information as a tool to achieve power and control over society. For example, Edward Herman and Noam Chomsky (1988), in their propaganda model of a mass media system, maintain that the elite class, governments, major media, and other corporate businesses are involved in the "manufacture of consent" within world society members and all together serve antidemocratic ends. By managing the information flow, they create in people's minds images and illusions of the surrounding world: a mental picture of something not real or present. As William Gamson and his collaborators (1992) state, the media (and their owners) generally operate in ways that promote apathy, cynicism, and quiescence rather than active citizenship and participation. The main danger here lies in people's mixing fiction with reality. Spontaneity is thus eliminated, critical thinking is "switched off," and an individual's original psychological acts are replaced with somebody else's feelings, thoughts, and desires (Fromm 1965). This threat prevents members of an information society from enjoying one of the most fundamental rights that democracy offers—the right to be broadly informed.

It is undeniable that such a vision of an information society turning quickly into reality has led to the creation of sophisticated tools that can be used to manipulate people's minds. Such visions of reality can be constructed in people's minds that will determine their preferences and attitudes, including those related to the social and political spheres. A certain construction of information can lead to increasing or decreasing people's sensitivity to certain social phenomena and controlling citizens' behavior.

Political marketing is criticized from the ethical standpoint as undermining democracy because of its ability to promote populism, and people with right appearances, and to manipulate and mislead the voter. Nicholas O'Shaughnessy (1990) argues that the rise of political marketing contributes to the misperception of political processes and the ease with which solutions can be traded and implemented. As campaigns are conducted primarily through mass media and citizens participate in them as a media audience, Phil Harris (2001a) states that we witness a shift from citizenship to spectatorship. Groups competing for power concentrate not on solving real problems, but on respecting symbolic commitments and showing competing desires and ambitions of parties interested in the programs. The area of anxiety is also the idea that opinion is being "bought" by the richest rather than the best, and this offends democratic notions (see Nelson 2009).

Those negative consequences and concerns related to an application of marketing in politics are also reinforced by some approaches that political marketing properly offers. Jennifer Lees-Marshment (2003) states that political marketing for politics means a significant transformation of the way the political world operates. It subjects politics to the consumer-like forces of business management and the market. According to her, politics could become more responsive to citizen's needs and demands, but also it might become consumer-led, a condition that would override professional judgment, lack ideology, and threaten the very essence of politics itself: "The ramifications of this phenomenon may indeed be phenomenal: marketing could transform, or may have already transformed, the nature of politics as we know it" (3). Kevin Moloney (2007) calls such relations between politics and marketing "policy-by-marketing." He believes that it is a reductionist approach to practice politics. It simplifies both political discourses as well as democracy. It should be stressed that political marketing is not an ideology, and it is not related to a particular ideology more than it is to another. It is "the processes of exchanges and establishing, maintaining, and enhancing relationships among objects in the political market (politicians, political parties, voters, interests groups, institutions), whose goal is to identify and satisfy their needs and develop political leadership" (Cwalina, Falkowski, and Newman 2009, 70; see also Chapter 1). It cannot and should not replace politics understood, as Lees-Marshment (2003, 3) notes, as "the area of people power, philosophy and ideology." The goal of the activities conducted during political campaigns is not to create a "new politics" but to determine how to generate and retain public support *for* party policies and programs (Baines, Brennan, and Egan 2003). Otherwise, as Bruce Newman (1999c) observes in the title of his book, democracy will change from its deliberative form into "an age of manufactured images," or, in other words, tabloidization. "Simulacra" will replace a reality that has no foundation in citizens' experience (Baudrillard 1981).

A threat to society may also be running government like a business. According to Neil Collins and Patrick Butler (2003; see also Butler, Collins, and Fellenz 2007), this model is popularized by the advocates and practitioners of the new public management (NPM) approach to reform the public service. NPM is based on an economic model of governance in which the market, or approximations to it, is the ideal mechanism for the allocation of public services. In marketing terms, NPM has two distinct strands: the development and operation of market (or market-like) mechanisms within the public sector, and the introduction of managerial techniques common in the private consumer sector. Central to this approach is the perception of citizens as consumers. The danger, however, is that NPM managers, seeing citizens merely as consumers, automatically utilize consumer-type models. In this manner, marketing approaches may regress to the analysis of consumer preferences rather than participation in the public political system. But the increased levels of customer service in government may actually lead to poorer government services in the broad sense—the substitution of political engagement with marketing research. The features of liberal representative democracy, particularly the role of deliberation, informed assent, and accountability, will be neglected.

Paradox of Freedom in Democratic Countries

The foundation of democratic societies is their citizens' freedom, which helps to create more and more sophisticated marketing strategies whose goal is to make the voter vote for a certain political option. We face then a paradoxical situation because a side product of these strategies is the limitation of the voter's choice in voting decisions (Cwalina and Falkowski 2008c).

The character of limiting freedom in democratic states is different from totalitarian states. In the latter, this limitation is imposed from outside. The whole legal structure, including state laws and rulings, had efficiently inhibited the freedom of citizens in East and Central Europe from 1945—the date of the Jalta Conference when Roosevelt and Churchill allowed East and Central Europe to be ruled by the USSR—until 1989 when the communist system collapsed. The citizens were aware of the limitations imposed by the state. In democratic countries, however, these limitations come from inside, through creating in people's minds a certain picture of a part of reality, stimulating certain behaviors. The character of such internal limitation is much more dangerous than external limitation, because citizens often do not realize that they are being limited in their freedom, and there are no formal ways to oppose these limits. As in totalitarian states, political organizations in democratic countries can achieve their goals through dishonest competition or falsifying the results of political elections. This falsifying, however, does not take place outside the voters but inside them, when false images and false memories of a candidate are created in their minds.

The problem of limiting voters' choice by political advertising and its threat to democracy were the subjects of a boisterous debate in the Australian Parliament at the beginning of the 1990s. Ian Ward and Ian Cook (1992) describe in detail the debate during which the Australian government, reaching similar conclusions on the paradoxical relationship between freedom and democracy, suggested a ban on political advertising. The authors do not agree with the sharp criticism of this ban and state that a ban on political advertising violates the right to freedom of thought. The authors do not agree with the sharp criticism of this ban according to which a ban on political advertising violates the right to freedom of thought.

Freedom of expression is guaranteed by the First Amendment to the U.S. Constitution, which declares that "Congress shall make no law . . . abridging the freedom of speech, or of the press." Interpreting this provision, Justice Oliver Holmes of the Supreme Court used the analogy of a "marketplace" with regard to election campaigns, when considering the need for ideas to be freely disseminated in the community: the freedom of speech promotes "a free circulation of ideas from which people could pick those which seemed most likely to be true" (Ward and Cook 1992, 23).

A healthy democracy means that voters are offered a number of ideas from which, based on their critical judgment, they reject those they do not accept. However, the market mechanisms allowing information to reach various voter segments permit the complete freedom in creating and broadcasting political messages to limit the expression of political ideas rather than facilitate it. The media can consciously publicize various problems in order to influence political evaluations through the psychological processes of remembering them (see Chapter 2). Joanne Miller and Jon Krosnick (2000) claim that democracy is threatened by such conduct. Intentional control of the evaluations of a politician's activities by the voters limits the voters' access to broad information and, by causing priming and activating heuristics, creates the illusion of a free and conscious choice. It is worthwhile to quote the authors' words here: "According to the theory of media priming, people are victims of the architecture of their minds—if a political issue is activated in people's memories by media attention to it, they presumably use the concept when asked to make political judgments—not by conscious choice, but merely because information about the issue appears automatically and effortlessly in consciousness" (Miller and Krosnick 2000, 302). But, as Ulrich Beck (1992) points out, what is publicized by the media, whose task is to look reliable and credible, is only single facts extracted from the excess of various hypothetical results. The point here is that the political sphere cannot afford to ignore "well-known common views" without losing votes.

On the other hand, the development of new information technologies and citizens' wider and wider access to the Internet are clear signs, as Doris Graber (2004, 563) puts it, of "the transformation of the age of news scarcity into the age of news abundance." Besides, various attempts of antipersuasion education for resisting citizens' manipulation are also made. It is the journalists and educators who mainly carry the burden of making the society aware of the threats resulting from the old or emerging power elites' use of manipulation techniques. Public journalism and special programs showing the mechanisms of constructing political advertising in adwatches (special TV programs that analyze the political ads according to their honesty) can be considered as promising attempts to make citizens aware of the threats of submitting to propaganda.

Public journalism is organized by people involved in journalism, and the intellectual leader of the movement is Jay Rosen (see Shepard 1994). The movement is based on a few major principles or dogmas (Glasser 1999; Rosen 1991). First, citizen concerns will be solicited and voiced. Only what is important for citizens is important for journalists as well. Second, media coverage will shift from polls and strategy to issues of public policy. Press articles or television programs cannot focus purely on the competition for power or influences. Their goal is to present the consequences of implementing various programs, not from the politicians' but from the citizens' perspective. Third, substantive reporting should prevail over short candidate sound bites. Only then will the citizens have a chance to understand what a political debate or conflict is all about. Fourth, partnership and solutions will be stressed over independence and professional detachment.

In 1992, during the presidential campaign in the United States, all the major television news programs presented, for the first time in history, "the adwatch" in which candidates' spots were analyzed according to their honesty and adherence to facts (Ansolabehere, Iyengar, and Simon 1995). The intention of such journalism is to stop candidates from using false and exaggerated statements. In the fall of 1991, Kathleen Hall Jamieson (1992), together with her research team and CNN employees, developed a visual grammar for such programs as the adwatch. Its goal was to develop some rules for presenting the critique of spots by the journalists. These techniques included a sequence of the following: (1) placing the offending commercials on a mock television screen and then moving the screen into the background (*distancing*), (2) attaching a new logo and a notice that this was an ad for a particular candidate (*disclaiming*), (3) stopping the commercial to comment on its content, and (4) commenting upon its content and putting print corrections on the screen (*displacing*). The purpose of these procedures was to encourage the audience to process the content of the critique rather than the content of the ad. It was hoped that the attitudinal effect of misleading, false, highly emotional, and demagogic commercials would be minimized by the contextualizing effects of the adwatch. The authors of the project developed a sample adwatch, supplemented it with a special guide, and distributed it with the help of the National Association of Broadcasters to all the television stations that were interested in it.

Obviously the methods of resisting voter manipulation may contribute to diminishing the influence of persuasion, but cannot eliminate it completely.

Ideological Extremity and Populism

A threat for the development of democracy may also be represented by the typology of the specific strategic posture a political party or candidate holds and their behavior on the political marketplace presented in Chapter 1. Stephan C. Henneberg (2006a, 2006b) argues that political parties have two different dimensions to choose from:

1. *Leading*. If the politicians try to lead, they know that their political concept (political product, ideology) is essentially right. Leading consists of trying to convince voters of the beneficial nature of a political offer and influencing others to do something to realize a political concept.
2. *Following*. If the politicians try to follow, they guess, anticipate, and analyze the wishes of the biggest possible number of voters. Here political marketing is not so much a managerial tool to execute strategies as the strategy itself to develop a political offering.

Depending on a party's or candidate's position relative to their focus on driving the political market (leading) or being driven by it (following), Henneberg distinguished four generic strategic postures: the Relationship Builder (high in market-driving and high in market-driven), the Convinced Ideologist (high/low), the Tactical Populist (low/high), and the Political Lightweight (low/low; in fact it does not participate in the competition). They exemplify in marketing terms how the party organization aspires to be perceived by citizens relative to its competitors. From the perspective of potential threats to democracy, the most significant ones seem to be the Convinced Ideologist and the Tactical Populist.

The Convinced Ideologist (CI) scores high on the leading-scale while its following capabilities are not fully developed. This posture is characterized by a clear focal point for policy-making—implementing ideological postulates. Preferences of voters or opinion shifts are secondary. The CI party concentrates on persuading and convincing voters to follow its proposals, without, however, paying too much attention to how they react to those proposals. The Tactical Populist (TP) party is characterized by following more than leading. Recognizing the political pulse of the electorate is its most important strategic aim. Therefore, strategic marketing techniques (microsegmentation and concentration on marginal seats and swing voters) are applied to ensure that its political propositions are best fitted to voters' current needs and opinions. It requires employing many electoral professionals—consultants, pollsters, and advisers—and handing over control of the whole campaign to them.

The consequence of adopting the CI strategy by a party or politician is that they may stop focusing on the needs and expectations of voters and focus mainly on the implementation of their own ideology—on satisfying their own needs. As such, ideology provides politicians with a broad conceptual map of politics into which political events, current problems, voters' preferences, and other parties' policies can be fitted (Budge 1994). The ideologies are the shared framework of mental models that groups of individuals possess and that provide both interpretation of the environment and a prescription as to how that environment should be structured (Denzau and North 1994). The ideological extremity then leads to a simplified vision of the world based on the following assumption: "Those who are not with us are against us." Therefore, in its extreme form the CI strategy leads to treating citizens as "us" and "them." In order to win electoral support, CIs use political marketing concepts only tactically. Their communication focuses on using mechanisms of persuasion to win power. Therefore, the evolution in party efforts to strengthen the area of leading and weaken following presents a significant threat to democracy, particularly if the party wins in the election. In extreme cases it may lead to authoritarian rule or even totalitarianism. It may also take a form of "missionary politics," as in the case of Venezuelan president Hugo Chávez (see Zúquete 2008).

In contemporary politics there are many parties that, to a smaller or larger degree, seem to take the CI strategy. The example offered by Henneberg (2006a) is the PDS in Germany, successor to the communist party of the German Democratic Republic. He says the CI is typically a party that did not shed its ideological baggage, but adopted a much more polished media appearance and used a sophisticated election campaign. Nevertheless, the essence of its political product remained largely unchanged. In this case, the threat to civil freedoms is determined externally.

At the other end of the spectrum there are parties and candidates adopting the TP strategy. The TP is characterized by following more than leading. It reacts, above all, to changes in the electorate's feeling, trying to fine-tune to the voters. Therefore, strategic marketing techniques are applied to ensure that the political propositions on offer are always in synchronization with public opinion. Such a party must be flexible with regard to the core characteristics of its political offer, which can change rapidly. In fact, it does not have its own political concept that would be stable and consistently presented to the voters. It creates an apparent political product, changed according to changes in society. It may be attractive for voters, but its practical implementation is not in fact possible. The most common examples of populist parties include the Freedom Party of Austria and Self-Defense of the Polish Republic.

As Nicholas O'Shaughnessy (2002) states, political marketing and its easily accessible public associations with the idea of manipulation has become one of those things it is fashionable to worry about—the political face of a cultural "dumbing down." Numerous ad watchers testify that this is a matter of public concern. "That there are thus ethical problems associated with political marketing is thus not in doubt. But what problems—and whose ethics?" (1079). O'Shaughnessy reviewed some of the principal contemporary and classical ethical theories of interest to marketing, including Kantian, utilitarian, contractarian, communitarian, objective, and cultural relativist theories. He questions whether they can discriminate usefully among the mass of criticisms of political marketing and offer enlightenment as to where the common interests are really being served and where anxieties should truly lie. In conclusion of this review, he states that the overall direction of the ethical critique is clear—that it is an error to proclaim a general anathema against political marketing and the key generic practices such as negative advertising most commonly associated with it. What is morally questionable is not so much the genre and its derivatives, but particularized individual cases of application, the specific instance that embodies the idea of excess: toxic individual negative campaigns, legislative seats merely purchased, allegation and video image merely fabricated. However, as he claims, the application of ethical frameworks does not generate any final answers, as no ethical debate is ever final.

Political marketing has also a positive influence on the stability and development of democracy. O'Shaughnessy (1987) points out that, at least to some extent, it can support the growth of an issue-oriented "political nation": distinguished from the older base of political support by greater commitment to narrower issues, and the possession of detailed and intimate information. Furthermore, political marketing contributes to filtering down the knowledge of marketing's various tools and techniques and transfusion of power from elected to nonelected, to staffers and civil service. Political marketing may be used for various purposes and is not, itself, a threat to democracy; the real threat is the intention of the people who decide to use it. Political marketing needs to be much concerned with being socially useful and with applying its knowledge and insights to the improvement of political processes and to human betterment.

References

Abelson, R.P., Kinder, D.R., Peters, M.D., and Fiske, S.T. 1982. Affective and semantic components in political person perception. *Journal of Personality and Social Psychology*, 42(4), 619–630.

Adams, W.C., and Smith, D.J. 1980. Effects of telephone canvassing on turnout and preferences: A field experiment. *Public Opinion Quarterly*, 44(3), 389–395.

Ahluwalia, R. 2000. Examination of psychological processes underlying resistance to persuasion. *Journal of Consumer Research*, 27(2), 217–232.

Alesina, A., and Cukierman, A. 1990. The politics of ambiguity. *Quarterly Journal of Economics*, 105(4), 829–850.

Andrews, L. 1996. The relationship of political marketing to political lobbying: An examination of the Devonport campaign for the trident refitting contract. *European Journal of Marketing*, 30(10/11), 68–91.

Ansolabehere, S., and Iyengar, S. 1994. Riding the wave and claiming ownership over issues: The joint effects of advertising and news coverage in campaigns. *Public Opinion Quarterly*, 58(3), 335–357.

———. 1995. *Going Negative: How Political Advertisements Shrink and Polarize the Electorate*. New York: Free Press.

Ansolabehere, S., Iyengar, S., and Simon, A. 1995. Evolving perspectives on the effects of campaign communication. In P. Warburn (ed.), *Research in Political Sociology*, vol. 7, 13–31. Greenwich, CT: JAI Press.

Aragonès, E., and Postlewaite, A. 2002. Ambiguity in election games. *Review of Economic Design*, 7(3), 233–255.

Aristotle. 1995. *Politics*. Oxford, UK: Oxford University Press/World's Classics.

Aronson, E. 1992. *The Social Animal*. New York: W.H. Freeman.

Aronson, E., Wilson, T.D., and Akert, R.M. 1994. *Social Psychology: The Heart and the Mind*. New York: HarperCollins.

Atkin, C.K., and Heald, G. 1976. Effects of political advertising. *Public Opinion Quarterly*, 40(2), 216–228.

Auer, J.J. 1962. The counterfeit debates. In S. Kraus (ed.), *The Great Debates: Carter vs. Ford, 1976*, 142–150. Bloomington: Indiana University Press.

Austin, E.W., and Pinkleton, B.E. 1995. Positive and negative effects of political disaffection on the less experienced voter. *Journal of Broadcasting & Electronic Media,* 39(2), 215–235.

Baines, P.R. 1999. Voter segmentation and candidate positioning. In B.I. Newman (ed.), *Handbook of Political Marketing*, 403–420. Thousand Oaks, CA: Sage.

———. 2005. Marketing the political message: American influences on British practices. *Journal of Political Marketing*, 4(2/3), 135–162.

Baines, P.R., Brennan, R., and Egan, J. 2003. "Market" classification and political campaigning: Some strategic implications. *Journal of Political Marketing*, 2(2), 47–66.

Baines, P.R., Harris, P., and Lewis, B.R. 2002. The political marketing planning process: Improving image and message in strategic target areas. *Marketing Intelligence & Planning*, 20(1), 6–14.

Baines, P.R., and Worcester, R.M. 2000. Researching political markets: Market-oriented or populistic? *International Journal of Market Research*, 42(3), 339–356.

Baines, P.R., Worcester, R.M., Jarrett, D., and Mortimore, R. 2003. Market segmentation and product differentiation in political campaigns: A technical feature perspective. *Journal of Marketing Management*, 19(1–2), 225–249.

———. 2005. Product attribute-based voter segmentation and resource advantage theory. *Journal of Marketing Management*, 21(9), 1079–1115.

Bale, T., and Sanders, K. 2001. "Playing by the book": Success and failure in John Major's approach to prime ministerial media management. *Contemporary British History*, 15(4), 93–110.

Barrett, A.W., and Peake, J.S. 2007. When the president comes to town: Examining local newspaper coverage of domestic presidential travel. *American Politics Research*, 35(1), 3–31.

Bartell, T., and Bouxsein, S. 1973. The Chelsea project: Candidate preference, issue preference, and turnout effects of student canvassing. *Public Opinion Quarterly*, 37(2), 268–274.

Bartels, L.M. 1986. Issue voting under uncertainty: An empirical test. *American Journal of Political Science*, 30(4), 709–728.

Bassili, J.N. 1993. Response latency versus certainty as indexes of the strength of voting intentions in a CATI survey. *Public Opinion Quarterly*, 57(1), 54–61.

Bassili, J.N., and Bors, D.A. 1997. Using response latency to increase lead time in election forecasting. *Canadian Journal of Behavioural Science*, 29(4), 231–238.

Bassili, J.N., and Fletcher, J.F. 1991. Response-time measurement in survey research: A method for CATI and a new look at nonattitudes. *Public Opinion Quarterly*, 55(3), 331–346.

Baudrillard, J. 1981. *Simulacra and Simulation: The Body in Theory*. Ann Arbor: University of Michigan Press.

Bauer, H.H., Huber, F., and Herrmann, A. 1996. Political marketing: An information-economic analysis. *European Journal of Marketing*, 30(10/11), 152–165.

Bavelas, J.B., Black, A., Bryson, L., and Mullett, J. 1988. Political equivocation: A situational explanation. *Journal of Language and Social Psychology*, 7(2), 137–145.

Beck, U. 1992. *Risk Society: Towards a New Modernity*. London, UK: Sage.

Benoit, W.L. 1995. *Accounts, Excuses, and Apologies: A Theory of Image Restoration Strategies*. Albany: State University of New York Press.

———. 1999. Bill Clinton in the Starr chamber. *American Communication Journal*, 2(2). http://acjournal.org/holdings/v012/Iss2/editorials/benoit/index.html.

———. 2000. Let's put "debate" into presidential debates. *Rostrum*, 74(9), 21–24.

———. 2006a. Image repair in President Bush's April 2004 news conference. *Public Relations Review*, 32(2), 137–143.

———. 2006b. President Bush's image repair effort on *Meet the Press:* The complexities of defeasibility. *Journal of Applied Communication Research*, 34(3), 285–306.

Benoit, W.L., and Davis, C. 2007. Newspaper coverage of U.S. Senate debates. *Speaker & Gavel*, 44, 13–26.

Benoit, W.L., and McHale, J. 1999. Kenneth Starr's image repair discourse viewed in *20/20*. *Communication Quarterly*, 47(3), 265–280.

Benoit, W.L., and Sheafer, T. 2006. Functional theory and political discourse: Televised debates in Israel and the United States. *Journalism & Mass Communication Quarterly*, 83(2), 281–297.

Benoit, W.L., Stein, K.A., and Hansen, G.J. 2004. Newspaper coverage of presidential debates. *Argumentation and Advocacy*, 41(1), 17–27.

Berry, L.L. 1980. Services marketing is different. *Business*, 30(3), 24–29.

Bittner, J.R. 1980. *Mass Communication: An Introduction*. Englewood Cliffs: Prentice-Hall.

Bloch, L.R. 2000. Mobile discourse: Political bumper stickers as a communication event in Israel. *Journal of Communication*, 50(2), 48–76.

Blumler, J.G., and Kavanagh, D. 1999. The third age of political communication: Influences and features. *Political Communication*, 16(3), 209–230.

Blumler, J.G., and Madge, J. 1967. *Citizenship and Television*. London: PEP Report.

Blumler, J.G., and McQuail, D. 1968. *Television in Politics*. London: Faber and Faber.

Boulding, W., Kalra, A., Staelin, R., and Zeithaml, V.A. 1993. A dynamic process model of service quality: From expectations to behavioral intentions. *Journal of Marketing Research*, 30(1), 7–27.

Boulding, W., Staelin, R., Ehret, M., and Johnston, W.J. 2005. A customer relationship management roadmap: What is known, potential pitfalls, and where to go. *Journal of Marketing*, 69(4), 155–166.

Bowen, L. 1994. Time of voting decision and use of political advertising: The Slade Gordon–Brock Adams senatorial campaign. *Journalism Quarterly*, 71(3), 665–675.

Bowler, S., Donovan, T., and Fernandez, K. 1996. The growth of the political marketing industry and the California initiative process. *European Journal of Marketing*, 30(10/11), 166–178.

Braithwaite, V. 1997. Harmony and security value orientations in political evaluation. *Personality and Social Psychology Bulletin*, 23(4), 401–414.

Bransford, J. 1979. *Human Cognition: Learning, Understanding, and Remembering*. Belmont, CA: Wadsworth.

Brennan, G., and Buchanan, J. 1984. Voter choice: Evaluating political alternatives. *American Behavioral Scientist*, 28(2), 185–201.

Brissender, J., and Moloney, K. 2005. Political PR in the 2005 UK general election: Winning and losing, with a little help from spin. *Journal of Marketing Management*, 21(9), 1005–1020.

British Election Study. 1992. Colchester, Essex: UK Data Archive, SN : 2981.

Bucy, E.P., and Newhagen, J.E. 1999. The emotional appropriateness heuristic: Processing televised presidential reactions to the news. *Journal of Communication*, 49(4), 59–79.

Budesheim, T.L., and DePaola, S.J. 1994. Beauty or the beast? The effects of appearance, personality, and issue information on evaluations of political candidates. *Personality and Social Psychology Bulletin*, 20(4), 339–348.

Budesheim, T.L., Houston, D.A., and DePaola, S.J. 1996. Persuasiveness of in-group and out-group political messages: The case of negative political campaigning. *Journal of Personality and Social Psychology*, 70(3), 523–534.

Budge, I. 1994. A new spatial theory of party competition: Uncertainty, ideology and policy equilibria viewed comparatively and temporally. *British Journal of Political Science*, 24(4), 443–467.

Burns, J.M. 1978. *Leadership*. New York: Harper and Row.

Butler, D., and Kavanagh, D. 1984. *The British General Election of 1983*. London: Macmilllan.

———. 1992. *The British General Election of 1992*. London: Macmillan.

Butler, P., and Collins, N. 1994. Political marketing: Structure and process. *European Journal of Marketing*, 28(1), 19–34.

———. 1999. A conceptual framework for political marketing. In B.I. Newman (ed.), *Handbook of Political Marketing*, 55–72. Thousand Oaks, CA: Sage.

Butler, P., Collins, N., and Fellenz, M.R. 2007. Theory-building in political marketing: Parallels in public management. *Journal of Political Marketing*, 6(2/3), 91–107.

Campbell, A., Gurin, G., and Miller, W. 1954. *The Voter Decides*. Evanston, IL: Row, Peterson.

Campbell, J.E. 1983. Ambiguity in the issue positions of presidential candidates: A causal analysis. *American Journal of Political Science*, 27(2), 284–293.

Campbell, J.E., Cherry, L.L., and Wink, K.A. 1992. The convention bump. *American Politics Quarterly*, 20(3), 287–307.

Canache, D., Mondak, J.J., and Conroy, A. 1994. Politics in multiparty context: Multiplicative specifications, social influence, and electoral choice. *Public Opinion Quarterly*, 58(4), 509–538.

Cantor, N., and Mischel, W. 1979. Prototypes in person perception. In L. Berkowitz (ed.), *Advances in Experimental Social Psychology*, vol. 12, 3–28. New York: Academic Press.

Caprara, G.V., and Zimbardo, P.G. 2004. Personalizing politics: A congruency model of political preference. *American Psychologist*, 59(7), 581–594.

Carlson, T., and Strandberg, K. 2007. Riding the Web 2.0 wave: Candidates on YouTube in the 2007 Finnish national elections. Paper presented at the 4th General Conference of the European Consortium of Political Research, Pisa, Italy, September 6–8, 2007. www.vasa.abo.fi/users/tcarlson/Carlson_Strandberg_YouTube.pdf.

Carmines, E.G., and Gopoian, J.D. 1981. Issue coalitions, issueless campaigns: The paradox of rationality in American presidential elections. *Journal of Politics*, 43(3), 1170–1189.

Case, C.E. 1992. Bumper stickers and car signs: Ideology and identity. *Journal of Popular Culture*, 26(3), 107–119.

Centrum Badania Opinii Społecznej [Public Opinion Research Center]. 1997. *Portrety liderów opozycji* [*Portraits of opposition leaders*]. BS/52/52/97.

Chaffee, S.H. 1978. Presidential debates: Are they helpful to voters? *Communication Monographs*, 45(4), 330–353.

Chaffee, S.H., and Choe, S.Y. 1980. Time of decision and media use during the Ford-Carter campaign. *Public Opinion Quarterly*, 44(1), 53–69.

Chaffee, S.H., and Rimal, R.N. 1996. Time of vote decision and openness to persuasion.

In D. Mutz, P. Sniderman, and R. Brody (eds.), *Political Persuasion and Attitude Change*, 267–291. Ann Arbor: University of Michigan Press.

Chanley, V.A., Rudolph, T.J., and Rahn, W.M. 2000. The origins and consequences of public trust in government: A time series analysis. *Public Opinion Quarterly*, 64(3), 239–256.

Cho, S., and Benoit, W. 2005. Primary presidential election campaign messages in 2004: A functional analysis of candidates' news releases. *Public Relations Review*, 31(2), 175–183.

Cohen, J. 1968. Multiple regression as a general data-analytic system. *Psychological Bulletin*, 70(6), 426–443.

Coleman, S. 2000. *Televised Election Debates: International Perspectives*. London: Macmillan.

Collins, N., and Butler, P. 2003. When marketing models clash with democracy. *Journal of Public Affairs*, 3(1), 52–62.

Conover, P.J., and Feldman, S. 1981. The origins and meaning of liberal/conservative self-identifications. *American Journal of Political Science*, 25(4), 617–645.

———. 1984. How people organize the political world: A schematic model. *American Journal of Political Science*, 28(1), 95–126.

———. 1989. Candidate perception in an ambiguous world: Campaigns, cues, and inference processes. *American Journal of Political Science*, 33(4), 912–940.

Converse, P.E. 2000. Assessing the capacity of mass electorates. *Annual Review of Political Science*, 3, 331–353.

Cwalina, W. 2000. *Telewizyjna reklama polityczna: Emocje i poznanie w kształtowaniu preferencji wyborczych* [Television political advertising: Emotions and cognition in forming voting preferences]. Lublin, Poland: Towarzystwo Naukowe KUL.

———. 2008a. Poland, Democratization. In L.L. Kaid and C. Holtz-Bacha (eds.), *Encyclopedia of Political Communication*, vol. 2, 552–556. Thousand Oaks, CA: Sage.

———. 2008b. Procesy samoregulacji w formowaniu wrażeń o politykach: Derywacja i racjonalizacja [Self-regulation processes in impression formation of politicians: Deriviation and rationalization]. *Czasopismo Psychologiczne* [*Psychological Journal*], 14(2), 167–186.

Cwalina, W., and Falkowski, A. 1999. Decision processes in perception in the political preferences research: A comparative analysis of Poland, France, and Germany. *Journal for Mental Changes*, 5(2), 27–49.

———. 2000. Psychological mechanisms of political persuasion: The influence of political advertising on voting behavior. *Polish Psychological Bulletin*, 31(3), 203–222.

———. 2003. Advertising and the image of politicians: National elections in Poland, France, and Germany. In F. Hansen and L.B. Christensen (eds.), *Branding and Advertising*, 205–231. Copenhagen: Copenhagen Business School Press.

———. 2005. *Marketing polityczny: Persepektywa psychologiczna* [*Political marketing: A psychological perspective*]. Gdańsk, Poland: Gdańskie Wydawnictwo Psychologiczne.

———. 2006. Political communication and advertising in Poland. In L.L. Kaid and C. Holtz-Bacha (eds.), *The Sage Handbook of Political Advertising*, 325–342. Thousand Oaks, CA: Sage.

———. 2007. Morality and competence in shaping the images of political leaders. Paper presented at 4th International Political Marketing Conference: Political

Marketing Concepts for Effective Leadership Behavior, Sinaia, Romania, April 19–21, 2007.

———. 2008a. Political TV advertising in forming voters' attitudes in Poland. In L.L. Kaid (ed.), *The EU Expansion: Communicating Shared Sovereignty in the Parliamentary Elections*, 101–120. New York: Peter Lang.

———. 2008b. Political branding: Political candidates' positioning based on interobject associative affinity index. Paper presented at 5th International Political Marketing Conference: Political Marketing: Theories Meet Practice, Marketing Meets Political Science, Manchester Business School, University of Manchester, March 27–29, 2008.

———. 2008c. Constructivist mind: False memory, freedom, and democracy. *Journal of Political Marketing*, 7(3/4), 239–255.

———. (in press). Cultural context of the perceptual fit of political parties' campaign slogans: A Polish case. In K. Gouliamos, A. Theocharous, B.I. Newman, and S.C.M. Henneberg (eds.), *Political Marketing: Cultural Issues and Current Trends*. New York: Haworth Press.

Cwalina, W., Falkowski, A., and Kaid, L.L. 2000. Role of advertising in forming the image of politicians: Comparative analysis of Poland, France, and Germany. *Media Psychology*, 2(2), 119–146.

———. 2005. Advertising and the image of politicians in evolving and established democracies: Comparative study of the Polish and the U.S. presidential elections in 2000. *Journal of Political Marketing*, 4(2/3), 19–44.

Cwalina, W., Falkowski, A., and Koniak, P. 2006. Advertising effects: Polish elections to the European Parliament. In M. Maier and J. Tenscher (eds.), *Campaigning in Europe–Campaigning for Europe: Political Parties, Campaigns, Mass Media and the European Parliament Elections 2004*, 371–386. Berlin: LIT Verlag.

Cwalina, W., Falkowski, A., and Newman, B.I. 2008. *A Cross-Cultural Theory of Voter Behavior*. New York: Haworth Press/Taylor & Francis Group.

———. 2009. Political management and marketing. In D.W. Johnson (ed.), *Routledge Handbook of Political Management*, 67–80. New York: Routledge.

Cwalina, W., Falkowski, A., Newman, B.I., and Verčič, D. 2004. Models of voter behavior in traditional and evolving democracies: Comparative analysis of Poland, Slovenia, and U.S. *Journal of Political Marketing*, 3(2), 7–30.

Cwalina, W., Falkowski, A., and Rożnowski, B. 1999. Television spots in Polish presidential elections. In L.L. Kaid (red.), *Television and Politics in Evolving European Democracies*, 45–60. Commack, NY: Nova Science.

Cwalina, W., and Koniak, P. 2007. Wpływ wieloznaczności przekazów politycznych na kształtowanie preferencji wyborczych [The effect of ambiguity of political messages on the formation of electoral preferences]. *Psychologia Społeczna [Social Psychology]*, 2(1), 23–41.

Dacey, R. 1979. The role of ambiguity in manipulating voter behavior. *Theory and Decision*, 10(1/4), 265–279.

Dahl, R. 2000. *On Democracy*. New Haven, CT: Yale University Press.

D'Alessio, D., and Allen, M. 2000. Media bias in presidential elections: A meta-analysis. *Journal of Communication*, 50(4), 133–156.

Dalton, R.J. 2007. Partisan mobilization, cognitive mobilization and the changing American electorate. *Electoral Studies*, 26(2), 274–286.

Dalton, R.J., and Wattenberg, M.P. (eds.). 2000. *Parties Without Partisans: Political Change in Advanced Democracies*. Oxford, UK: Oxford University Press.

Danielian, L.H., and Page, B.I. 1994. The heavenly chorus: Interest group voices on TV news. *American Journal of Political Science*, 38(4), 1056–1078.

Dann, S., Harris, P., Mort, G.S., Fry, M.L., and Binney, W. 2007. Reigniting the fire: A contemporary research agenda for social, political and nonprofit marketing. *Journal of Public Affairs*, 7(3), 291–304.

Davidson, S. 2005. Grey power, school gate mums and the youth vote: Age as a key factor in voter segmentation and engagement in the 2005 UK general election. *Journal of Marketing Management*, 21(9), 1179–1192.

Davies, P.J., and Newman, B.I. (eds.). 2006. *Winning Elections With Political Marketing*. Binghamton, NY: Haworth Press.

Day, G.S. 1994. The capabilities of market-driven organizations. *Journal of Marketing*, 58(1), 37–52.

———. 1998. What does it mean to be market-driven? *Business Strategy Review*, 9(1), 1–14.

Dayan, D., and Katz, E. 1992. *Media Events: The Live Broadcasting History*. Cambridge, MA: Harvard University Press.

de Chernatony, L. 2001. *From Brand Vision to Brand Evaluation: Strategically Building and Sustaining Brands*. Oxford, UK: Butterworth Heinemann.

de Chernatony, L., and White, J. 2002. New Labour: A study of the creation, development and demise of political brand. *Journal of Political Marketing*, 1(2/3), 45–52.

De Marez, L., Vyncke, P., Berte, K., Schuurman, D., and De Moor, K. 2007. Adopter segments, adoption determinants and mobile marketing. *Journal of Targeting, Measurement and Analysis for Marketing*, 16(1), 78–95.

Denzau, A.T., and North, D.C. 1994. Shared mental models: Ideologies and institutions. *Kyklos*, 47(1), 3–31.

Diamanti, I., and Lello, E. 2005. The Casa delle Libertà: A house of cards? *Modern Italy*, 10(1), 9–35.

Diamond, E., and Bates, S. 1992. *The Spot: The Rise of Political Advertising on Television*. Cambridge, MA: MIT Press.

Dimitrova, D.V., Connolly-Ahern, C., Williams, A.P., Kaid, L.L., and Reid, A. 2003. Hyperlinking as gatekeeping: Online newspaper coverage of the execution of an American terrorist. *Journalism Studies*, 4(3), 401–414.

Djupsund, G., and Carlson, T. 2003. Catching the "wired voters"? Campaigning on the Internet. *Nordicom-Information*, 25(1/2), 39–50.

Donaldson, T., and Preston, L.E. 1995. The stakeholder theory of the corporation: Concepts, evidence, and implications. *Academy of Management Review*, 20(1), 65–91.

Dorling, D., Eyre, H., Johnston, R., and Pattie, C. 2002. A good place to bury bad news? Hiding the detail in the geography on the Labour Party's website. *Political Quarterly*, 73(4), 476–492.

Downs, A. 1957. *An Economic Theory of Democracy*. New York: Harper.

Doyle, P. 1975. Brand positioning using multidimensional scaling. *European Journal of Marketing*, 9(1), 20–34.

Druckman, J.N. 2003. The power of television images: The first Kennedy-Nixon debate revisited. *Journal of Politics*, 65(2), 559–571.

———. 2004. Priming the vote: Campaign effects in a U.S. senate elections. *Political Psychology*, 25(4), 577–594.

Druckman, J.N., and Nelson, K.R. 2003. Framing and deliberation: How citizens' conversations limit elite influence. *American Journal of Political Science*, 47(4), 728–744.

Druckman, J.N., and Parkin, M. 2005. The impact of media bias: How editorial slant affects voters. *Journal of Politics*, 67(4), 1030–1049.

Dulio, D.A., and Towner, T.L. 2009. The permanent campaign. In D.W. Johnson (ed.), *Routledge Handbook of Political Management*, 83–97. New York: Routledge.

Egan, J. 1999. Political marketing: Lessons from the mainstream. *Journal of Marketing Management*, 15(6), 495–503.

Ekman, P. 1992. *Telling Lies: Clues to Deceit in the Marketplace, Politics and Marriage*. New York: W.W. Norton.

Entman, R.M. 2007. Framing bias: Media in the distribution of power. *Journal of Communication*, 57(1), 163–173.

Eshbaugh-Soha, M., and Peake, J.S. 2006. The contemporary presidency: "Going local" to reform Social Security. *Presidential Studies Quarterly*, 36(4), 689–704.

Eysenck, H.J. 1956. The psychology of politics and the personality similarities between fascists and communists. *Psychological Bulletin*, 53(6), 431–438.

Faas, T., and Maier, J. 2004. Chancellor-candidates in the 2002 televised debate. *German Politics*, 13(2), 300–316.

Faber, R.J. 1992. Advances in political advertising research: A progression from if to when. *Journal of Current Issues and Research in Advertising*, 14(2), 1–18.

Faber, R.J., and Storey, M.C. 1984. Recall of information from political advertising. *Journal of Advertising*, 13(3), 39–44.

Faber, R.J., Tims, A.R., and Schmitt, K.G. 1990. Accentuate the negative? The impact of negative political appeals on voting intent. In P. Stout (ed.), *Proceedings of American Academy of Advertising*, 10–16. Austin, TX: American Academy of Advertising.

Falkowski, A. 1995. *A Similarity Relation in Cognitive Processes: An Ecological and Information Processing Approach*. Delft, Netherlands: Eburon.

Falkowski, A., and Cwalina, W. 1999. Methodology of constructing effective political advertising: An empirical study of the Polish presidential election in 1995. In B.I. Newman (ed.), *Handbook of Political Marketing*, 283–304. Thousand Oaks, CA: Sage.

Farrell, D.M., and Wortmann, M. 1987. Parties' strategies in the electoral market: Political marketing in West Germany, Britain and Ireland. *European Journal of Political Research*, 15(3), 297–318.

Farwell, L., and Weiner, B. 2000. Bleeding hearts and the heartless: Popular perceptions of liberal and conservative ideologies. *Personality and Social Psychology Bulletin*, 26(7), 845–852.

Fazio, R.H. 2007. Attitudes as object-evaluation associations of varying strength. *Social Cognition*, 25(5), 603–637.

Fein, S., Goethals, G.R., and Kugler, M.B. 2007. Social influence on political judgments: The case of presidential debates. *Political Psychology*, 28(2), 165–192.

Feldman, S., and Conover, P.J. 1983. Candidates, issues and voters: The role of inference in political perception. *Journal of Politics*, 45(4), 810–839.

Fenno, R.F., Jr. 1978. *Home Style: House Members in Their Districts*. Boston: Little, Brown.

Festinger, L., Schachter, S., and Back, K. 1950. *Social Pressures in Informal Groups: A Study of Human Factors in Housing*. Palo Alto, CA: Stanford University Press.

Fiedler, J.A., and Maxwell, R.A. 2000. Perceptual mapping and campaign. Paper presented at 8th Sawtooth Software Conference on Quantitative Methods in Marketing Research. Hilton Head Island, South Carolina, March 23, 2000.

Fiske, S.T., Cuddy, A.J.C., and Glick, P. 2006. Universal dimensions of social cognition: Warmth and competence. *TRENDS in Cognitive Sciences*, 11(2), 77–83.

Fiske, S.T., and Neuberg, S.L. 1990. A continuum of impression formation, from category-based to individuating processes: Influences of information and motivation on attention and interpretation. In M.P. Zanna (ed.), *Advances in Experimental Social Psychology*, vol. 23, 1–74. San Diego, CA: Academic Press.

Fiske, S.T., and Taylor, S.E. 2008. *Social Cognition: From Brains to Culture*. New York: McGraw-Hill.

Forgas, J.P., Kagan, C., and Frey, D. 1977. The cognitive representation of political personalities: A cross-cultural comparison. *International Journal of Psychology*, 12(1), 19–30.

Forgas, J.P., Laszlo, J., Siklaki, I., and Moylan, S.J. 1995. Images of politics: A multidimensional analysis of implicit representations of political parties in a newly emerging democracy. *European Journal of Social Psychology*, 25, 481–496.

Forma, P. 2000. Comparing class-related opinions between MP candidates and party supporters: Evidence from Finland. *Scandinavian Political Studies*, 23(2), 115–137.

Fournier, P., Nadeau, R., Blais, A., Gidengil, E., and Nevitte, N. 2004. Time-of-voting decision and susceptibility to campaign effects. *Electoral Studies*, 23(4), 661–681.

Freeman, R.E., and Evan, W.M. 1990. Corporate governance: A stakeholder interpretation. *Journal of Behavioral Economics*, 19(4), 337–359.

Freestone, O.M., and McGoldrick, P.J. 2007. Ethical positioning and political marketing: The ethical awareness and concerns of UK voters. *Journal of Marketing Management*, 23(7/8), 651–673.

Fridkin, K.L., Kenney, P.J., Gershon, S.A., Shafer, K., and Woodall, G.S. 2007. Capturing the power of a campaign event: The 2004 presidential debate in Tempe. *Journal of Politics*, 69(3), 770–785.

Fromm, E. 1965. *Escape From Freedom*. New York: Avon Books.

Gaber, I. 1999. Government by spin: An analysis of the process. *Contemporary Politics*, 5(3), 263–275.

———. 2004. Alastair Campbell, exit stage left: Do the "Phillis" recommendations represent a new chapter in political communications or is it "business as usual"? *Journal of Public Affairs*, 4(4), 365–373.

Gamson, W.A., Croteau, D., Hoynes, W., and Sasson, T. 1992. Media images and the social construction of reality. *Annual Review of Sociology*, 18, 373–393.

Gamson, W.A., and Modigliani, A. 1996. The changing culture of affirmative action. In R.A. Braumgart (ed.), *Research in Political Sociology*, vol. 3, 137–177. Greenwich, CT: JAI Press.

Garramone, G.M. 1983. Issue versus image orientation and effects of political advertising. *Communication Research*, 10(1), 59–76.

———. 1984. Audience motivation effects: More evidence. *Communication Research*, 11(1), 79–96.

———. 1985. Effects of negative political advertising: The roles of sponsor and rebuttal. *Journal of Broadcasting & Electronic Media*, 29(2), 147–159.

Garramone, G.M., and Atkin, C.K. 1986. Mass communication and political socialization: Specifying the effects. *Public Opinion Quarterly*, 50(1), 76–86.

Geer, J.G., and Geer, J.H. 2003. Remembering attack ads: An experimental investigation of radio. *Political Behavior*, 25(1), 69–95.

Gerber, A.S., and Green, D.P. 2001. Do phone calls increase voter turnout? A field experiment. *Public Opinion Quarterly*, 65(1), 75–85.

Gibson, J. 1999. Political timing: A theory of politicians' timing of events. *Journal of Theoretical Politics*, 11(4), 471–496.

Gibson, R.K. 2004. Web campaigning from a global perspective. *Asia-Pacific Review*, 11(1), 95–126.

Gibson, R.K., and Ward, S.J. 1998. UK political parties on the Internet: "Politics as usual" in the new media? *Harvard International Journal of Press/Politics*, 3(3), 14–38.

Glasser, T. (ed.). 1999. *The Idea of Public Journalism*. New York: Guilford Press.

Gold, G.J., and Raven, B.H. 1992. Interpersonal influence strategies in the Churchill-Roosevelt bases-for-destroyers exchange. *Journal of Social Behavior and Personality*, 7(2), 245–272.

Goldstein, K., and Freedman, P. 2002. Lessons learned: Campaign advertising in the 2000 elections. *Political Communication*, 19(1), 5–28.

Goodhart, C. 1984. *Monetary Theory and Practice: UK Experience*. London: Macmillan.

———. 1989. The conduct of monetary policy. *Economic Journal*, 99(396), 293–346.

Grabe, M.E., Zhou, S., Lang, A., and Bolls, P.D. 2000. Packaging television news: The effects of tabloid on information processing and evaluative responses. *Journal of Broadcasting & Electronic Media*, 44(4), 581–598.

Graber, D. 1990. Seeing is remembering: How visuals contribute to learning from television news. *Journal of Communication*, 40(3), 134–155.

———. 2004. Mediated politics and citizenship in the twenty-first century. *Annual Review of Psychology*, 55, 545–571.

Green, D.M., and Swets, J.A. 1966. *Signal Detection Theory and Psychophysics*. New York: John Wiley.

Groeling, T., and Kernell, S. 1998. Is network coverage of the president biased? *Journal of Politics*, 60(4), 1063–1087.

Grönroos, C. 1994. From marketing mix to relationship marketing: Towards a paradigm shift in marketing. *Management Decision*, 32(2), 4–20.

———. 1996. Relationship marketing: Strategic and tactical implications. *Management Decision*, 34(3), 5–14.

———. 1997. Value-driven relational marketing: From products to resources and competencies. *Journal of Marketing Management*, 13(5), 407–419.

———. 1998. Marketing services: The case of a missing product. *Journal of Business & Industrial Marketing*, 13(4/5), 322–338.

Groseclose, T., and Milyo, J. 2005. A measure of media bias. *Quarterly Journal of Economics*, 80(4), 1191–1237.

Gummesson, E. 2002. Relationship marketing in the New Economy. *Journal of Relationship Marketing*, 1(1), 37–57.

Hallahan, K. 1999. Seven models of framing: Implications for public relations. *Journal of Public Relations Research*, 11(3), 205–242.

Hampson, S.E., John, O.P., and Goldberg, L.R. 1986. Category breadth and hierarchical structure in personality: Studies of asymmetries in judgments of trait implications. *Journal of Personality and Social Psychology*, 51(1), 37–54.

Harris, P. 2001a. To spin or not to spin—that is the question: The emergence of modern political marketing. *Marketing Review*, 2(1), 35–53.

———. 2001b. Machiavelli, political marketing and reinventing government. *European Journal of Marketing*, 35(9/10), 1136–1154.

Harris, P., Gardner, H., and Vetter, N. 1999. "Goods over God": Lobbying and political marketing—A case study of the campaign by the Shopping Hours Reform Council to change Sunday trading laws in the United Kingdom. In B.I. Newman (ed.), *Handbook of Political Marketing*, 607–626. Thousand Oaks, CA: Sage.

Harris, P., Kolovos, I., and Lock, A. 2001. Who sets the agenda? An analysis of agenda setting and press coverage in the 1999 Greek European elections. *European Journal of Marketing*, 35(9/10), 1117–1135.

Harris, P., and Lock, A. 1996. Machiavellian marketing: The development of corporate lobbying in the UK. *Journal of Marketing Management*, 12(4), 313–328.

———. 2002. Sleaze or clear blue water? The evolution of corporate and pressure group representation at the major UK party conferences. *Journal of Public Affairs*, 2(3), 136–151.

———. 2005. Political marketing funding and expenditure in UK general election campaign of 2005. *Journal of Marketing Management*, 21(9), 1117–1133.

Harris, P., McGrath, C., and Harris, I. 2009. Machiavellian marketing: Justifying the ends and means in modern politics. In D.W. Johnson (ed.), *Routledge Handbook of Political Management*, 537–554. New York: Routledge.

Harris, P., and O'Shaughnessy, N.J. 1997. BSE and marketing communication myopia: Daisy and the death of the sacred cow. *Risk Decision and Policy*, 2(1), 29–39.

Harris, P., and Rees, P. 2000. Pictures at an exhibition: Milton, Machiavelli, Monet, Mussorgsky and marketing. *Marketing Intelligence & Planning*, 18(6/7), 386–373.

Harrison, M. 1992. Politics on the air. In D. Butler and D. Kavanagh (eds.), *The British General Election of 1992*, 155–179. London: Macmillan.

Harrison, T.M., Stephen, T.D., Husson, W., and Fehr, B.J. 1991. Images versus issues in the 1984 presidential election: Differences between men and women. *Human Communication Research*, 18(2), 209–227.

Hayes, B.C., and McAllister, I. 1996. Marketing politics to voters: Late deciders in the 1992 British election. *European Journal of Marketing*, 30(10/11), 127–139.

Hellweg, S.A., Pfau, M., and Brydon, S.R. 1992. *Televised Presidential Debates: Advocacy in Contemporary America*. New York: Praeger.

Henneberg, S.C. 2003. Generic functions of political marketing management. University of Bath, School of Management, Working Paper Series 2003.19.

———. 2006a. Leading or following? A theoretical analysis of political marketing postures. *Journal of Political Marketing*, 5(3), 29–46.

———. 2006b. Strategic postures of political marketing: An exploratory operationalization. *Journal of Public Affairs*, 6(1), 15–30.

———. 2008. An epistemological perspective on research in political marketing. *Journal of Political Marketing*, 7(2), 151–182.

Henneberg, S.C., and O'Shaughnessy, N.J. 2007. Theory and concept development in political marketing: Issues and an agenda. *Journal of Political Marketing*, 6(2/3), 5–31.

Herman, E., and Chomsky, N. 1988. *Manufacturing Consent: The Political Economy of the Mass Media*. New York: Pantheon Books.

Hilgard, E.R. 1962. *Introduction to Psychology*. 3rd edition. New York: Harcourt.

Hills, S.B., and Sarin, S. 2003. From market driving to market driven: An alternate paradigm for marketing in high technology industries. *Journal of Marketing Theory and Practice*, 11(3), 13–24.

Ho, D.E., and Quinn, K.M. 2008. Measuring explicit political positions of media. *Quarterly Journal of Political Science*, 3(4), 353–377.

Holbrook, A.L., Krosnick, J.A., Visser, P.S., Gardner, W.L., and Cacioppo, J.T. 2001. Attitudes toward presidential candidates and political parties: Initial optimism, inertial first impressions, and focus on flaws. *American Journal of Political Science*, 45(4), 930–950.

Holbrook, T.M. 1996. *Do Campaigns Matter?* Thousand Oaks, CA: Sage.

———. 1999. Political learning from presidential debates. *Political Behavior*, 21(1), 67–89.

Holler, M.J., and Skott, P. 2005. Election campaigns, agenda setting and electoral outcomes. *Public Choice*, 125(1/2), 215–228.

Homer, P.M., and Batra, R. 1994. Attitudinal effects of character-based versus competence-based negative political communications. *Journal of Consumer Psychology*, 3(2), 163–185.

Hooley, G.J. 1980. Multidimensional scaling of consumer perceptions and preferences. *European Journal of Marketing*, 14(7), 436–448.

Houston, D.A., and Doan, K. 1999. Can you back that up? Evidence (or lack thereof) for effects of negative and positive political communication. *Media Psychology*, 1(3), 191–206.

Houston, D.A., Doan, K., and Roskos-Ewoldsen, D. 1999. Negative political advertising and choice conflict. *Journal of Experimental Psychology: Applied*, 5(1), 3–16.

Howard, J., and Sheth, J.N. 1969. *The Theory of Buyer Behavior*. New York: John Wiley.

Howard, P.N. 2006. *New Media Campaigns and the Managed Citizen*. New York: Cambridge University Press.

Huckfeldt, R. 2001. The social communication of political expertise. *American Journal of Political Science*, 45(2), 425–438.

Huckfeldt, R., Beck, P.A., Dalton, R.J., and Levine, J. 1995. Political environments, cohesive social groups, and the communication of public opinion. *American Journal of Political Science*, 39(4), 1025–1054.

Huckfeldt, R., Beck, P.A., Dalton, R.J., Levine, J. and Morgan, W. 1998. Ambiguity, distorted messages, and nested environmental effects on political communication. *Journal of Politics*, 60(4), 996–1031.

Huckfeldt, R., Johnson, P.E., and Sprague, J. 2002. Political environment, political dynamics, and the survival of disagreement. *Journal of Politics*, 64(1), 1–21.

Huckfeldt, R., Levine, J., Morgan, W., and Sprague, J. 1999. Accessibility and political utility of partisan and ideological orientations. *American Journal of Political Science*, 43(3), 888–911.

Huntington, S.P. 1991. *The Third Wave: Democratization in the Late Twentieth Century*. Norman: University of Oklahoma Press.

Ingram, P., and Lees-Marshment, J. 2002. The Anglicization of political marketing: How Blair "out-marketed" Clinton. *Journal of Public Affairs*, 2(2), 44–56.

Ireland, E. 2009. Campaigning online. In D.W. Johnson (ed.), *Routledge Handbook of Political Management*, 166–176. New York: Routledge.

Irving, D. 1996. *Goebbels: Mastermind of the Third Reich*. London: Focal Point Publications.

Iyengar, S. 1991. *Is Anyone Responsible? How Television Frames Political Issues.* Chicago: University of Chicago Press.

Iyengar, S., and Kinder, D.R. 1987. *News That Matters: Television and American Opinion.* Chicago: University of Chicago Press.

Iyengar, S., Kinder, D.R., Peters, M.D., and Krosnick, J.A. 1984. The evening news and presidential evaluations. *Journal of Personality and Social Psychology,* 46(4), 778–787.

Jagoda, K., and Nyhan, N. 1999. *E-Voter 98: Measuring the impact of online advertising for a political candidate. A case study.* Westhill Partners. www.e-voter98.com/overview.html.

Jamieson, K.H. 1992. *Dirty Politics: Deception, Distraction, and Democracy.* New York: Oxford University Press.

Jamieson, K.H., and Birdsell, D.S. 1988. *Presidential Debates: The Challenge of Creating an Informed Electorate.* New York: Oxford University Press.

Janis, I.L., and Feshbach, S. 1953. Effects of fear-arousing communication. *Journal of Abnormal and Social Psychology,* 48(1), 78–92.

Janiszewski, C. 1990a. The influence of print advertisement organization on effect toward a brand name. *Journal of Consumer Research,* 17(1), 53–65.

———. 1990b. The influence of nonattended material on the processing of advertising claims. *Journal of Marketing Research,* 27(3), 263–278.

Jankowski, N.W., Foot, K., Kluver, R., and Schneider, S. 2005. The Web and the 2004 EP election: Comparing political actor Web sites in 11 EU Member States. *Information Polity,* 10(3/4), 165–176.

Jansen, H.J. 2004. Is the Internet politics as usual or democracy's future? Candidate campaign Web sites in the 2001 Alberta and British Columbia provincial elections. *Innovation Journal: The Public Sector Innovation Journal,* 9(2). www.innovation.cc/scholarly-style/jansen-9–2.pdf.

Jaworski, B.J., and Kohli, A.K. 1993. Market orientation: Antecedents and consequences. *Journal of Marketing,* 57(3), 53–70.

Johnson, R.M. 1971. Market segmentation: A strategic management tool. *Journal of Marketing Research,* 8(1), 13–18.

Johnson-Cartee, K.S., and Copeland, G.A. 1991. *Negative Political Advertising: Coming of Age.* Hillsdale, NJ: Lawrence Erlbaum.

Johnston, R.J., Pattie, C.J., and Allsopp, J.G. 1988. *A Nation Dividing? The Electoral Map of Great Britain 1979–1987.* London: Longman.

Jost, J.T., Glaser, J., Kruglanski, A.W., and Sulloway, F.J. 2003. Political conservatism as motivated cognition. *Psychological Bulletin,* 129(3), 339–375.

Kahle, L.R., Beatty, S.E., and Homer, P. 1986. Alternative measurement approaches to consumer values: The list of values (LOV) and values and life styles (VALS). *Journal of Consumer Research,* 13(3), 405–409.

Kahneman, D., and Tversky, A. 1979. Prospect theory: An analysis of decision under risk. *Econometrica,* 47(2), 267–291.

———. 1984. Choices, values, and frames. *American Psychologist,* 39(4), 341–350.

Kaid, L.L. 1997. Effects of television spots on images of Dole and Clinton. *American Behavioral Scientist,* 40(8), 1085–1094.

———, (ed.). 1999a. *Television and Politics in Evolving European Democracies.* Commack, NY: Nova Science.

———. 1999b. Political advertising: A summary of research findings. In B.I. Newman (ed.), *Handbook of Political Marketing,* 423–438. Thousand Oaks, CA: Sage.

Kaid, L.L., and Chanslor, M. 1995. Changing candidate images: The effects of political advertising. In K.L. Hacker (ed.), *Candidate Images in Presidential Elections*, 83–97. Westport, CT: Praeger.

Kaid, L.L., Chanslor, M., and Hovind, M. 1992. The influence of program and commercial type on political advertising effectiveness. *Journal of Broadcasting & Electronic Media*, 36(3), 303–320.

Kaid, L.L., and Hirsch, R.O. 1973. Selective exposure and candidate image: A field study over time. *Central States Speech Journal*, 24(1), 48–51.

Kaid, L.L., and Holtz-Bacha, C. (eds.). 1995. *Political Advertising in Western Democracies: Parties and Candidates on Television*. Thousand Oaks, CA: Sage.

———. 2006. *The Sage Handbook of Political Advertising*. Thousand Oaks, CA: Sage.

Kaid, L.L., and Johnston, A. 1991. Negative versus positive television advertising in U.S. presidential campaigns, 1960–1988. *Journal of Communication*, 41(3), 53–63.

Kalafatis, S.P., Tsogas, M.H., and Blankson, C. 2000. Positioning strategies in business markets. *Journal of Business & Industrial Marketing*, 15(6), 416–437.

Kaufmann, K.M., and Petrocik, J.R. 1999.The changing politics of American men: Understanding the sources of the gender gap. *American Journal of Political Science*, 43(3), 864–887.

Kavanagh, D. 1996. Speaking truth to power? Pollsters as campaign advisors. *European Journal of Marketing*, 30(10/11), 104–113.

Kearsey, A., and Varey, R.J. 1998. Managerialist thinking on marketing for public services. *Public Money & Management*, 18(2), 51–60.

Keller, K.L. 1993. Conceptualizing, measuring, managing customer-based brand equity. *Journal of Marketing*, 57(1), 1–22.

———. 1999. Brand mantras: Rationale, criteria and examples. *Journal of Marketing Management*, 15(1–3), 43–51.

———. 2001. Building customer-based brand equity: A blueprint for creating strong brands. *Marketing Management*, 28(1), 35–41.

———. 2003. Brand synthesis: The multidimensionality of brand knowledge. *Journal of Consumer Research*, 29(4), 595–600.

Kern, M. 1989. *30-Second Politics: Political Advertising in the Eighties*. New York: Praeger.

Kinder, D.R. 1986. Political character revisited. In R.R. Lau and D.O. Sears (eds.), *Political Cognitions*, 233–256. Hillsdale, NJ: Lawrence Erlbaum.

Kinder, D.R., and Sears, D.O. 1987. Public opinion and political action. In G. Lindzey and E. Aronson (eds.), *Handbook of Social Psychology*, vol. 2, 659–741. New York: Random House.

King, K.N. 2002. The art of impression management: Self-presentation in local-level campaign literature. *Social Science Journal*, 39(1), 31–41.

Kinsey, D.E. 1999. Political consulting: Bridging the academic and practical perspectives. In B.I. Newman (ed.), *Handbook of Political Marketing*, 113–127. Thousand Oaks, CA: Sage.

Kiousis, S., Bantimaroudis, P., and Ban, H. 1999. Candidate image attributes: Experiments on the substantive dimension of second level agenda setting. *Communication Research*, 26(4), 414–429.

Kiousis, S., and Shields, A. 2008. Intercandidate agenda-setting in presidential elections: Issue and attribute agendas in the 2004 campaign. *Public Relations Review*, 34(4), 325–330.

Kleine, R.E., III, and Kernan, J.B. 1988. Measuring the meaning of consumption objects: An empirical investigation. *Advances in Consumer Research*, 15(1), 498–504.

Klinenberg, E., and Perrin, A. 1996. *Symbolic politics in the Information Age: The 1996 presidential campaigns on the web.* http://demog.berkeley.edu/~aperrin/infosociety.html.

Klotz, R. 1998. Virtual criticism: Negative advertising on the Internet in the 1996 Senate races. *Political Communication*, 15(3), 347–365.

Kochan, M. 2002. *Slogany w reklamie i polityce* [Slogans in advertising and politics]. Warsaw: Wydawnictwo TRIO.

Kohli, A.K., and Jaworski, B.J. 1990. Market orientation: The construct, research propositions, and managerial implications. *Journal of Marketing*, 54(2), 1–18.

Kosslyn, S.M., and Rosenberg, R.S. 2004. *Psychology: The Brain, the Person, the World.* Boston: Allyn & Bacon.

Kotler, P. 1975. Overview of political candidate marketing. *Advances in Consumer Research*, 12(2), 761–769.

Kotler, P., and Andreasen, A. 1991. *Strategic Marketing for Nonprofit Organizations.* Englewood Cliffs, NJ: Prentice Hall.

Kotler, P., and Armstrong, G. 1990. *Marketing: An Introduction.* Englewood Cliffs, NJ: Prentice Hall.

Kotler, P., Armstrong, G., Brown, L., and Adam, S. 1998. *Marketing.* 4th edition. Sydney, Australia: Prentice Hall.

Kotler, P., and Keller, K.L. 2006. *Marketing Management.* 12th edition. Upper Saddle River, NJ: Pearson Prentice Hall.

Kotler, P., and Kotler, N. 1999. Political marketing. Generating effective candidates, campaigns, and causes. In B.I. Newman (ed.), *Handbook of Political Marketing*, 3–18. Thousand Oaks, CA: Sage.

Kotler, P., and Levy, S.J. 1969. Broadening the concept of marketing. *Journal of Marketing*, 33(1), 10–15.

Kramer, G.H. 1970/1971. The effects of precinct-level canvassing on voter behavior. *Public Opinion Quarterly*, 34(4), 560–572.

Kraus, S., and Davis, D.K. 1981. Political debates. In D. Nimmo and K.R. Sanders (eds.), *Handbook of Political Communication*, 273–296. Beverly Hills, CA: Sage.

Krosnick, J.A., Boninger, D.S., Chuang, Y.C., Berent, M.K., and Carnot, C.G. 1993. Attitude strength: One construct or many related constructs? *Journal of Personality and Social Psychology*, 65(6), 1132–1151.

Kuklinski, J.H., and Hurley, N.L. 1996. It's a matter of interpretation. In D.C. Mutz, P.M. Sniderman, and R.A. Brody (eds.), *Political Persuasion and Attitude Change*, 125–144. Ann Arbor: University of Michigan Press.

Lamb, C.W. 1987. Public sector marketing is different. *Business Horizons*, 30(4), 56–60.

Lastovicka, J.L., and Bonfield, E.H. 1982. Do consumers have brand attitudes? *Journal of Economic Psychology*, 2(1), 57–75.

Latané, B. 1981. The psychology of social impact. *American Psychologist*, 36(4), 343–356.

Lau, R.R. 1985. Two explanations for negativity effects in political behavior. *American Journal of Political Science*, 29(1), 119–138.

Lau, R.R., and Schlesinger, M. 2005. Policy frames, metaphorical reasoning, and support for public policies. *Political Psychology*, 26(1), 77–114.

Lau, R.R., Sigelman, L., and Rovner, I.B. 2007. The effects of negative political campaigns: A meta-analytic reassessment. *Journal of Politics*, 69(4), 1176–1209.

Lazarsfeld, P., Berelson, B., and Gandet, H. 1944. *The People's Choice: How the Voter Makes Up His Mind in a Presidential Campaign*. New York: Columbia University Press.

Leary, M. 1996. *Self-Presentation: Impression Management and Interpersonal Behavior*. Boulder, CO: Westview Press.

Lebel, G.G. 1999. Managing volunteers: Times have changed—or have they? In B.I. Newman (ed.), *Handbook of Political Marketing*, 129–142. Thousand Oaks, CA: Sage.

Le Bon, G. 2002/1895. *The Crowd: A Study of the Popular Mind*. Mineola, NY: Dover.

Lees-Marshment, J. 2001a. The marriage of politics and marketing. *Political Studies*, 49(4), 692–713.

———. 2001b. The product, sales and market-oriented party: How Labour learnt to market the product, not just the presentation. *European Journal of Marketing*, 35(9/10), 1074–1084.

———. 2003. Political marketing: How to reach that pot of gold. *Journal of Political Marketing*, 2(1), 1–32.

———. 2004. Mis-marketing the Conservatives: The limitations of style over substance. *Political Quarterly*, 75(4), 392–397.

Lees-Marshment, J., and Quayle, S. (2001). Empowering the members or marketing the party? The Conservative reforms of 1998. *Political Quarterly*, 72(2), 204–212.

Lemert, J.B. (1993). Do televised presidential debates help inform voters? *Journal of Broadcasting & Electronic Media*, 37(1), 83–94.

Levitt, T. 1960. Marketing myopia. *Harvard Business Review*, 38(4), 45–56.

Lilleker, D.G. 2005. Local campaign management: Winning votes or wasting resources? *Journal of Marketing Management*, 21(9), 979–1003.

Lindsay, B. 1999. Interest groups and the political process: Gender issues. In B.I. Newman (ed.), *Handbook of Political Marketing*, 643–660. Thousand Oaks, CA: Sage.

Lipset, S.M. 1981. *Political Man: The Social Bases of Politics*. Baltimore: Johns Hopkins University Press.

Lizza, R. 2006. The YouTube election. *New York Times*, August 20. www.nytimes.com/2006/08/20/weekinreview/20lizza.html.

Lloyd, J. 2005. Square peg, round hole? Can marketing-based concepts such as "product" and the "marketing mix" have a useful role in the political arena? In W.W. Wymer Jr. and J. Lees-Marshment (eds.), *Current Issues in Political Marketing*, 27–46. Binghamton, NY: Haworth Press.

Lock, A., and Harris, P. 1996. Political marketing–*vive la différence!* *European Journal of Marketing*, 30(10/11), 14–24.

Lord, C.G., Ross, L., and Lepper, M.R. 1979. Biased assimilation and attitude polarization: The effects of prior theories on subsequently considered evidence. *Journal of Personality and Social Psychology*, 37(11), 2098–2109.

Lott, B., Lott, A., and Saris, R. 1993. Voter preference and behavior in the presidential election of 1988. *Journal of Psychology*, 127(1), 87–97.

Mackiewicza, R., and Cwalina, W. 1999. Przetwarzanie informacji słownych i obrazowych przez telewidzów: Psychologiczne badania nad komunikatywnością

telewizyjnych programów informacyjnych [Visual and verbal information processing by television viewers: Psychological research on the communicative value of
television news coverage]. In W.P. Francuz (red.), *Psychologiczne aspekty odbioru
telewizji [Psychological aspects of television viewing]*, 183–210. Lublin, Poland:
Towarzystwo Naukowe KUL.

Madden, M., and Fox, S. 2006. *Riding the waves of "Web 2.0."* Washington, DC: Pew
Internet & American Life Project. www.pewinternet.org/pdfs/PIP_Web_2.0.pdf.

Mahajan, V., and Wind, Y. 2002. Got emotional product positioning? *Marketing
Management*, 11(3), 36–41.

Manzer, L.L., Ireland, R.D., and Van Auken, P.M. 1980. Image creation in small
retailing: Applications of newspaper advertising. *Journal of Small Business Management*, 18(2), 18–23.

Margolis, M., Resnick, D., and Wolfe, J.D. 1999. Party competition on the Internet
in the United States and Britain. *Harvard International Journal of Press/Politics*,
4(4), 24–47.

Marland, A. 2003. Marketing political soap: A political marketing view of selling
candidates like soap, of electioneering as a ritual, and of electoral military analo-
gies. *Journal of Public Affairs*, 3(2), 103–115.

Mathur, L.K., and Mathur, I. 1995. The effect of advertising slogan changes on market
values of firms. *Journal of Advertising Research*, 35(1), 59–65.

Mauser, G. 1983. *Political Marketing: An Approach to Campaign Strategy*. New
York: Praeger.

McAllister, I. 1985. Campaign activities and electoral outcomes in Britain 1979 and
1983. *Public Opinion Quarterly*, 49(4), 489–503.

McAllister, I., and Studlar, D.T. 1995. New Politics and partisan alignment: Values,
ideology and elites in Australia. *Party Politics*, 1(2), 197–220.

McCombs, M.E. 1981. The agenda-setting approach. In D.D. Nimmo and K.R.
Sanders (eds.), *Handbook of Political Communication*, 121–140. Beverly Hills,
CA: Sage.

McCombs, M.E., Llamas, J.P., Lopez-Escobar, E., and Rey, F. 1997. Candidate image in Spanish elections: Second level agenda setting effects. *Journalism & Mass
Communication Quarterly*, 74(4), 703–717.

McCombs, M.E., and Shaw, D.L. 1972. The agenda-setting function of mass media.
Public Opinion Quarterly, 36(2), 176–185.

McCurley, C., and Mondak, J.J. 1995. Inspected by #1184063113: The influence of
incumbents' competence and integrity in U.S. House elections. *American Journal
of Political Science*, 39(4), 864–885.

McGinniss, J. 1969. *The Selling of the President*. New York: Trident.

McGrath, C. 2007. Framing lobbying messages: Defining and communicating political
issues persuasively. *Journal of Public Affairs*, 7(3), 269–280.

McNair, B. 2004. PR must die: Spin, anti-spin and political public relations in the
UK, 1997–2004. *Journalism Studies*, 5(3), 325–338.

McNicol, D. 1972. *A Primer of Signal Detection Theory*. London: George Allen
& Unwin.

McQuail, D. 1994. Mass communication and the public interest: Towards social theory
for media structure and performance. In D. Crowley and D. Mitchell (eds.), *Communication Theory Today*, 235–253. Cambridge, UK: Polity Press.

Menon, G., and Johar, G.V. 1997. Antecedents of positivity effects in social versus
nonsocial judgments. *Journal of Consumer Psychology*, 6(4), 313–337.

Merritt, S. 1984. Negative political advertising: Some empirical findings. *Journal of Advertising*, 13(3), 27–38.

Messaris, P. 1997. *Visual Persuasion: The Role of Images in Advertising*. Thousand Oaks, CA: Sage.

Milavsky, R., and Zhu, J.H. 1996. Equal time within televised presidential debates. In M.E. Stuckey (ed.), *The Theory and Practice of Political Communication Research*, 95–119. Albany: State University of New York Press.

Miller, D. 1987. Politics. In D. Miller (ed.), *The Blackwell Encyclopaedia of Political Thought*, 430–431. Oxford, UK: Blackwell.

Miller, J.M., and Krosnick, J.A. 2000. News media impact on the ingredients of presidential evaluations: Politically knowledgeable citizens are guided by trusted source. *American Journal of Political Science*, 44(2), 301–315.

Miller, J.M., and Peterson, D.A.M. 2004. Theoretical and empirical implications of attitude strength. *Journal of Politics*, 66(3), 847–867.

Mitchell, J.P., Macrae, C.N., and Banaji, M.R. 2005. Forming impressions of people versus inanimate objects: Social-cognitive processing in the medial prefrontal cortex. *NeuroImage*, 26(1), 251–257.

Moloney, K. 2000. *Rethinking Public Relations: The Spin and the Substance*. New York: Routledge.

———. 2001. The rise and fall of spin: Changes of fashion in the presentation of UK politics. *Journal of Public Affairs*, 1(2), 124–135.

———. 2007. Is political marketing new words or new practice in UK politics? *Journal of Political Marketing*, 6(4), 51–65.

Mondak, J.J. 1995a. Media exposure and political discussion in U.S. elections. *Journal of Politics*, 57(1), 62–85.

———. 1995b. Elections as filters: Term limits and the composition of the U.S. House. *Political Research Quarterly*, 48(4), 701–727.

———. 1995c. Competence, integrity, and the electoral success of congressional incumbents. *Journal of Politics*, 57(4), 1043–1069.

Mondak, J.J., and Huckfeldt, R. 2006. The accessibility and utility of candidate character in electoral decision making. *Electoral Studies*, 25(1), 20–34.

Moran, M. 1986. *The Politics of Banking: The Strange Case of Competition and Credit Control*. 2nd edition. London: Macmillan.

Morgan, R.M., and Hunt, S.D. 1994. The commitment-trust theory of relationship marketing. *Journal of Marketing*, 58(3), 20–38.

Morgenstern, S., and Zechmeister, E. 2001. Better the devil you know than the saint you don't? Risk propensity and vote choice in Mexico. *Journal of Politics*, 63(1), 93–119.

Morris, D. 1997. *Behind the Oval Office: Winning the Presidency in the Nineties*. New York: Random House.

Mosley, P. 1978. Images of the "floating voter": Or, the "political business cycle" revisited. *Political Studies*, 26(3), 375–394.

Mowen, J.C., and Minor, M. 1998. *Consumer Behavior*. Upper Saddle River, NJ: Prentice Hall.

Mueller, J.E. 1973. *War, Presidents and Public Opinion*. New York: John Wiley.

Mylona, I. 2008. SMS in everyday political marketing in Greece. *Journal of Political Marketing*, 7(3/4), 278–294.

Narver, J.C., and Slater, S.F. 1990. The effect of a market orientation on business profitability. *Journal of Marketing*, 54(4), 20–35.

Negrine, R. 1994. *Politics and the Mass Media in Britain*. London: Routledge.

Neisser, U. 1967. *Cognitive Psychology*. New York: Appleton-Century-Crofts.

Nelson, C.J. 2009. Ethics in campaigns and public affairs. In D.W. Johnson (ed.), *Routledge Handbook of Political Management*, 555–563. New York: Routledge.

Newman, B.I. 1994. *The Marketing of the President: Political Marketing as Campaign Strategy*. Thousand Oaks, CA: Sage.

———. 1999a. Preface. In B.I. Newman (ed.), *Handbook of Political Marketing*, xiii–xiv. Thousand Oaks, CA: Sage.

———. 1999b. A predictive model of voter behavior: The repositioning of Bill Clinton. In B.I. Newman (ed.), *Handbook of Political Marketing*, 259–282. Thousand Oaks, CA: Sage.

———. 1999c. *The Mass Marketing of Politics: Democracy in an Age of Manufactured Images*. Thousand Oaks, CA: Sage.

———. 1999d. Politics in an age of manufactured images. *Journal of Mental Changes*, 5(2), 7–26.

Newman, B.I., and Sheth, J.N. 1984. The "gender gap" in voter attitudes and behavior: Some advertising implications. *Journal of Advertising*, 13(3), 4–16.

———. 1985. A model of primary voter behavior. *Journal of Consumer Research*, 12(2), 178–187.

Niffenegger, P.B. 1988. Strategies for success from the political marketers. *Journal of Services Marketing*, 2(3), 15–21.

Nimmo, D. 1999. The permanent campaign: Marketing as a governing tool. In B.I. Newman (ed.), *Handbook of Political Marketing*, 73–86. Thousand Oaks, CA: Sage.

Nisbett, R.E., and Ross, L. 1980. *Human Inference: Strategies and Shortcomings of Social Judgment*. Englewood Cliffs, NJ: Prentice Hall.

Noelle-Neumann, E. 1974. Spiral of silence: A theory of public opinion. *Journal of Communication*, 24(2), 43–51.

———. 1977. Turbulences in the climate of opinion. *Public Opinion Quarterly*, 41(2), 58–88.

Nordhaus, W.D. 1975. The political business cycle. *Review of Economic Studies*, 42(2), 169–190.

O'Cass, A. 1996. Political marketing and the marketing concept. *European Journal of Marketing*, 30(10/11), 37–53.

———. 2001. The internal-external orientation of a political party: Social implications of political party marketing orientation. *Journal of Public Affairs*, 1(2), 136–152.

Oehler, C.M. 1944. Measuring the believability of advertising claims. *Journal of Marketing*, 9(2), 127–131.

O'Keefe, G.J., Mendelsohn, H., and Liu, J. 1976. Voter decision making 1972 and 1974. *Public Opinion Quarterly*, 40(3), 320–330.

Ormrod, R.P. 2005. A conceptual model of political market orientation. In W.W. Wymer Jr. and J. Lees-Marshment (eds.), *Current Issues in Political Marketing*, 47–64. Binghamton, NY: Haworth Press.

———. 2006. A critique of the Lees-Marshment market-oriented party model. *Politics*, 26(2), 110–118.

Ormrod, R.P., and Henneberg, S.C. 2009. Different facets of market orientation: A comparative analysis of party manifestos. *Journal of Political Marketing*, 8(3), 190–208.

OSCE/ODIHR Election Assessment Mission Final Report. 2008. Republic of Poland: Pre-term parliamentary elections, October 21, 2007. www.osce.org/documents/odihr/2008/03/30354_en.pdf.

O'Shaughnessy, N. 1987. America's political market. *European Journal of Marketing*, 21(4), 60–66.

———. 1988. The peevish penmen: Direct mail and US elections. *European Journal of Marketing*, 22(6), 36–44.

———. 1990. High priesthood, low priestcraft: The role of political consultants. *European Journal of Marketing*, 24(2), 7–23.

———. 2001. The marketing of political marketing. *European Journal of Marketing*, 35(9/10), 1047–1057.

———. 2002. Toward an ethical framework for political marketing. *Psychology and Marketing*, 19(12), 1079–1094.

———. 2004. *Politics and Propaganda: Weapons of Mass Seduction*. Manchester, UK: Manchester University Press.

O'Shaughnessy, N.J., and Henneberg, S.C. 2009. The selling of the president 2004: A marketing perspective. In D.W. Johnson (ed.), *Routledge Handbook of Political Management*, 177–193. New York: Routledge.

Ottati, V., Fishbein, M., and Middlestadt, S.E. 1988. Determinants of voters' beliefs about the candidates' stands on the issues: The role of evaluative bias heuristics and the candidates' expressed message. *Journal of Personality and Social Psychology*, 55(4), 517–529.

Page, B.I. 1976. The theory of political ambiguity. *American Political Science Review*, 70(3), 742–752.

Pancer, S.M., Brown, S.D., and Barr, C.W. 1999. Forming impression of political leaders: A cross-national comparison. *Political Psychology*, 20(2), 345–368.

Pancer, S.M., Brown, S.D., Gregor, P., and Claxton-Oldfield, S.P. 1992. Causal attributions and the perception of political figures. *Canadian Journal of Behavioural Science*, 24(3), 371–381.

Pandora, K. 1998. "Mapping the new mental world created by radio": Media messages, cultural politics, and Cantril and Allport's *The Psychology of Radio*. *Journal of Social Issues*, 54(1), 7–27.

Pankowski, K. 1997. Wpływ debat telewizyjnych na preferencje i zachowania wyborcze [Influence of televised debates on voters' preferences and behaviors]. In L. Kolarska-Bobińska and R. Markowski (eds.), *Prognozy i wybory: Polska demokracja '95 [Forecasts and voters' choices: Polish democracy '95]*, 147–166. Warsaw: Wydawnictwo Sejmowe.

Parasuraman, A., Zeithaml, V.A., and Berry, L.L. 1985. A conceptual model of service quality and its implications for future research. *Journal of Marketing*, 49(4), 41–50.

———. 1988. SERVQUAL: A multiple-item scale for measuring consumer perceptions of service quality. *Journal of Retailing*, 64(1), 12–40.

Parker, G.R. 1977. Some themes in congressional unpopularity. *American Journal of Political Science*, 21(1), 93–109.

———. 1989. The role of constituent trust in congressional elections. *Public Opinion Quarterly*, 53(2), 175–196.

Parker, S.L., and Parker, G.R. 1993. Why do we trust our congressman? *Journal of Politics*, 55(2), 442–453.

Patterson, M.L., Churchill, M.E., Burger, G.K., and Powell, J.L. 1992. Verbal and nonverbal modality effects on impressions of political candidates: Analysis from the 1984 presidential debates. *Communication Monographs*, 59(3), 231–242.

Pattie, C., and Johnston, R. 1999. Context, conversation and conviction: Social networks and voting at the 1992 British general election. *Political Studies*, 47(5), 877–889.

————. 2000. "People who talk together vote together": An exploration of contextual effects in Great Britain. *Annals of the Association of American Geographers*, 90(1), 41–66.

Payne, A., and Frow, P. 2005. A strategic framework for customer relationship management. *Journal of Marketing*, 69(4), 167–176.

Peake, J.S. 2007. Presidents and front-page news: How America's newspapers cover the Bush administration. *Press/Politics*, 12(4), 52–70.

Peake, J.S., and Eshbaugh-Soha, M. 2008. The agenda-setting impact of major presidential TV addresses. *Political Communication*, 25(2), 113–137.

Peeters, G. 1992. Evaluative meanings of adjectives in vitro and in context: Some theoretical implications and practical consequences of positive-negative asymmetry and behavioral-adaptive concepts of evaluations. *Psychologia Belgica*, 32(2), 211–231.

Peterson, D.A.M. 2005. Heterogeneity and certainty in candidate evaluations. *Political Behavior*, 27(1), 1–24.

Petrenko, V., Mitina, O., and Brown, R. 1995. The semantic space of Russian political parties on a federal and regional level. *Europe-Asia Studies*, 47(5), 835–858.

Petrocik, J.R. 1996. Issue ownership in presidential elections, with a 1980 case study. *American Journal of Political Science*, 40(3), 825–850.

Pinkleton, B.E., Um, N.H., and Austin, E.W. 2002. An exploration of the effects of negative political advertising on political decision making. *Journal of Advertising*, 31(1), 13–25.

Plasser, F. 2009. Political consulting worldwide. In D.W. Johnson (ed.), *Routledge Handbook of Political Management*, 24–41. New York: Routledge.

Plasser, F., Scheucher, C., and Senft, C. 1999. Is there a European style of political marketing? A survey of political managers and consultants. In B.I. Newman (ed.), *Handbook of Political Marketing*, 89–112. Thousand Oaks, CA: Sage.

Powell, F.C., and Wanzenried, J.W. 1993. Perceptions of Bush, Clinton, and Perot in relation to frequency of presidential debate viewing. *Perceptual and Motor Skills*, 77, 35–41.

Prete, M.I. 2007. M-politics: Credibility and effectiveness of mobile political communication. *Journal of Targeting, Measurement and Analysis for Marketing*, 16(1), 48–56.

Price, V., and Allen, S. 1990. Opinion spirals, silent and otherwise: Applying small-group research to public opinion phenomena. *Communication Research*, 17(3), 369–392.

Pryor, K., and Brodie, R.J. 1998. How advertising slogans can prime evaluations of brand extensions: Further empirical results. *Journal of Product & Brand Management*, 7(6), 497–508.

Rahn, W.M. 1993. The role of partisan stereotypes in information processing about political candidates. *American Journal of Political Science*, 37(2), 472–496.

Rahn, W.M., Krosnick, J.A., and Breuning, M. 1994. Rationalization and derivation processes in survey studies of political candidate evaluation. *American Journal of Political Science*, 38(3), 582–600.

Randall, V. 1987. *Women and Politics*. Chicago: University of Chicago Press.

Raven, B.H. 1990. Political applications of the psychology of interpersonal influence and social power. *Political Psychology*, 11(3), 493–520.

————. 1999. Influence, power, religion, and the mechanisms of social control. *Journal of Social Issues*, 55(1), 161–186.

Reece, B.B. 1984. Children's ability to identify retail stores from advertising slogans. In T.C. Kinnear (ed.), *Advances in Consumer Research*, vol. 11, 320–323. Provo, UT: Association for Consumer Research.

Reece, B.B., Vanden Bergh, B.G., and Li, H. 1994. What makes a slogan memorable and who remembers it. *Journal of Current Issues and Research in Advertising*, 16(2), 41–57.

Reeder, G.D., and Brewer, M.D. 1979. A schematic model of dispositional attributions in interpersonal perception. *Psychological Review*, 86(1), 61–79.

Rees, P., de Chernatony, L., and Carrigan, M. 2006. Building a political brand: Ideology or voter-driven strategy. *Brand Management*, 13(6), 418–428.

Reid, D.M. 1988. Marketing the political product. *European Journal of Marketing*, 22(9), 34–47.

Roch, C.H. 2005. The dual roots of opinion leadership. *Journal of Politics*, 67(1), 110–131.

Roddy, B.L., and Garramone, G.M. 1988. Appeals and strategies of negative political advertising. *Journal of Broadcasting & Electronic Media*, 32(4), 415–427.

Roediger, H.L., III. 2008. Relativity of remembering: Why the laws of memory vanished. *Annual Review of Psychology*, 59, 225–254.

Rogers, E. 1995. *Diffusion of Innovations*. New York: Free Press.

Rokeach, M. 1973. *The Nature of Human Values*. New York: Free Press.

Roscoe, D.D., and Jenkins, S. 2005. Meta-analysis of campaign contributions' impact on roll call voting. *Social Science Quarterly*, 86(1), 52–68.

Rosen, J. 1991. Making journalism more public. *Communication*, 12(4), 267–284.

Ross, J.R.E. 1999. The machine was alive and well and living in Skokie. In B.I. Newman (ed.), *Handbook of Political Marketing*, 521–538. Thousand Oaks, CA: Sage.

Rychlak, J.F. 1968. *A Philosophy of Science for Personality Theory*. Boston: Houghton Mifflin.

Ryfe, D.M. 1999. Franklin Roosevelt and the fireside chats. *Journal of Communication*, 49(4), 80–103.

Sanders, D. 1991. Government popularity and the outcome of the next general election. *Political Quarterly*, 62(2), 235–261.

Sanders, K., and Kaid, L.L. 1981. Political rallies: Their uses and effects. *Central States Speech Journal*, 32(1), 1–11.

San Martín, S., Gutiérrez, J., and Camarero, C. 2004. Trust as the key to relational commitment. *Journal of Relationship Marketing*, 3(1), 53–77.

Sartori, G. 1970. Concept misformation in comparative politics. *American Political Science Review*, 64(4), 1033–1053.

Savage, L.J. 1954. *The Foundations of Statistics*. New York: John Wiley.

Saxer, U. 1993. Public relations and symbolic politics. *Journal of Public Relations*, 5(2), 127–151.

Scammell, M. 1996. The odd couple: Marketing and Maggie. *European Journal of Marketing*, 30(10/11), 114–126.

———. 1999. Political marketing: Lessons for political science. *Political Studies*, 47(4), 718–739.

Scharl, A., Dickinger, A., and Murphy, J. 2005. Diffusion and success factors of mobile marketing. *Electronic Commerce Research and Applications*, 4(2), 159–173.

Schneider, S.M., and Foot, K.A. 2002. Online structure for political action: Exploring presidential campaign web sites from the 2000 American election. *Javnost (The Public)*, 9(2), 43–60.

Schoenwald, M. 1987. Marketing a political candidate. *Journal of Consumer Marketing*, 4(2), 57–63.

Schulz, W., Held, T., and Laudien, A. 2005. Search engines as gatekeepers of public communication: Analysis of the German framework applicable to internet search engines including media law and anti-trust law. *German Law Journal*, 6(10), 1419–1431.

Schwartz, T. 1973. *The Responsive Chord*. Garden City, NY: Anchor Press.

Semetko, H.A., and Valkenburg, P.M. 2000. Framing European politics: A content analysis of press and television news. *Journal of Communication*, 50(2), 93–109.

Shama, A. 1975. Applications of marketing concepts to candidate marketing. *Advances in Consumer Research*, 2(1), 793–801.

Shapiro, M.A., and Lang, A. 1991. Making television reality: Unconscious processes in the construction of social reality. *Communication Research*, 18(5), 685–705.

Shaw, D.R. 1999. A study of presidential campaign event effects from 1952 to 1992. *Journal of Politics*, 61(2), 387–422.

Shepard, A. 1994. The gospel of public journalism. *American Journalism Review*, 16(7), 28–34.

Shepard, R. 1961. The analysis of proximities: Multidimensional scaling with unknown distance function. *Psychometrika*, 27(2), 125–140.

Shepsle, K.A. 1972. The strategy of ambiguity: Uncertainty and electoral competition. *American Political Science Review*, 66(2), 555–568.

Sherif, M. 1937. The psychology of slogans. *Journal of Abnormal and Social Psychology*, 32, 450–461.

Sherman, E. 1999. Direct marketing: How does it work for political campaigns? In B.I. Newman (ed.), *Handbook of Political Marketing*, 365–388. Thousand Oaks, CA: Sage.

Sherman, R.C., and Ross, L.B. 1972. Liberalism-conservatism and dimensional salience in the perception of political figures. *Journal of Personality and Social Psychology*, 23(1), 120–127.

Shikiar, R. 1976. Multidimensional perceptions of the 1972 presidential election. *Multivariate Behavioral Research*, 11(2), 259–263.

Shostack, G.L. 1977. Breaking free from product marketing. *Journal of Marketing*, 41(2), 73–80.

Sigelman, L., and Buell, E.H. 2003. You take the high road and I'll take the low road? The interplay of attack strategies and tactics in presidential campaigns. *Journal of Politics*, 65(2), 518–531.

Sigelman, L., and Shiraev, E. 2002. The rational attacker in Russia? Negative campaigning in Russian presidential elections. *Journal of Politics*, 64(1), 45–62.

Sigelman, L., and Sigelman, C.K. 1984. Judgments of the Carter-Reagan debate: The eyes of the beholder. *Public Opinion Quarterly*, 48(3), 624–628.

Sigelman, L., Sigelman, C.K., and Walkosz, B.J. 1992. The public and the paradox of leadership: An experimental analysis. *American Journal of Political Science*, 36(2), 366–385.

Singh, K., Leong, S.M., Tan, C.T., and Wang, K.C. 1995. A theory of reasoned action perspective of voting behavior: Model and empirical test. *Psychology and Marketing*, 12(1), 37–51.

Skoko, B. 2005. Role of TV debates in presidential campaigns: Croatia's case of 2005. *Politička Misao*, 42(5), 97–117.

Skowronski, J.J., and Carlston, D.E. 1989. Negativity and extremity biases in impression formation: A review of explanations, *Psychological Bulletin*, 105(1), 131–142.

Slater, S.F., and Narver, J.C. 1994. Market orientation, customer value, and superior performance. *Business Horizons*, 37(2), 22–27.

Smith, G. 2001. The 2001 general election: Factors influencing the brand image of political parties and their leaders. *Journal of Marketing Management*, 17(9/10), 989–1006.

———. 2005. Positioning political parties: The 2005 UK general election. *Journal of Marketing Management*, 21(9), 1135–1149.

Smith, G., and Hirst, A. 2001. Strategic political segmentation: A new approach for a new era of political marketing. *European Journal of Marketing*, 35(9/10), 1058–1073.

Smith, G., and Saunders, J. 1990. The application of marketing to British politics. *Journal of Marketing Management*, 5(3), 295–306.

Smudde, P.M., and Courtright, J.L. 2008. Time to get a job: Helping image repair theory begin a career in industry. *Public Relations Journal*, 2(1). www.prsa.org/prjournal/V012N01/SmuddeCourtright.pdf.

Squire, P., and Smith, E.R.A.N. 1988. The effect of partisan information on voters in nonpartisan elections. *Journal of Politics*, 50(1), 169–179.

Steen, J.A. 1999. Money doesn't grow on trees: Fund-raising in American political campaigns. In B.I. Newman (ed.), *Handbook of Political Marketing*, 159–173. Thousand Oaks, CA: Sage.

Stephens, N., and Merrill, B.D. 1984. Targeting the over sixty-five vote in political campaigns. *Journal of Advertising*, 13(3), 17–20 & 49.

Stewart, M.C., and Clarke, H.D. 1992. The (un)importance of party leaders: Leader images and party choice in the 1987 British election. *Journal of Politics*, 54(2), 447–470.

Stromer-Galley, J. 2000. On-line interaction and why candidates avoid it. *Journal of Communication*, 50(4), 111–132.

Stromer-Galley, J., and Foot, K.A. 2002. Citizen perceptions of online interactivity and implications for political campaign communication, *Journal of Computer-Mediated Communication*, 8(1). http://jcmc.indiana.edu.

Sullivan, D.G., and Masters, R.D. 1988. "Happy warriors": Leaders' facial displays, viewers' emotions, and political support. *American Journal of Political Science*, 32(2), 345–368.

Sullivan, J.L., Aldrich, J.H., Borgida, E., and Rahn, W. 1990. Candidate appraisal and human nature: Man and superman in the 1984 election. *Political Psychology*, 11(3), 459–484.

Sundar, S.S., Kalyanaraman, S., and Brown, J. 2003. Explicating web site interactivity: Impression formation effects in political campaign sites. *Communication Research*, 30(1), 30–59.

Swinyard, W.R., and Coney, K.A. 1978. Promotional effects on high- versus low-involvement electorate. *Journal of Consumer Research*, 5(1), 41–48.

Szalay, L.B., and Bryson, J.A. 1973. Measurement of psychosocial distance: A comparison of American Blacks and Whites. *Journal of Personality and Social Psychology*, 26(2), 166–177.

Szalay, L.B., and Deese, J. 1978. *Subjective Meaning and Culture: An Assessment Through Word Associations*. Hillsdale, NJ: Lawrence Erlbaum.

Tanner, J.F., Jr., Hunt, J.B., and Eppright, D.R. 1991. The protection motivation model: A normative model of fear appeals. *Journal of Marketing*, 55(3), 36–45.

Thaler, R.H. 1985. Towards a positive theory of consumer choice. *Journal of Economic Behavior and Organization*, 1(1), 39–60.

Thompson, J.B. 1994. Social theory and the media. In D. Crowley and D. Mitchell (eds.), *Communication Theory Today*, 27–49. Cambridge, UK: Polity Press.

Toffler, A., and Toffler, H. 1994. *Creating a New Civilization: The Politics of the Third Wave*. Atlanta: Turner.

Trammell, K.D. 2007. Candidate campaign blogs: Directly reaching out to the youth vote. *American Behavioral Scientist*, 50(9), 1255–1263.

Trammell, K.D., Williams, A.P., Postelnicu, M., and Landreville, K.D. 2006. Evolution of online campaigning: Increasing interactivity in candidate Web sites and blogs through text and technical features. *Mass Communication & Society*, 9(1), 21–44.

Tversky, A. 1977. Features of similarity. *Psychological Review*, 84(4), 327–352.

Vargo, S.L., and Lusch, R.F. 2004. Evolving to a new dominant logic for marketing. *Journal of Marketing*, 68(1), 1–17.

Varoga, C. 1999. Ballot position: Recycling slogans. *Campaign & Election*, October/December, 69.

Ward, I., and Cook, I. 1992. Televised political advertising, media freedom, and democracy. *Social Alternatives*, 11(1), 21–26.

Wattenberg, M.P. 1987. The hollow realignment: Partisan change in a candidate-centered era. *Public Opinion Quarterly*, 51(1), 58–74.

———. 1991. *The Rise of Candidate-Centered Politics: Presidential Elections of the 1980s*. Cambridge, MA: Harvard University Press.

Weiner, B., Graham, S., Peter, O., and Zmuidinas, M. 1991. Public confession and forgiveness. *Journal of Personality*, 59(2), 281–312.

Wells, W.D. 1975. Psychographics: A critical review. *Journal of Marketing Research*, 12(5), 196–213.

West, D.M. 1994. Political advertising and news coverage in the 1992 California U.S. Senate campaigns. *Journal of Politics*, 56(4), 1053–1075.

———. 1994/1995. Television advertising in election campaigns. *Political Science Quarterly*, 109(5), 789–809.

Wheatley, J.J., and Oshikawa, S. 1970. The relationship between anxiety and positive and negative advertising appeals. *Journal of Marketing Research*, 7(1), 85–89.

White, D.M. 1950. The "gate keeper": A case study in the selection of news. *Journalism Quarterly*, 27(4), 383–390.

Wilkes, R.E. 1977. Product positioning by multidimensional scaling. *Journal of Advertising Research*, 17(4), 15–19.

Wilkie, W.L. 1994. *Consumer Behavior*. New York: John Wiley.

Williams, A.P., Trammell, K.D., Postelnicu, M., Landreville, K.D., and Martin, J.D. 2005. Blogging and hyperlinking: Use of the Web to enhance viability during the 2004 US campaign. *Journalism Studies*, 6(2), 177–186.

Williams, B.A., and Delli Carpini, M.X. 2000. Unchained reaction: The collapse of media gatekeeping and the Clinton-Lewinsky scandal. *Journalism*, 1(1), 61–85.

Wind, Y. 1978. Issues and advances in segmentation research. *Journal of Marketing Research*, 15(3), 317–337.

Winter, D.G., and Carlson, L.A. 1988. Using motive scores in the psychobiographical study of an individual: The case of Richard Nixon. *Journal of Personality*, 56(1), 75–103.

Wirthlin Worldwide. 1996. *Election '96: Defining Mr. Right.* Wirthlin Quorum Online. www.wirthlin.com/publicns/quorum/wq9607.htm.

Wisconsin Advertising Project. 2008. Pres. TV advertising spending continues to grow: Over $28 million spent from September 28–October 4. http://wiscadproject. wisc.edu/wiscads_release_100808.pdf.

Wojciszke, B. 1994. Multiple meanings of behavior: Construing actions in terms of competence or morality. *Journal of Personality and Social Psychology,* 67(2), 222–232.

———. 1997. Parallels between competence- versus morality-related traits and individualistic versus collectivistic values. *European Journal of Social Psychology,* 27(3), 245–256.

———. 2005. Affective concomitants of information on morality and competence. *European Psychologist,* 10(1), 60–70.

Wolfsfeld, G. 1992. Voters as consumers: Audience perspectives on the election broadcast. In A. Arian and M. Shamir (eds.), *The Elections in Israel 1992,* 235–253. Albany: State University of New York Press.

Woodworth, R.S., and Schlosberg, H. 1954. *Experimental Psychology.* New York: Holt, Rinehart & Winston.

Worcester, R.M., and Baines, P.R. 2004. Voter research and market positioning: Triangulation and its implications for policy development. www.ipsos-mori.com/ publications/rmw/two-triangulation-models.pdf.

Worcester, R.M., and Mortimore, R. 2005. Political triangulation: Measuring and reporting the key aspects of party and leader standing before and during elections. *Journal of Political Marketing,* 4(2/3), 45–72.

Wray, J.H. 1999. Money and politics. In B.I. Newman (ed.), *Handbook of Political Marketing,* 741–758. Thousand Oaks, CA: Sage.

Wring, D. 1997. Reconciling marketing with political science: Theories of political marketing. *Journal of Marketing Management,* 13(7), 651–663.

———. 1999. The marketing colonization of political campaigning. In B.I. Newman (ed.), *Handbook of Political Marketing,* 41–54. Thousand Oaks, CA: Sage.

Wu, H.D. 2000. Systemic determinants of international news coverage: A comparison of 38 countries. *Journal of Communication,* 50(2), 110–130.

Wymer, W.W., Jr., and Lees-Marshment, J. (eds.). 2005. *Current Issues in Political Marketing.* Binghamton, NY: Haworth Press.

Yorke, D.A., and Meehan, S.A. 1986. ACORN in the political marketplace. *European Journal of Marketing,* 20(8), 63–76.

Zeithaml, V.A., Parasuraman, A., and Berry, L.L. 1985. Problems and strategies in service marketing. *Journal of Marketing,* 49(2), 33–46.

Zhu, J.H., Milavsky, J.R., and Biswas, R. 1994. Do televised debates affect image perception more than issue knowledge? A study of the first 1992 presidential debate. *Human Communication Research,* 20(3), 302–333.

Ziegler, R., Arnold, F., and Diehl, M. 2007. Communication modality and biased processing: A study on the occasion of the German 2002 election TV debate. *Basic and Applied Social Psychology,* 29(2), 175–184.

Ziff, R. 1971. Psychographics for market segmentation. *Journal of Advertising Research,* 11(2), 3–9.

Zillmann, D., Harris, C.R., and Schweitzer, K. 1993. Effects of perspective and angle manipulations in portrait photographs on the attribution of traits to depicted persons. *Mediapsychologie,* 5(2), 106–123.

Żukowski, T. 1997. Polska widownia polityczna w lutym 1997 roku [Polish political scene in February 1997]. Unpublished OBOP data study, February, Warsaw.

Zullow, H.M., Oettingen, G., Peterson, C., and Seligman, M.E.P. 1988. Pessimistic explanatory style in the historical record: CAVing LBJ, presidential candidates, and East versus West Berlin. *American Psychologist*, 43(9), 673–682.

Zullow, H.M., and Seligman, M.E.P. 1990. Pessimistic rumination predicts defeat of presidential candidates, 1900 to 1984. *Psychological Inquiry*, 1(1), 52–61.

Zúquete, J.P. 2008. The missionary politics of Hugo Chávez. *Latin American Politics and Society*, 50(1), 91–121.

Internet Sources

www.china.org.cn
www.debates.org

Name Index

Subject Index

ABC, 60
ACORN (A Classification of Residential
   Neighbourhoods) (Great Britain),
   90–91
Adwatch campaign (United States),
   284–85
Aestheticization, 52
Agenda-setting, 59–61
Almanac of American Politics, 148
Ambiguity strategy, 116–20
  allocation theory, 118
  illustration, 117*f*
Anguita, Julio, 61
Apartisans, 91
Apoliticals, 91
A priori voter segmentation, 82–83,
   88, 89, 92, 102–3
Ashdown, Paddy, 236
Attitude accessibility, 86–87
Attitude certainty, 87, 219–24
Azmar, Jose Maria, 61

Beatty, Warren, 134
Bentson, Lloyd, 173*t*
Billboards, 203, 204–5
Blair, Tony
  candidate image, 131
  market-driven orientation, 24
  market-oriented party, 43
Blogs, 242–44

Bovine Spongiform Encephalopathy
   (BSE), 68, 80*n*1
Brand equity pyramid, 24–27
  brand association, 26
  brand image, 26
  brand resonance, 26
  brand response, 26
  brand salience, 24–25
  model illustration, 25*f*
  party self-identification, 25–26
Brand identity, 121
Brochures, 202–3
Bush, George H.W.
  candidate image, 154, 155*f*
  emotional voting, 159
  ideal leadership, 137
  political advertising, 207
  political debate, 172, 173*t*, 179, 180*f*
Bush, George W.
  candidate image, 153
  media bias, 58
  political advertising, 210, 211–12, 214,
    215*t*, 226, 229–30
  political blog, 243–44
  political debate, 172, 173*t*, 187–89,
    190*f*, 192–94
  rally-around-the-flag strategy, 249,
    250*f*
  war strategy
By-elections, 261, 266–68

325

About the Authors

Wojciech Cwalina is a professor in the Department of Marketing Psychology at the Warsaw School of Social Sciences and Humanities in Poland. His research specialty is social psychology, including political marketing, person perception, and media psychology. He is the author of *Television Political Advertising* (in Polish) and coauthor of *Political Marketing* (in Polish, with Andrzej Falkowski), *A Cross-Cultural Theory of Voter Behavior* (with Andrzej Falkowski and Bruce I. Newman), and numerous articles (*Media Psychology, Journal of Political Marketing, Journalism Studies, Polish Psychological Bulletin*) and book chapters. He is a member of the editorial boards of *Psychologia Społeczna* (Social Psychology) and *Journal of Political Marketing*. He is a marketing consultant and media adviser in Polish political campaigns.

Andrzej Falkowski is a professor of psychology and marketing and the head of the Department of Marketing Psychology at the Warsaw School of Social Sciences and Humanities in Poland. His research specialty is cognitive psychology, including consumer behavior, marketing, and political advertising. He has been a Fulbright Scholar at the University of Michigan. His publications include numerous articles in consumer behavior, political marketing, and cognitive psychology journals, as well as chapters and books including *Television and Politics in Evolving European Democracies* (with Wojciech Cwalina) and *A Cross-Cultural Theory of Voter Behavior* (with Wojciech Cwalina and Bruce I. Newman). He is advisory editor of the *Handbook of Political Marketing* and an editorial board member of *Journal of Political Marketing*.

Bruce I. Newman is currently a professor of marketing at DePaul University. He was a visiting scholar at the Institute of Government at the University of California-Berkeley (2001–2002); in the Department of Political Science at

.ord University (2002–2003); and a William Evans Visiting Fellow in J6 at the University of Otago in New Zealand. He is the founding editor .n chief of the *Journal of Political Marketing* (2001), published by Taylor & Francis in London. He has published over ten books and numerous articles on the subjects of political marketing and consumer psychology, including *The Marketing of the President*, published in 1994, and, more recently, *A Cross-Cultural Theory of Voter Behavior* (with Wojciech Cwalina and Andrzej Falkowski). In 1993 Dr. Newman received the Ehrenring (Ring of Honor) from the Austrian Advertising Research Association in Vienna for his research in political marketing. In March 1995, he was invited to the White House to advise senior aides to President Clinton on communication strategy and subsequently met with them on several occasions.